T0334001

Health Research Governance in Africa

The globalisation of research has resulted in the increased location of research involving humans in developing countries. Countries in Africa, along with China and India, have seen research grow significantly. With emerging infectious diseases, such as Ebola and Zika, emphasising the risk of public health crises throughout the world, a further increase in health research, including clinical research in developing countries, which are often the sites of these diseases, becomes inevitable. This growth raises questions about domestic regulation and the governance of health research.

This book presents a comprehensive and systemic view of the regulation of research involving humans in African countries. It employs case studies from four countries in which research activities continue to rise, and which have taken steps to regulate health research activity: South Africa, Nigeria, Kenya, and Egypt. The book examines the historical and political contexts of these governance efforts. It describes the research context, some of the research taking place, and the current challenges. It also looks at the governance mechanisms, ranging from domestic ethical guidelines to legal frameworks, the strengthening of existing regulatory agencies to the role of professional regulatory bodies. The book analyses the adequacy of current governance arrangements within African countries, and puts forward recommendations to improve the emerging governance systems for health research in African and other developing countries. It will be a valuable resource for academics, researchers, practitioners, and policymakers working in the areas of health research, biomedical ethics, health law, and regulation in developing countries.

Cheluchi Onyemelukwe-Onuobia is Associate Professor at the Babcock School of Law and Security Studies, Babcock University, Nigeria, and Managing Partner at Health Ethics and Law Consulting, Nigeria. She is also a member of Nigeria's National Health Research Ethics Committee.

Biomedical Law and Ethics Library

Sheila A. M. McLean

Professor Sheila A.M. McLean is Professor Emerita of Law and Ethics in Medicine, School of Law, University of Glasgow, UK.

Scientific and clinical advances, social and political developments and the impact of healthcare on our lives raise profound ethical and legal questions. Medical law and ethics have become central to our understanding of these problems, and are important tools for the analysis and resolution of problems – real or imagined.

In this series, scholars at the forefront of biomedical law and ethics contribute to the debates in this area, with accessible, thought-provoking, and sometimes controversial, ideas. Each book in the series develops an independent hypothesis and argues cogently for a particular position. One of the major contributions of this series is the extent to which both law and ethics are utilised in the content of the books, and the shape of the series itself.

The books in this series are analytical, with a key target audience of lawyers, doctors, nurses, and the intelligent lay public.

Available titles:

The Umbilical Cord Blood Controversies in Medical Law
Karen Devine

The Fetus as a Patient
A Contested Concept and its Normative Implications
Dagmar Schmitz, Angus Clarke and Wybo Dondorp

Revisiting Landmark Cases in Medical Law
Shaun D. Pattinson

Health Research Governance in Africa
Law, Ethics, and Regulation
Cheluchi Onyemelukwe-Onuobia

For more information about this series, please visit: www.routledge.com/ Biomedical-Law-and-Ethics-Library/book-series/CAV5

Health Research Governance in Africa
Law, Ethics, and Regulation

Cheluchi Onyemelukwe-Onuobia

Routledge
Taylor & Francis Group

LONDON AND NEW YORK

First published 2019
by Routledge

2 Park Square, Milton Park, Abingdon, Oxfordshire OX14 4RN
52 Vanderbilt Avenue, New York, NY 10017

Routledge is an imprint of the Taylor & Francis Group, an informa business

First issued in paperback 2019

British Library Cataloguing-in-Publication Data
A catalogue record for this book is available from the British Library

Library of Congress Cataloging-in-Publication Data
Names: Onyemelukwe-Onuobia, Cheluchi, 1978–
Title: Health research governance in Africa : law, ethics, and regulation /
Cheluchi Onyemelukwe-Onuobia.
Description: Abingdon, Oxon ; New York, NY : Routledge, 2018. |
Series: Biomedical law and ethics library | Includes index. | Based in part
on author's thesis (doctoral - Dalhousie University (Canada), Faculty of
Law, 2010) issued under title: Governance of health research involving
humans in developing countries : the Nigerian example.
Identifiers: LCCN 2018020319
Subjects: LCSH: Human experimentation in medicine—Law and
legislation—Africa.
Classification: LCC KQC698.5 .O59 2018 | DDC 344.604/196—dc23
LC record available at https://lccn.loc.gov/2018020319

ISBN: 978-1-138-03677-2 (hbk)
ISBN: 978-0-367-48189-6 (pbk)

Typeset in Galliard
by codeMantra

Contents

Acknowledgement

A book, several years in the making, is often the product of many thoughts, ideas, handholding, foundations and even disruptions. While I cannot document every support received, I am truly thankful for all the assistance that has directly and indirectly brought this book into being.

This book began its life as a doctoral thesis at Dalhousie University's Schulich School of Law, over a decade ago. I received much support from my thesis committee, led by my primary supervisor Prof Jocelyn Downie (OC) of the Schulich School of Law. I thank her for her thoughtful steering and incisive comments which helped inspire the direction of the thesis which has now been expanded in this book. Her optimism, encouragement, support and generosity, helped make the doctoral journey a positive experience. I also thank Prof Bill Lahey, formerly Director of the Health Law Institute, now President of University of Kings College, Nova Scotia. Our discussions exposed me to the rich and diverse field of regulation and governance and helped shape my reflections on the regulation of health research in Africa. Prof Chidi Oguamanam, now of the University of Ottawa brought critical insights, robust critiques of several of the arguments, a thorough knowledge of the context, and moral support, and I am grateful. I also thank Prof Benard Dickens, Emeritus Professor for insightful comments as examiner of the thesis, which have been put to work in this book. I would also like to acknowledge gratefully the financial support provided to me during the course of my doctoral studies by the Canadian Institutes of Health Research Training Programme in Health Law, Ethics, and Policy, the Schulich School of Law, and the Faculty of Graduate Studies.

I thank my colleagues at Babcock University School of Law and Security Studies for their support. In particular, I am grateful the academically stimulating environment provided by the Emeritus Prof Agbede, Prof Sodipo, Prof G. Elias, Prof D Olanrewaju, Prof N Udombana, and Prof K Ajayi. I also thank Mrs Louisa James, Dr Ayoyemi Arowolo, and Dr T Aderibigbe for their support and encouragement.

I thank also members of the National Health Research Ethics Committee, a statutory oversight body for health research involving human in Nigeria, in particular, the Chair, Prof Zubairu Iliyasu for opportunities to support different aspects of our work that have provided some of the insights in this book. Over the years, I have had opportunity to travel to different countries in Africa and, being unable to mention names, I thank each person who answered my questions on research ethics and culture, and all who responded to my requests for articles on various aspects. I acknowledge with gratitude the research assistance of Amarachi Okonkoh, Associate at Health Ethics and Law Consulting.

My family deserves specific mention. My husband, Fred Onuobia, provided me his support and encouragement, and various materials for this project in the early stages. I thank him for the insightful discussions we had on various points in the book. His love for and faith in me, his unwavering desire for my success, and the home we have built together, have consistently made seemingly impossible goals attainable, and dreams possible. My children, Kelechi, Oluchi and Udochi, endured long hours I spent tapping away on the computer or researching aspects of this book. I appreciate them and the endless joy, love and meaning they bring to my life.

I thank my parents, Prof. Obidinma Onyemelukwe and Dr. Rebecca Onyemelukwe for their love, support, and encouragement, and for their unwavering belief in my abilities. They nurtured my educational ambitions from the beginning and inspired me to go this route by their example. No one could have better parents. I thank also my siblings Akaoma, Ijendu and Soke for their love and encouragement.

I acknowledge with gratitude the support of the publishers, Routledge. I thank Prof Sheila Maclean, Prof Emerita of Law and Ethics, School of Law, the University of Glasgow and Editor of the Biomedical Law and Ethics Series for receptive audience when I broached the idea of this book for the series. I thank Alison Kirk, editor at Routledge, for patiently shepherding the book through the publishing process, her assistant, Alexandra Buckley for all her help, and the anonymous reviewer for insights that inspired me to work further on various aspects of the book.

Finally, thank you, my God and Comfort, for everything.

I accept responsibility for all errors.

1 Introduction

The globalisation of research has resulted in increased location of research in developing countries. Countries in Africa, and developing countries like China and India, have seen research grow significantly. With emerging infectious diseases such as Ebola and Zika raising the spectre of public health crises throughout the world, an increase in clinical and other kinds of research in developing countries, often the sites of these diseases, becomes inevitable.[1] But how is this research regulated? How are the regulatory, safety, and public health concerns of research addressed within domestic contexts?

From the late nineties to now, the questions concerning health research involving human participants have expanded to encompass the matter of ethics and whether or not the ethics practised by health researchers in resource-constrained settings should differ from the ethics of research in richer countries. Health research in developing countries, including countries in Africa, has also raised questions of health and economic justice: the effects of economic inequality on what diseases receive attention. The results of the soul-searching of experts have spilled over from the pages of academic journals into amendments of international ethics guidelines, such as the World Medical Association's Helsinki Declaration,[2] and into efforts by organisations such as the United States National Institutes of Health to train bioethicists in African countries.[3]

The increase in externally sponsored research in developing countries, including African countries, has only intensified the need for a proper scrutiny of the regulation and governance of such research. Important questions of global justice and equity, and the arguably greater vulnerability of research participants in poor countries continue to be raised. What naturally follows, then, is concern

---

1 Several of the trials for vaccine development for Ebola took place in African countries: Ghana, Senegal, Guinea, Tanzania, and Uganda. See World Health Organisation, online: <www.who. int/medicines/emp_ebola_q_as/en/> (April 15, 2016).

2 Fogarty International Center, online: <https://www.fic.nih.gov/programs/pages/bioethics. aspx>.

3 WMA *Declaration of Helsinki – Ethical Principles for Medical Research Involving Human Subjects* (2013).

about how adequately research participants in such countries are protected and the existence and sufficiency of any governance mechanisms for that purpose.

Historical events in several countries, including developed countries, have underscored the need for regulation and oversight of health research involving humans. These include the oft-cited examples of human experimentation atrocities during the Second World War in Germany, the United States Tuskegee Syphilis Study,[4] the Willowbrook studies,[5] the Jewish Chronic Hospital Disease Study in Brooklyn,[6] and the Cameron experiments in Canada.[7] The controversies surrounding the Zidovudine trials in several developing countries in the late 1990s[8] brought to the fore that poorer countries could not be excluded from discussions of how best to protect human participants within research. Further, some evidence of such research has only recently been uncovered, such as the Guatemalan syphilis studies.[9]

The local examples within African countries further underscore the need to ensure appropriate research governance. From the Pfizer incident in Nigeria in the mid-nineties, where it was alleged that Pfizer acted unethically in its testing of a drug during a meningitis epidemic,[10] (including failure to obtain informed consent and lack of ethics review approval) to the conviction of a doctor in Zimbabwe for failure to seek relevant approvals and for failure to obtain informed consent for human experimentation in the 1990s,[11] the need to protect participants in health research is a widespread concern. The recent movement towards genomic research, such as was captured in the H3Africa project, further

---

4 Experiments on African American men in the United States where the research subjects were prevented from getting effective treatment while participating in a study on syphilis long after a cure was discovered for the disease. See Allan M Brandt, "Racism and Research: The Case of the Tuskegee Syphilis Study" (1978) 8:6 Hastings Cent Rep 21–29.

5 Where children with intellectual disabilities were injected with hepatitis. See Henry K Beecher, "Ethics and Clinical Research" (1966) 274:24 N Engl J Med 1354–1360; Saul Krugman, "The Willowbrook Hepatitis Studies Revisited: Ethical Aspects" (1986) 8:1 Clin Infect Dis 157–162. Web.

6 In which the patients hospitalised with debilitating chronic diseases were injected with live cancer cells without their consent. See a detailed review of some historical cases in Jay Katz, *Experimentation with Human Beings* (New York: Russell Sage Foundation, 1972).

7 Where electric shock experiments were tested on mentally ill patients.

8 Paquita De Zulueta, "Randomised Placebo-Controlled Trials and HIV-Infected Pregnant Women in Developing Countries: Ethical Imperialism or Unethical Exploitation?" (2001) 15:4 Bioethics 290 at 293–296. See also George Annas "Human Rights and Maternal-Fetal HIV Transmission Prevention Trials in Africa" (1998) 88 Am J Public Health 560; Marcia Angell, "The Ethics of Clinical Research in the Third World" (1997) 337 N Engl J Med 847–849; and Abdool Q Karim et al, "Informed Consent for HIV Testing in a South African Hospital: Is It Truly Informed and Truly Voluntary?" (1998) 88 Am J Public Health 637.

9 In which persons were injected with syphilis without their knowledge or consent. See Michael A Rodriguez & Robert Garcia, "First Do No Harm: The US Sexually Transmitted Disease Experiments in Guatemala" (2013) 103:12 Am J Public Health 2122.

10 Discussed extensively in Chapter 6.

11 See Karl Maier, "Race-row Doctor Faces Trial over Patients' Deaths," *Independent* (July 3, 2018), online: <https://www.independent.co.uk/news/world/race-row-doctor-faces-trial-over-patients-deaths-1411503.html>.

highlights the potential benefits of research and emphasises the need for understanding and enforcing ethics in health research.

Several factors, both global and local, have had a significant impact on the adoption of domestic governance research governance frameworks. The combination of the increase in externally funded research, greater cognizance of research scandals, increased awareness of the need to protect research participants, more bioethics expertise and capacity, and the drive towards the use of clinical trials registries has resulted in more formalised governance frameworks within some African countries, including through legislation, strengthening of drug regulatory authorities, and ethics review mechanisms. In this regard, a number of African countries have developed instruments for guiding and regulating health research involving humans. These instruments form the basis of governance of research in these countries, and this seems to be an appropriate time, therefore, to consider the governance of health research in Africa.[12]

What are the governance mechanisms currently employed in African countries? While some aspects of research governance have received attention, others have only begun to receive attention, such as the legal frameworks. What is the contribution of law to health research governance in Africa? Professional regulatory bodies, often functioning under the shadow of law, could also play an important role in health research governance. What is their place in the current health research governance matrix? Other institutions potentially involved in research governance such as non-governmental organisations and civil society bodies have not received much attention in current literature. Evidence from other areas of health indicates that these organisations are a powerful force in the health space in many African countries. What is their place, if any, in current health research governance structure? What role could they or ought they to play? Can research participants find a voice through civil society organisations as has happened in some developed countries? What challenges do African countries face in regulating research?

The issues

There continues to be considerable interest in health research involving humans in developing countries, including African countries. The increasing awareness of the difference in the circumstances of developing countries and developed countries; the higher burden of disease; and the higher level of vulnerability of persons in developing countries, including African countries, to exploitation have, at the same time, prompted concerns about the ethical conduct of research involving humans in these countries. The conduct of external researchers in developing countries has been criticised by several commentators for failing in some cases to meet the ethical standards which such researchers would have

---

12 H3Africa Consortium et al, "Research Capacity: Enabling the Genomic Revolution in Africa" (2014) 344 Science 1346.

been compelled to adopt in developed countries. There have also been a number of claims that multinational pharmaceutical companies have conducted trials in developing countries not using the same ethical standards that they would adopt abroad and possibly endangering the lives of the research participants involved in such trials.[13]

Previous research has focussed in part on examining the ways in which the economic inequalities and disparity in access to healthcare between developing countries and developed countries have affected the types of research conducted in developing countries by external sponsors and who dictates the research agenda, including the types of research to be conducted.[14] Earlier research also focussed on how these inequalities, and the difficulties in applying the international ethical guidelines, give rise to ethical concerns and controversies.[15] The literature has therefore focussed on several ethical concerns in research in developing countries, including the adequacy of informed consent procedures in developing countries, the standard of care to be offered to persons involved in randomised clinical trials, access to the benefits of the research, and the inadequacy of ethics review in developing countries.[16]

Although these challenges have become well recognised, and the need to balance ethical requirements and sociocultural differences is understood, there is little consensus on precisely how they are to be addressed by researchers in practical situations. For instance, when, if ever, is it appropriate to deviate from international ethical guidelines? Does cultural relativity justify ethical relativism? Is ethical relativism permissible in particular instances? Does it constitute "ethical imperialism" to impose the requirements of the international ethical guidelines, regardless of differing circumstances, or is a universal standard the only justifiable standard? These questions also have great relevance for concerns surrounding the standard of care issue, an ethical concern that has received much attention in the literature.

The standard of care[17] issue can rightly be said to be the issue that thrust ethical issues in research involving humans in developing countries into the limelight

13 See, for example, Thomas Pogge, "Testing Our Drugs on the Poor Abroad" in Jennifer Hawkins & Ezekiel Emanuel, eds, *Exploitation and Developing Countries: The Ethics of Clinical Research* (Princeton: Princeton University Press, 2008) at 105–141. Adriana Petryna, "Ethical Variability: Drug Development and Globalizing Clinical Trials" (2005) 32:2 Am Ethnol 183.

14 Nuffield Council on Bioethics, The Ethics of Research Related to Healthcare in Developing Countries *(London:* Nuffield Council on Bioethics, 2002). Ruth Macklin, *Double Standards in Medical Research in Developing Countries* (Cambridge: Cambridge University Press, 2004).

15 See, for example, Reidar K Lie et al, "The Standard of Care Debate: The Declaration of Helsinki versus the International Consensus Opinion" (2004) 30 J Med Ethics 190.

16 See, for example, Macklin, *supra* Note 14.

17 Although it is employed profusely in the literature, several different meanings may be attributed to the phrase "standard of care." Some of these include the ethical standards that should generally apply in health research involving humans in different countries, "the types or level of treatments provided to patients in the clinical setting, but it might not serve as a justification for what *ought* to be provided to participants in research." It can also be described as "the nature of the care and treatment that will be provided to participants in research," and the term might also mean what

in recent years. It is perhaps the most hotly debated issue in internationally sponsored research in developing countries. This concern revolves mostly around the nature of the care and treatment provided during research, including all the preventive or therapeutic treatment that ought to be provided to participants in the course of the research.[18] The debate originates from the basic ethical requirement that participants in research should not be exploited. But how this basic ethical requirement is to be translated into actual practice, especially in developing countries, which have more limited healthcare options, has created heated debate in the literature. Several broad issues arise with regard to standard of care in research. In view of the limited healthcare options available in many developing countries, what standard of care should be offered to participants in the control arm of clinical research? Should this differ in any respect from the standard of care offered within similar research elsewhere in the world, particularly in developed countries? Should the same ethical standards apply across borders, irrespective of the different contexts, including poverty and poor healthcare systems? Is a different standard justifiable on the grounds that the results of the research will ultimately benefit wider populations in developing countries?[19]

The debates surrounding the issue of standard of care were ignited by the 1997 article of Lurie and Wolfe in the *New England Journal of Medicine*.[20] In this, they objected to the apparently unethical nature of clinical trials conducted by the United States National Institutes of Health (NIH) and the Center for Disease Control (CDC) for the prevention of perinatal transmission of HIV involving HIV-positive women in South Africa, Uganda, Thailand, and other developing countries. The women were not provided with antiretroviral treatment, thereby arguably allowing many infants to contract HIV unnecessarily. The trials were argued to be against international ethical guidelines, notably the Helsinki Declaration, which at that time required that "every patient, including those of a control group, if any ... should be given the best proven diagnostic and therapeutic method."[21] Commentators insisted that since the

---

actually obtains in a particular setting. See National Bioethics Advisory Commission, *Ethical and Policy Issues in International Research: Clinical Trials in Developing Countries Volume1 – Report and Recommendations of the National Bioethics Advisory Commission* (Bethesda, MD: National Bioethics Advisory Commission, 2001), (hereafter NBAC) at 13 (emphasis mine). See also Alex J London, "The Ambiguity and the Exigency: Clarifying 'Standard of Care' Arguments in International Research" (2000) 25 J Med Philos 379; Ruth Macklin, *Double Standards in Medical Research in Developing Countries* (Cambridge: Cambridge University Press, 2004).

18 As Macklin succinctly notes, the ethical issue focusses on "what is ethically acceptable to provide to a control group in research with the standard of care in the developing country – whatever is routinely provided to people in that country with that medical condition? Or must a control group be provided with the best treatment available elsewhere – the 'standard of care' in the sponsoring country?" Macklin (2004), 34.

19 *Ibid.* at 36.

20 Peter Lurie and Sidney M. Wolfe, "Unethical Trials of Interventions to Reduce Perinatal Transmission of the Human Immunodeficiency Virus in Developing Countries" (1997) 337:12 N Engl J Med 853.

21 Principle 30 of the 1996 Amendment.

use of a placebo would have been unethical in the United States, the use of placebos in zidovudine trials in these developing countries was also unethical.[22] Critics countered that placebo-controlled trials were necessary to produce faster, clearer, and more reliable results than would otherwise be obtained through the use of active controls, which would be more expensive and less efficient. There have been other cases, for instance, the Surfaxin trials in several Latin American countries, in which a placebo was to be used, although effective treatment was available in the United States[23] and other allegations of improper placebo use in South Africa.[24] This issue remains problematic. For example, a rotavirus vaccine study with infants in India in which placebos were used, reported in *The Lancet* in 2014, has raised concern.[25]

Ethical issues arise also with respect to issues such as informed consent in situations where people are vulnerable because of their economic circumstances, their levels of education, or the lack of health infrastructure. Other ethical concerns include privacy and confidentiality in different cultural contexts and access to the benefits of the research when it is over. Thus, despite the provisions of the international ethical guidelines on these issues, there continues to be controversy in this area and a diversity of thinking on the issues,[26] and new revisions of international guidelines do not appear to have solved all the controversial issues.[27]

22 Marcia Angell, "The Ethics of Clinical Research in the Third World" (1997) 337:12 N Engl J Med Journal of Medicine 847–849.

23 See James V Lavery et al, ed, *Ethical Issues in International Biomedical Research: A Casebook* (Oxford: Oxford University Press, 2007) at 151–159. See Macklin (2004), at 17–18; or the Hepatitis A vaccine trials conducted in Thailand in 1991 (see R Lie, "Justice and International Research" in R Levine, S Gorovitz & J Gallagher, eds, *Biomedical Research Ethics: Updating International Guidelines* (Geneva: CIOMS-WHO, 2000) at 27–40.). For differing views on the exploitative nature of the Surfaxin trials, see Robert J Temple, "Benefit to the Trial Participants or Benefit to the Community? How Far Should the Surfaxin Trial Investigators' and Sponsors' Obligations Extend?" in Lavery et al, at 155–159; and Peter Lurie & Sidney Wolfe, "The Developing World as the Answer to the Dreams of Pharmaceutical Companies: The Surfaxin Story" in Lavery et al, *ibid.* at 159–168.

24 Wemos, The Clinical Trials Industry in South Africa: Ethics, Rules and Realities (Wemos, 2013), online: <https://www.wemos.nl/wp-content/uploads/2016/06/Clinical_Trials_Industry_South_ Africa_2013.pdf>.

25 Michael Carome, "Unethical Clinical Trials Still Being Conducted in Developing Countries" *The Huffington Post* (October 3, 2014), online: <www.huffingtonpost.com/michael-carome-md/ unethical-clinical-trials_b_5927660.html>.

26 Is a global and universal standard of care the only acceptable ethical standard? Does this amount to ethical imperialism? Is a local standard of care (treatment based on the standard available in the local or regional context) permissible in some cases, allowing local circumstances and existing conditions to be taken into consideration? Or does this amount to exploitation? Is there a midway between a universal standard of care and a local standard of care?

27 See, for example, Annette Rid and Harald Schmidt, "The 2008 Declaration of Helsinki — First among Equals in Research Ethics?" (2010) J Law Med Ethics 143; L J Burgess, D Pretorius, "FDA Abandons the Declaration of Helsinki: The Effect on the Ethics of Clinical Trial Conduct in South Africa and Other Developing Countries" (2012) 5:2 South S Afr J Bioeth Law 87.

More recently, newer ethical issues are also emerging, for example, around access to experimental medicines, especially in the wake of the Ebola epidemic;[28] privacy and confidentiality; and informed consent in relation to genomic research and biobanking.[29] Aspects of the governance mechanisms and instruments have also become more prominent.[30]

In this book, I focus on what the current and emerging governance frameworks say about these issues. What effect have these debates had on the domestic governance frameworks of African countries? Do the ethical guidelines differ from international ethical guidelines, such as the Helsinki Declaration and the Council for International Organizations of Medical Sciences *International Ethical Guidelines for Human Research involving Humans*, 2016 (CIOMS Guidelines)[31] on these issues? What ethical frameworks govern externally sponsored researchers in African countries at this time? What is the role of the international ethical guidelines? Are they a descriptive standard of what is to be done or an aspirational ideal? Is the world evolving to a unified standard? Do domestic policies reflect such a unified standard?

Apart from the ethical concerns and the difficulties in applying the international guidelines, another concern is whether regulation or oversight, broadly speaking, is keeping pace with the increase in research in developing countries. Where governance frameworks have been put in place, how effective are they in addressing the regulatory challenges? Research in previous years had identified a major vacuum in health research regulatory capacity. As an example, almost 20 years ago, the Regional Committee for Africa of the World Health Organization (WHO) observed that studies involving humans in the Africa region were not subjected to ethics review. Previous research indicated that several developing countries did not have research ethics review boards and relevant legislation. As ethics review boards began to be established, the capacity of ethics review bodies to adequately do their work came into question, including their knowledge of the policies and guidelines, and the relevant legal frameworks.[32]

---

28 Cheluchi Onyemelukwe, "Access to Experimental Drugs, Fundamental Rights and Clinical Trials Regulation in Nigeria" (2017) 10:2 Asia Pac J Health L & Ethics 81–114.

29 See, for example, Jantina De Vries et al, "Regulation of Genomic and Biobanking Research in Africa: A Content Analysis of Ethics Guidelines, Policies and Procedures from 22 African Countries" (2017) 18:8 BMC Med Ethics; Obiajulu Nnamuchi, "H3Africa: An Africa Exemplar? Exploring Its Framework on Protecting Human Research Participants" (2017) Dev World Bioeth 1–9.

30 See, for example, Raffaella Ravineto, "The Revision of the ICH-Good Clinical Practice Guidelines: A Missed Opportunity?" (2017) 2:4 Indian J Med Ethics 255-259.

31 WHO, Council for International Organizations of Medical Sciences *International Ethical Guidelines for Human Research involving Humans*, 2016, online: https://cioms.ch/wp-content/uploads/2017/01/WEB-CIOMS-EthicalGuidelines.pdf. This replaces the earlier CIOMS, *International Ethical Guidelines for Biomedical Research Involving Human Subjects*, 2002.

32 See Cecilia Milford, Douglas Wassenaar & Catherine Slack, "Resources and Needs of Research Ethics Committees in Africa: Preparations for HIV Vaccine Trials" (2006) 28:2 IRB: Ethics & Hum Res 1 at 9.

This situation has changed significantly over the past 20 years. Several African countries have taken steps to address gaps in the oversight of research and to provide protection for participants in research by establishing or formalising domestic regulatory regimes and governance structures. These steps include establishing national ethics review boards and enacting, or amending, previously existing guidelines, and even legislation governing research involving humans. Nigeria is one example. About ten years ago, it produced a national code for ethics in health research.[33] Other countries have done the same: Uganda (1997),[34] Malawi (2002),[35] South Africa (2004, 2015),[36] Tanzania (2002),[37] and Kenya (2004).[38] Several have adopted legislation: Kenya (1979, 2014), South Africa (2003), Nigeria (2014), Zambia (2014), Liberia (2016), and so on. Some countries have created a national clinical trials registry. Internationally, ClinicalTrials. gov provides an overview of clinical trials registered by several investigators around the world. Regionally, the Pan African Clinical Trials Registry (PACTR) has been developed for clinical trials conducted in Africa.[39] There have also been efforts to harmonise regulations in regard to drug registration to increase access to medicines on the continent, which may potentially affect new drugs research. This effort is supported by the economic arm of the African Union – New Partnership for Africa's Development (NEPAD) through the initiative African Medicines Regulatory Harmonization (AMRH).[40] These are exciting and important developments fuelled by previous debate and grants by organisations such as the European and Developing Countries Clinical Trials Partnership (EDCTP)[41] and the United States National Institute of Health's Fogarty International Center Grants, which have provided training for several

---

33 NHREC, *National Code for Health Research Ethics* (2006), online: <www.nhrec.net/nhrec/index.html>.
34 Uganda, *Guidelines for the Conduct of Health Research Involving Human Subjects in Uganda* (National Consensus Conference, 1997).
35 National Research Council of Malawi, *Procedures and Guidelines for the Conduct of Research in Malawi* (2002).
36 National Health Research Ethics Council, Department of Health, *Ethics in Health Research: Principles, Structures and Processes Guidelines* (Pretoria: Department of Health, 2004); National Health Research Ethics Council, Department of Health, *Ethics in Health Research: Principles, Structures and Processes Guidelines* (Pretoria: Department of Health, 2015).
37 Tanzania set up a national ethics review committee in 2002. See JKB Ikingura, M Kruger & W Zeleke, "Health Research Ethics Review and Needs of Institutional Ethics Committees in Tanzania" (2007) 9:3 Tanzan Health Res Bull 154.
38 National Council for Science and Technology, *Guidelines for Ethical Conduct of Biomedical Research Involving Human Subjects in Kenya* (2004); Ministry of Health: *Kenya National Guidelines for Research and Development of HIV/AIDS Vaccines* (2005) *Science and Technology Act* (2001).
39 The Pan African Clinical Trials Registry, online: <www.atmregistry.org/> (September 17, 2009).
40 African Medicines Regulatory Harmonisation (AMRH), online: <www.nepad.org/content/african-medicines-regulatory-harmonisation-armh-programs>.
41 European & Developing Countries Clinical Trials Partnership (EDCTP), online: <www.edctp.org/>.

bioethicists; they have also been supported by the uptake of technological innovations, such as virtual databases. These databases include the United Nations Educational Scientific and Cultural Organisation (UNESCO) Global Ethics Observatory (launched in 2005),[42] the Health Research Web,[43] annual editions of the International Compilation of Human Subjects Standards assembled by the United States Office of Human Research Protections, the Training and Resources in Research Ethics Evaluation (TRREE) database, the United States National Institute of Allergy and Infectious Disease's ClinRegs database launched in 2014, and the Canadian Global Health Research Harmonization Database.[44] The work of international development agencies in African countries such as the WHO, UNESCO, and Family Health International (FHI) have helped to propel the establishment of bioethics bodies and national ethics review committees.

While the interest in health research involving humans and in its governance in developing countries has increased over the years, with many recent publications considering ethics review systems in developing countries, the emergent policies and the structures they create need more investigation. Thus, while some literature has emerged, studying in some degree the strengths, weaknesses, and challenges of ethics review committees,[45] there are comparatively few publications that examine the governance of research in these countries in a comprehensive way, including the specific role of government, the legal system in regulating research, or civil society's role in advocating for participants. As for regulatory agencies that approve new drugs in African countries, these have been largely overlooked in the literature. It is not clear what role they play or how effective they are in protecting any research participants who participate in trials for drugs. While many drug regulatory authorities in African countries rely on already completed studies in developed countries,[46] there are trials currently being undertaken in several African countries for various new drugs and vaccines not yet approved in developing countries, including vaccines for HIV/AIDS and vaccines for the Ebola Virus Disease. With increasing publications on research ethics and governance by African and international researchers, this is changing.

However, there is certainly room, and need, for greater representation and for more analysis from a governance and legal perspective[47] which critically

---

42 <www.unesco.org/new/en/social-and-human-sciences/themes/global-ethics-observatory/>.
43 Health Research Web, < *https://www.healthresearchweb.org/*
44 See Canadian Global Health Research Harmonization Database, online: <www.ccghr.org>.
45 They further note that "Additional information on how African RECs function, including their staffing, operating procedures, strengths, and challenges would be useful for African and international researchers working within Africa, and for growing efforts to enhance ethics capacity on this vast continent." See Nancy Kass et al, "The Structure and Function of Research Ethics Committees in Africa: A Case Study" 4:1 PLoS Med e3, online: <http://medicine.plosjournals.org/archive/1549-1676/4/1/pdf/10.1371_journal.pmed.0040003-S.pdf> (June 9, 2007).
46 Florencia Luna, "Research in Developing Countries" in Bonnie Steinbock, ed, *The Oxford Handbook of Bioethics* (Oxford: Oxford University Press, 2007) at 329–330.
47 Remigius N Nwabueze, *Legal and Ethical Regulation of Biomedical Research in Developing Countries* (Aldershot: Ashgate, 2013); Pamela Andanda et al, "The Ethical and Legal Regulation

examines the structure and adequacy of any existing governance systems and the potential effect of these systems on the protection of human participants in these countries. What legal and governance arrangements are in place, and what gaps remain in research governance? As pointed out earlier, much of the literature on research involving humans in developing countries previously focussed on internationally sponsored research in developing countries. Discussions on the ethics of international research or research supported by developed country sponsors in developing countries and particular ethical concerns remain important, not least because they address important issues of global equity and the practical application of ethical principles. However, there is need for more research addressing the ethics and regulation of indigenous or domestic research, that is, research sponsored by entities within developing countries nor how research participants in this type of research (no matter how little) are protected. An understanding of domestic governance systems is especially important because such systems govern all research involving humans, not only internationally sponsored research but also indigenous or domestically sponsored research.

Perhaps in recognition of this, some researchers and organisations are now focussed on analysing the domestic governance of health research. Emerging research now focusses on key domestic governance issues.[48] Some organisations have developed databases on research governance systems, as mentioned earlier, but these typically do not analyse gaps and weaknesses. Other recent research engages in some analysis of the governance structures, but there is still some way to go in regard to a systemic and comprehensive analysis. Understanding the governance arrangements currently in place in developing countries seems particularly important at this time because of these recent steps taken by many developing countries, including African countries. This need is not lessened by the fact that these systems are relatively recent and, it may thus be argued, allow insufficient time to analyse in any great detail their adequacy and effectiveness in protecting research participants. Critical changes may be made before problems become entrenched. Such evaluation is also especially crucial because African countries without governance systems or in the process of establishing governance systems may want to adopt the procedures and systems now in use in developing countries that have taken early steps in this respect. For instance, as I describe in the following chapters, national research ethics review committees are becoming entrenched, as are institutional review committees. As another example, Nigeria and several other African countries appear to have replicated some of the same concepts that apply in South Africa, including enacting

---

of HIV-Vaccine Research in Africa: Lessons from Cameroon, Malawi, Nigeria, Rwanda and Zambia" (2011) 10:4 Afr J AIDS Res 451–463 at 463.

48 See, for example, Olubunmi Ogunri, Folasade Daniel & Victor Ansa, "Knowledge of the Nigerian Code of Health Research Ethics among Biomedical Researchers in Southern Nigeria" (2015) 11:5 J Empir Res Hum Res Ethics 397–407; Obi Nnamuchi, "Biobank and Genomic Research in Uganda: Are Extant Privacy and Confidentiality Regimes Adequate?" (2015) 44:1 J L Med & Ethics 85.

legislation which establishes a national ethics review committee. Indeed, national ethics review committees are increasingly now the norm, often having the responsibility of accrediting lower-level regional or institutional ethical committees. Whether this is a practicable model, with resource challenges persisting, remains to be seen.

Examining these systems from a governance perspective is also important, not only because such examination provides much-needed descriptive information on the emerging governance systems in developing countries but because it moves the discourse from identification of issues to proffering of solutions. The discussion about ethical concerns is important because it addresses the ways in which the conduct of research affects participants. To put these concerns into a context in which action can be taken, however, there is a need for domestic governance structures and systems, including policy guidelines, legislation, and ethics review mechanisms.

In a similar vein, there is some focus in the literature on the provision of equivalent protections by developed countries when their citizens or companies sponsor or conduct research in developing countries.[49] These are undoubtedly important and even morally desirable. But discussion of domestic governance systems allows room for consideration of developing countries' ownership in the protection of their citizens who become research participants. This shift in focus could also allow for more participation of researchers from the developing world in these important debates.

Examining research involving humans from a governance perspective is also helpful because it allows one to ask the crucial question: what regulatory tools and institutions are required to effectively govern research involving humans? The first tool that typically comes to mind is ethics review. Ethics review is now a central part of the research governance systems of many countries, and the ethics review system may therefore be mistakenly considered the governance system. The literature tends, therefore, to examine mainly the work of ethics review committees, particularly in developed countries where they have been established for a longer period but increasingly now also in developing countries, including African countries. But an important gap persists. What, for instance, is the role of drug regulatory authorities? How or do they work in conjunction or apart from the well-acknowledged ethics review committees? What is the impact of foreign funding aimed at improving the regulatory capacity of ethics review committees on the structure of the emerging governance systems? There is a need to expand the focus on research involving humans in developing countries to include a consideration of not only the ethical issues but also fuller examinations of the existing and emerging governance structures and arrangements in

---

49 See, for example, United States, Department of Health and Human Services, 'Report of the Equivalent Protections' (2003), online: <www.hhs.gov/ohrp/international/EPWGReport2003. pdf>. See also "Biomedical Research Projects in Developing Countries" (Denmark) (2006), online: <www.cvk.im.dk/cvkEverest/Publications/cvkx2Eimx2Edk%20x2D%20dokumenter/ English/20061130095326/CurrentVersion/ulandssagerENG.pdf> (April 3, 2007).

developing countries, including African countries. This book aims to make some contribution in this area.

A broader and more inclusive view of research governance systems may include other components apart from the ethics review system, such as a legal framework, including formal legislation and other forms of law; national and international ethics guidelines; professional associations and codes of conduct; national regulatory bodies, such as the ones which regulate pharmaceutical production and the use of human participants, departments of health; civil society, including non-governmental organisations which promote patients' rights; the general public; the research participants themselves; and the interactions between these entities.[50]

The context: the need for health research and research governance in Africa

With particular regard to the governance of health research involving humans, understanding the context within which such research takes place is important for a proper appreciation of some of the peculiar issues that may arise in analysing the need for oversight and the obstacles that may beset the governance systems. A word is perhaps necessary here on the use of the term "Africa." The term "Africa" is used rather loosely here to refer to the continent. The countries in the continent, and more specifically those discussed in this book, are by no means a homogenous group, and important differences exist between them, including in terms of economic development and health research capacity.[51] There are, however, important similarities which make a group analysis possible, including but not limited to typically weaker regulatory capacities than there are in other parts of the world. Further, generally speaking, regulation and governance take place against a backdrop of, in many cases, relatively new, fragile, or developing democracies in which regulatory institutions are still in the process of development. The health systems are typically weak, health indices of many of these countries are poor, universal health coverage in many cases is still a faraway prospect, and the majority of citizens may find it difficult to pay for medical treatments that become available. Furthermore, research funding and trained researchers may be in shorter supply than they may be elsewhere. The analysis undertaken in the book discusses governance within this context.

The group analysis that creates the background for the book is, however, nuanced and made more specific by a focus on specific African countries. Some of these countries have been chosen as case studies because they have a relatively high capacity for research, that is, are research-active and have had a longer

---

50 See Ann Strode, Catherine Slack, & Muriel Mushariwa, "HIV Vaccine Research – South Africa's Ethical-Legal Framework and Its Ability to Promote the Welfare of Trial Participants" (2005) 95:8 S Afr Med J 598.
51 See Macklin (2004), at 10–11.

experience of regulating research. This is the case in South Africa, which has been the site of some of the HIV drug trials and controversies but has an older, more sophisticated system of governance. This is also the case with Kenya. Other countries, like Egypt and Nigeria, have also had some experience with research but are firming up governance arrangements. Nigeria had a research ethics scandal with the mid-nineties clinical trial conducted by Pfizer. Each of these countries has developed policies for research ethics and put in place some governance structures. However, there is no gainsaying the fact that the physical and regulatory infrastructure in these countries could do with some improvement. This is discussed in detail in the book. An analysis of the emerging domestic regulatory and governance regimes in these countries is necessary to understand the context for the local application of ethical principles; to provide information on these recent developments; and, as mentioned earlier, to proactively identify and draw attention to national systems and practices, and the potential issues, weaknesses, and problems that may arise in these new regimes. The analysis recognises differences in context and identifies how this affects research governance in each of the countries. More generally, there are also differences with regard to political governance, healthcare systems and priorities, and organisation of the legal system, which have potential effects on the governance of health research. For instance, while Nigeria runs a common-law system, South Africa runs a hybrid system, comprising the civil and common-law system, yet legislation plays a key role, sometimes limiting the differences in the way law applies in the research governance system. Subsequent chapters will engage in identifying and contextualising these similarities and differences, and exploring the impact of these on research governance in these countries.

Research governance is also discussed in this book, bearing in mind the need for more health research in improving health outcomes in Africa. In developing countries, including African countries, where an estimated 80 per cent of the world's population live, there is a high burden of disease and high levels of poverty, including communicable diseases; non-communicable diseases; and health-related social issues, such as violence and low levels of life expectancy. In these countries, health research is particularly important to finding ways of reducing that burden and, where possible, doing so by the least expensive means. Research into the factors that determine good health is also important. Although many of the diseases in developing countries require simple interventions that perhaps do not necessitate extensive health research, such as improved sanitation, adequate nutrition, and clean water, the high incidence of diseases such as HIV/AIDS and malaria means that continued health research remains crucial.[52] Also, therapies that have already proven effective elsewhere may need to be tested specifically in developing countries because of genetic and environmental differences.[53]

---

52 Nuffield Council on Bioethics, *The Ethics of Clinical Research in Developing Countries* (London: Nuffield Council on Bioethics 1999) at 2.
53 *Ibid*. at 15.

Research undertaken in the past in many African countries into diseases such as malaria, yellow fever, and trypanosomiasis has contributed immensely to knowledge about the prevention and treatment of these diseases. Clinical trials conducted in developing countries have contributed to public health knowledge and practice in both developing and developed countries.[54] The HIV/AIDS epidemic in particular – with an estimated 36.7 million people infected worldwide in 2015 and the majority of these people living in sub-Saharan Africa[55] – emphasises the need for research. HIV/AIDS research has made it possible to discover the cause of the disease and interventions, such as antiretroviral drugs that have made the disease a manageable condition rather than a death sentence. Pharmaceutical companies also sponsor research into new drugs in developing countries. The development of new drugs may be targeted for the needs of developing countries or may simply be undertaken for the development of new interventions for diseases which may not necessarily be prevalent in developing countries. The dependence on foreign sponsors creates its own problems, raising questions about the motives of such sponsors,[56] research priorities and how responsive research projects are to the health needs of the population, who sets the agenda for research in the developing world, and whether or not developing countries benefit adequately from such research efforts.

However, there has been an increase in the volume of research in these countries, a trend frequently referred to as the "globalization of research."[57] Some steps have been taken towards a reversal of the '10/90 gap:' the fact that 10 per cent of global resources went to 90 per cent of diseases which occur in the developing world.[58] The amount of research conducted in developing countries has since improved significantly, with much effort by many organisations.[59] Still the amount

---

54 See David Mabey, "Importance of Clinical Trials in Developing Countries" (1996) 348 Lancet 1113 for examples of trials in developing countries that have influenced clinical and public health practice in the developed world.

55 WHO, Global Health Observatory (GHO) data, online: <www.who.int/gho/hiv/en/> (September 9, 2017).

56 Reduced costs and a legislative and regulatory vacuum resulting in fewer delays and requirements, the availability and treatment of more willing and naïve participants, and foreign market development have been identified as possible motivations for multinational pharmaceutical companies' interest. See David M Carr, "Pfizer's Epidemic: A Need for International Regulation of Human Experimentation in Developing Countries" (2002) 35 Case W Res J Int'l L 15.

57 See Seth W Glickman et al, "Ethical and Scientific Implications of the Globalization of Clinical Research" (2009) 360:8 N Engl J Med 816.

58 Previous studies, particularly the study published by the Commission on Health Research for Development in 1990, had shown that only 10 per cent of the resources available globally are devoted to diseases that account for 90 per cent of global diseases, principally affecting poor people in developing countries – the "10/90 gap." Commission on Health Research for Development, *Health Research: Essential Link to Equity in Development* (New York: Oxford University Press, 1990). See also *The 10/90 Report on Health Research 2003–2004* (Geneva: Global Forum for Health Research, 2004) at 107–126.

59 Governmental organisations such as the NIH, the Centers for Disease Control (CDC) in the United States, the Canadian International Development Agency (CIDA), the International Development Research Centre (IDRC), the Canadian Institutes of Health Research (CIHR),

of research in developing countries trails behind research in developed countries and is still very much below optimal levels.[60] Even with the resources provided by sponsors in the developed world, there is still a wide gap in the resources for, and therefore the level of, health research conducted in Africa.[61] The increase in research has been noted to be uneven between countries and even between diseases.[62] With respect to new drugs, there is an inadequacy of effective, safe, and affordable medicines to control infectious diseases that cause high morbidity and mortality in developing countries.[63] Where treatments exist, they are sometimes old, toxic and difficult to administer, and unsuitable for the challenging conditions in developing countries.[64] Although there appears to be, in recent years, an increase in drug development in developing countries, pharmaceutical companies have frequently ignored diseases that occur in these countries because investment in research and development (R&D) would yield only poor, if any, returns.[65] The state of drug development in developing countries arguably shows both a failure of public policy (governments in both developing and developed countries have paid insufficient attention to this issue, including providing the necessary support and funding) and a shirking of ethical responsibility (pharmaceutical companies have consistently placed profit ahead of the lives of the poor).[66]

Research findings in developed countries, where more resources are expended on research, may not be easily transferable to developing country settings for

---

the United Kingdom Medical Research Council (MRC) and the United Kingdom Department for International Development (DfID), France's Agence Nationale de Recherches sur le Sida (ANRS), and the EDCTP; international organisations such as the WHO and United Nations Development Programme/World Bank/WHO 'Special Programme for Research and Training in Tropical Diseases' (TDR); and non-profit organisations originating in developed countries such as the Wellcome Trust and the Bill and Melinda Gates Foundation sponsor research on areas such as HIV/AIDS, tuberculosis, malaria, diabetes, hypertension, cardiovascular disease, and sexual and reproductive health in many developing countries.

60 See Mauricio L Barreto, "Health Research in Developing Countries" (2009) 339 BMJ b4846; Global Forum for Health Research, *10/90 Report on Health Research 2003–2004* (Geneva: Global Forum for Health Research, 2004), at 122. For health spending in general see Christopher Murray & Joseph Dieleman, "Global Health Funding Reaches New High as Funding Priorities Shift" Institute of Health Matrics and Evaluation, online: <www.healthdata.org/news-release/global-health-funding-reaches-new-high-funding-priorities-shift>.

61 Bernard Lown & Amitava Banerjee, "The Developing World in the New England Journal of Medicine" (2007) Globalization and Health, online: <www.globalizationandhealth.com/content/2/1/3>.

62 Sadie Regmi et al, "Research and Development Funding for 13 Neglected Tropical Diseases: An Observational Economic Analysis" (2014) 384:S20 The Lancet

63 Patrice Trouiller et al, "Drug Development for Neglected Diseases: A Deficient Market and a Public Policy Failure" (2002) 359:9324 Lancet 2188.

64 See Beatrice Stirner, "Stimulating Research and Development of Pharmaceutical Products for Neglected Diseases" (2008) 15 Eur J Health L 391 at 394.

65 One study pointed out that of 1,393 new chemical entities marketed between 1975 and 1999, only 16 were for tropical diseases and tuberculosis, and observed that there is a 13-fold greater possibility of bringing a drug for central-nervous-system disorders or cancer to the market than for a neglected disease. *Ibid.*

66 See Lavery, 87–85.

various reasons, including the facts that communicable diseases which are prevalent in developing countries are not typically prevalent and thus are not the focus of research in the developed world, sociocultural and economic circumstances differ, and interventions developed in the Western world do not always work as effectively in the developing world.[67] Genetics, cost factors, and climatic conditions may require different interventions to be developed for African countries.

Despite the obvious need for health research in developing countries, resources for undertaking such research are sadly lacking. Many African countries lack sufficient numbers of trained researchers, infrastructure, and general resources to allocate to health research.[68] They often lack the political will to devote the resources available to them to health research. Where resources are allocated within national research policies, they are sometimes not expended. There is a high level of dependence, therefore, on foreign sponsors in the developed world. The book addresses this in more detail in subsequent chapters.

In sum, although some increase in resources and in the volume of health research has been noted, as the previous discussion indicates, the disequilibrium in resources devoted to health research in developing countries persists. In the discussion that follows regarding the governance of research in developing countries, one cannot lose sight of the fact that there is need for more health research in African countries. More research remains necessary to address public health needs, improve health outcomes, increase life expectancy, and promote human rights and economic development. Hopefully, the growing trend in health research in developing countries will continue and will extend to African countries and to neglected diseases. The emergence of public health problems such as Ebola Virus Disease and the Zika virus the increased risk of the travel which is shrinking the world, and the consequent globalisation of diseases indicates that this would benefit not only Africa but the world.

The need for more research in developing countries should, however, be balanced with the necessity of adequate oversight in African countries. Finding this balance is likely to be tricky; a potential conflict of interest situation may arise between getting ready research funding or pharmaceutical R&D and tightening regulations. Governance of health research is necessary in developing countries, alongside the need for increased research on neglected diseases in developing countries. External help from developed countries and international organisations may be necessary to address issues of costs and gain increased understanding of regulatory and governance systems from countries which have had them for longer. Such external help recognises the fact that developed countries have an interest in disease eradication in developing countries because many diseases do not respect geographic boundaries. Diseases such as HIV/AIDS require research, which should realistically occur in many developing

---

67 Global Forum on Health Research, at 124–125.
68 Trudie Lang et al, "Clinical Research in Resource-Limited Settings: Enhancing Research Capacity and Working Together to Make Trials Less Complicated" (2010) 4:6 PLoS Negl Trop Dis e619. doi:10.1371/journal.pntd.0000619.

countries as there is a greater burden of that disease in such countries. Yet such research would benefit developed countries too as they seek to provide treatments and cures to their own citizens. Effective regulation of such research in developing countries would therefore benefit developed countries. As will become clear in the discussions that follow, some external assistance from foreign countries has been forthcoming and is increasingly a key component of the steps that some African countries have taken in regard to the domestic governance of research.[69] By some accounts, an estimated 19 million dollars was spent on ethics review between 2002 and 2012, targeted at establishing new ethics review committees and building research ethics capacity.[70] All told, however, the issue of costs does not negate the need for domestic governance systems. In addition, some of the critical health problems which developing countries face require research, and such research would occur more safely within a regulated environment which takes into consideration the peculiarities of the developing world context.

It would of course be naïve to ignore or gloss over global inequalities and how these may affect the steps that African countries are willing to take to protect their citizens while encouraging that beneficial health research be undertaken. There is a need to better understand the relationship between the two sides of the debate. That is, there is conceivably a relationship between the need for increased resources for beneficial research in developing countries and the regulation of such research. It can be argued that appropriate governance structures may create more room to undertake, and manage, such research. To explain further, there is the possibility that such structures may ensure that such research operates within safe, clearly established parameters. This, in turn, may help create trust between researchers and research participants and the wider community, thus potentially making increased room for research that is more likely to be beneficial to the target population. This way, everyone stands to gain – researchers, research participants, and the wider community. It may also create more bureaucratic structures to give a semblance of regulation – more ethics review committees, more documents to file, to meet international and foreign sponsor requirements – without necessarily protecting research participants effectively.

Trust is a particularly important factor to consider in the African context. This is because the erosion of trust affects not only the potential participation

69 These include research ethics capacity-building programs developed by the Fogarty International Center of the United States National Institutes of Health and the European-based European and Developing Countries Clinical Trials Partnership (EDCTP). See Paul Ndebele et al, "Research Ethics Capacity Building in Sub-Saharan Africa: A Review of NIH Fogarty-Funded Programs 2000–2012" (2014) 9:2 J Empir Res Hum Res Ethics 24–40; Nancy E Kass et al, "Bioethics Training Programmes for Africa: Evaluating Professional and Bioethics-Related Achievements of African Trainees after a Decade of Fogarty NIH Investment" (2016) 6:9 BMJ e012758.

70 Carel Ijsselmuiden et al, "Mapping African Ethical Review Committee onto Capacity Needs: The MARC Initiative and HR Web's Interactive Database of RECs in Africa" (2012) 12 Dev World Bioeth 74.

in health research[71] but also participation by the general population in important and beneficial health programmes. For instance, the rejection in 2004 of the polio vaccine in Northern Nigeria (a disease that has largely been eradicated in many countries around the world) has been attributed, in part, to the fears engendered by the Pfizer incident.[72] The unanticipated costs of failure to ensure that governance structures are effective may be catastrophic to much-needed health research and may therefore exceed the costs of proper governance. Research governance, as defined in this book, does not therefore draw a strict dichotomy between increasing research and ensuring the protection of research participants. Indeed the view is taken that better research protections will help to ensure the safety, and preserve the trust, of research participants in developing countries, which might, in turn, facilitate greatly needed health research in those countries. What does this mean in practice? Does this mean an increase in bureaucracy and layers of administrative procedures which may have the attendant effect of limiting much-needed research?[73] Or does it mean regulation of research to prevent fraudulent practices?[74] Thus, how to balance the two competing priorities, regulating research and attracting research investment, remains a key question for African countries.

A note on the term "Health Research"

It is important to note that, although there tends to be a focus in the literature, and even in research governance systems, on biomedical or clinical research (perhaps because of the more obvious physical risk involved in such research), health research involving humans is not restricted to such research. Health research involving humans also extends to social science or behavioural research and research in the humanities in which humans are the subjects, which may have health implications. For instance, the example of the Tudor study,[75] in which it was sought to determine if children could be induced to stutter by being labelled as stutterers, may, strictly speaking, not be considered clinical research,

---

71 See, for example, Irene Jao et al, "Involving Research Stakeholders in Developing Policy on Sharing Public Health Research Data in Kenya: Views on Fair Process for Informed Consent, Access Oversight, and Community Engagement" (2015) 10:3 J Empir Res Hum Res Ethics, online: <http://journals.sagepub.com/doi/full/10.1177/1556264615592385> noting that in collaborative international research in African countries "an important underlying issue is one of maintaining the trust of researchers, community stakeholders, and the wider public."

72 See Ayodele Samuel Jegede, "What Led to the Nigerian Boycott of the Polio Vaccination Campaign?" (2007) 4:3 PLoS Med e73. doi:10.1371/journal.pmed.0040073 (April 3, 2007). See also Ebenezer Obadare, "A Crisis of Trust: History, Politics, Religion and the Polio Controversy in Northern Nigeria" (2005) 39:3 Patterns of Prejudice 265 at 278–279.

73 See Trudie Lang & Sisira Siribaddana, "Clinical Trials Have Gone Global: Is This a Good Thing?" (2012) 9:6 PLoS Med e1001228. doi:10.1371/journal.pmed.1001228.

74 See, for example, the BMJ's exposé of fraudulent clinical trials in China – "80% of China's Clinical Trial Data Are Fraudulent, Investigation Finds" (2016) 355 BMJ i5396.

75 Nicoline Grinager Ambrose & Ehud Yairi, "The Tudor Study: Data and Ethics" (2002) 11 Am J Speech Lang Pathol 190–203.

and yet it caused harm to children. Other examples may include a study of the effect of sexual violence on women during a civil war; the effect of domestic violence on the mental health status of women; a study of stigmatisation as a result of infection with leprosy, mental illness, or HIV; studies on sexual behaviours of persons who have undergone HIV testing and counselling, aimed at reducing high-risk sexual behaviour; or studies of the health effects of domestic violence and emotional abuse against women. Such research also includes studies involving children with learning disabilities or cognitive impairments or studies involving access to records of personal or confidential information, including genetic or other biological information, concerning identifiable persons. These scenarios can all, in a broad understanding of "health," be considered health research involving humans. In these kinds of research, there is also the possibility of harm. For instance, failure to obtain informed consent or disclosure of private information obtained over the course of the research may cause harm to research participants. Other harms may include psychological stress or an experiencing of anxiety or humiliation.

As Downie points out, and as the previous examples show, research risks are not so neatly identified with disciplines. The discipline, by itself, does not determine the presence or absence of ethical considerations but rather whether or not the methodology employed (which is not determined by the discipline) results in the research having a direct impact on human beings.[76] Moreover, with the increasingly interdisciplinary nature of investigations of health accompanying the recognition that the determinants of health not only come from health therapies and technologies but are also dependent on social and economic factors, focussing governance only on biomedical research seems faulty. In any event, many institutions and countries have adopted the gradation of risk, including the concept of "minimal risk," in an attempt to provide a system where research is reviewed according to the intensity of the risk.

With respect to risks, Waring and Lemmens classify the risks accompanying health research involving humans into two broad categories: risks to the person and risks to social values. Risks to the person might be physical, such as death or injury resulting from interventions or unexpected responses to environmental, genetic, pharmacological, or environmental factors. Risks to the person might also be psychological harms, including psychological stress or an experiencing of anxiety or humiliation. Risks to social values include risks to the objectivity and scientific integrity of research that are posed by conflicts of interest and to public trust in the ethical conduct of research.[77] Research risks may also be collective in the sense that research may potentially harm a community

---

76 See Jocelyn Downie, "Contemporary Health Research: A Cautionary Tale" (2003) Health L J (Special Edition) at 1.

77 Duff R Waring & Trudo Lemmens, "Integrating Values in Risk Analysis of Biomedical Research: The Case for Regulatory and Law Reform" (2004) 54:3 U Toronto L J 249 at 251. See also Baruch A Brody, Laurence B McCullough, & Richard R Sharp, "Consensus and Controversy in Clinical Research Ethics" (2005) 294:11 JAMA 1411 at 1412.

instead of an individual. The results of research may cause significant harm in the community, for instance, in situations where the results are used to justify discrimination against or within a community or support harmful stereotypes or social perceptions. Such harm is of particular issue in already vulnerable and disadvantaged communities in various countries, including African countries. The dangers of research can also include the possibility of suffering wrongs, as noted by Macklin. Wrongs, in this case, may be defined as harms to one's interests.[78] For example, a participant may have feelings of having their privacy invaded or may feel wronged by virtue of a loss of control where tissue travels or is used in a manner not anticipated by a research participant due to insufficient understanding during the informed consent process. These risks are the main reason why health research involving humans requires regulation by effective governance mechanisms. They can also occur in different types of health research. All told, therefore, it may not be wise to draw a strict line between the types of research – biomedical research or social science research which has health implications – particularly since there are risks in these types (although the risks are perhaps more conspicuous in biomedical research and less easy to assess in social and behavioural research). This strict demarcation is avoided in this book.

Thrust

Part of the aim in conducting this analysis is to describe and set out in detail the emergent research governance systems in Africa. The descriptions are then employed in assessing and evaluating the adequacy of some systems in place and in making suggestions for further improvement. Several questions are raised, and an attempt is made to answer them in this book. Such questions include: how have the debates about certain provisions of the international guidelines affected the governance of health research involving humans in these countries? What are the emergent policies? How effective are the emergent national policies? What are the mechanisms for regulating research? Are there differences between national policies and international ethical guidelines and funding guidelines? If there are, how do these differences impact the protection of research participants in these countries? What is the role of law, if any, in these systems, and what are the implications of this role or lack thereof on the protection of research participants? What ought to be the role of law? Other key governance issues include: the current challenges African countries face in regulating research, the strengths and weaknesses of the governance system currently under development in African countries, and the improvements needed to ensure good research governance. This book addresses these issues in order to provide a comprehensive and systemic view of the governance of research involving humans in African countries.

---

78 Ruth Macklin, *Ethics in Global Health: Research, Policy and Practice* (New York: Oxford University Press, 2012) at 239.

2 Governance as an analytical framework for health research involving humans

Governance, law, and regulation

Health research involving humans in developing countries has been the subject of much ethical analysis, particularly in the area of biomedical research. In Chapter 1, I argued that more work is needed to understand emerging research governance systems in African countries and link the various parts of the governance of research into a comprehensive whole. This chapter explores one way to address this vacuum by taking an in-depth look at governance and its relevance to research regulation in Africa.

Health research involving humans is one area of human endeavour in which the areas of governance and regulation have particular relevance. As explained briefly in the preceding chapter, formal and informal mechanisms are employed in the regulation of research involving humans to ensure, among other things, that research is conducted within ethically acceptable and safe parameters. This chapter seeks then to propose an analysis of health research involving humans using a governance analytical framework. This understanding is then applied throughout the book in the discussion of the governance of health research in African countries.

The term "governance" is applied liberally with respect to research involving humans. Sometimes it is used interchangeably with the related term "regulation." Do they mean the same thing? Can they mean the same thing in the particular context of regulating the conduct of research involving humans? And how effectively can governance be deployed as an analytical framework for health research involving humans in African countries?

Governance: definitional concerns

Governance and regulation have become very relevant and interesting areas of consideration for scholars in recent years. 'Governance' is a term used liberally not only in relation to regulation or organisational management but in political administration internationally and domestically as well as in the field of development. As a concept, it appears to be subject to many interpretations. And the increasing recognition of 'new' governance arrangements has added to confusion as to the meaning of the term. In particular, these "new" governance arrangements have spurred whole schools of thought devoted to understanding the concept of governance within political and social science.[1]

The concept of governance has been used in academic and other literature in various ways. In discussions about states in general, and developing countries in particular, governance is frequently employed in discussions relating to democracy and the rule of law, and the challenges that developing countries face in these areas. The reference to democracy and rule of law may allow us to view this idea of governance as "democratic governance," a system by which governments are selected or changed and the interactions of the governments various organs and institutions. Apart from the democratic nature of any specific government, governance is also used in reference to the responsibilities of governments and the capacity of civil society to articulate its interests and exercise legal rights and obligations prompting the term, "good governance" often employed by international development agencies.[2] In promoting the idea of good governance, these institutions have taken steps to encourage democracy and free-market reforms, promote institutional and regulatory reforms, shift power from the public sector or government to the private sector, and engage civil society in the process of achieving public goals in an efficient manner. This usage of governance draws together strands from the political, administrative, and economic values of legitimacy and efficiency.[3]

The term "governance" has also been used particularly in academic literature in referring to the changes associated with transformations in the regulatory landscape, the different roles now adopted by governments (or the state), and private and non-state actors. In this sense, governance, also described as "new" governance, refers to "a basically nonhierarchical mode of governing, where non-state, private corporate actors (formal organizations) participate in the formulation and

1 Kees Van Kersbergen & Frans Van Waarden, "'Governance' as a Bridge between Disciplines: Cross-Disciplinary Inspiration Regarding Shifts in Governance and Problems of Governability, Accountability and Legitimacy" (2004) 43:1 Eur J Polit Res 141. See also Oliver Treib, Holger Bähr, & Gerda Falkner, "Modes of Governance: Towards a Conceptual Clarification" (2007) 14:1 J Eur Pub Pol'y 1.

2 UNDP, *Reconceptualising Governance* (New York: UNDP, 1997), online: <www.pogar.org/publications/other/undp/governance/reconceptualizing.pdf> at 9.

3 See Cynthia Hewitt de Alcantra, "Uses and Abuses of the Concept of Governance" (1998) 50:155 Int'l Soc Sci J 105 at 106. de Alcantra notes that the increasing reliance of international development agencies on the concept of governance signifies an intellectual shift from complete reliance on free-market policies to a more social and development-oriented approach. She points out that

> By talking about 'governance' – rather than 'state reform' or 'social and political change – multilateral banks and agencies within the development establishment were able to address sensitive questions that could be lumped together under a relatively offensive heading and usually couched in technical terms, thus avoiding any implications that these institutions were exceeding their statutory authority by intervening in the internal political affairs of sovereign affairs.

implementation of public policy,"[4] "the investigation of a plurality of sites of non-state regulatory activity,"[5] or "activities related to public purposes that are undertaken jointly by multiple actors, including those 'beyond government,' or at the very least beyond the organizational boundaries of a single government."[6] This conception of governance involves several core ingredients, including the accomplishing of public goals through collaboration with other organisations, such as private-sector and non-profit organisations, and employing non-hierarchical, informal, and extraconstitutional means.[7] This understanding is different from what may be referred to as the "old" or traditional governance, which denotes a process of steering and controlling activities in the economy and the society in which the state plays a central role.[8]

Beyond any specific understanding of the concept, however, governance has a generic meaning which underlies the different understandings held in particular fields of thought. "Governance, at whatever level of social organization it occurs, refers to the systems of authoritative norms, rules, institutions, and practices by means of which any collectivity, from the local to the global, manages its common affairs."[9] It is this generic sense of governance, applicable to regulation and management activities in a variety of institutions and organisations, that is frequently applied to our understanding of the need for controlling health research involving humans. In this respect, according the University of Ottawa Centre on Governance, governance is, broadly speaking, "about the processes by which human organizations, whether private, public or civic, steer themselves."[10] In a

---

4 Renate Maynzt, "From Government to Governance: Political Steering in Modern Societies." Paper presented at the Summer Academy on IPP: Wuerzburg, September 7–11, 2003, online: <www.ioew.de/governance/english/veranstaltungen/Summer_Academies/SuA2Mayntz.pdf>.

5 Peter Swan, "Governing at a Distance: An Introduction to Law, Regulation and Governance" in Michael Mac Neil, Neil Sargent, & Peter Swan, eds, *Law, Regulation, and Governance* (Ontario: Oxford University Press, 2002) at 10.

6 RAW Rhodes, "The New Governance: Governance without Government" (1996) 44 Pol Stu 652 at 653.

7 Karen Mossenberger, "The Many Meanings of Governance: How Should We Develop Research and Theory?" (2007). Draft Paper Prepared for the Conference: "A Global Look at Urban and Regional Governance: The State-Market –Civic Nexus" January 18–19, 2007, at 2.

8 Jon Pierre, "Introduction: Understanding Governance" in Jon Pierre, ed, *Debating Governance* (Houndmills, Basingstoke, Hampshire: Palgrave Macmillan, 2000) at 3.

9 John Gerard Ruggie, "Global Governance and "New Governance Theory": Lessons from Business and Human Rights" (2014) 20:1 Global Governance: A Review of Multilateralism and International Organizations 5–17. See also de Alcantra, noting that "In the English speaking world, 'governance' is a word routinely used over the course of many centuries to refer to the exercise of authority within a given sphere. It has often been employed as a synonym for the efficient management of a broad range of organisations and activities, from the modern corporation (corporate governance) or university (the governance of Vassar College) to the ocean depths." De Alcantra, at 105. See also Luca Gnan, Alessandor Hinna, & Fabio Monteduro, *Conceptualizing and Researching Governance in Public and Non-Profit Organisations* (Bingley, UK: Emerald Group Publishing, 2013) at x.

10 Quoted in M McDonald, *The Governance of Health Research Involving Human Subjects* (Ottawa: Law Commission of Canada, 2000) at 22.

description that presents a holistic conception of governance, a Law Commission of Canada study explains the concept of governance as pertaining

> not only to organizations, but also to the complex ways in which private, public and social organizations interact and learn from one another, the manner in which citizens contribute to the governance system, directly and indirectly, through their collective participation in civil, public and corporate institutions; and the instruments, regulations and processes that define the 'rules of the game.'[11]

These generic descriptions of governance, which are applicable to any activity that requires some control, perhaps explain the liberal use of the term, with particular regard to research involving humans, and are helpful for the purpose of analysis in this book. Thus, the concept may be seen by some as allowing some form of control over activities, without necessarily requiring governmental input or intervention. On the other hand, as exemplified by its usage in the context of democratic governance or even the idea of good governance, the role of the state in the process of governance cannot simply be ignored. The generic understanding of governance is pivotal to the analysis conducted in the book. However, the specific understandings of governance are helpful in trying to develop a suitable and useful framework for analysing the systems that regulate research involving humans in African countries.

The commonalities in the different approaches to governance are captured effectively in the generic definition which I have adopted for this book: "the processes by which human organizations, whether private, public or civic, steer themselves,"[12] with a core element of regulation and control to achieve certain goals. In this respect, "Governance, within the socio-legal frame, is an overarching concept to describe the complex and multi-faceted social processes – official and unofficial, intended and unintended, visible and invisible – that together mediate social behaviour and conduct."[13] From this generic perspective, governance not only is about achieving goals and objectives through positive and negative control but also includes the provision of policies, facilities, processes, instruments (such as statutes and policy mandates), available resources, institutions, and institutionalised rules and norms by which these goals are to be realised.[14]

The terms "governance" and "regulation" are frequently used interchangeably and sometimes together. However, regulation is, broadly speaking, a process of imposing order and prescribing acceptable conduct.[15] The term, like governance,

---

11 *Ibid.* at 4.
12 From the University of Ottawa Centre on Governance, quoted in M McDonald, *ibid.*
13 Chotray and Stoker, at 14.
14 McDonald, *supra* Note 10 at 208. See also Frederickson & Smith, *supra* Note 60 at 214.
15 See Christine Parker et al, eds, "Introduction" in *Regulating Law* (Oxford: Oxford University Press, 2004) at 4. See also Anthony Ogus, *Regulation: Legal Form and Economic Theory* (Oxford: Clarendon Press, 1994) at 1.

is also used in a variety of situations, but it is more often than not understood as the command-and-control techniques by which the state, typically through the use of legally backed sanctions, prescribes acceptable conduct. Regulation is conceived, by traditionalists, as a product of the state or government. This concept of regulation locates its basis in the theory of legal positivism.[16] Thus one could, as Majone does, define regulation as "sustained and focused control exercised by a public agency, on the basis of a legislative mandate, over activities that are generally regarded as desirable to society" or, as Hood and others do, "the use of public authority to set and apply rules and standards."[17] This understanding of regulation is associated with, and mostly limited to, law in the form of formal legislation or legal regulations or a set of authoritative rules, often administered by a governmental agency for monitoring and enforcing compliance.[18] Regulation as rule-making and rule enforcement by governments, according to King, has its roots in the early stages of modern statehood and is a function undertaken by all states.[19] However, although this view of regulation as rule making and enforcement has been predominant (especially in legal circles), it is becoming increasingly outdated as many begin to accept the notion of regulation as a wider activity encompassing more than command and control.

Regulation is widely acknowledged as including different types of regulation, such as regulation by law, economic or fiscal regulation (for example, through the use of taxes or licensing), market regulation (or regulation by market forces), or self-regulation within a particular industry or profession (which may be acknowledged by law). Further, different disciplines have different conceptions of regulation. For instance, for economists, regulation may be the means by which private firms are compelled to adopt anticompetitive behaviour. Some therefore view economics, law, and politics as intertwined from a regulatory perspective, while some distinguish between economic regulation and social regulation.[20] A more contemporary and arguably more comprehensive and appropriate view of regulation

16 See discussion in Roderick MacDonald, "The Swiss Army Knife of Governance" in Pearl Eliadas, Margaret Hill & Michael Howlett, *Designing Government: From Instruments to Governance* (Montreal & Kingston: McGill-Queens University Press, 2005), hereafter *Designing Government*.

17 G Majone, *Regulating Europe* (London: Routledge, 1996) at 9; C Hood et al, *Regulation inside Government: Waste-Watchers, Quality Police and Sleaze- Busters* (Oxford: Oxford University Press, 1999) at 3. See also Julia Black, "Critical Reflections on Regulation" (2002) 27 Austl J Legal Phil 1 at 11–12.

18 See, for example, Hans J Kleinsteuber, "The Internet between Regulation and Governance: Self-Regulation, Co-Regulation, State Regulation" in *The Media Freedom Internet Cookbook* (Organization for Security and Co-operation in Europe, 2004) at 63.

19 Roger King, *The Regulatory State in an Age of Governance: Soft Words and Big Sticks* (Houndmills, Basingstoke & Hampshire: Palgrave Macmillan, 2007) at 13.

20 See Macgregor observing that regulation is "a process in which economics, politics and law are inextricably intertwined." L McGregor, T Prossert, & C Villiers, eds, *Regulation and Markets Beyond* (Aldershot: Ashgate, 2000) at 3. See also M Minogue, "Governance-Based Analysis of Regulation" (2003) 73:4 Ann Public & Coop Econ 649. See generally R Baldwin, C Scott, & C Hood, *A Reader on Regulation* (New York: Oxford University Press, 1998).

includes both state and non-state actors, legislation, and other non-formal forms of law and social rules.[21] This understanding of regulation identifies more closely with the understanding of the "new governance," described in detail in the following sections. It may be fruitful to consider regulation as an intentional attempt to control, order, or influence the behaviour of others. Indeed some consider regulation as always intentional, even though its results and outcomes may be unintended.[22] In this sense, regulation is not limited to state intervention in the economy or society or targeted rules, and it includes the basic prerequisites for a regulatory regime: namely, the setting of standards, processes for monitoring compliance with the standards, and mechanisms for enforcing standards.[23]

The view of regulation as controlling of conduct or imposing of order leads to thinking that it may only be an aspect of governance which emphasises a wide variety of actors and the coordination of different mechanisms in managing a policy sphere. This is particularly true if one considers regulation as a product of the state. For instance, Swan observes that "governance defined as any strategy, process, procedure, or program for controlling, regulating, or exercising authority over animate or inanimate objects or populations, is regarded as being much broader than the conception of state-centred regulation."[24] A review of the literature shows that although some may still regard regulation as 'what states do,' increasingly, governance is used to indicate the fact that non-state bodies do something similar (particularly in the context of the 'new' governance). Many authors then extrapolate from this to employ governance as the overarching term and 'regulation' as a subset of governance.[25]

As only an aspect of governance, regulation may not completely capture all the activities or all the actors which a governance framework anticipates, including, for instance, citizens and their participation in the process. Governance may therefore be a higher-order or more encompassing activity that includes regulation (involving the setting of standards, processes for monitoring compliance with the standards, and mechanisms for enforcing standards) but also many other kinds of actions, policy options, and approaches.[26] Indeed, some describe governance broadly as "the regulation of social activities utilizing a variety of modes and mechanisms of societal regulation"[27] and as "all the forms of regulation that are neither market nor state: it is civil society minus the market... plus

---

21 Fiona McDonald, *Patient Safety, Governance and Regulation* (Unpublished thesis submitted to Dalhousie University, 2009) at 13.

22 Alan Hunt, *Explorations in Law and Society: Toward a Constitutive Theory of Law* (New York: Routledge, 1993) at 315.

23 See Parker et al, *supra* Note 15 at 4.

24 Swan, Note 5 at 11.

25 Thanks to Professor Julia Black of the London School of Economics for her helpful attempt to clarify these terms.

26 Thanks to Professor Lahey of the Schulich School of Law, Dalhousie University, for this concise summary.

27 Volker Schneider & Johannes M Bauer, "Governance: Prospects of Complexity Theory in Revisiting System Theory" (2007). Paper presented at the Annual Meeting of the Midwest Political Science Association, Palmer House Hotel, Chicago, IL, April 12, 2007, online: <www.quello.msu.edu/images/uploads/wp-07-01.pdf>.

local political society."[28] The governance of research involving humans could thus be argued to include all regulatory activities affecting such research. Conceived in this way, then, regulation is subsumed in, and is only a component of, governance. Agreeing with this view, Braithwaite, Coglianese, and Levi-Faur describe 'governance' as a broader term than 'regulation.' To them,

> Governments and governance are about providing, distributing, and regulating. Regulation can be conceived as that *large subset of governance* that is about steering the flow of events and behavior, as opposed to providing and distributing. Of course, when regulators regulate, they often steer the providing and distributing that regulated actors undertake as well.[29]

However, even if one assumes that regulation is not an activity engaged in only by the state in a top-down, command-and-control fashion but an activity which involves a controlling of conduct by other actors, governance could still be argued to be a broader domain. This is because, perhaps more than regulation, governance allows for a wide range of actors and institutions; permits the examination of the distribution of rights obligations and power that support the organisational system and the patterns of coordination that support its activities and sustain coherence; establishes benchmarks, and allows the sharing of knowledge to ensure restoration when there are signs that the system requires repair.[30]

---

28 Bob Jessop, "The Regulation Approach, Governance and Post-Fordism: Alternative Perspectives on Economic and Political Change?" (1995) 24 Econ & Soc 307 at 313; Georges Benko & A Lipietz, "De la Régulation des Espaces aux Espaces de Régulation" in R Boyer, eds, *Théorie de la Régulation: L'état des Savoirs* (Paris: La Découverte, 1994) at 293–303.

29 John Braithwaite, Cary Coglianese, & David Levi-Faur, "Can Regulation and Governance Make a Difference?" (2007) 1:1 Regulation & Governance 1 at 3, (emphasis mine). Lobel adds that regulation as a concept carries with it the problematic issues of boundaries and predetermined solutions but that the concept of governance is "open, dynamic, and diverse with a built-in temporal dimension." Braithwaite and Parker further point out that "Governance is a more general theoretical domain than regulation in that governance is also about allocating resources in ways that are not intended to steer the flow of events" and that "regulatory theory is becoming an increasingly central part of the theory of governance." Orly Lobel, "The Renewal Deal: The Fall of Regulation and the Rise of Governance" (2004) 89 Minn L Rev 342. However, others, particularly those who view governance only from the perspective of "new" governance, see it as being narrower than regulation. In this vein, Vincent-Jones notes that

> Thus, there is sufficient common ground in regulation and governance theories to suggest that a synbook is possible and may be useful in the analysis of central-local relations. However, while the approaches share a concern with processes of social control, direction and influence, there are fundamental differences in the form of inquiry and scope of explanation. In the regulation approach, the motivating force is the state as a 'purposeful actor.' Governance theorists studying the exercise of political power through governmentality, on the other hand, address the narrower issue of what authorities of various sorts want to happen, in relation to problems defined how, in pursuit of what objectives, and through what strategies and techniques.

Peter Vincent-Jones, "Values and Purpose in Government: Central-Local Relations in Regulatory Perspective" (2002) 29 J L & Soc 27 at 31.

30 *Ibid.*

In any event, whatever views one holds, there is certainly a significant correlation between governance and regulation. This book employs the term 'governance' as involving regulation (with the ingredients of standard-setting, compliance-monitoring, and standards enforcement) as a core element. Regulatory theory is therefore drawn on significantly in the analysis undertaken in this book. It is, however, convenient to employ primarily the term (and framework of) governance, especially given that it is used quite frequently in the literature dealing with research involving humans. But beyond this convenience, the generic understanding of governance, the different meanings which one can attach to the term, and the literature on the 'new governance,' which I employ in my analysis later, affords broad room for understanding, analysing, and making recommendations on the emerging research governance systems in developing countries.

It may also be necessary to distinguish law from governance because law, however conceived, also deals with the controlling of behaviour, both in a normative and positivist sense. Considered in the positivist sense advocated by Hart, law represents rules articulated and enforced by an institutionalised authority which regulates conduct or behaviour.[31] In this sense, law, as an official product of the state and as a set of rules articulated by the state and usually backed by sanctions (hard law), is a critical part of the much-maligned command-and-control regulation. The state, then, is clearly an actor (perhaps the most important actor) in regulation and governance. As I will argue in the following subsections, in some circumstances, despite the increasing acknowledgement of the role of other actors in regulation and governance, the state (with its function of developing formal law) remains a very important actor. Whether or not one views regulation as broader than the positivist view of the top-down use of state authority to control conduct, law performs some regulatory and instrumental functions (which Black refers to as "regulatory law"[32]). It is a mechanism or one of the policy options envisaged by governance. Law, then, is a lever of action with the object or purpose of changing or controlling behaviour with prescriptions.[33] The concerns attached to seeing law as a tool of governance in the form of legislation and legal regulations would thus relate to how the state seeks to achieve compliance and may also include creating mechanisms in legislation or legal regulations for allowing self-regulation by the persons or organisations which need to be regulated.

Since it regulates conduct, it is obvious that there is a close relationship between law, governance, and regulation. This relationship is perhaps clearer to sociolegal scholars, who consider law in social contexts, than legal scholars who take an internal view of law and focus on doctrine.[34] For sociolegal scholars,

---

31 Julia Black, "Law and Regulation: The Case of Finance" in Parker et al, Note 23 at 34.

32 *Ibid.*

33 Roderick A Macdonald, "The Swiss Army Knife of Governance" in Pearl Eliadis, Margaret M Hill, & Michael Howlett, *Designing Government: From Instruments to Governance* (Montreal & Kingston: McGill-Queen's University Press, 2001) at 219.

34 See Angus Corbett & Stephen Bottomley, "Regulating Corporate Governance" in Parker et al, Note 23 at 37.

then, the linkages between law, governance, and regulation are not limited to the objective of controlling conduct in order to achieve certain social goals. In this regard, looking at law through a regulatory lens may also involve understanding the interactions between hard law and soft law, doctrines and legislation, and public and private law as well as the effect that common law doctrines may have on the operation of statutory law intended to regulate conduct and vice versa.[35] It would also involve looking at the ways in which legal norms affect the regulatory environment. In subsequent sections of this chapter and in the following chapter, I consider the role of law in the governance of research involving humans in developing countries.

Governance: old, new, hybrid

Concerns about overregulation, inefficiency of regulating institutions, legalism, inflexibility and costs of regulation, and arguments in favour of deregulation have gained ground in recent years. Much has thus been made of the concept of "new" governance, which allows greater participation of private actors in social regulation. Much of the literature dealing with the new governance, in attempting to define this concept, thus identifies and elaborates an increasing de-emphasis on hierarchical regulation by the state through strictly command-and-control methods to governance through partnerships between the government and private entities, with the aim of achieving public goals. It describes the increasingly networked nature of the actors in governance; the proliferation of different tools in governance; and governments acting more indirectly, shifting lawmaking and other regulatory processes from a command-and-control framework to a more responsive approach tailored to local circumstances. It also describes the use of less traditional regulatory instruments and more creative means to achieve public objectives, including robust public participation, benchmarking, and information sharing, to solve public problems.[36] Partnerships between the state, industry, and civil society are thus one of the main hallmarks of the new governance.[37] Within the "new governance" concept, traditional ways of achieving regulatory goals yield not only to participative approaches but also to innovative approaches. These include voluntary approaches under which regulators work with industry associations to develop practice codes, information sharing practices, sharing of best practices, self-auditing that involves evaluation of compliance by regulated entities or third parties, management-based systems that entail firm responsibility for adhering to plans that limit regulated harms, and performance-based approaches that put emphasis on regulation for results.[38] In terms of regulation

---

35 Parker, Note 23 at 5.
36 Jason M Solomon, "Law and Governance in the 21st Century Regulatory State" (2008) 86 Tex L Rev 819 at 822.
37 Lobel, Note 41 at 374–375.
38 Peter J May, "Regulatory Regimes and Accountability" (2007) 1 Regulation & Governance 8 at 8.

in the new governance, "the scope of regulation as command shrinks while the parameters of regulation as self-governance unfold."[39] New governance systems may therefore include, in certain respects, systems of self-regulation, that is, systems where private actors, such as professional associations, regulate their members on issues delegated to them directly or indirectly by government.[40] Such self-governance typically takes place in the "shadow of hierarchy" (the state).[41] New governance tools or instruments also include soft law, that is, guidelines, benchmarks, and standards that have no formal sanctions rather than hard law, such as legislation (which in a positivist sense can be regarded as a top-down projection of state authority),[42] as key components of governance.[43]

As has been pointed out elsewhere, these systems are not necessarily new, as the term implies, and have had a long life in policymaking and literature,[44] but recognition of the concept and interest in the new ways in which government works to achieve public goals may be more recent.[45] Likewise, Trubek notes that the word "new" refers to the "widespread and explicit use of nonconventional forms of governing" and in the sense of being different from traditional modes of governing, rather than its novelty.[46]Lobel, for her part, considers the "newness" of the new governance approach to be an essential feature of this emerging approach, a dynamic innovation that allows the regime to constantly renew itself.[47] In any event, such governance aspires to being more open-textured, flexible, and participatory, involving all stakeholders in the regulatory process and responsive to contributions from those being regulated. The idea of regulation as the state's top-down control of behaviour through certain means, including the enactment and enforcement of legal rules, has increasingly given way to a growing reliance on private actors and non-legal rules. But the appropriate role of government in not only economic regulation but also social regulation remains open to debate.

In the African context, aspects of the "new" governance are clearly on display in various sites of regulation. The role of the business sector is increasingly recognised in the development of regulation. In Nigeria, for example, apart from collaborations in the areas of infrastructural development between the government

---

39 Swan, *supra* Note 5 at 14.
40 In such cases, state involvement is indirect if self-regulation takes place as a response to threats by government that if nothing is done, state action will follow. See Robert Baldwin & Martin Cave, *Understanding Regulation: Theory, Strategy, and Practice* (New York: Oxford University Press, 1999) at 126. See also Maynzt, at 4.
41 Maynzt, *ibid.*
42 McDonald, *supra* Note 10 at 209.
43 See Louise G Trubek, "New Governance and Soft Law in Health Care Reform" (2006) 3 Ind Health L Rev 139 at 158.
44 Jeremy Richardson, "New Governance or Old Governance? A Policy Style Perspective" in David Levi-Faur, ed, *Oxford Handbook of Governance* (New York: Oxford University Press, 2012) at 311–325.
45 See Lester M Salomon, "The New Governance and the Tools of Public Action: An Introduction" (2001–2002) 28 Fordham Urb L J 1611.
46 Trubek, *supra* Note 43.
47 Lobel, *supra* Note 29 342 at 348.

and the private sector in the form of public-private partnerships, for instance, the private health sector has established stakeholder groups to advocate for its interests. The private health sector has had representation on technical working groups developing health policy, health investments regulation, and so on. Furthermore, the impact of funding organisations like the Bill and Melinda Gates Foundation on regulation is by no means insignificant. Moreover, non-governmental organisations now form a key part of the governance institutions – working with governments, challenging governments to live up to their responsibilities, advocating for patients and other groups.[48] While several of these entities have been involved in healthcare provision and health research in Africa for a long time,[49] they are increasingly also involved in the policymaking sphere. Beyond the wider policy arena, these organisations – funding organisations, civil society organisations, professional regulatory bodies – all regulate research and other health activities internally, providing other sites of governance.

Even in the era of "new" governance, however, a clear role for the state remains in the governance of health research involving humans in Africa. As discussed in subsequent chapters examining some African countries' research governance systems, a role for the state persists through regulation via legislation that provides regulatory requirements. Researchers and research institutions must comply with these requirements, which often involve continuing relationships. Thus it has been observed that the state remains central in health issues, including research, and that

> the state has not disappeared…, it remains tangible in the many people enrolled in its workforce, its buildings and circulations, and its habitual procedures and paper trails; it also remains present in people's claims for care, in state providers' determination to define policies and standards, and even in foreign donors' insistence on working through state "partners." … All this is not quite the same as the developmental state of old, but it is not yet something altogether different either.… the state's place in biopolitical order has changed, not diminished.[50]

The reason the state remains a critical actor with its paraphernalia of legislation and other policy instruments yet operating more than ever in a "new" governance way in the health research sphere is captured succinctly by Geissler:[51]

> Why is the state still necessary for para-statal science? The answer is that it provides legitimacy and rationale to the scientific undertaking: the national

48 The Treatment Action Campaign in South Africa is a key example. The Socio-Economic Rights Action Program (SERAP) in Nigeria is another example.

49 P Wenzel Geissler, "Introduction: A Life Science in Its African Para-State" in *Para-States and Medical Science: Making African Global Health* (Durham, NC: Duke University Press; 2015).

50 *Ibid.* at 9.

51 Id at 9.

government retains legal responsibility and liability for research activities; it underwrites regulatory rules and provides ethics approval; it sets laboratory, pharmaceutical, and professional standards (although increasingly transnational standards such as iSo and Good Clinical Practice [GCP] are adhered to). It allows legitimate access to citizens' bodies and avails public medical facilities for the recruitment of participants, for clinical trial procedures, and for the referral of participants after the end of research projects. And finally, it serves as the ultimate destination of findings, which ideally translate—after circulation through global scientific journals and health policy agencies—into national health policies. Thus the state remains crucial to the activities, but it no longer functions as one center around and from which activities are assembled.[52]

Governance as an analytical framework for research involving humans

Health research involving humans, given its nature and the issues connected therewith, has been the subject of much ethical analysis. There is certainly a preoccupation in the literature with research ethics and institutional and research practice. Although this is not out of place, understanding the subject of health research involving humans beyond the ethical standards or even the work of ethics review committees requires a broader perspective. Analysing this subject comprehensively from the perspective of controlling and managing it requires a broader framework of analysis than a strictly ethical framework or even a legal framework or one that considers only an organisational framework. It requires a framework that is able to marry these different angles effectively to provide a broad and wide-ranging analysis, and offer an encompassing account of the regulation of health research in African countries.

As an analytical framework, then, governance (particularly the new governance perspective and its variants) takes a systems approach, permitting the discussion of steering of activities in terms of the interrelated parts of that activity, that is, the institutions and organisations involved in a particular policy field. It recognises the institutions within a system and all the actors in the policy field, including those being regulated, as potentially active actors in the governance process.[53] Thus it allows for the study of the configuration of particular institutions, organisations, and agencies involved in various ways in a system (such as the research governance system) and the interactions of, and relationships between, these bodies.[54]

The contribution of the governance perspective to theory, argues Stoker, is not at the level of causal analysis, nor does it offer a new normative theory.

---

52 P Wenzel Geissler, A Life Science in Its African Para- State at 13.
53 Bjoern Niehaves, Karstern Klose, & Joerg Becker, "Governance Theory Perspectives on IT Consulting Projects: The Case of ERP Implementation" (2006) 5:1 E-Service J 5 at 9.
54 McDonald, *supra* Note 10 at 22.

Instead, its significance lies in serving as an organising framework and providing a framework for understanding changing processes of governing.[55] As a theoretical framework, it is rather broad and thus may be considered too wide as an analytical framework.[56] This breadth might be seen as a weakness in terms of depth, but this is also its strength, especially as a framework for investigating a system such as that of health research involving humans, which consists of different actors, systems, and institutions. As Schneider and Bauer assert, the major advantage of governance is "that it provides a rather abstract frame in order to cover a broad array of institutional arrangements and mechanisms by which the coordination, regulation and control of social systems and subsystems can be conceptualized."[57] As an analytical framework, then, governance has descriptive, explanatory, organising, and normative value that not only allows us, in my view, to examine the policy response to any particular field of activity, in this case, health research involving humans, but also compels us to think more broadly in terms of the systems governing that field and the constellation of actors and institutions that come together to make up the systems, and to question what the appropriate relationships and interactions between them should be.

Further, as a concept, governance focusses on the tools or instruments employed in achieving public objectives. Thus beyond the perspective taken on governance – whether traditional or new – many theories of governance focus on the tools or instruments of governance. Each theoretical understanding may favour or emphasise a different set of tools for achieving public objectives.[58] Several tools are generally used in the governance of research involving humans, including ethics review committees, a legal framework that may include legislation, and a policy framework that may include ethics guidelines and guidelines for the operation of ethics review committees. For the purposes of this book, the question would be what tools or instruments are required to effectively govern research involving humans in developing countries? If one accepts certain actors and tools in governance as necessary, the question arises: against what criteria can the actors and tools be measured?

With specific regard to a sensitive area such as research involving humans, the subject under consideration, agendas may differ in terms of what counts as beneficial research and how to facilitate it. Also, the vulnerability of research participants, particularly in the developing world context, to potential exploitation is palpable. Self-regulation by professional organisations of physicians and medical researchers may be helpful in determining the manner in which research should be conducted. However, professional organisations regulate members who may have other interests that conflict fundamentally with the interests of those who subject themselves to such research. Funding agencies' requirements may also be helpful.

55 Gerry Stoker, "Governance as Theory: Five Propositions" (1998) 50:155 Intl Soc Sci J 17–28 at 18.
56 Schneider & Bauer, *supra* Note 27 at 3–4.
57 *Ibid.* at 3.
58 See Salomon, *supra* Note 45 at 1611.

But since these requirements could vary from one funding agency to the next, and from one funded organisation to another, these requirements will not only be non-comprehensive in facilitating research and setting appropriate parameters but can also only offer at best patchy and incomplete protection to research participants.

Thus, in an area such as that which I describe later which had previously been dominated by non-state actors, the mediating role of the government as a protector of its citizens remains essential still. Given that governments should ideally work for the citizens' best interests, they may, if they actively exercise appropriately the powers at their disposal, be a more effective negotiator on behalf of the citizens. This does not suggest that the government itself is not an interested party – it may, for instance, be interested in attracting foreign research and the accompanying jobs and monies, an interest that may conflict with the paramount objective of ensuring the safety of participants in research. Indeed, although there have been no empirical studies to support this, some have accused developing world governments of refusing to adopt legal regulations in order to retain the interest of research sponsors.[59] And it is not unusual (and this is the case in several African countries contexts) that the state may be run by a corrupt or even despotic government. Also, economic constraints may mean that the scarce resources are devoted to myriad problems. Leadership challenges, where the state fails to lead in providing basic amenities, may abound[60] such that other actors, such as non-governmental organisations, are becoming more relevant in providing basic services, including healthcare.[61] The relevant capacity for reviewing and monitoring research, important aspects of research governance, may not be found within developing country bureaucracies. For some, therefore, the weaknesses of the state, especially in a developing country context, may mean that a system without the active input of the government, except perhaps in some kind of facilitative role, may be best.

However, other actors that may be involved in the research governance systems are not necessarily free from some of these concerns.[62] More importantly, my

59 See, for example, RN Nwabueze, "Ethical Review of Research Involving Human Subjects in Nigeria: Legal and Policy Issues" (2003–2004) 14 Ind Int'l & Comp L Rev 87.
60 Kenneth L. Leonard, "When Both States and Markets Fail: Asymmetric Information and the Role of NGOs in African Health Care" (2002) 22 Intl Rev L & Econ 61 at 62, noting the various challenges associated with governments in Africa.
61 *Ibid.*
62 See, for example, with respect to non-governmental organisations, Daniel Jordan Smith, "AIDS NGOS and Corruption in Nigeria" (2012) 18:3 Health Place 475-480; Daniel Jordan Smith, "Corruption, NGOs, and Development in Nigeria" (2010) 31:2 Third World Quarterly, online: <https://www.ncbi.nlm.nih.gov/pmc/articles/PMC3832995/pdf/nihms524535.pdf> Raymond c Offenheiser, "Enhancing NGO Effectiveness in Africa: Re-Evaluating the Potential for Genuine Partnerships 7 Oxfam America (Working Paper No. 4, 1999), noting that African NGOs are viewed as lacking, amongst other things, legitimacy and may be prone to cronyism. See also Henry Zakumumpa, "Are NGOs the New Colonial Power in Africa?" *Daily Monitor* (June 3, 2009), online: <www.monitor.co.ug/artman/publish/opinions/Are_NGOs_the_new_colonial_power_in_Africa_85863.shtml>. Yet others argue in relation to the delivery of healthcare services in Africa that NGOs offer better services. See Leonard, *supra* Notes 60, 61 at 62.

arguments in Chapter 1 regarding the importance of a domestic context and the need to create national governance systems also feed into my arguments here about the importance of the state in an area such as that of health research involving humans. The active involvement of the state in the governance of health research would, in my view, result in a more organised, less fragmentary system. Reliance only on funding requirements or conditions in employment contracts or institutional ethics review committees which are not coordinated in any fashion and which face inherent conflict of interest issues, or on drug regulatory authorities which are typically government agencies, will not be comprehensive and may be inadequate. In any event, to dismiss an actor with perhaps the most resources, however imperfect, especially in a developing country, is, in my view, unhelpful and counterproductive. Instead of dismissing the state, it is necessary to seek ways to clearly delimit its authority and encourage its active and effective input, if only to add legitimacy to the system (for instance, through the creation of a national ethics review system, set up by government but not a part of government bureaucracy).[63] Also necessary are ways to build the necessary expertise and capacity in specific areas, such as ethics review and encouraging advocacy by interested groups.

Further, mechanisms for providing inducement, checks, and balances are needed. Creating relevant arms-length processes, addressing issues relating appointments into, and the composition of, the relevant regulatory bodies created by the state are all avenues through which the independence, integrity, and ultimately the effectiveness of the system can be ensured. To these would be added the active participation of other actors, such as civil society, including research participants; patients' rights organisations; and even institutions, such as the media, which may not have a formal or explicit role in research governance. They should complement and act as a check on government, boosting the effectiveness of the governance process. Indeed, they may actively induce the state or government to perform and utilise the appropriate resources. These steps emphasise that a strictly top-down framework will not suffice (and, as I discuss further in this chapter, is increasingly not the case, even in developing countries) and that other actors are necessary but necessary in addition to the state.

Additionally, a formal legal framework is an instrument which the government should ideally bring to the governance table. The legal framework should establish a system of governance (facilitative) that details the obligations of all parties involved in the process. But it should go further, even beyond the protections that could be provided through the retrospective decisions of courts, and the possible administrative law applications to the work of ethics review committees, to offer prospective and specific safeguards for participants and sanctions for non-compliance (protective and regulative). In addition, allowing for guidelines (soft law) in areas where specificity could be elusive potentially offers not only

---

63 Some have therefore argued, for instance, with respect to national research ethics review committees in the developing world, that an attachment to the ministry of health may be more effective and legitimate. See Carl H Coleman & Marie Bousseau, "Strengthening Local Review of Research in Africa: Is the IRB Model Relevant?" (2006), online: <www.thehastingscenter.org/strengthening-local-review-of-research-in-africais-the-irb-model-relevant/>.

more legitimacy but also a greater level of accountability than would otherwise be the case. One could reasonably argue that law is an important underpinning for the governance of research involving humans, not least because law, more often than not, implies a role for government, is wide-ranging, thus potentially regulating and imposing accountability on all the actors in the governance systems, including the government. It confers a certain legitimacy on public actions, including governance systems and choice of governing instruments. This legitimacy arises when law operates in a democratic context such that resulting legislation and/or regulations have indirect input from the citizens who place representatives in government.[64] Further, the threat of sanctions in this context may serve as an incentive for complying not only with the legislation but also with the guidelines.[65]

Consequently, rather than seeing the governance context in African countries as simply a command-and-control condition or a situation in which the government has a minimal role, it is perhaps more useful to draw on both traditional governance (by which I mean state control) and the new governance (the newer recognition of a partnership between all the stakeholders). This relates to the sustainable governance concept or the good governance approach mentioned earlier: governance would be carried out with an explicit role for government as well as a space in which private actors could contribute to governance.[66] One could then reasonably ask such important questions as how the characteristics of traditional governance (including formal or hard law) can be fruitfully blended with, or be complementary to, less traditional forms of governance (such as soft law or increased civil society participation) for greater effect where necessary. One could also ask what benefits the different actors – government, research sponsors, researchers, professional bodies, and research participants – bring to the table and how these can be more effectively managed to ensure better governance of research.

In this way, the new governance concept, with its emphasis on utilising all the actors and institutions, along with taking cognisance of multiple sites of regulation and addressing the relationship between state intervention and societal autonomy, in combination with traditional approaches by the state (command and control), becomes helpful in creating an effective framework in the context of health research involving humans in developing countries. While this may obviously not have the same purchase in all settings, or be suitable for all situations requiring governance, a hybrid framework that adopts a generic understanding to which both traditional and new governance contribute their strengths, harnesses the synergies of different actors and

---

64 See generally Pierre Issalys, "Choosing among Forms of Public Action: A Question of Legitimacy" in *Designing Government*, particularly at 169–171.

65 David M Trubek & Louise G Trubek, "New Governance and Legal Regulation: Complementarity, Rivalry, and Transformation" (2007) 13 Colum J Eur L at 547.

66 The good governance approach recognises the important role of the state and the rule of law while emphasising the importance of the private sector and the civil society.

institutions, and takes into account the political and socio-economic contexts as well as the best interests of African countries is needed in such countries as Nigeria.

Governance is thus a very useful analytical framework for health research involving humans because of the importance of the comprehensive systems macro perspective (or what McDonald calls a 'second-order' perspective)[67] on the actors, institutions, mechanisms, rules, and processes that are involved in, and manage, health research involving humans. Taking the comprehensive perspective afforded by the governance framework also allows an evaluation of what these instruments convey about the nature of the relationships between all the policy actors and institutions, including such actors and institutions as the government and the legal system, civil society and patients rights' organisations, researchers and ethics review committees, and research participants. This perspective thus affords, for example, freedom to examine law in the context of different disciplines that bear on research involving humans, such as biomedicine and social science. It permits an inquiry into not only the role and place of law in the system (for instance, is it facilitative?) but also its relationship with other components and key institutions frequently employed in the oversight of research involving humans, such as ethics review committees (for instance, does it create legal obligations for these institutions?), in achieving the public policy objectives of enabling beneficial research while ensuring the safety and dignity of research participants.

Thus, within the perspective of a hybrid framework of governance, that is, a mid-ground between the "old" and "new" governance, one could fruitfully ask whether, based on available evidence, these institutions and actors work separately or together and if so how harmoniously. In many countries, developed and developing, the systems of research participants' protection (with respect to standards, structures, regulations, and policies) are not necessarily ordered as a coherent, cohesive, and organised structure, and consist of fragmented institutions and policies involved in the governance process.[68] To explain this point further, the different actors in research governance may employ different forms of governance. For example, funding agencies may have separate criteria for funding eligibility different from those utilised in research institutes, which may themselves have no coercive control over researchers. The universities may also have different guidelines and ways of ensuring compliance, including clauses in researchers' employment contracts, which may be different from those employed by self-regulating professional bodies, which may exercise significant influence and control over their members, and which may also differ from the powers exercised by departments of health.

---

67 McDonald, *supra* Note at 23.
68 See Jocelyn Downie, "The Canadian Agency for the Oversight of Research Involving Humans: A Reform Proposal" (2006) Accountability in Research 75 where she points out that in Canada "Numerous bodies are tasked with various aspects of what can really only loosely be called a 'system.'"

The normative weight of international organisations such as the World Medical Association and the guidance they provide, as well as how these organisations have influenced the development of the governance systems in developing countries, also provide a source of governance.[69] What are the contributions of these different bodies to the research governance system? And how do these different sources of regulation affect how adequately research participants are protected? Do they work cohesively or not, and how does this affect the effectiveness and adequacy of the system? A governance framework helps to identify and analyse these sources and determine the interplay between the different players and the forms of governance, and how harnessing these subsystems could provide greater effectiveness in research governance. One could then reasonably attempt to answer such important questions as how the characteristics of traditional governance (including formal or hard law) can be fruitfully blended with, or be complementary to, less traditional forms of governance (such as soft law or increased civil society participation) for greater effect where necessary. One could also try to determine what benefits the different actors – government, research sponsors, researchers, professional bodies, and research participants – bring to the table and how these can be more effectively managed to ensure better governance of research.

Further, I am of the view that when employed appropriately, and without overstretching what might be considered an already diffuse concept, governance not only has an explanatory and organising value but also has prescriptive value. In this regard, one can consider simply the organisation of the system and the actors within that system or how the system is changing to accommodate different types of actors, instruments, and processes. But one can also go beyond that to question whether the system is working effectively, which then requires us to question what the system (whether organised coherently or cohesively or not) is set up to achieve and even further what the system should achieve. One can also ask whether the right interests are involved in decision-making in research governance. One can also question if the right instruments or tools are being utilised, a central concern in governance literature. We could also question if the current governance arrangements in any country help the delivery of better outcomes. In other words, governance as an analytical framework allows us to inquire normatively but also prescriptively as to what the goals of regulation and governance are, should, or ought to be; the necessary actors and instruments or tools; and the criteria by which to evaluate governance.

Just as importantly, the actors, institutions, instruments, and processes involved in research governance work within a sociopolitical context which may affect their effectiveness. A hybrid governance framework not only allows the evaluation of these contexts but also permits one to address normatively the ideal context for the institutions, actors, and processes to function effectively. A governance framework is also helpful in raising important questions relating to the legitimacy of governance actions within any given sociopolitical context: for

---

69 See Adèle Langlois, "The UNESCO Universal Declaration on Bioethics and Human Rights: Perspectives from Kenya and South Africa" (2008) 16:1 Health Care Analysis 39.

example, in determining the source(s) of authority for relevant matters such as lawmaking and production of national guidelines.

In employing this hybrid idea of governance, it is important to admit some assumptions, the most important of which is that governance will take place within a democracy, no matter how imperfect, such that any resulting legislation is the product (however indirectly) of the people's wishes. But it may limit the applicability of such a framework in other contexts where this may not be so. Thus, there would, of course, be more difficulties in an undemocratic setting. It is also not possible within the scope of this book to examine big questions relating to the challenges that law presents in the sense that, as described by Hunt, it can be both a mechanism that contributes to social domination (as in, for instance, law enacted in a military regime) and a mechanism that contributes to the potential of human emancipation.[70] This book dwells more on the positive aspects of law, but I address in more particular detail the role of law and any possible objections in the context of research governance in the next chapter. Also, the political context in terms of the division of authorities and the organisation of the legal system also matter. Analyses of the African countries' research governance thus take into consideration their constitutional and political contexts.

This framework would be incomplete, however, without a consideration of what the goals of governance for research should be and the criteria by which to measure the attainment of those goals.

Goals and criteria for governance of health research involving humans

In the application of any kind of framework to the subject of research governance in African countries, it is important to question: what are the goals of the governance of research involving humans? Although this is addressed summarily in Chapter 1, it bears reiteration here. Downie and McDonald carefully list the main objectives of the governance of health research involving humans. In their insightful review, the goals of governance arrangements are to:

- Respect the dignity and rights of research participants;
- Protect the safety of all research participants as much as it is possible to do so;
- Build and maintain trust between the researchers, research institutions, research participants, and society as a whole;
- Promote potentially beneficial research;
- Promote safe and effective research;
- Analyse, balance, and distribute harms and benefits;
- Pursue all of these in a way that is administratively and financially efficient and fair.[71]

---

70 Hunt, *supra* Note 22 at 327.
71 Jocelyn Downie & Fiona McDonald, "Revisioning the Oversight of Research Involving Humans in Canada" (2004) 12 Health L J 159 at 160.

These goals can be summarised as yielding three main goals: namely, first, the goal of ensuring that research is potentially beneficial and, second, that while inherent risks exist in the process, efforts are made to minimise them and to protect the safety, dignity, and well-being of research participants. A third important goal is the maintenance of trust between the research community and society as a whole, which flows from the first two goals.[72]

Thus, the major reason for conducting research is that it has the potential to provide benefits, whether in terms of providing effective (or more effective) therapeutic interventions for diseases or information which influences health policies. In the developing world, as I discussed in Chapter 1, the need for health research and the potential benefits attached therewith cannot be overstated.

In the process of obtaining these benefits, the safety of research participants must be actively ensured. Research participants who volunteer themselves for research for the purpose of potentially obtaining benefits for the society deserve to have their safety, rights, and welfare protected to the greatest extent possible. Research ethics, as articulated in the international guidelines discussed in Chapter 1, makes this abundantly clear. Where there are conflicts between these goals, the goal of ensuring the safety of the participants and minimising any risk to them clearly takes precedence. The Helsinki Declaration clearly states that "While the primary purpose of medical research is to generate new knowledge, this goal can never take precedence over the rights and interests of individual research subjects."[73] The precedence of research participants in the scale of priorities represents an important value. The normative goals for research governance can then be framed thus: there is value in ensuring that the health of people in general is improved. The protection of the rights, safety, dignity, and welfare of research participants is, however, of greater value. In ensuring the rights of research participants, the trust of the community is preserved, and, in turn, more beneficial research is made possible.

All the governance arrangements and structures put in place therefore have to achieve these goals and reflect these values, respecting the paramount importance of not jeopardising the health and well-being of research volunteers. Furthermore, the governance arrangements, as Downie and McDonald rightly note, need to be operated in an efficient manner, which, in the final analysis, will affect the effectiveness of the arrangements.

If the goals of research governance are clear, what about the criteria by which the attainment of these goals are measured? Governance literature is also very helpful in this regard. Salomon discusses several criteria, some of which are particularly helpful in my analysis: namely, effectiveness, efficiency, equity, manageability, and legitimacy and political feasibility.[74] Others have proposed such criteria as clear mission, responsibility, accountability, transparency, stewardship,

---

72 McDonald, Governance of Health Research Involving Humans in Canada, at 51.
73 Article 8 of the Helsinki Declaration, 2013.
74 Salomon, *supra* Note 45 1611 at 1647–1649.

flexibility, succession, representation, and simplicity.[75] From the good governance approach, which fundamentally links democracy, development, and health promotion, we have such criteria as participation, consensus orientation, accountability, transparency, responsiveness, effectiveness, equity, and respect for the rule of law.[76] Hirtle links the good governance criteria to health research involving humans, observing that

> To address research ethics issues from the perspective of public governance is to focus on elements of good governance. These include accountability, oversight and transparency, clear government roles and responsibilities, clear relationships, structures and standards, and public processes, mechanisms and participation.[77]

From these various discussions, I derive eight criteria, which encapsulate the aforementioned prescriptions. The criteria are: effectiveness, legitimacy, clarity, comprehensiveness, efficiency, adequacy, uniformity, and simplicity. I discuss the criteria against which the actors, instruments, and mechanisms applied in attaining the goals of health research involving humans can be assessed respectively in the following.

Effectiveness is arguably the most fundamental and basic measure for assessing the success of public action. "It essentially measures the extent to which an activity achieves its objectives."[78] The criterion of effectiveness in the context of the governance of health research thus raises the question of whether the objectives of the system are being met – promoting beneficial research and protecting research participants. Questions of compliance also fall under the criterion of effectiveness. This criterion therefore applies to all the tools or instruments and institutions employed in the governance of health research involving humans. All the other criteria are important only to the extent that they contribute to meeting this criterion. Thus, while I engage in an examination of each of the other criteria in examining specific mechanisms of research governance, the criterion of effectiveness runs through the entire examination and will be an intrinsic part of the analysis of each of the tools. In other words, I will be asking if the degree of uniformity or clarity or comprehensiveness of standards, actors, tools, and institutions involved in research governance is effective in meeting the goals of promoting socially beneficial research and protecting research participants in developing countries, specifically Nigeria.

75 McDonald, *supra* Note 54 at citing *The Canadian Institutes for Health Research (CIHR) Public Report on Governance*.

76 Helmut Brand, "Good Governance for the Public's Health" (2007) 17:6 Eur J Public Health 561, citing the United Nations Economic and Social Commission for Asia and the Pacific (UNESCAP) at 1.

77 Marie Hirtle, "The Governance of Research Involving Human Participants in Canada" (2003) 11 Health L J 137 at 138–139. See Stephanie J Poustie et al, "Implementing a Research Governance Framework for Clinical and Public Health Research" (2006) 185 Med J Austl 623.

78 Salomon, at 1647.

Working within a governance framework, therefore, the book will consider what tools ought to be employed in the research governance system and examine their potential effectiveness in achieving the goals of research governance in Chapter 3. The assessment of effectiveness is certainly not easy, even in this case, where the goals are fairly clear. Systems are usually shown to be ineffective when an incident occurs (in the case of research governance, research participants die or are harmed). It is perhaps more accurate to state that what we are concerned with here is both actual and potential effectiveness. In other words, what potential does the system have to work effectively?

Within the criterion of effectiveness also comes the related criterion of legitimacy, which is also a criterion that runs through each of the rest of the criteria. Legitimacy raises issues of rights, obligation, and power, and of acceptance of authority. In a general sense, legitimacy has been described as being about

> the moral grounding of power and therefore involves social and cultural norms and expectations concerning proper behaviour of those that govern, the social relationship between rulers and ruled, the role of trust, reputation and force, and the balance between authority and obeisance. Such norms and expectations vary across time and space. They can refer to the output or input of policymaking, to the procedures or legality of decision making or to its content, to the performance or to the status of rulers, and to limited or ultimate criteria of justice.[79]

Thus legitimacy refers not only to power and authority but also to the internal and external processes of exercising that authority in a policy sphere. Legitimacy is crucial to garnering wide support for the measures taken to govern a particular activity, in this case health research involving humans, and thus ensure its effectiveness. A legitimate tool is more likely to be accepted and to be effective in achieving its ends. Thus Issalys frames the issue of the choice of governance tools in terms of legitimacy. He observes that legitimacy "resides in the acceptance both of an authority and of the rules laid out by this authority, it has obvious repercussions for the effectiveness and even for the efficiency of any mechanism of public intervention."[80] Effectiveness and efficiency of governance actions are therefore closely linked to legitimacy as are public participation, accountability, and transparency.[81]

Questions about the independence, transparency, and credibility or conflicts of interest in ethics review committees thus provoke questions about legitimacy.

---

79 NWO Research Programme, "Shifts in Governance: Problems of Legitimacy and Accountability" (The Hague: Netherlands Organisation for Scientific Research, 2004).

80 Pierre Issalys, "Choosing Among Forms of Public Action: a Question of Legitimacy" in *Designing Government*, describing the various perspectives adopted in discourse relating to the criteria for choosing the tools for public action, particularly with respect to legitimacy at 154.

81 Baldwin & Cave also referring to legitimacy point out the benchmarks for regulation: namely, legislative mandate, accountability, due process, expertise, and efficiency. Baldwin & Cave, *supra* Note 40 at 77–84. These criteria are similar to those laid out by Issalys, Note 80 at 171.

Several issues addressed in this book are by implication questions of legitimacy. For instance, questions about the origins of research governance in African countries, such as whether recent research governance systems established for the principal purpose of receiving research funding from developed countries, or to address research ethics scandals, involve an examination of legitimacy. Questions about the sufficiency of public participation in research governance, or questions about the role of law in research governance or the role of government generally or even in the context of national ethics review committees, necessarily engender an examination of legitimacy. Thus, like effectiveness, questions of legitimacy implicitly undergird much of the discussion that follows in analysing the mechanisms of research governance in Nigeria.

The other criteria raise specific issues as to the organisation and operation of the research governance system. Clarity in the context of research governance requires that the roles; responsibilities; rights of all the stakeholders in the research governance system, including research sponsors, research funders, research institutions, professional bodies, research regulators, and research participants; and lines of accountabilities be clear and unambiguous to ensure greater effectiveness.

Related to this is the need for uniformity or consistency and adequacy. The legal and ethical standards applied within the research governance system must be both adequate and consistent, and not dependent, for instance, on the institution in which research is taking place or the organisation which is funding the research. Adequacy is also important in the consideration of the authority of the different institutions. They must have adequate independence, adequate resources, and adequate authority to operate and carry out tasks within the research governance system, including standard setting and standards implementation.

The system also needs to be comprehensive, including the whole spectrum of actors and different types of health research involving humans; to provide protections for a wide scope of research participants; and should be encompassing in terms of the relevant issues. It should include not only ethical standards and legal regulations but prescriptions relating to other indirect factors (for instance, the training of researchers or the creation of clinical trial registries), which may affect the conduct of health research. These should be addressed comprehensively within the various legal and policy instruments which govern research. As Downie and McDonald note, non-comprehensive systems (for instance, in terms of what kinds of health research are covered or what receives ethics review) pose threats to research participants, may impose increased costs on society, increase adherence or compliance problems, and put public trust in the research process at risk.[82]

The system needs to be efficient. Efficiency is a criterion that considers the balance of results against costs.[83] It questions how best to achieve results with minimum financial, human, and time resources. Particularly in the context of

---

82 Downie & McDonald, at 8.
83 Salomon, at 1648.

a developing country, the available resources, financial, infrastructural, and human, must be utilised efficiently. These should permit seamless relationships between different actors and instruments, and proper coordination between structures, and allow no duplication or waste of scarce resources. Efficiency, however, can only be contributory to the effectiveness of the system; it cannot be a goal in itself, otherwise the protection of research participants may be jeopardised.

Despite the wide range of actors involved in what is increasingly a complex activity, the organisation of the governance system, and the processes employed therewith, although there are underlying complexities, should aim to permit a relative ease of operation and the clarity of roles and lines of accountability mentioned earlier. Clarity and simplicity logically make it more likely that actors will know their obligations, making compliance easier. Studies in some countries currently indicate that the complexity of existing regulations in human research creates room for layers of organisations to operate,[84] possibly creating a diversity of interests that may not necessarily promote protections for research participants. In subsequent chapters of this book, and in the specific context of the research governance systems of Nigeria, I will be making assessments using these criteria.

Conclusion

The specific framework adopted in this book for the analysis of health research governance in Africa is a generic understanding of governance that includes all the actors, comprising the government, research sponsors, and citizens, as active participants in the process and finds merit in a hybrid form that includes the strengths of both traditional and new governance. Many of the problems arising from research involving humans in the developing world are problems of governance. The fundamental questions that this book attempts to answer in the specific context of African countries are clearly questions of governance: namely, how ought health research involving humans, a clearly beneficial and public activity which also has risks, be managed? By what criteria ought the current systems be assessed? In what ways can the systems be improved? The preceding discussion shows the clear value of governance as a means of understanding the controlling of activities in order to achieve public goals and objectives. The issues that arise in the context of these questions, for instance, the consistency of ethical and legal standards, the comprehensiveness of any regulatory standards, compliance with those standards, and effectiveness of any regulations, are all issues of governance.[85] One could certainly focus on a specific actor, such

---

84 See, for instance, E Helminki, "Actors Involved in the Regulation of Clinical Research: Comparison of Finland to England, Canada, and the USA" (2015) 13 Health Syst Pol'y Res 20, online: <https://www.ncbi.nlm.nih.gov/pmc/articles/PMC4391597/>.

85 See Jocelyn Downie, "Contemporary Health Research: A Cautionary Tale" (2003) Health L J (Special Edition) 1 at 5, describing several governance issues.

as the state or the government, or the impact of the judicial system or medical institutions or ethics review committees, and there are many emerging studies on these issues. However, health research involving humans is an activity managed by different institutions and mechanisms, and which has effects beyond a specific group managed by a specific medical institution or a specific research sponsor. Further, as McDonald observes, "governance issues arise with respect to the appropriate division of responsibilities for the protection of human subjects amongst the agencies and organizations that conduct, sponsor, and regulate research."[86] A comprehensive look at the interactions of these organisations is a worthwhile venture, especially in African countries where this has only been undertaken focussing to some degree on discrete components, particularly ethics review. Extrapolating from this, research governance requires an examination of the scope and structure of the system, the responsibilities and composition of the institutions within the system, accountability, and compliance mechanisms within the system, all of which have implications for ensuring the protection of participants and promoting beneficial research, and all of which come clearly under the umbrella of governance.

The analytical framework of the book therefore takes a three-pronged approach, consisting of ethical, legal, and performance approaches, to the investigation of research governance arrangements and mechanisms in Nigeria. Beyond gaining an understanding of the ethical framework of the governance system, the legal context, and the institutional instruments of governance, another important issue that requires consideration is the current and potential functioning of the systems for research governance in African countries. How well is the system working in practice, and what potential does it have to work well?

In sum, the governance of health research involving humans in developing countries requires a more comprehensive analysis than has hitherto been undertaken. The aim of this chapter has been to discuss the analytical framework within which a detailed examination of this subject can be undertaken. In the foregoing pages, I have attempted to set out a governance framework which, in my view, will allow for the comprehensive and wide-ranging analysis required here. The framework draws considerably from work already done by scholars of regulation and governance but attempts to set out a hybrid framework which I consider to be more suitable for the purposes of the book. I have addressed the rationale for adopting this framework. I have also, in the foregoing pages, indicated how this framework will be applied in the rest of the book. The subsequent chapters will provide more details and put this framework further in the specific context of African countries.

---

86 Michael McDonald, "Canadian Governance of Health Research Involving Human Subjects: Is Anybody Minding the Store?" (2001) 9 Health L J 1 at 4.

3 Components of health research governance systems

Introduction

The governance of health research involving humans is a wide-ranging subject. In many countries, research governance typically operates through different institutions, instruments, and processes, all of which I term "components of research governance." The components may include drug regulatory authorities, funding agencies, a legal framework, the ethics review system, and policy guidelines that detail the ways in which research should be conducted. Several key questions may arise in examining the components and tools of research governance: namely, what are the components of research governance currently in use in countries around the world, and how do they operate to govern health research? What should the components of governance of health research in African countries be? Do these components act, and should they act, in a coordinated fashion?

In this chapter, I answer the first question: namely, what are the components of research governance systems currently in use around the world? The objectives of this chapter are therefore to identify and describe briefly the components of research governance systems widely accepted both in the literature and in actual operation as a precursor to our analysis of the research governance arrangements around the world and in African countries. In my view, these are important components, and there is no need to reinvent the wheel in African countries. In essence, these components are also essential in African countries.

However, while there is clear understanding in the literature and in the actual operation of governance systems that these are necessary components for the governance of health research, there may be some debate about their content. Thus, for instance, there is broad acceptance of the need for an ethical framework, but there may be disagreement about the content of domestic or international ethical guidelines or how they should be implemented in African countries.

Another example of a widely accepted component, both in the literature and in the actual operation of governance systems, is the central role of ethics review committees.[1] Although widely accepted, these committees are structured differently in

---

1 P Veerus, J Lexchin & E Hemminki, "Legislative Regulation and Ethical Research Governance of Medical Research in Different European Union Countries" (2014) 40:6 J Med Ethics 409–413.

countries around the world (national, regional, or institutional structures),[2] sometimes established statutorily and in other countries not,[3] and regulated by a national mechanism in some but not all countries. There are also systemic issues that may limit their functionality and effectiveness in protecting research participants.

Less articulated in the literature is the inclusion of civil society organisations in the institutional framework. Civil society organisations are omitted in most accounts of the components of research governance. This is understandable because these organisations may be argued not to be, strictly speaking, part of the formal research governance system. But in light of the hybrid framework proposed in Chapter 2, the balancing purpose that such organisations can serve, and the need to provide a more complete picture of research governance components, as this book proposes, I argue that organisations that advocate for research participants' safety may be a helpful component of the institutional framework.

In providing a description of the institutional framework, I identify systemic issues that may limit the effectiveness of the different organisations involved in research governance in different countries, many of which are articulated in the literature on research governance. It is necessary to identify these concerns because they are matters that need to be addressed in research governance systems, including the emerging governance systems of African countries. These systemic issues are considered in more detail in the specific context of African countries in subsequent chapters. Descriptions undertaken in this chapter are drawn from various jurisdictions around the world.

The discussion is undertaken with the macro perspective discussed in Chapter 2 in mind, allowing for breadth of analysis rather than specificity. Thus, although some specific issues are identified, a detailed description of *all* the specific issues and concerns that arise in the context of an ethical framework or an institutional framework is not undertaken here. In essence, no one country has a perfect system. The problematic issues identified in the discussion undertaken here indicate some of the issues that need to be addressed in the contexts of African countries.

The chapter commences with this introduction as the first section. The second section considers the ethical framework, examining the role of national and international guidelines in creating an ethical framework for the governance of health research involving humans. It notes that establishing domestic guidelines in African countries may be one way to address issues that have been controversial in the international ethical guidelines. The third section considers the role of different institutions and organisations involved in the governance of research involving humans, such as ethics review committees. It identifies some of the systemic issues that have been problematic in countries around the world and those that may pose difficulties in African countries. The fourth section considers the role of the legal framework. The fifth section concludes the chapter.

---

2 AS Walanj, "Research Ethics Committees: Need for Harmonization at the National Level, the Global and Indian Perspective" (2014) 5 Perspect Clin Res 66–70.

3 Veerus, Lexchin & Hemminki, *supra* Note 1 at 409–413.

Ethical framework

Research governance and bioethics are inextricably linked. The ethical framework of the governance of research involving humans is a vital and foundational component of research governance systems. Indeed, an ethical framework should be a core part of the governance of research involving humans. It is within the ethical framework that the true goals and objectives of research governance are located – the goals of ensuring beneficial research and protecting the safety of research participants. Thus governance involves not only procedures and processes but also the underlying values that require the adoption of these procedures. And although governance and regulatory structures are important, active aspects of protecting research participants, their procedural aspects and institutional mechanisms must be built on an ethical foundation. This ensures that there are not merely governance mechanisms operating formalistically without any ethical directions or compliance with procedural requirements divorced completely from the ethical principles which necessitate the governance structures to begin with.[4] Hence, ethical standards and principles have been an important underpinning for research governance both internationally and locally. Any serious discussion of the governance of research must therefore consider ethical foundations and values, and begin with the discussion of the ethical framework. It must not only begin with but also permeate the governance framework such that all governance processes are channelled to the primary goal of research participant protections and trust. Otherwise, we may resort to checking of boxes and surface in compliance with the rules. Ethics provides the "why" and to a significant degree the "how."

Research governance and ethics are inextricably linked. The ethical framework typically consists of research ethics principles which may be located in the international ethical guidelines and in the national ethical guidelines. Many of these guidelines are amended at intervals in light of evolving understanding of ethical issues. The ethical framework may also derive from values articulated in other important national sources, such as constitutions of countries.

The international ethical guidelines, including the Helsinki Declaration; the Council for International Organizations of Medical Sciences (CIOMS) *International Ethical Guidelines for Health-Related Research involving Humans*, 2016 (CIOMS Guidelines); International Conference on Harmonization (ICH) Technical Requirements for Registration of Pharmaceuticals for Human Use; ICH Harmonized Tripartite Guideline and, more recently, United Nations on Educational, Scientific and Cultural Organisation (UNESCO) Declaration on Bioethics and Human Rights, have therefore been primary instruments for regulating research involving humans. While they have no formal legal character and cannot, by themselves, be considered law, these guidelines have been incorporated

---

4 Anne Slowther, Petra Boynton & Sara Shaw, "Research Governance: Ethical Issues" (2006) 99 J R Soc Med 65 at 65.

into domestic law[5] around the world. But even where they are not so incorporated, they contain some provisions that may bind researchers and research institutions, requiring them to adopt certain standards. While these international guidelines have provided a form of governance, national guidelines also play a crucial role in research governance in many countries, including African countries. We discuss this further in the case studies in subsequent chapters.

The international ethical guidelines play an important role in the domestic governance systems of many countries, operating as soft law in the regulation and governance of health research. The governance approach fits well into the new governance approach because these international ethical guidelines provide, to a large extent, open-ended guidance as opposed to rules and very few formal sanctions.[6] Further, the origin, development, and effect of these guidelines are prototypical examples of the new governance approach: for instance, the Helsinki Declaration, which is a form of self-regulatory guidance drawn up by the World Medical Association but which has now become an authoritative reference point for other guidelines, national and international. Many countries employ these guidelines either directly or indirectly, drawing upon them in national regulations, policies, and guidelines.[7] A brief overview of the international ethical guidelines is therefore necessary. More importantly, I argue that African countries should consider developing national guidelines to address any areas of weakness in the international ethical guidelines and to provide the national position on issues in the international ethical guidelines that may be controversial.

The overview of current international ethical guidelines begins with the Nuremberg Code. Although the principles enunciated in the Code were part of the judgement at the Nuremberg Trials[8] and were therefore not intended to be a code of medical research ethics, the Code is of major historical importance. It codified, for the first time, the ethical tenets governing scientific research on

---

5 See, AC Campbell & KC Glass, "The Legal Status of Clinical and Ethics Policies, Codes, and Guidelines in Medical Practice and Research" (2001) 46 McGill L J 473 at 478.

6 O Lobel, "The Renew Deal: The Fall of Regulation and the Rise of Governance in Contemporary Legal Thought" (2004) 89 Minn L Rev 342 at 363.

7 See Delon Human & Sev S Fluss, "The World Medical Association's Declaration of Helsinki: Historical and Contemporary Perspectives" (2001) World Medical Association, online: <www.wma.net/e/ethicsunit/pdf/draft_historical_contemporary_perspectives.pdf>.

8 The origins of modern international bioethics can be traced to the abuse of research participants in concentration camps in the Second World War and the subsequent enunciation of the *Nuremberg Code*, the first international declaration of ethical standards for research outlined by the judges at the Nuremberg Trials of Nazi doctors in 1947. See generally GJ Annas & MA Grodin, *The Nazi Doctors and the Nuremberg Code: Human Rights in Experimentation* (New York: Oxford University Press, 1992); Evelyne Shuster, "Fifty Years Later: The Significance of the Nuremberg Code" (1997) 337 N Engl J Med 1436; Jochen Vollman, "Informed Consent in Human Experimentation before the Nuremberg Code" (1996) 313 BMJ 1445; Pascal Arnold & Dominique Sprumont, "The 'Nuremberg Code': Rules of Public International Law" in Ulrich Trohler & Stella Reiter-Theil, eds, *Ethics Codes in Medicine: Foundations and Achievements of Codification Since 1947* (Aldershot: Ashgate Publishing Ltd., 1998).

human beings[9] and marked the beginning of a larger consciousness of the need to establish standards for the ethical conduct of human research. It brought the issue of the ethical conduct of research involving humans to global awareness.[10] The Nuremberg Code's major contribution to contemporary research ethics is its requirement for informed consent, now widely accepted as a core requirement for research involving humans.[11] It was largely responsible for the inclusion of a provision on the need for informed consent in human experimentation in the *International Covenant on Civil and Political Rights*.[12] Some have even argued, perhaps due to its origins as part of a court judgement and the moral force of its principles, that the Nuremberg Code is part of customary international law binding on states.[13] And a United States court decided in 2009 that violation of the requirement for informed consent in human experimentation was a violation of customary international law.[14]

Although it remains an influential document, the Nuremberg Code has largely been superseded in practical application by the *Helsinki Declaration*.[15] Since 1964, when it was adopted, the severally revised *Helsinki Declaration* has provided the primary guiding principles for regulating medical research involving human participants for the purpose of guiding physicians and others conducting biomedical research involving humans.[16] It contains a number of requirements for the ethical conduct of research, such as provisions requiring informed consent from participants in medical research, which reflects the value of respect of persons.[17]

The Helsinki Declaration is widely applied and referenced in different national and international guidelines.[18] It has not only been instrumental to the governance and regulation of biomedical research by providing guiding principles but has also been influential in the establishment of ethical review committees, a key component of research governance. In establishing a requirement for independent ethical review committees in the 1975 amendment and requiring

9 Annas & Grodin, *ibid.*
10 See Sharon Perley et al, "The Nuremberg Code: An International Overview" in Annas & Grodin *ibid.* at 152–155.
11 See Jay Katz, "The Consent Principle of the Nuremberg Code: Its Significance Then and Now" in Annas & Grodin, *supra* Note 40 at 227–238; Arnold & Sprumont, *supra* Note 8.
12 G.A. res. 2200A (XXI), 21 U.N. GAOR Supp. (No. 16) at 52, U.N. Doc. A/6316 (1966), 999 U.N.T.S. 171, *entered into force* March 23, 1976. See Perley et al, *ibid.* at 153.
13 See Arnold & Sprumont, *supra* Note 8.
14 See Markus Schott, "Medical Research on Humans: Regulation in Switzerland, the European Union, and the United States" (2005) 60 Food & Drug L J 45. See *Rabi Abdullahi v Pfizer, Inc* Docket Nos. 05-4863-cv (L), 05-6768-cv (CON), 2009 WL 214649 (2d Cir January 20, 2009).
15 World Medical Association, *Declaration of Helsinki – Ethical Principles for Medical Research Involving Human Subjects* (last revised: 2013), online: <https://www.wma.net/wp-content/uploads/2016/11/DoH-Oct2013-JAMA.pdf>.
16 See Introduction, Article 1 of the Helsinki Declaration.
17 Principle 24.
18 See Snezana Bosnjak, "The Declaration of Helsinki – The Cornerstone of Research Ethics" (2001) 9:3 Arch Oncol 179.

that reports of experimentation violating the Declaration's ethical principles not be accepted for publication, it took steps to give teeth to substantive standards through procedural mechanisms,[19] but, as Dickens notes, it remains procedurally undeveloped.[20]

The issues that have arisen with the Helsinki Declaration, particularly in the context of the developing world, have been issues of interpretation and application in the special circumstances that may arise in that context. Charges of ethical imperialism levelled against the ethical standards set in the Helsinki Declaration, and opposing arguments about ethical relativism, have raised questions about the universality of the principles contained in the Declaration and whether or not it can truly represent a broad and international spectrum of opinion on ethical standards such as would be necessary to guarantee its legitimacy.[21] Some authors[22] have taken issue particularly with its statement of primacy over other regulatory instruments, as contained in Article 10 of the Declaration:

> Physicians must consider the ethical, legal and regulatory norms and standards for research involving human subjects in their own countries as well as applicable international norms and standards. *No national or international ethical, legal or regulatory requirement should reduce or eliminate any of the protections for research subjects set forth in this Declaration.*[23]

In this regard, issues around the vagueness of some provisions, the lack of consensus on some key ethical issues like "standard of care" in randomised clinical trials, and little allowance for exceptions have been considered problematic.[24]

In this regard, one of the most controversial requirements of the Declaration in recent years in the context of research involving humans in African countries has been the requirement relating to the standard of care to be provided to participants in randomised clinical trials. It currently provides that the effectiveness of a new method should be tested against those of the best current prophylactic, diagnostic, and therapeutic methods,[25] and that "[t]he benefits, risks, burdens and effectiveness of a new intervention must be tested against those of the best proven intervention(s)."[26] However, the CIOMS Guidelines contain slightly

---

19 James F Childress, "Nuremberg's Legacy: Some Ethical Reflections" (2000) 43:3 Perspect Biol & Med 347 at 351.

20 Bernard Dickens, "The Challenge of Equivalent Protection" in *National Bioethics Advisory Commission Ethical and Policy Issues in International Research: Clinical Trials in African countries Volume II – Report and Recommendations of the National Bioethics Advisory Commission* (Bethesda, MD: National Bioethics Advisory Commission, 2001) at A-3.

21 See Plomer, *supra* Note 27 at 4.

22 Annette Rid & Harald Schmidt, "The 2008 Declaration of Helsinki — First among Equals in Research Ethics?" (2010) 38:1 J Med L & Ethics 143.

23 Article 10 of the Helsinki Declaration.

24 *Ibid.*

25 Principle 32.

26 Principle 33.

different language, requiring that control groups be provided the "established effective intervention" under certain specified conditions.[27] (Some of the concerns around this have been touched upon in Chapter 1 in the context of HIV research.) The broad ethical question for African countries is should trial participants receive the "best" proven treatment as their counterparts in other parts of the world or the "best local standard" in view of the resource constraints and the possibility of obtaining quicker scientific answers which may ultimately benefit wider populations in African countries? And what does any chosen option mean for the equality and safety of participants where the local standard of care is nothing at all? The debate is by no means settled. The clarifications which have been added to the Declaration in recent years as a result of these concerns have, according to some commentators, threatened to weaken the authority of the principles contained therein.[28]

Further, although it has set procedural and substantive standards for the ethical conduct of biomedical research and carries great moral and normative authority, the scope of the Declaration is limited by the fact that it is binding only on medical researchers. Its legal status in many countries is also uncertain.[29] However, where the guidelines, such as the Helsinki Declaration, are adopted by legislation, they become legally binding. Moreover, courts may consider the Helsinki Declaration or other guidelines in examining the standard of conduct which may be expected from researchers. For instance, the Quebec Supreme Court in Canada referred to the Helsinki Declaration in *Weiss v Solomon* in trying to determine the standard of care required of a researcher and a hospital through the approval of the protocol by the hospital's ethics review committees[30] The Helsinki Declaration has also informed legislation and has been incorporated in the regulations and guidelines of some countries.[31]

Despite being influential in the development of national and international ethical guidelines and legal regulations, the legal force of the Helsinki Declaration is by no means clear. It frequently depends on whether or not it is explicitly recognised by or incorporated by reference or directly into domestic legislation or professional regulations. An uncertain legal status in various countries notwithstanding, the Helsinki Declaration, as previously stated, is a primary reference document with regards to ethical standards in health research. This uncertainty, however, indicates that a national ethical policy may be useful as a guidance document in African countries, especially when supported directly or indirectly by domestic law.

---

27 CIOMS, *International Ethical Guidelines for Biomedical Research Involving Human Subjects* (2002) (CIOMS Guidelines).
28 See, for example, "Dismantling the Helsinki Declaration" (2003) 169:10 CMAJ Editorial.
29 See the Nuffield Council on Bioethics, *supra* Note 5 at 64; Plomer, *supra* Note 27 at 5.
30 *Weiss v Solomon* (1989) 48 CCLT 280 (Quebec Supreme Court). The researcher was found liable for not adequately disclosing the risks of involvement in a biomedical research project, in which the research participant subsequently died.
31 See Fluss & Human, *supra* Note 45. See S Gevers, "Medical Research Involving Human Subjects: Towards an International Legal Framework?" (2001) 8 Eur J Health L 293 at 294, noting the indirect legal significance of the Helsinki Declaration. See Campbell & Glass, *supra* Note 5 at 473.

The Council for International Organisation for Medical Sciences (CIOMS),[32] in conjunction with the World Health Organisation, has also adopted guidelines for ethical research: the *International Ethical Guidelines for Biomedical Research Involving Human Subjects*[33] (CIOMS Guidelines). They were first drafted in 1982 to propose ways in which the principles set out in the Helsinki Declaration could be effectively applied in African countries.[34] The guidelines have historical foundations in the Helsinki Declaration.[35] They were most recently revised in 2016, after revisions in 2002, following the intense debates about the standard of care issue (briefly discussed in Chapter 1).[36] They are designed to be useful to countries in defining national policies on the ethics of biomedical research involving human subjects. They contain ethical guidelines and standards which apply specifically to the circumstances of African countries. For instance, the guidelines state that the ethical justification of biomedical research is the prospect of discovering new ways of benefiting people's health and can only be ethically justifiable if it is carried out in ways that respect, protect, are fair to, and are morally acceptable within the communities in which the research is conducted. It also requires that all research be submitted to an ethics review committee, which must be independent of the research team. It contains specific provisions relating to establishing or improving ethical review mechanisms, particularly within African countries, taking into consideration the lack of resources and other peculiar conditions.

Other ethical guidelines deal with specific issues in research. They draw from, and build on, the major guidelines described briefly earlier, primarily the Helsinki Declaration. These include WHO's *Standards and Operational Guidance for Ethics Review of Health-Related Research with Human Participants*,[37] which replaced the earlier *Operational Guidelines for Ethics Committees that Review Biomedical Research*, the UNESCO Declaration on Bioethics and Human Rights.[38]

---

32 The Council for International Organizations of Medical Sciences (CIOMS) is an international, non-governmental, non-profit organisation established jointly by WHO and United Nations Scientific and Cultural Organization (UNESCO) in 1949. See online: <www.cioms.ch>.

33 The Council for International Organizations of Medical Sciences, *International Ethical Guidelines for Biomedical Research Involving Human Subjects* adopted 1993, revised 2002, latest revision, 2016.

34 The "Background Note" of the 1993 edition of the CIOMS Guidelines stated that their main purpose was "to indicate how the ethical principles...as set forth in the Declaration of Helsinki, could be effectively applied, particularly in African countries, given their socioeconomic circumstances, laws and regulations, and executive and administrative arrangements."

35 *Ibid.*

36 See Trudo Lemmens et al, "CIOMS' Placebo Rule and the Promotion of Negligent Medical Practice" (2004) 11 Eur J Health L 153.

37 WHO, *Standards and Operational Guidance for Ethics Review of Health-Related Research with Human Participants* (Geneva: WHO, 2011).

38 Tropical Disease Research and World Health Organisation, *Operational Guidelines for Ethics Committees that Review Biomedical Research*, online: WHO <www.who.int/tdr/publications/publications/ethics.htm>; James Lavery, "The Challenge of Regulating International Research with Human Subjects" (2004) Science and Development Network, online: <www.scidev.net/dossiers/index.cfm?fuseaction=policybrief&policy=52&section=265&dossier=5>.

These guidelines also include the International Conference on Harmonisation's *Harmonised Tripartite Guidelines for Good Clinical Practice* (GCP),[39] revised last in 2016, which aims to "provide a unified standard for the European Union, Japan and the United States to facilitate the acceptance of clinical data by the regulatory authorities in these jurisdictions."[40] The GCP establishes scientific and ethical quality for drug trials internationally.[41] The existence of the GCP reflects increasing recognition of the need for a harmonisation of rules between countries to ensure easier facilitation of the ethical review of research as well as increased foreign market access for pharmaceuticals.[42] The GCP contains mainly regulatory and administrative procedures but also addresses such ethical issues as informed consent. Many countries, including African countries, now require compliance with the GCP as part of their drug approval processes. The GCP's positions on matters such as standard of care and the use of placebos are arguably looser than the Helsinki Declaration's.[43]

These international ethical guidelines aim to provide general guidance for the ethical conduct of research in countries around the world. They provide a new governance approach to the regulation and governance of health research, with the attendant benefits of a voluntary model of adoption and flexibility. As guidelines, they are flexible and so can address a wide variety of issues in a broad manner. They provide soft law guidance rather than hard law regulation. Instead of penal sanctions, there are other methods of enforcement, including, for instance, non-publication by journals where a research project clearly violates a principle of the guidelines.[44] As discussed in Chapter 2, such flexibility, voluntariness, and lack of penal sanctions would appeal to proponents of the new governance. In a complex enterprise, comprising diverse perspectives held by different stakeholders, often with conflicting interests, the guidelines may be argued to provide a basic standard. In my view, their moral authority, particularly the Helsinki Declaration, provides a form of governance and regulation which may go beyond obedience to black letter laws.

However, views on their practical application remain divergent. Their provisions can sometimes conflict, as, for instance, on the use of placebos. Moreover, since compliance with the guidelines is mainly voluntary, uniformity in practice is not guaranteed, which may lead to less protections for research participants in some countries. Further, the same flexibility which allows room for addressing

---

39 International Conference on Harmonisation of Technical Requirements for Registration of Pharamceuticals for Human Use, ICH Harmonised Tripartite Guideline – *Guideline for the Good Clinical Practice* (#6 (R2) (ICH-GCP Guideline)) (Geneva: 2016).

40 *Ibid.*

41 Para 3.

42 Adriana Petryna, "Ethical Variability: Drug Development and Globalizing Clinical Trials" (2005) 32:2 Am Ethnol 183 at 185.

43 See, for example, NAFDAC, Good Clinical Practice Guidelines, 2016 (Nigeria).

44 See, for instance, Article 30 of the Helsinki Declaration, which requires researchers to report research results, including sources of funding, conflicts of interest, and institutional affiliations.

issues broadly means that there is little precision in the guidance that they give, and application in practice may sometimes prove difficult.

As Plomer observes, the increasing globalisation of medical research brings to light the tension between the aspiration to the universality of the ethical principles in the international guidelines and the reality of the plurality of cultures.[45] As the ethical concerns in African countries described briefly in Chapter 1 clearly show, even though the international guidelines, particularly the Helsinki Declaration, carry great normative weight and have informed national policies and guidelines for research involving humans around the world, it is not always clear what is required to satisfy the rules in these guidelines. It has also been argued that they provide insufficient consideration of issues of global inequality, social justice, and inclusion of all groups in the benefits and burdens of research,[46] and that there is limited representation by resource-limited countries in their drafting processes, thus limiting their legitimacy[47] and ultimately making it difficult for courts in African countries to look to them for guidance.[48] Others have noted the differences in terms of who draws up the guidelines – the World Medical Association (which developed the Helsinki Declaration) is a body consisting of over 80 medical associations in the world, while the ICH-GCP was established by a few developed countries, including the United States, the European Union, Japan, and Canada.[49]

The conflict regarding the application of the international ethical guidelines is most particularly highlighted by the United States' decision in 2008 to cease applying the Helsinki Declaration in foreign clinical trials if they are used to support applications for the registration of products in the United States, relying instead on the ICH-GCP.[50] This effectively permits the greater use of placebos, even in the absence of the "best proven" intervention in foreign clinical trials,[51] and allows less stringent requirements in the areas of post-trial benefits for trial participants, conflicts of interest, and publication of trial results.[52] Some have noted that pharmaceutical companies doing clinical research in poorer countries

45 Plomer, *supra* Note 22 at 13.
46 See Lisa Eckenweiler et al, "The Declaration of Helsinki through a Feminist Lens" (2008) 1:1 Intl J Fem Approaches Bioeth 162.
47 Lavery, *supra* Note 81 at 204. See Jonathan Kimmel, Charles Weijer & Eric Meslin, "Helsinki Discords: FDA, Ethics, and International Drug Trials" (2009) 373:9657 Lancet 13.
48 Lemmens, *supra* Note 72 at 156.
49 Food and Drug Administration, HHS, "Human Subject Protection; Foreign Clinical Studies not Conducted under an Investigational New Drug Application. Final rule" (2008) 73:82 Fed Regist 22800–22816. See LJ Burgess & D Pretorius, "FDA Abandons the Declaration of Helsinki: The Effect on the Ethics of Clinical Trial Conduct in South Africa and Other Developing Countries" (2012) 5:2 S Afr J Bioeth & L 87.
50 Silvia Camporesi, "The FDA decision to Shelve the Helsinki Declaration: Ethical considerations" (2008).
51 See Kimmel, Weijer & Meslin, *supra* Note 50 at 13; Michael E Goodyear et al, "Does the FDA have the Authority to Trump the Declaration of Helsinki?" (2009) 338 BMJ 1559.
52 See Burgess & Pretorius, *supra* Note 53.

are beginning to omit reference to the Helsinki Declaration.[53] Recent debates about whether or not to limit the provision of access to PrEP to control groups, despite the WHO's recommendation to make PrEP available to all persons at significant risk of HIV infection, including women, on various grounds emphasise that these ethical dilemmas remain unresolved and that domestic discussions of these issues in African countries remain necessary.[54]

The decision raises questions about the general applicability of the international ethical guidelines but even more so about what African countries are doing or should do to take ownership of the protection of research participants in those countries. One way to address the complex concerns about ethical principles, and the contents and legitimacy of the international guidelines, may be an engagement between all interested agents and parties in continuous dialogue, negotiation, and reflection in an open, transparent way.[55] Moreover, collective consideration and acceptance of standards by countries will generally prevent accusations of hegemony which may arise where one country imposes its own standards and procedures, even where such standards and procedures are effective in protecting the rights of research participants.[56] The debates about the ethics of externally sponsored research in African countries and subsequent attempts at the revision and clarification of both the CIOMS and Helsinki Declaration, if not entirely resolved or successful, indicate a willingness to consider different perspectives. In this respect, it would be helpful to include more representatives and perspectives from African countries in the process of creating and amending these guidelines as well as in developing research protocols to be employed in African countries.

But going beyond these suggestions, national ethical policies or guidelines, in my view, are especially necessary to address areas that have proved contentious in the international guidelines. Countries are required to provide the highest protections to their citizens, especially from a human rights perspective.[57] National guidelines and policies can also ensure that any gaps in the international guidelines are specifically addressed in a national context. It is thus necessary for African countries to establish national policies, guidelines, and regulations which address in more depth the specific contexts and ethical issues which arise in them. This does not suggest that the international ethical guidelines have no further use. Their moral authority (particularly the Helsinki Declaration)

53 See Burgess & Pretorious, *supra* Note 53 at 88.
54 F Durueke, G Adeyemo & M Folayan, "Echoes from South Africa: Relevance to Nigeria: Standard of Care for Clinical Trials" (2017) *NHVMAS* online: <http://nhvmas-ng.org/site/echoes-from-south-africa-relevance-to-nigeria-standard-of-care-for-clinical-trials/>.
55 Konrad, *supra* Note 22 at 13. See also Michael DE Goodyear, Karmela Krleza-Jeric & Trudo Lemmens, "The Declaration of Helsinki: Mosaic Tablet, Dynamic Document, or Dinosaur?" (2007) 335 BMJ 625 at 626.
56 See Godfrey Tangwa, "Moral Agency, Moral Worth and the Question of Double Standards in Medical Research in African Countries" (2001) 1:2 Dev World Bioeth 156 at 67.
57 Fatma E Marouf & Bryn Espin, "Setting a Minimum Standard of Care in Clinical Trials: Human Rights and Bioethics as Complementary Frameworks" (2015) 17:1 Health & Hum Rts J 31.

remains considerable, their universality provides a baseline for protections, and the debates throw light onto the varying viewpoints in human participants' protection. But in view of the limitations discussed earlier, and the potential benefits of domestic guidance, national guidelines are essential. The contexts of these national guidelines and the pressures that domestic governments may be put under, especially resource-challenged governments, which may be led to adopt unfavourable national policies, must not be glossed over. However, there are limited alternatives to African countries' becoming educated on the issues and choosing what works best for protecting research participants within their countries while allowing beneficial research to take place.

Some African and other developing countries are already taking this route: South Africa,[58] Kenya, Uganda,[59] Nepal,[60] and India.[61] These countries have adopted national guidelines that are "tailored to their national contexts, with specific provisions addressing the vulnerabilities that may have enabled past abuses."[62] For instance, the South African national ethical guidelines adopt a broad meaning of the term "standard of care" and state exceptions that allow the use of placebos in arguably more specific terms than the Helsinki Declaration.[63] In Kenya, the guidelines make special provisions concerning research with underdeveloped communities, prisoners, married women in rural areas, and pregnant or lactating women.[64] Other countries, like Ghana, The Gambia, and Liberia, however, still do not have national guidelines.

Apart from addressing contentious issues and gaps, national guidelines and policies often provide specific requirements regarding the structure and organisation of the governance system. They may also set out the actors in the governance system, their responsibilities, and a system of accountability. The *UK Policy Framework for Health and Social Care Research* is applicable to the health authorities in the United Kingdom – England, Wales, Scotland, and Northern Ireland[65] – and specifies the responsibilities of research participants, research sponsors, and ethics review committees. In a like manner, Canada's Tri-Council

---

58 National Health Research Ethics Council, *Ethics in Health Research: Principles, Structures and Processes Guidelines* (Pretoria: Department of Health, 2004).

59 Uganda, *Guidelines for the Conduct of Health Research Involving Human Subjects in Uganda* (National Consensus Conference 1997).

60 Nepal Health Research Council, *National Ethical Guidelines for Health Research in Nepal* (2001).

61 Indian Council of Medical Research (ICMR), *"Ethical Guidelines for Biomedical Research on Human Subjects"* (2000). See also Nandini Kumar et al, "The Indian Experience" (2008) 6:4 J Acad Ethics.

62 Adèle Langlois, "The UNESCO Universal Declaration on Bioethics and Human Rights: Perspectives from Kenya and South Africa" (2008) 16:1 Health Care Analysis 39 at 43–44.

63 National Health Research Ethics Council, Ethics in Health Research: Principles, Structures and Processes Guidelines (Pretoria: Department of Health, 2015).

64 National Council for Science and Technology, *Guidelines for Ethical Conduct of Biomedical Research Involving Human Subjects in Kenya* (NCST No. 45, 2004). See paras 9–13.

65 *UK Policy Framework for Health and Social Care Research* (United Kingdom, 2017). See Appendix 1.

Policy Statement[66] specifies, among other things, the operation of ethics review committees, including the conditions under which an expedited review may take place and the requirement for institutions to establish a standing committee to hear appeals when a researcher is dissatisfied with an ethics review committee's decision, matters that are not addressed in the Helsinki Declaration. Both ethical principles and procedural or structural matters may be contained in the same guidance document (as is the case with Canada's Tri-Council Policy Statement and the Australian *National Statement on Ethical Conduct in Human Research 2007* (updated May 2015))[67] or in separate documents. Given the gaps that exist in the international guidelines and the procedural matters that need to be attended to, there is need to provide for both substantive ethical matters and organisational or structural issues, and procedural issues and processes in domestic policy documents.

Finally, national policies can provide a further layer of protection for research participants beyond any protections offered by the international ethical guidelines. They may provide this by clarifying the application of certain ethical principles in the local context, specifying appropriate procedural mechanisms, and making reference to local legal requirements and standards; African countries therefore need to consider creating national guidance, where it is not already in place, to allow for clearer and more direct application.

In a hybrid framework of governance, as proposed in Chapter 2, such national policy guidance will retain the positive attributes of a new governance approach (including flexibility and ease of amendment) while operating within a domestic context. Such flexibility is important because of changes that may need to be made in line with international developments, ongoing evolution in research ethics, and changes in domestic circumstances. With wide consultations between stakeholders in the research enterprise, these guidelines could also promote legitimacy. As I argued in Chapter 2, allowing for guidelines (soft law) in areas where specificity could be elusive potentially offers not only more legitimacy but a greater level of accountability than would otherwise exist. However, national guidelines, like international guidelines, typically lack enforcement mechanisms, relying instead on moral suasion in African countries. Thus, as I have argued elsewhere, hard law is also necessary, given the need to protect research participants in African countries.[68] Certain basic requirements, in my view, need to be enforceable in law. Still, some controversial ethical issues, like the standard of care issue, may best be dealt with in national guidelines rather than legislation

---

66 Canadian Institutes of Health Research, Natural Sciences and Engineering Research Council of Canada, and Social Sciences and Humanities Research Council of Canada, Tri-Council Policy Statement: Ethical Conduct for Research Involving Humans, December 2014.

67 NHMRC, *National Statement on Ethical Conduct in Human Research* 2007 (Updated May 2015). The United Kingdom's previous *Research Governance Framework for Health and Social Care* (2005) focussed mainly on processes and procedural matters.

68 Cheluchi Onyemelukwe, "Research Involving Humans in Africa: A Case for Domestic Legal Frameworks" (2008) 16:2 Afr J Intl & Comp L 152.

because of the evolving understanding of such issues. Emerging ethical issues, such as how to deal with and store biological samples, research involving traditional and alternative medicines, and access to experimental medicines in the age of epidemics, to name a few, may also benefit from focus at a national level. In the following chapters, I consider in greater detail the national guidelines that have recently been adopted in some African countries and their impact on research governance.

Institutional framework

Beyond the ethical standards detailed in the ethics guidelines described earlier, an institutional framework is required, and has developed in countries around the world, to provide a system of governance. Different institutions act as the active mechanisms which implement the ethical framework. Principal among these institutions is the ethics review committee. Other institutions, such as the national drug regulatory authorities and professional associations, also play an active role in the implementation of ethical standards and principles.

In the following I describe briefly the institutions that govern health research involving humans in countries around the world. The account given of these institutions is by necessity condensed to provide only the most essential details. Also, while this subsection addresses some of the issues that arise in the deployment of these institutions in research governance, the analysis undertaken here is necessarily broad. However, the identification of systemic issues which affect the functioning and effectiveness of these institutions is necessary for an understanding of issues that may arise in African countries.

Ethics review committees

Ethics review is a fundamental part of the research governance systems of many countries and is now widely recognised as a necessary safeguard and a formal mechanism for the protection of research participants. A detailed history of the origins of ethics review has been undertaken elsewhere.[69] McNeill, for instance, traces the history of ethics review committees in several countries,[70] and it is unsurprising that, particularly in the United States, where they first began as a system of peer review,[71] these committees were established in response to several unethical experiments involving humans. Such experiments include the 1963 Jewish Chronic Disease Hospital incident, where chronically ill patients were

---

69 Paul M McNeill, *The Ethics and Politics of Human Experimentation* (Cambridge: Cambridge University Press, 1993) at 53–84. See also Ruth R Faden & Tom L Beauchamp, *A History of Informed Consent* (New York and Oxford: Oxford University Press, 1986).

70 The United States, Britain, Ireland, Australia, New Zealand, and Canada.

71 See Charles McCarthy, "The Institutional Review Board: Its Origins, Purpose, Function and Future" in David N Weisstub, ed, *Research on Human Subjects: Ethics, Law and Social Policy* (Oxford: Elsevier Science Ltd., 1998) at 307.

injected with cancer cells without their knowledge or consent.[72] In the following, I reflect briefly on the ethics review process and its significance in research governance. From a systems perspective, I also describe briefly some of the issues that affect its effectiveness as a crucial part of research governance, including composition, structure, and financial support, with illustrations from different countries. I then consider, briefly, ethics review in African countries.

The ethics review process, one of the principal means of ensuring that any proposed research is ethical, requires that investigators or researchers submit the proposed research project or protocol to a committee, prior to research commencement. Such a committee enquires into its ethical acceptability. Thus it is different from (though it may include) peer review of the scientific aspects of research. The ethics review committee is charged with assessing the risks and benefits of the proposed research, ensuring that its potential benefits outweigh any foreseeable risks attached thereto and in this process weighing the interests of the research participants, the society, and the investigators.[73] In carrying out these functions, ethics review committees provide a means of accountability and boost public trust and confidence in the research enterprise. In this way, these committees also play an important role in facilitating research.

Ethics review committees typically have the authority to decide whether research proposals are reasonable and ethically acceptable, and can proceed; whether they are not and should therefore not proceed; whether they can proceed with some modification; or, if research has already commenced, whether it is to be terminated. The extensive powers of ethics review committees have attracted criticisms from many researchers and commentators, including complaints that they sometimes prevent and delay beneficial research, that they unnecessarily limit academic and research freedom, that they are particularly unhelpful in the social sciences, and that the process is expensive.[74] However, ethics review is, and remains likely to continue being, a critical part of research governance as a direct oversight mechanism for health research. At any rate, the international ethical guidelines, including the Helsinki Declaration, require that health research involving humans passes through the ethics

---

72 See McNeill for a fuller history of origins of the ethics review system. See McNeill, *supra* Note 72 at 57.

73 WHO, *Research Ethics Committees: Basic Concepts for Capacity-Building* (Geneva: WHO, 2009) at 14.

74 See Zachary M Schragg, "The Case against Ethics Review in the Social Sciences Research Ethics" (2011) 7:4 Res Ethics 120–131; M Schuman, "Clinical Trials: The Balance between Protecting Participants and Promoting Drug and Product Development" (2009) 180:6 CMAJ 603; DS Wald, "Bureaucracy of Ethics Applications" (2004) 329 BMJ 282–284; Alysun M Jones & Bryony Bamford, "The Other Face of Research Governance" (2004) 329:7460 BMJ 280; CK Gunsalus et al, "Mission Creep in the IRB World" (2006) 312 Science 1441; Norman Fost & Robert J Levine, "The Dysregulation of Human Subjects Research" (2007) 298 JAMA 2196; Jon Nicholls, "The Ethics of Research Ethics Committees" (2000) 320:7243 BMJ 1217.

review process.[75] The committees that carry out such review (referred to here as ethics review committees[76]) are now regarded as key in most countries for the purpose of providing independent ethics assessment of research protocols and protecting research participants. Some countries, like Denmark,[77] South Africa,[78] and Nigeria,[79] have even taken the additional step of making it a legal requirement that all health research, with certain specified exceptions, passes through ethics review. Other countries, including the United States, Canada, and the United Kingdom, legally require ethics review specifically for clinical trials of drugs. Research governance, for the most part then, is built around the committees which carry out ethics review, ensuring, amongst other things, that research is conducted in an ethical manner and that the rights, safety, and welfare of research participants are protected. Even systems which lack a formal legal underpinning typically consist of institutional ethics review committees as the centrepiece around which governance revolves.

The requirements of most research sponsors and international journals, particularly journals which publish biomedical research, that ethics review approval must be obtained for funding or publication[80] further cements the centrality of ethics review in research governance. These mechanisms – funding requirements and publications – are soft law mechanisms favoured in new governance thinking and are thus part of the hybrid framework proposed in this book for the effective governance of health research involving humans.

The decisions taken during review by these committees, whether to approve or disapprove a proposed research protocol, or terminate an ongoing project, are influenced by international, national, and institutional policy and guidelines; by law; by institutional culture; and, significantly, by the views, values, and decision-making processes of individual members as well as group dynamics.[81] Thus, from a systemic perspective, the composition or membership of committees,

75 Article 23. Helsinki Declaration 2013.
76 Different countries have different nomenclature: Institutional Review Boards in the United States, Research Ethics Boards (REB) in Canada, Health Research Ethics Committees (HREC) in Nigeria and South Africa. But all have basically the same functions.
77 See Section 1 and Section 8 of the *Act on a Biomedical Research Ethics Committee System and the Processing of Biomedical Research Projects*.
78 Section 73 of the *National Health Act*. Sweden also legally mandates ethics review of research involving humans. See *The Swedish Ethical Review Act*, (Lag (2003:460) om etikprövning av forskning som avser människor) issued June 5, 2003 (SFS no 2003:460), implemented in January 2004 and amended in 2008. The Swedish Ethical Review Act was revised in 2008 (SFS 2008:192).
79 National Health Act (Nigeria).
80 International Journal of Medical Journal Editors, "Uniform Requirements for Manuscripts Submitted to Biomedical Journals: Ethical Considerations in the Conduct and Reporting of Research: Protection of Human Subjects and Animals in Research" online: <www.icmje.org/ethical_6protection.html>.
81 CA Schuppli & D Fraser, "Factors Influencing the Effectiveness of Research Ethics Committees" (2007) 33 J Med Ethics 294.

the structure and organisation of ethics review committees, and the financial support that the committees receive to undertake their work as a fundamental part of the research governance system are some of the factors which can affect their functioning. The composition and competency or expertise of individual members on matters of ethics, their understanding of scientific, and research processes are key matters. There is therefore the need to have a broad membership. Such membership should include adequate expertise necessary to appropriately evaluate the soundness and scientific validity of research protocol, the capability to examine research projects for ethical soundness, and the ability to take into account the values of the community in which the research is to take place. The composition of committees varies in different countries, ranging from at least five members in countries like Canada,[82] the United States,[83] South Africa,[84] and Nigeria[85] to at least seven members in Denmark[86] and eight members in Australia.[87] There is a general recognition that there should be members that are familiar with the research methods that are being proposed.[88] It is also now recognised that, in order to achieve a diversity of values and perspectives, and to counter any predisposition by institutional members towards research or institutional interests, not only should the committee be comprised of members drawn from the institution (in an institutional ethics committee) but also there should be lay members. These members represent the community in which the research is to take place as well as the research participants.[89] In this regard, they are necessary to advance dialogue with, and accountability to, local communities[90] and provide a diversity of perspectives. In Denmark, half of the regional committee is required to be drawn from lay members.[91] These may include non-medical clinical staff who have not practiced as such for at least five years, and at least half of the lay members must be persons who are not and have never been involved in carrying out research on humans.[92] In a hybrid governance framework, lay membership, that is, membership drawn from outside the institution and from the community, enhances accountability and responsiveness.

---

82 Section 1, Article B- 1.3- Membership of REBs of the TCPS.
83 Department of Health and Human Services. Protection of Human subjects. 1991; Title 45 CFR & 46.45 CFR 46.107.
84 South Africa – Section 4.1 of *Ethics in Health Research: Principles, Structures and Processes* (Composition).
85 NHREC, *National Code for Health Research Ethics* (2006), Section D.
86 Section 3.
87 Chapter 5.1. 29 of the National Statement.
88 See, for instance, Canada – Section 1, Article B- 1.3 (TCPS)- Membership of REBs.
89 See, for instance, South Africa – Section 4.1 of *Ethics in Health Research: Principles, Structures and Processes* (Composition).
90 TCPS – Article 1.3 (see discussion).
91 McNeill, *supra* Note 103 at 102. See also Soren Holm, "The Danish Research Ethics Committee System—Overview and Critical Assessment" in NBAC, *Ethical and Policy Issues in Research Involving Human Participants Commissioned Papers and Staff Analysis* (Washington: NBAC, 2001) at F-10.
92 Section 6 of the *Governance Arrangements for NHS Research Ethics Committees.*

Questions continue to be raised in the literature, however, regarding whether ethics review members should be part-time volunteers or dedicated professionals;[93] the need for ethicists on ethics review committees;[94] the need for representation of research participants on ethics review committees;[95] and what lay membership really means, especially given that what is considered lay membership varies in each jurisdiction. Is a lay member merely one with no scientific expertise or one with no connection to the institution?[96] Questions also arise regarding the role that laypersons can and should play in the ethics review process and whether or not laypersons can effectively contribute to the process, especially in the absence of a certain level of education and training in matters of research and research ethics.[97] Apart from lay participation, some jurisdictions require an ethics expert,[98] others require a lawyer,[99] and others underscore the desirability of gender balance in the composition of such committees.[100] Other related issues include the provision of education and training for ethics review committee members in the different disciplines, methodologies, approaches, and ethical issues implicated in health research. There are more detailed discussions of these issues in other literature.[101] A fuller description and discussion in the context of African countries follow.

93 "Choosing a Research Ethics Committee System amongst the Existing Models? Critical Decision of a Middle Income Country (Chile)" online: <www.gfbronline.com/PDFs/Eighth_Casestudy1.pdf>.

94 Nathan Emmerich, "On the Ethics Committee: The Expert Member, the Lay Member and the Absentee Ethicist" (2009) 5:1 Res Ethics Rev 9; Downie & McDonald, *supra* Note 118.

95 Hadskis, Michael, "Giving Voice to Research Participants: Should IRBs Hear from Research Participant Representative?" (2007) 14:3 Account Res 155; McNeill, *supra* Note 103 at 7.

96 Denise Avard et al, "Research Ethics Boards and Challenges for Public Participation" (2009)17:2–3 Health L Rev 66 at 67, describing the vagueness of the definition of lay membership in the Canadian TCPS. What is considered lay membership varies in each jurisdiction. In South Africa, two laypersons are required. Laypersons are defined as those who have no affiliation to the institution, are not currently involved in medical, scientific or legal work and are preferably from the community in which the research is to take place." Section 4.1 of the *Ethics in Health Research: Principles, Structures and Processes Guidelines.*

97 Avard, *ibid.*

98 Canada – Section 1, Article B- 1.3- Membership of REBs.

99 South Africa – Section 4.1 of *Ethics in Health Research: Principles, Structures and Processes* (Composition). See also Canada, *ibid.* The lawyer, however, is required only in the cases of biomedical research. The second edition, which is still under consultation, however, makes no distinction between biomedical and other types of research. Both editions state that the lawyer is not to give legal advice or serve as counsel to the committee but to address the legal issues that arise in connection with the proposed research.

100 See the United States: 45 CFR 46.107.

101 See generally McNeill, *supra* Note 103; Michael, *supra* Note 98 at 155; Raymond de Vries & Carl Forsberg, "Who Decides? A Look at Ethics Committee Membership" (2002) 14:3 HEC Forum 252; Henry B Dinsdale, "The Composition of Research Ethics Boards" online: <www.chrcrm.org/main/modules/pageworks/index.php?page=015&id=231>; Sohini Sengupta & Bernard Lo, "The Roles and Experiences of Non-affiliated and Non-scientist Members of Institutional Review Board" (2003) 14 Acad Med 212; Emily E Anderson, "A Qualitative Study

The structure of the ethics review system is another factor that impinges on the effectiveness of the ethics review process because it has implications for the integrity and independence of the system, and for its efficiency. Two main types of structures of ethics review systems – the institutional system of ethics review or the regional system of ethics review – exist. These may operate in a centralised or decentralised system. The institutional system of ethics review involves ethics review committees in different institutions in which health research takes place. The United States model of Institutional Review Boards (IRBs) represents the pioneering approach of the "local" review of research, that is, conducting review within the institutions in which the research will take place.[102] The strength of the institutional model lies, then, in the ease of conducting local review, taking into consideration the local context, values, and issues, including cultural issues.

Regulation, as provided by institutional ethics review committees is, effectively, self-regulation.[103] In this respect, institutional committees are typically composed of a majority of members who are drawn from the institutions. Institutional ethics review committees, with many members from the institution, typically have members with expertise in different fields and in methodologies that may be used in health research. And, as mentioned earlier, they can conduct review, taking into account the local context, values, and issues, including cultural issues. Also, institutional ethics review committees can closely monitor ongoing studies.[104] Further, an institutional system makes it easier to locate the responsibility for ethical review close to where the research is conducted.[105]

However, many committees are funded by the institutions within which they operate. The institutions themselves frequently depend on research funding from external sources. Inherent conflict of interest issues thus arise from a structure where the institution which seeks to attract research is in some ways the same institution which will review the research, albeit through an ostensibly independent ethics committee.[106] Members of ethics review committees, even in

---

of Nonaffiliated, Non-scientist Institutional Review Board Members" (2006) 13 Accountability in Research 135; Joan P Porter, "How Unaffiliated/Non-scientist Members of Institutional Review Boards See Their Roles" (1987) 9:6 IRB: Ethics & Hum Res 1; Schuppli & Fraser, *supra* Note 84 at 294; PE Bauer, "A Few Simple Truths about Your Community IRB Members" (2001) 23 IRB 7; Avard, *supra* Note 99 at 66.

102 "Choosing a Research Ethics Committee System amongst the Existing Models? Critical Decision of a Middle Income Country(Chile)" online: < www.gfbronline.com/PDFs/Eighth_Casestudy1.pdf>.

103 For the advantages of self-regulation, see generally Ian Ayres & John Braithwaite, *Responsive Regulation: Transcending the Deregulation Debate* (New York: Oxford University Press, 1992) at 103.

104 Ayres & Braithwaite, *ibid.* at 104, noting that self-regulation can achieve greater inspectorial depth.

105 MH Walsh, JJ McNeil & KJ Breen, "Improving the Governance of Health Research" (2005) 182 Med J Aust 468.

106 Ezekiel J Emmanuel et al, "Oversight of Human Participants Research: Identifying Problems to Evaluate Reform Proposals" (2004) 141:1 Ann Intern Med 282 at 283. In these countries, ethics review committees can also be independent from the institutions and provide ethics review in exchange for payment.

the absence of financial conflict of interest, may have secondary interests, such as approving research in their own area of specialty or disapproving research which may draw research participants from their own research.[107]

Thus, the possibility of regulatory capture increases significantly under the institutional system of ethics review. In this respect, the direct regulators of research, that is, the ethics review committees, may be directly or indirectly interested in attracting research funds to the institution. Such interest creates a greater possibility of capture by the researchers and research sponsors whom they are supposed to regulate. The inherent conflict of interest issues arising from self-regulation in the context of institutional systems of ethics review thus calls into question the independence of committees. Actual, potential, or perceived conflict of interest permits regulatory capture. This not only endangers the safety of participants but also has the potential to mar the promotion of health research by eroding public confidence and trust in the research process.

A regional ethics review committee, on the other hand, is a model of committee review that is not based solely at the local institutional level, such as in a hospital or a university. These broader regional systems are typically responsible for "a distinct region, a distinct group of research subjects, a distinct disease, or projects related to a distinct funding agency."[108] A country may, therefore, have institutional committees but also specialised regional committees that review specialised research.[109] Other countries, like Denmark,[110] have regional systems that are typically responsible for a distinct region, and all the research conducted in that region is reviewed by one regional committee.

The regional model, as employed in countries like Denmark,[111] would appear to be free from the criticisms of the institutional model because members are drawn region-wide, and there is less likelihood of conflict of interest issues arising in the context of the institutional model. As has been argued in detail elsewhere the "local context" is not lost by regionalisation.[112] Also, there may be more balance between local insight and the necessary distance from personal prejudice. Riis has therefore noted that "It is more appropriate – and a clear advantage for countries having the chance to start from scratch – to create a *regional* system instead of an institutional one from the very beginning."[113]

---

107 Eric Campbell, "Concerns about IRBs in the Enterprise of Clinical Research" (2004) 4 Lancet Oncology 326.

108 Alison Shea, "Regional Research Ethics Boards: Canadian and International Models" (2004), online: via <www.nshrf.ca> at 3.

109 For example Canada. Shea, *ibid.*

110 And other Scandinavian countries, like Sweden and Norway.

111 The regional model is also employed in other Scandinavian countries: Sweden and Norway. See European Network of Research Ethics Committees (EUREC), "National Information: Sweden" online: <www.eurecnet.org/information/sweden.html>.

112 Downie, *supra* Note 150 at 93–94.

113 Povl Riis, "Ethical Review of Biomedical Research in Europe: Suggestions for Best National Practices" (1998), online: <www.coe.int/T/E/Legal_Affairs/Legal_co-operation/Bioethics/Activities/Biomedical_research/CDBI-INF(1998)6E-ManualDebra.pdf> at 4.

Where appropriately set up, a regional system may be more manageable and efficient, and ensure more uniformity of standards and thus more protection of research participants. This is because there will likely be fewer ethics review committees and less chance of duplication, inconsistency in reviews, and "forum shopping."

Both institutional and the regional committees may operate in a centralised or decentralised atmosphere, or in a dual system that combines both.[114] A centralised system,[115] consisting frequently of a national committee, is recommended by some commentators to address issues which institutional or regional committees may be inadequate to deal with. These include the increase in applications for review and multisite or multi-jurisdictional research; the need to ensure faster, more efficient, consistent ethics review processes; and the need to ensure coordination between different institutional or regional ethics review committees and the standardisation of the ethics review process.[116] Several African countries have adopted this approach, notably, Nigeria, South Africa, Ethiopia, and Kenya. The trend from my research in African countries appears to continue to be in favour of such a national agency, even in countries that are yet to have such structure, such as Liberia and The Gambia. The United States, the United Kingdom, and Canada, on the other hand, continue to have a decentralised approach. The functions of auditing ethics review committees and providing guidelines and standards, hearing appeals from the local committees which national ethics review committees typically have, are helpful in creating a uniform system of research governance, with clear reporting relationships and accountability. Such a national committee would essentially provide what Ayres and Braithwaite call "enforced self-regulation"[117] or regulation of self-regulation. In other words, institutional or regional committees may develop their own policies and function independently. A national or central committee would serve as an "enforcer," monitoring institutional or regional committees to ensure that they function as required. Some commentators have, however, suggested that centralised systems may exacerbate the burden on researchers and ethics com-

---

114 Maureen H Fitzgerald & Paul A Phillips, "Centralized and Non-Centralized Ethics Review: A Five Nation Study" (2006)13 Account Res 47.

115 Fitzgerald & Philips describe a centralised system: "In the centralized system all applications, other than possibly undergraduate research, would go to a centralized committee or an over-arching national body, and the review process would be conducted by committees associated with and administered by this body. In this system, the committee that reviews the application may or may not be located within the geographical region where the researcher is located. " See Fitzgerald & Phillips, *ibid.* at 63.

116 See Walsh, McNeil & Breen, *supra* Note 108 468 at 470; ZJ Penn & PJ Steer, "Local Research Ethics Committees: Hindrance or Help?" (1995) 102 Br J Obstet Gynaecol 1–2; Department of Health, *Ethics Committee Review of Multi-Centre Research* (London: Department of Health, 1997); J Blunt, J Savulescu & AJM Watson, "Meeting the Challenges Facing Research Ethics Committees: Some Practical Suggestions" (1998) 316 British Med J 58–61; Fitzgerald & Phillips, *supra* Note 117 at 47; DC Whiteman et al, "National Ethics Committee Urgently Needed" (2003) 178 MJA 187; MC Christian et al, "A Central Institutional Review Board for Multi-Institutional Trials" (2000) 346 N Engl J Med 1405.

117 Ayres & Braithwaite, *supra* Note 147.

mittees by adding another level of bureaucracy, and that their effectiveness has yet to be determined.[118]

It is uncommon for countries to run a fully centralised system in which all administrative systems and review activities are centralised.[119] It is more common for countries to operate either a dual system or a decentralised system. Thus, some developed countries, like Denmark, and African countries, like Nigeria and South Africa, operate a dual system and therefore have a national ethics review committee. The national ethics review committee may, amongst other things, register, audit the institutional committees (in the case of Nigeria and South Africa) or regional committees (as in Denmark), act as an appeal body, and review some types of research.[120] Accreditation is becoming a necessary part of standardisation, and most national ethics review bodies have an accreditation function.

Similarly, others, like the United Kingdom and New Zealand, operate a dual system, with multiregional and institutional committees and a central committee that vets multisite research protocols (in the case of New Zealand) and a committee for ensuring coordination between the different regions (in the case of the United Kingdom).[121] However, some countries with institutional committees, such as Australia,[122] Canada,[123] and the United States,[124] although

---

118 Davina Ghersi, "Research Ethics Committees and the Changing Research Environment" (2005) 5 Lancet Oncology 325; K Alberti, "Multicentre Research Ethics Committees: Has the Cure Been Worse Than the Disease?" (2000) 320 BMJ 1157–1158.

119 Fitzgerald & Philips cites the example of Tasmania in Australia. Some African countries until recently also had systems where research was reviewed by the national ministry of health and which could thus be considered a centralised system. See Fitzgerald & Philips, *supra* Note 157.

120 Denmark has a national ethics review committee: the Danish National Committee on Biomedical Research Ethics. See Section 24 of the Act for its functions. See also online: <www.cvk. sum.dk/CVK/Home/English.aspx> Sweden operates a similar system. See EUREC, *supra* Note 154.

121 See generally AS Walanj, "Research Ethics Committees: Need for Harmonization at the National Level, the Global and Indian Perspective" (2014) 5:2 Perspect Clin Res 66; A Hedgecoe et al, "Research Ethics Committees in Europe: Implementing the Directive, Respecting Diversity" (2006) 32 JME 484. See generally Fitzgerald & Phillips, *supra* Note 117 at 47.

122 In Australia, HRECs function within institutions. Although it also has a national ethics committee, the Australian Health Ethics Committee (AHEC), a principal committee of the NHMRC, this does not act as a national ethics review committee as in South Africa, Nigeria, and Denmark. AHEC is established under Sections 35 and 36 of the *National Health and Medical Research Council Act* 1992 and is required to oversee the operation of the HREC system. (National Statement 1999 Principles 2.46–2.48). AHEC does not act as an overall review body and does not audit HRECs or review particular projects like the NHREC in Nigeria. Further, it has no power to impose sanctions on non-compliant HRECs or researchers.

123 In Canada, REBs operate within individual institutions such as universities and within Health Canada. There is no national ethics review committee. Newfoundland has set up its own Health Research Ethics Authority for Newfoundland and Labrador which appoints an REB and approves other research ethics bodies. Some REBs also function on a regional basis, such as the Ontario Research Cancer Board. See Downie & McDonald, *supra* Note 118 at 6. Section 3 (1), 7 and 8 of the NewFoundLand Health Research Ethics Authority Act, 2006.

124 In the United States, IRBs operate within institutions. The *National Research Act* 1974 requires each institution conducting federally supported research involving human subjects to establish an IRB to review the ethical aspects of all research protocols within the institution.

there may be certain specialised ethics review committees, operate in a mostly decentralised atmosphere, with the institutional ethics review committees reporting only to their home institutions, and multisite or multicentre research is reviewed by different institutional committees.

Which is the best ethics review structure for the protection of participants – institutional/regional, centralised/decentralised, national/no national committee? Not much empirical work has been done on this issue.[125] However, a key aspect of making that choice would also depend on sustainability. Ethics review systems can be costly, including expenditures for documentation, necessary equipment, training, project monitoring, and site visits. They must therefore have adequate financial support.[126] Denmark stands out from the other jurisdictions in detailing in law a system of funding for ethics review committees within its legislation.[127] Many countries do not legally require that ethics review committees be provided with adequate funding to carry out their work. Yet it is clear that funding is needed for administrative support, for seeking expert support where necessary. Insufficient funding may hamper the speed of ethics review, creating a preventable obstacle to research, and may jeopardise the protection of the participants with which ethics review committees are charged.[128] Given the paucity of resources in African countries, this issue is of particular concern.

The increase in research activities in African countries, especially as the HIV/AIDS epidemic expanded in the continent and international health research increased, instigated a push for more reliable ethics review. While some African countries have a relatively long history of ethical review of studies involving human participants, for example, South Africa (since 1966); Kenya (some form of oversight since 1979);[129] and Nigeria, having institutional ethics review committees since the 1980s, some earlier studies noted the absence of ethics review committees in some countries.[130] In 2001, for instance, the Regional Committee for Africa, WHO pointed out that about a quarter of the studies involving humans in the

125 Empirical work has focussed on the lengths of time and the results of ethics review in national contexts. See, for example, E Hemminki, JI Virtanen & E Regushevskaya, "Decisions by Finnish Medical Research Ethics Committees: A Nationwide Study of Process and Outcomes" (2015) 10:4 J Empir Res Hum Res Ethics 404–413; L Abbott & C Grady, "A Systematic Review of the Empirical Literature Evaluating IRBs: What We Know and What We Still Need to Learn" (2011) 6 J Empir Res Hum Res Ethics 3–19. doi:10.1525/jer.2011.6.1.3. Google Scholar, Link; EL Angell et al, "An Analysis of Decision Letters by Research Ethics Committees: The Ethics/Scientific Quality Boundary Examined" (2008) 17 Quality & Safety in Health Care 131–136.
126 LE Bain, "Rethinking Research Ethics Committees in Low- and Medium-Income Countries" (2017) Research Ethics 1–7, online: <http://journals.sagepub.com/doi/pdf/10.1177/1747016117692026>.
127 *Act on a Biomedical Research Ethics Committee System and the Processing of Biomedical Research Projects* 2003 (as amended), online: <www.cvk.sum.dk/English/actonabiomedicalresearch.aspx>, Section 28.
128 Downie & McDonald, *supra* Note 118 at 24.
129 M Kruger, P Ndebele & L Horn, eds, *Research Ethics in Africa: A Resource for Research Ethics Committees* (Stellenbosch: Sun Press, 2014) at 6.
130 See K Ahmad, "African Countries Need Effective Ethics Review Committees" (2003) 362 Lancet 627–628.

Africa Region were not subjected to ethics review.[131] As the amount of research conducted in the developing world increases, concerns have also arisen with regard to the existence, functioning, effectiveness, and independence of ethics review committees in African countries. Previous studies have suggested that even where conducted, ethics review may not be rigorous due to lack of capacity and infrastructure.[132] Earlier studies had also identified problems, including lack of standardisation, insufficient funding, inadequate facilities and equipment for work, understaffing[133] imbalance in composition,[134] conflict of interest, lack of transparency, inadequate training and capacity to review research,[135] inadequate or non-existent post-approval monitoring systems,[136] lack of standard operating procedures,[137] as well as inactivity in the ethics review committees in African countries.[138] Given such issues as possible political interference, the understandable yet inappropriate desire of some committees to attract funding and other perceived benefits to the community from proposed research projects, ad hoc establishment of committees to satisfy foreign requirements,[139] and the dependence of some ethics review committees on foreign funding for meeting routine costs, the independence of ethics review committees in African countries has also been questioned.[140]

Other studies on the structure and function of ethics review committees found that conflicts of interest arose in the context of reviewing the protocols

131 AA Hyder et al, "Ethical Review of Health Research: A Perspective from Developing Country Researchers" (2004) 30 J Med Ethics 30; J Kiriga, C Wambebe & A Baba-Mousa, "Status of National Bioethics Committees in the WHO African Region" (2005) 6 BMC Med Ethics E10; D Zhang et al, "An Assessment of the Quality of Randomized Controlled Trials Conducted in China" (2008) 9 Trials 22. See also EE Abbas "Industry-Sponsored Research in African countries" (2007) 28:6 Contemp Clin Trials 677.

 Other studies undertaken by the NBAC on research in African countries found that some research undertaken by researchers from the United States in African countries had not undergone any ethics review in the host countries. Other studies undertaken by the NBAC on research in African countries found that some research undertaken by researchers from the United States in African countries had not undergone any ethics review in the host countries. Zhang et al, *supra* Note 134 at 22. See also Abbas, *supra* Note 134 at 677.

132 A Nyika et al, Composition, Training Needs and Independence of Ethics Review Committees across Africa: Are the Gate-Keepers Rising to the Emerging Challenges?" (2009) 35 J Med Ethics 189.

133 JKB Ikingura, M Kruger & W Zeleke, "Health Research Ethics Review and Needs of Institutional Ethics Committees in Tanzania" (2007) 9:3 Tanzan Health Res Bull 154.

134 Keymanthri Moodley & Landon Myer, "Health Research Ethics Committees in South Africa 12 Years into Democracy" (2007) 8 BMC Med Ethics 1.

135 See Milford et al, *supra* Note 5. See also Nancy Kass et al, "The Structure and Function of Research Ethics Committees in Africa: A Case Study" 4:1 PLoS Med e3, online: <http://medicine. plosjournals.org/perlserv/?request=get-document&doi=10.1371/journal.pmed.0040003> (May 3, 2009).

136 Kass & Hyder, *supra* Note 163 at B-109.

137 A Nyika et al, "Capacity Building of Ethics Review Committees Across Africa Based on the Results of a Comprehensive Needs Assessment Survey" (2009) 9:3 Dev World Bioeth 149.

138 "A Rapid Assessment of Strategic Information Systems for Lesotho's HIV/AIDS Programme" (2005), online: <www.rhap.org.za/resources/240.pdf?PHPSESSID=c765d08831c119ea0b51da 8863412bf2> at 40, noting the inactive state of the ethics review board.

139 See Kass & Hyder, *supra* Note 314 at B-108.

140 Nuffield Council on Bioethics, *supra* Note 5 at 104–106; *supra* Note 17; Lavery, *supra* Note 19 at 233–237.

of departmental colleagues and protocols which would bring money into the institutions. In such cases, questions are sometimes not raised to allow the projects to proceed quickly.[141] Given the paucity of resources in institutions in such countries, the likelihood of conflict of interest and the harm that could result from such conflict are amplified. Such conflict of interest issues would affect the independence of the committee and consequently the protection of the participants with which the committee is charged. Some commentators therefore argue against the wholesale adoption of the institutional models operated in some developed countries.[142] The alternative would be for African countries to consider their circumstances and study different systems around the world to determine what model of ethics review structure best suits their needs. Several studies have been undertaken of the functioning of ethics review committees in African countries.[143]

The number of ethics review committees have grown significantly. A recent mapping of African ethics review committees indicates that at least 167 committees are currently operating on the continent.[144] This number is likely conservative as the mapping was undertaken on a voluntary basis, and the numbers operating may be up to double the figure stated.[145] More concern about delays in ethics review is being expressed, and potential solutions through the use of web-based technologies are being developed,[146] indicating a growing norm of ethics review and an acceptance of this norm as a key part of the governance of health research in African countries.

Even so, current studies suggest that ethics review is still not being done consistently across African countries. A study conducted in Cameroon, an African country, observed that out of 174 theses on HIV in Cameroon, only 17 had documented ethics approvals.[147] A systematic review of literature on biomedical

---

141 Kass et al, *supra* Note 138 at e3.
142 Carl H Coleman & Marie Bousseau, "Strengthening Local Review of Research in Africa: Is the IRB Model Relevant?" (2006), online: <www.bioethicsforum.org/ethics-review-of-medical-research-in-Africa.asp>.
143 Examples of previous studies on ethics review committees in African countries include Ikingura, Kruger & Zeleke, *supra* Note 136 *at 154;* Kass et al, *supra* Note 138 at e3; Cecilia Milford, Douglas Wassenaar & Catherine Slack, "Resources and Needs of Research Ethics Committees in Africa: Preparations for HIV Vaccine Trials" (2006) 28:2 IRB: Ethics & Hum Res 1; JM Kirigia, C Wambebe & A Baba-Mousa, "Status of National Research Bioethics Committees in the WHO African Region" (2005) 6 BMC Med Ethics 10.
144 B Mokgatla et al, "Mapping of Research Ethics Committees in Africa: Evidence of the Growth of Ethics Review of Health Research in Africa" (2017) 00 Dev Word Bioeth 1 (epub ahead of publication).
145 *Ibid.* at 2.
146 Boitumelo Mokgatla, Prince Bahati & Carel I Jsselmuiden, "Enhancing the Efficiency and Quality of African Research Ethics Review Processes – Through an Automated Review Platform" (2017) 6:2 J AIDS Clin Res 1.
147 NS Munung et al, "Are Students Kidding with Health Research Ethics? The Case of HIV/AIDS Research in Cameroon" (2012) 13:1 BMC Med Ethics 12.

research in Cameroon also showed similar results.[148] More recent research has also noted challenges in the areas of

> inadequately developed ethics review committees (erratic meetings, poor leadership, etc.); lack of resources (computers, office space, etc.); limited or outdated legislation; overworked, and/or untrained committee members; low awareness of ethics guidelines, and lack of training in bioethics and research ethics.[149]

Other research points out subsisting challenges in the area of composition (limited diversity), inadequate capacity, and lack of national ethics guidelines.[150]

Even in the face of these challenges, an estimated 19 million dollars was spent on ethics review between 2002 and 2012, targeted at establishing new ethics review committees and building research ethics capacity.[151] One of the products of such funding is the publication of a resource text in 2014 aimed at building the capacity of research ethics committees in Africa.[152]

It is essential to consider how recent developments in research governance in African countries affect the structuring of the system of ethics review committees; the composition of the committees; the process of appointing members into the committees; the functions of the committees; the adequacy of their powers and authority; and, ultimately, their effectiveness in carrying out their assigned functions. I consider these issues in more detail in the context of several African countries in subsequent chapters.

National drug regulatory agencies

National drug regulatory agencies or authorities are institutions that protect public health by regulating the efficacy and safety of drugs consumed by people, implementing legislation, generating rules, and developing enforcement strategies with regards thereto. They are typically a national creation, established by legislation. Their functions are usually dictated by the statute that establishes them. These functions may include developing appropriate standards for

---

148 NS Munung et al, "How Often Are Ethics Approval and Informed Consent Reported in Publications on Health Research in Cameroon? A Five-Year Review" (2011) 6:3 J Empir Res Hum Res Ethics 93–97; R Fombo, "Review of Research and Research Ethics in Cameroon" (2017) 1:2 Intl J of Res Culture Soc'y 19.

149 Kruger, Ndebele & Horn, *supra* Note 132 at 8.

150 See Blessing Silgawai & Douglas Wassenar, "Biomedical Research Ethics Committees in Sub-Saharan Africa: A Collective Review of Their Structure, Functioning, and Outcomes" (2015) 10:2 J Empir Res Ethics Rev 169.

151 C Ijselmudden et al, "Mapping African Ethical Review Committee onto Capacity Needs: The MARC Initiative and HR Web's Interactive Database of RECs in Africa" (2012) 12 Dev World Bioeth 74.

152 M Kruger, P Ndebele & L Horn, eds, *supra* Note 132.

the manufacture, import, supply, promotion, and use of drugs. Their functions may also include facilitating access to drugs, inspecting manufacturing facilities and distribution channels, and monitoring adverse drug reactions. More relevant for the purpose of this book, national drug regulatory authorities typically evaluate the safety of clinical trials. The drug development process necessarily requires that new drugs be tested on human beings in clinical trials prior to approval for general use. Related risk regulation is usually undertaken by a national regulatory authority, pursuant to domestic legislation and regulations. These detail legal requirements for the conduct of clinical trials and typically include GCP requirements, such as ethics review approval, recruitment requirements, consent procedures, the qualifications of investigators, and the duties of sponsors. The duties of sponsors include the reporting of adverse reactions to an intervention during a clinical trial to ethics review committees and the regulatory authority.[153] These requirements aim to ensure that clinical trials are credible and that research participants are protected.[154]

All functions relating to drug regulation may come under a single agency (as in Nigeria – National Agency for Food and Drug Administration and Control (NAFDAC), and United States' Food and Drug Administration (FDA), which may or may not be part of a country's department or ministry of health (Australia – Therapeutic Goods Administration (Department of Health and Ageing), United Kingdom (Medicines and Healthcare Products Regulatory Agency – a part of the Department of Health), and Canada (Therapeutic Products Directorate, Health Canada), Morocco – The Ministry of Health)).[155] Whether or not it is an independent agency is a significant factor because "if a national drug regulatory authority (DRA) is an arm of an existing ministry, its director may not be able to make major policy decisions on his/her own. It may well be that many drug regulation activities are carried out by another agency with overlapping jurisdictions and functions."[156]

However organised, the role of national regulatory authorities is essential, especially in light of the fact that the interests of the pharmaceutical companies which usually sponsor clinical trials for new drugs may sometimes diverge significantly from the interests of those who participate in research, public health, and public interests.[157] National regulatory authorities regulate the procedures for the commencement and the implementation of clinical trials, and monitor the post-clinical trials phases for adverse outcomes. These authorities monitor the clinical trial process, with the aim of ensuring not only the safety of

---

153 The ICH-GCP has been adopted in many countries around the world. See the earlier discussion on the Ethical Framework.
154 Robert H Rowland, "How Are Drugs Approved? Part 3. The Stages of Drug Development" (2008) 46:3 J Psychosoc Nurs 17 at 18.
155 In many African countries, such as Ghana, Botswana, Uganda, Kenya, and so on, the Ministry of Health conducts review of clinical trials.
156 WHO, *The World Medicines Situation* (Geneva: World Health Organisation, 2004), at 14.
157 John Abraham, "The Pharmaceutical Industry as a Political Player" (2002) 360 Lancet 1498 at 1500.

medicines but the safety of trial participants. These authorities typically have to give approval before the commencement of clinical trials.[158] Drug regulatory authorities may regulate the manner in which ethics review committees operate in regard to the review of clinical trials.[159] They may also conduct inspections of trials to ensure that appropriate safety and ethical standards are maintained. They are also usually required to maintain records of clinical trials data submitted by research sponsors.

Several systemic issues arise with respect to the governance of drug research involving humans, mostly revolving around the effectiveness of such authorities in carrying out their mandate, including the protection of research participants. Whether or not drug regulatory authorities in a given country play a sufficiently active role in research governance is dependent on such factors as sufficient political and legislative support; the possibility of regulatory capture of national regulatory authorities by some interested parties; the funding of such agencies; the relationship of the national drug regulatory authorities and the other interested stakeholders, such as the department of health, or any other related governmental body, such as a national ethics body or ethics review committee; and how well the aforementioned entities regulate sponsors of clinical trials and ethics review committees in relation to clinical trials of drugs and devices.

Although African drug markets have been for the most part generic rather than innovator markets,[160] there is evidence that neglected diseases are getting a little more (if still insufficient) attention.[161] Many of these still pass through developed countries' drug approval processes, but there is greater room for participation by domestic drug regulatory authorities.[162] It is thus essential to study the role of drug regulatory authorities, given the increase in international research and some increase in the focus on neglected diseases, many of them medicines-related research. The recent trials of HIV and Ebola vaccines are also a reminder that clinical drug trials in African countries will remain necessary. Amidst the advantages for multinational pharmaceutical companies of cost reduction; shorter timelines for testing; the availability of a greater number of treatment-naïve participants; and, very significantly, lesser regulatory hurdles, questions will continue to arise regarding the possible exploitation of research participants in African countries. Furthermore, the global biological norms may not necessarily fit with specific African contexts and the individual health status

---

158 See, for instance, United Kingdom – MHRA, "Medicines and Medical Devices Regulation: What You Need to Know" online: <www.mhra.gov.uk/home/groups/comms-ic/documents/websiteresources/con2031677.pdf>.

159 See Trudo Lemmens, "Federal Regulation of REB Review of Clinical Trials: A Modest But Easy Step towards an Accountable REB Review Structure in Canada" (2005) 13:2 and 3 Health L Rev 39.

160 WHO, *Assessment of Medicines Regulatory Systems in sub-Saharan African Countries: An Overview of Findings from 26 Assessment Reports* (WHO, 2010) at 6.

161 Mary Moran et al, "Registering New Drugs for Low-Income Countries: The African Challenge" (2011) 8:2 PLoS Med e1000411. https://doi.org/10.1371/journal.pmed.1000411

162 *Ibid.*

of participants in African countries.[163] The work of drug regulatory authorities in African countries is therefore becoming even more essential with respect to providing a system for the availability of safe drugs while ensuring the safety of research participants in this era of globalisation.

Earlier studies found that many drug regulatory authorities in Africa lacked well-developed drug regulation capacity.[164] This persists.[165] Drug regulatory authorities in African countries face many challenges, including "operating in an environment with insufficient political support, resulting in inadequate legislative mechanisms, inadequate financial resources, inconsistent application processes and corruption of an appropriate regulatory culture" as well as access to high levels of scientific expertise necessary for the effective assessment or registration of drugs.[166] The limited resources available have to be expended to attend to the other problems with which African countries are besieged, including managing the challenges of counterfeit drugs.

Drug approval processes in African countries also tend to be less sophisticated than in developed countries. Drug regulatory authorities in developed countries are often only required to consider the quality of clinical trial data and the safety of drugs entering their domestic markets (although this is changing to some degree, as noted earlier). Thus, they typically have little information on the manner of research conducted in African countries, whether ethical or unethical,[167] necessitating domestic oversight in African countries. A 2010 WHO report noted that the majority of some sub-Saharan African countries had guidelines in place to regulate the ethical aspects of clinical trials. However, few drug regulatory authorities actually "authorized the performance of clinical trials in their countries, and therefore very few authorities monitored clinical trials after approval. Links with ethics committees were often weak or non-existent."[168] Indeed where ethics review committees were involved, the drug regulatory authorities retained little control, mostly due to lack of capacity.[169] In some cases, the links are tenuous, and the ethics guidance for ethics review committees and in relation to drug regulatory authorities are inconsistent.

---

163 Benhards Ogutu, "Are Current Biological Norms Adapted for Clinical Research in Africa?" in *The Road to Regulatory Harmonization for Africa: Accelerating Access to Essential Medicines and Vaccines*, DNDi Meeting Report Nairobi, Kenya, June 4, 2013.

164 WHO, *Use of the WHO Certification Scheme on the Quality of Pharmaceutical Products Moving in International Commerce* (Geneva: World Health Organization, 1995) quoted in the *World Medicines Situation*, *supra* Note 196 at 94.

165 WHO, "Regulatory Harmonisation. Updating Medicines Regulatory Systems in Sub-Saharan African Countries" (2010) 24:1 WHO Drug Information at 6–20.

166 Suzanne Hill & Kent Johnson, "Emerging Challenges and Opportunities in Drug Registration and Regulation in African Countries" (2004) DFID Health Systems Resource Centre, online: <www.dfidhealthrc.org/publications/atm/Hill.pdf> at 40; Warren A Kaplan & Richard Laing, "Paying for Pharmaceutical Registration in African Countries" (2003) 18:3 Health Pol'y & Plan 237.

167 Seth W Glickman et al, "Ethical and Scientific Implications of the Globalization of Clinical Research" (2009) 360:8 N Engl J Med 816 at 818.

168 WHO, *supra* Note 163 at 6.

169 *Ibid.* at 22.

These point to a serious vacuum in the regulation of research and the protection of research participants from a drug regulation perspective. However, there is considerable variation in level of regulation and capacity to regulate. South Africa, for instance, has a legal framework and GCP guidelines that provide a foundation for clinical trials regulation and clinical trials registration, and demonstrate much capacity for doing so. Nigeria has a legal framework and GCP guidelines, and mandates clinical trial registration, while Sudan does not mandate clinical trial registration.[170] Burundi, it has been observed, lacks the capacity to regulate clinical trials due to lack of a legal framework and technical, financial, and human capacity.[171] Further, as a recent text notes,

> Of particular importance in Africa is vaccine research, especially in view of the HIV epidemic. Currently only SA's Medicines Regulatory Authority (MRA) is capable of adequate provision of national oversight for vaccine research, while other national MRAs need to be strengthened or established.[172]

The inadequacies of African countries' drug regulatory systems have serious implications in light of the increase in clinical trials' exportation by multinational pharmaceutical companies. The financial power and influence of multinational pharmaceutical companies, the resource constraints of African countries, and the high level of dependence on donor support and dependence on user fees to maintain regulatory processes make conflicts of interest and regulatory capture a serious concern in the contexts of these countries.[173]

Others have argued for more regional cooperation between African countries.[174] Pharmaceutical companies currently find it difficult to register medicines in many African countries due to the variability in the registration requirement. Some efforts are being undertaken in this regard with the harmonisation of medicines registration proposed under the auspices of New Partnership for Africa's Development (NEPAD) through the African Regulatory Harmonisation Initiative (AMRHI).[175]

---

170 See Paul Ashigbie, "Pharmaceutical Regulation: A 12 Country Study" (Boston University School of Public Health, 2010). These points are discussed in greater detail in subsequent chapters.

171 PATH, "Medicines Regulation in the East African Community: Landscape Summary Report" (PATH, 2016).

172 Kruger, Ndebele & Horn, *supra* Note 155 at 6.

173 See Abraham, "The Pharmaceutical Industry as a Political Player" (2004) 360:9344 The Lancet 1498-1502 discussing the regulatory capture by pharmaceutical companies in the context of the United States. See also Hill & Johnson, *supra* Note 202. Some have therefore argued that African countries, when considering applications for new drugs, should, and in many cases do, rely on the assessments of drug regulatory authorities in developed countries, including those in Europe and the United States. Shani & Yahalom, *supra* Note 182 at 709; Gray, *supra* Note 182 at 2; Piero L Olliaro et al, "Drug Studies in African countries" (2001) 79:9 Bull World Health Organ 894.

174 See the example of Norplant described in *The World Medicines Situation, supra* Note 196 at 99.

175 K Narsai et al, "Impact of Regulatory Requirements on Medicine Registration in African Countries – Perceptions and Experiences of Pharmaceutical Companies in South Africa" (2012) 5:1 South Med Rev 31.

However, as shown by the evidence presented in subsequent chapters, there are efforts to improve on this in the context of some African countries.

In sum, drug regulatory authorities are a crucial part of the governance of research involving humans because they directly regulate clinical trials. In subsequent chapters we focus on the specific systemic issues that arise with respect to the work of drug regulatory authorities in African countries with respect to research governance.

Policymaking structures

Other institutions involved in the governance of research are what could be considered domestic policymaking structures. These may be government departments or ministries of health. The ministry of health is usually a site of policymaking with its own planning and research department of unit. In some cases in African countries (The Gambia, for example), the ministry of health also has a reviewing function, conducting a prior review before the ethics review or conducting the ethics review. Such a reviewing function may assess a proposal for benefits to the country, national interest, and funding considerations. Specifically, ministries of health may develop a research agenda and related policies. These roles can be conflicting (for example, protecting national interests which may violate human rights versus facilitating research which interrogates those very issues), raising issues that may make the research enterprise more complicated for researchers.[176]

Apart from government departments, the policymaking structure may be a national ethics review committee with a mandate to provide research ethics policy as well as an ethics review function, as, for example, in Nigeria. The policymaking structures may also be a national policymaking body specifically established for that purpose, which may or may not have a statutory base and may or may not have direct regulatory functions.[177] Thus, for instance, in Australia, the Australian Health Ethics Committee (AHEC), established under the *National Health and Medical Research Council Act* 1992, is mandated to issue guidelines for human research.[178] In South Africa, the National Health Research Ethics Council has a clear policymaking role as well. It has the mandate under the National Health Act to determine guidelines for the functioning of health research ethics committees and set norms and standards for conducting research on humans and animals, including norms and standards for conducting

---

176 Robert Klitzman, "Reviewing HIV-Related Research in Emerging Economies: The Role of Government Reviewing Agencies" (2016) 16:1 Dev World Bioeth 4.

177 For instance, national ethics review committees may audit and accredit local committees but also make national guidelines, thus combining regulatory and policymaking functions.

178 Section 35 (3) (b). Susan Dodds & Colin Thomson, "Bioethics and Democracy: Competing Roles of National Bioethics Organisations" (2006) 20:9 Bioethics 326 at 330.

clinical trials.[179] In Canada, the Interagency Advisory Panel on Research Ethics, created by the three major federal funding agencies, helps develop, interpret, and implement the *Tri-Council Policy Statement on Research on Ethical Conduct of Research Involving Humans,* Canada's major research ethics policy.[180] While it has a direct role in policymaking, preparing draft policies with input from various stakeholders, it is not independent from the government funding agencies who have the final say on the policies.

These policy structures may be active policymaking bodies in the sense that they have the mandate to devise or create policies that govern health research involving humans and other areas of bioethics. The policies made by either these bioethics policy bodies or government ministries of health may have a direct impact on the way research is conducted and regulated. However, there may also be national bioethics advisory councils or commissions whose impact on research governance may be more indirect and limited. These advisory councils or commissions are typically mandated to make policy recommendations to the government, including policies and guidelines on research involving humans. Acting in such an advisory capacity, the government may or may not follow the recommendations of advisory councils on policy options to adopt, allowing them only an indirect role on research governance, as in such countries as Denmark. The Danish Council of Ethics is an independent body established under a statute which advises the Danish Parliament and raises public debate about ethical problems in the field of biomedicine, including biomedical research relating to human beings.[181] Countries such as the United States have had several successive bioethics advisory councils, which typically exist at the pleasure of the executive in power. Such advisory councils may help create policy, although this may not be their direct function.

Policy structures assist in articulating and elaborating on issues and divergent views, permitting the reaching of consensus on areas where there may be scientific and moral uncertainty and controversy.[182] The establishment of such policymaking structures brings the state into the arena of research governance and helps define the role that the state has chosen to play in such governance. In a manner that is clearly part of the new governance approach, such policies may

---

179   Other advisory bodies include the Belgian Advisory Committee on Bioethics, the Finnish National Advisory Board on Health Care Ethics, the French National Consultative Ethics Committee for Health and Life Sciences, and the Portuguese National Council of Ethics for the Life Sciences.

180   Panel on Research Ethics, "About Us: Terms of Reference" online: <http://pre.ethics.gc.ca/eng/panel-group/about-apropos/reference>.

181   Danish Council on Ethics (Det Etiske Råd), online: <www.etiskraad.dk/sw293.asp>. The legislation is *The Act on The Danish Council of Ethics,* Act No. 440 of June 9, 2004. See particularly Section 2 of the Act.

182   But some argue that bioethics commissions can sometimes prevent a serious debate about issues by putting on the appearance of reaching a false consensus. See Jonathan D Moreno, "Do Bioethics Commissions Hijack Public Debate?" (1996) 26:3 Hastings Cent Rep 47.

also provide conditions for funding[183] and may even influence legislation.[184] And in countries where no research-related legislation has been enacted, the policies made by such organisations may be the only substantive guide that sets parameters for health research involving humans. Deliberations by such bodies, and any publications put forth, also assist in keeping the public informed on issues arising in research ethics and governance. These deliberations may also signal the directions which government regulation or policymaking more broadly may take and shape the ultimate policy, even where the council or commission is only advisory, because members of such committees tend to be persons regarded as experts in research ethics and governance issues.[185]

Some of the systemic issues which arise with respect to policy structures and their role in research governance in both developed and African countries include issues around legitimacy, community engagement or public participation, transparency, accountability, representation, and effectiveness. For instance, in terms of legitimacy, accountability, representation, and community engagement, broad-based consultation of the public is necessary. What is the nature of public participation in the development of research ethics policies?[186] How broad are attempts to ensure public participation, and how much influence does such participation have on the resulting policies? Are there inherent conflict of interest issues that may undermine the effect of the policies developed and, more generally, research governance? As an example, in Canada, it has been argued that an inherent conflict of interest exists with respect to the creation of an ethics guideline by the major funding agencies whose major purpose is to promote research, and who have also created the Interagency Panel Advisory Panel on Research Ethics, the policy-making body.[187] These issues have an impact on the effectiveness of these policymaking bodies; the resulting policies developed; and, ultimately, on research governance.

These issues also arise specifically in such areas as the process of appointment into such bioethics councils. Who appoints members of these councils? Does the membership of these councils or committees reflect a broad range, or diversity, of persons? And how does this affect the work that the councils do? In the United States, for example, President Bush appointed members of the President's Council on Bioethics who were viewed by some as mainly researchers who supported his conservative views on stem cell research, and whose recommendations were considered to be therefore ideological rather than scientific or objective.[188]

---

183 Dodds & Thomson, *supra* Note 177 at 329.

184 See Moreno, *supra* Note 181.

185 Weiman Rei & Jiunn-Rong Yeh, "Steering in the Tides: National Bioethics Committee as an Institutional Solution to Bio-politics?" in *Asian Bioethics in the 21st Century* (2003) Eubios, online: <www.eubios.info/ABC4/abc4363.htm>.

186 Charles Weijer, "Book Review: *Society's Choices: Social and Ethical Decision Making in Biomedicine*" online: <www.ncehr-cnerh.org/english/communique/npubs_e.html>.

187 See Downie, *supra* Note 150.

188 Elizabeth Blackburn & Janet Rowley, "Reason as Our Guide" (2004) 2:4 PLos Biol. This was disputed by others. Elizabeth Blackburn, "Bioethics and the Political Distortion of Biomedical

In terms of effectiveness, particularly with respect to advisory councils or commissions, how much do they really affect the direction of policy towards promoting research and protecting research participants, especially if established for political purposes? And are they granted sufficient resources to carry out their mandate?

These systemic issues arise in different countries, developed and developing, but perhaps more so in African countries with less established democracies. Specifically in African countries, policies should be made with an understanding of the context of resource challenges, global inequities, the limited awareness of rights by many who may participate in research, and the effect of these challenges on the promotion of research and the protection of research participants. International development agencies such as UNESCO have been involved in developing national bioethics committees in several African countries.[189]

Are these policymaking structures sufficiently empowered with the necessary mandate, resources, and expertise to take these factors into account in crafting research ethics policies? Can their potential functions be merged with those of the national ethics review committees in view of important considerations of sustainability? I consider these issues in more depth in the context of specific African countries.

Other institutional actors: universities, research institutes, research sponsors, professional associations

In addition to those described earlier, other institutions, such as universities and research institutes, are also involved in the governance of health research. The role that the institutions described here play or should play indicates that they have to be a part of the governance framework. This adds further justification for the necessity of a hybrid governance framework in analysing the governance of health research in African countries.

Many universities, teaching hospitals, and research institutes have research ethics policies that govern the ethical conduct of research. These policies may require ethics review of research and prescribe the manner in which ethics review committees are organised, administered, and funded. In some cases, these policies are a requirement from research sponsors who sponsor research in those institutions. For instance, in Canada, where the major research ethics policy is a product of the federal funding agencies, institutions are required to draw up policies in line with the Tri Council Policy Statement. The inherent conflict of

---

Science" (2004) 350:14 N Engl J Med 1379. President Obama subsequently issued an order in March 2009 to lift the ban on the federal funding of embryonic stem cell research; this may be argued to advance his more liberal approach to bioetechnology, particularly stem cell research.

189 Monique Wasunna & Christine Wasunna, "Bioethics Development in Africa: The Contributions of the UNESCO International Bioethics Committee" in Alireza Bagheri, Jonathan D Moreno & Stefano Semplici, eds, *Global Bioethics: The Impact of the UNESCO Bioethics Committee* (New York: Springer, 2016) at 175–183.

interest issues arising from institutional requirements for and efforts to obtain funding, and the possible impact on ethics review in these institutions have been discussed earlier.

In other cases, research sponsors, which may include government funding agencies, pharmaceutical companies, universities, research institutes, and non-governmental organisations, draw up policies and provide funding conditions to ensure the ethical conduct of research. Under those conditions, research sponsors typically require compliance with the conditions for continued funding eligibility.

Professional regulatory organisations also regulate research conducted by their members, not only in terms of ensuring quality assurance, establishing professional standards, and educating and certifying their members[190] but in establishing specific requirements regarding the ethical conduct of research. Professional codes of conduct in the health professions (and indeed other professions) are now common and set standards of conduct for professionals. For health professionals these may include matters of dealings with patients and each other; matters of dress; and, specifically for our purposes, the conduct of experimental studies involving animals, humans, and social or population groups.

Professional associations' responsibilities to regulate research may originate from a statutory basis, a duty to maintain professional standards and promote public trust and confidence, or fiduciary obligations.[191] In Canada, for instance, the Alberta College of Physicians and Surgeons requires physicians and surgeons in that province to submit their research activities for ethics review and has set up a centralised Research Ethics Review Committee to oversee such activities.[192] The College of Physicians and Surgeons of Manitoba has also put in place a similar measure.[193] In Nigeria, the Medical and Dental Council of Nigeria, a professional association of doctors and dentists, has drawn up a code of ethics which includes requirements for the ethical conduct of research under legislative mandate.[194]

Systemic issues arise with respect to each of these institutions, including the limitations of the scope of the research governed by them, which is necessarily determined by the scope of their authority and interest. Some pertinent issues and some kinds of research may thus fall outside their scope. In the case of professional associations, while there is an opportunity to regulate some kinds of research that may fall outside the scope of other policies, for instance, research that takes place in doctor's offices, they cannot provide comprehensive protections

---

190 Henry Dinsdale, "Professional Responsibility and the Protection of Human Research Subjects in Canada" (2005) 13:2 and 3 Health L Rev 80 at 80.

191 See Timothy Caulfield et al, "Research Ethics and the Role of the Professional Bodies: A View from Canada" (2004) 32 J L Med & Ethics 365.

192 See *Ibid.*

193 College of Physicians and Surgeons or Manitoba (CPSM). (2005), online: <www.cpsm. mb.ca/>.

194 Section 1 of the Medical and Dental Practitioners' Act, Cap M4 Laws of the Federation of Nigeria, 2004.

for all health research.[195] Also, there may be inadequate interest in research governance and a limited understanding of the potential role of the professional association in research governance.[196] Further, apart from medicine, other professional regulatory bodies who may be involved in the research process may not regulate research, even though their members may be involved in research. The thinking appears to be that medical doctors are the primary actors in research. This is not always the case. But, even where it is the case, others, like nurses, may be involved in caring for patients or others, while others may be involved in data collection and management.

In the case of research sponsors, their requirements may conflict with the interests of research participants. Such conflict of interest also arises in universities, which may be desirous of facilitating research and require continued research funding but also have to protect research participants within university-affiliated research. The death of a research participant in the United States, Jesse Gelsinger, in a gene therapy trial, exposed such conflict of interest issues. In that instance, the principal investigator and the university had an undisclosed financial interest in the outcome of the trial. The university benefited substantially from donations made by the research sponsor to its gene therapy programs.[197] Similarly, the case of Dr Nancy Olivieri, a researcher at the University of Toronto whose contract with a research sponsor, Apotex, precluded publication of adverse findings during a trial, and who did not receive appropriate support from the university, highlights concerns about conflicts of interest.[198] These concerns are, of course, likely exacerbated in the resource-challenged settings of African countries.

Civil society organisations and community groups

In the hybrid framework that I proposed in Chapter 2, I discussed the possibility that civil society organisations and community groups (disease communities or geographical communities) may serve as checks on other actors in governance. Although they may lack the type of accountability required of government or state entities, they may bring a balance to the research governance system that would otherwise be lacking. They may also, as watchdogs, serve as the voice of

---

195 See Caulfield, *supra* Note 190.
196 See, for instance, Dinsdale, *supra* Note 230 at 82 describing the inadequacy of professional associations' interest in research governance in Canada. See also Aceme Nyika, "Professional Ethics: An Overview from Health Research Ethics Point of View" (2009) 112:Suppl 1 Acta Tropica S84.
197 See DR Waring & T Lemmens, "Integrating Values in Risk Analysis of Biomedical Research: The Case for Regulatory and Law Reform" (2004) 54:3 U Toronto L J 249; WM Kong, "Legitimate Requests and Indecent Proposals: Matters of Justice in the Ethical Assessment of Phase 1 Trials Involving Competent Patients" (2005) 31 J Med Ethics 205. See also Barry Schwartz, "Safety in Human Research: Past Problems and Current Challenges from a Canadian Perspective" (2008) 20:3 HEC Forum 277.
198 Downie, *supra* Note 150.

research participants and possibly prevent regulatory capture, which can jeopardise the interests of research participants and the general public. Thus, from the
perspective of new governance or the proposed hybrid governance framework,
civil society organisations could – along with community and lay participation in
ethics review committees – serve as the entry point for non-state actors, including those on behalf of whom governance arrangements are employed. In this
section, I consider these organisations as a potential and important constituent
of research governance.

Under the umbrella of civil society organisations, as defined in this book,
are organisations such as patients' rights groups, consumer organisations, non-
governmental organisations, and community groups. Although they typically
do not feature in accounts of the institutional framework of research governance
and may not be considered a formal part of the framework, in my view, they
are particularly necessary because they provide an avenue for past and potential
research participants, and citizens to participate in research governance in an
organised fashion. They also provide an important means of providing checks
and balances on other institutions by, among other things, publicising unethical
research (in other words, naming and shaming). They are also particularly essential in African countries where weak or fledgling democracies and corruption
are major concerns.

In developed countries, many patients' rights organisations are focussed
mainly on advocacy for funding for clinical research on different diseases, on
gaining access to clinical trials, and on speeding up drug approval processes.[199]
These types of organisations have very often

> expressed an enthusiasm for 'the bright side' of research, and a willingness
> to assume risk, that many scientific investigators did not share... These ad-
> vocates have tended to avoid REBs that examine the risks faced by research
> participants. They have regarded ethics review as a paternalistic distraction
> from the main goal of promoting benefits to patients.[200]

But there are others, such as the Alliance for Human Research Protection[201]
in the United States, and Wemos, based in the Netherlands,[202] who advocate
for the protection of participants in research.[203] Alliance for Human Research

---

199 An example of such an organisation is the Abigail Alliance for Better Access to Developmental
 Drugs, see online: <http://abigail-alliance.org/>. Another example is AIDS Coalition to Un-
 leash Power (ACT UP). See Mark Harrington, "Community Involvement in HIV and Tuberculosis Research" (2009) 52:S1 J Acquir Immune Defic Syndr S63.
200 Waring & Lemmens, at 200.
201 Alliance for Human Research Protection, online: <www.ahrp.org/cms/content/view/18/87/>.
202 <www.wemos.nl>.
203 Another example is the Public Citizen's Health Research Group, also based in the United
 States, which was one of the organisations that raised concerns about the standard of care
 issue in the zidovudine trials in African countries mentioned in Chapter 1. See P Lurie & SM
 Wolfe, "Unethical Trials of Interventions to Reduce Perinatal Transmission of the Human/

Protection is a "network of lay and professional people with a mandate to advance ethical research practices; to ensure that the human rights, dignity, and welfare of research participants are protected; and to minimise the risks associated with such endeavours."[204] Another such organisation is the Citizens for Responsible Care and Research,[205] whose mission is to raise the level of ethical and professional conduct of research involving humans, especially with respect to the protection of vulnerable participants, like the mentally challenged and children.[206]

In African countries, non-governmental organisations typically act as a buffer between the government and citizens, acting as the voice of the latter, including in areas such as human rights. The activist and advocacy efforts of such organisations have assisted in the changing of old laws and the enactment of new legislation. Such efforts have brought the need to accommodate consultations with civil society groups in such legislative processes to the fore.[207] They may deliver healthcare services. They may also engage in activism around health issues including, but not limited to, promoting access to essential medicines for HIV/AIDS and other diseases, reducing disease-related stigma and discrimination, and liaising with international organisations such as the WHO in health-related activities. With respect to research governance, civil society organisations in African countries have been engaged in presenting community views on ethical issues in health research and are increasingly consulted in designing research protocols.[208] In South Africa, civil rights organisations have successfully challenged government research policies through legal action.[209]

Civil society organisations can ask key questions such as those related to how the research potentially impacts quality of life and possible barriers to participation, such as travel distances and related costs, management of work responsibilities while participating, and any supports that may be available to participants.[210]

Immunodeficiency Virus in African countries" (1997) 337 N Engl J Med 853. The authors are members of the Public Citizen's Health Research Group.

204 Waring & Lemmens, *supra* Note 200 at 281.

205 Citizens For Responsible Care and Research (CIRCARE), online: <www.circare.org/>.

206 *Ibid.*

207 See, for example, Obiora Chinedu Okafor, "Modest Harvests: On the Significant but Limited Impact of Non-Governmental Organisations on Legislative and Executive Behaviour in Nigeria" (2004) 48:1 J Afr L 23 at 24.

208 In Thailand, community groups consisting of sex workers and their representatives, and drug users protested the trial of tenoforvir, a microbicide, in 2004, on the grounds that participants were not afforded enough protections, including provision of treatment, in the event that they got infected. See Seree Jintarkanon et al, "Unethical Clinical Trials in Thailand: A Community Response" (2005) 365:9471 The Lancet 1617; JA Singh & EJ Mills "The Abandoned Trials of Pre-Exposure Prophylaxis for HIV: What Went Wrong?" (2005) 2:9 PLoS Med 234; and A Chua et al, "The Tenofovir Pre-Exposure Prophylaxis Trial in Thailand" (2005) 2:10 PloS Med 346.

209 For prominent examples, see Jerome Amir Singh, "Using the Courts to Challenge Irrational Health Research Policies and Administrative Decisions" (2009) 112:Suppl 1 Acta Tropica S76.

210 Mary J Scroggins, "Perspective of an Advocate: A Case and Framework for Research Advocacy in Africa" (2013) 8:Suppl 1 Infectious Agents and Cancer S4.

Civil society organisations (CSOs) can assist in the very essential work of educating research participants at the grass-roots levels where most research activities take place and where the burden of research is most felt.[211] At such a grass-roots level, there is less likelihood of education and awareness of the rights of participants. CSOs could also engage in advocacy to strengthen regulations and establish and implement research governance policies and legislation. CSOs may be well placed to act with respect to drawing attention to the requirements of justice and access to benefits contained in many ethical guidelines. CSOs are also well positioned to use social media, a useful tool for engaging many people at once, in advocating for research regulations, ethical conduct of research, and access to experimental medicines.[212]

While CSOs may be helpful in the governance of health research in African countries, they may also face systemic challenges. For example, there may be too few of these organisations focussed on research governance. Where they do exist, sufficient resources in terms of funding and training on the relevant issues may be lacking. Conflict of interest and regulatory capture issues may also arise where such organisations are involved in advocacy not only for the ethical conduct of research but also for access to participation in research or access to experimental medicines, two potentially conflicting goals. The possibility also exists of their being captured by other stakeholders whose interests may not necessarily be aligned with those of research participants, including the interests of patients who have few alternatives and therefore seek faster approval processes or pharmaceutical companies who may want to circumvent existing ethical and procedural requirements.[213] In African countries, where the adequacy of resources in any sector, including the non-profit sector, is almost always a concern, the possibility of the capture of advocacy groups raises serious potential issues. A continuous evaluation and appraisal of their functions is therefore necessary.

Legal framework

It is clear that the ethical framework, discussed earlier, is a foundational component of research governance as is an institutional framework which actuates the ethical framework. Similarly, a legal framework is an important component of research governance because of the special characteristics of law which differentiate it from ethics or bioethics, the broader domain of research ethics.[214]

---

211 Temidayo O Ogundiran, "Enhancing the African Bioethics Initiative" (2004) 4 BMC Med Educ 21.
212 See, for example, Cheluchi Onyemelukwe, "Access to Experimental Medicines, Fundamental Rights and Clinical Trials Regulation" (2017) 10:2 Asia Pac J Health L & Ethics 81 at 82.
213 *Ibid.* Daniel Jordan Smith, "AIDS NGOS and Corruption in Nigeria" (2012) 18:3 Health Place 475–480; Daniel Jordan Smith, "Corruption, NGOs, and Development in Nigeria" (2010) 31:2 Third World Q, online: <https://www.ncbi.nlm.nih.gov/pmc/articles/PMC3832995/pdf/nihms524535.pdf>
214 See Cheluchi Onyemelukwe, "Research Involving Humans in African Countries: A Case for Domestic Legal Frameworks" (2008) 16:2 Afr J Intl & Comp L 152 at 167.

But there are also connections in the two fields that allow both to influence each other and to provide value in the specific area of research governance.[215] In this regard, the law (in part)[216] reflects society's idealism; morality; and some consensus, at any given point in time, of what society views as acceptable, ethically appropriate behaviour.[217] In a sociolegal sense, law's most important reason for existing is as a communal resource[218] which society imbues with power (including coercive power) to express and regulate the basic values that it holds important. Bioethics (and ethics more generally) is concerned with such values as autonomy, equity, fairness, and justice. To achieve these lofty ideals, society chooses the vehicle of law, which acts as an enforcer of social values.[219] Thus law, in its role as the principal instrument for protecting and upholding human rights, ought to promote (although there have been instances where it has fallen short of promoting) equity, fairness, and justice.[220] Law is also a principal means of enforcing policies, including health policies, and a crucial medium for deciding differences about public policy.[221]

In general, then, law may be considered, as Schneider so concisely summarises it,

> essentially a device for social regulation. It is the means by which society through its government seeks to establish a framework for human interactions. This framework helps set minimum standards for human behavior (criminal law and tort law exemplify this function), helps establish and support the institutions and practices people use in organizing their relations with each other (this is what contract and commercial law, for instance, do), and helps people resolve their disputes (which is a primary function of civil courts). In this century, the law has broadened that framework by providing some minimum assurances of human well-being (what we call the welfare state).[222]

Governance and regulation through law thus has several uses, including facilitating certain socially and morally acceptable actions, and setting norms and protecting citizens, including through setting penalties and sanctions for

---

215 *Ibid.* See also Hendrick, Note 8.
216 Legal positivists would argue differently – morality is separate from law. However, law, while not simply equated with morality, must show to some extent a reflection of the morality of the society.
217 Scott, *supra* Note 10 at 245.
218 Roger Cotterrell, "Subverting Orthodoxy, Making Law Central: A View of Sociolegal Studies" (2002) 29:4 J L & Soc'y 632 at 642–643.
219 Scott, *supra* Note 10 at 257.
220 *Ibid.* at 246.
221 BR Dworkin, *Limits: The Role of Law in Bioethical Decision-Making* (Indiana: Indiana University Press 1996) at 2.
222 Schneider at 16. Another useful definition for the purposes of this book is the one given by Dworkin, who describes law in terms of procedure and processes for correcting or refusing to correct social ills and for the purpose of deciding whether to intervene, who should intervene, and in what way in relationships between persons and the government. See Dworkin, *ibid.* at 8.

unacceptable action or behaviour, and regulating or declaring standards, thus providing clarity and certainty in handling controversial areas.[223] Formal regulation by means of statutes is particularly useful where the interests of the weak and vulnerable are at stake.[224]

In the case of health research involving humans, ethical concerns relate principally to the safety and welfare of research participants, an area in which the law can play, and has played, a crucial role. The legal framework of research governance in different jurisdictions typically consists of common and civil law principles in the areas of tort, administrative law, criminal law, and intellectual property law[225] but may also include formal, specific legislation. Several African countries have legislation governing research generally (Nigeria, South Africa); some have legislation governing specific aspects of research, such as public health research (Liberia); while in many others, formal legislation governing many aspects of research involving humans is absent (The Gambia). Legislation can provide a legal basis for ethics review, making it a legal requirement, creating the different levels of ethics review committees, and assigning them remits. This imbues the ethics review process with legal status and authority, potentially allowing ethics review committees to do their work more effectively. I have made a case for legislation in research governance in African countries elsewhere.[226]

Apart from legislation, the law of negligence plays a key role in the protection of participants, with its focus on the standard of care that ought to be provided to research participants and the legal consequences of researchers' breach of that care. Thus, in the Canadian case of *Halushka v University of Saskatchewan*, a student at the University of Saskatchewan was offered 50 dollars to participate in a clinical trial, over the course of which he suffered cardiac arrest. The student had been told that a catheter would be inserted into a vein in his arm but was not told that it would be advanced to and through his heart. The court found that the researcher had not informed the student of the purpose of the research and associated procedures. It held that "the subject of medical experimentation is entitled to a full and frank disclosure of all the facts, probabilities and options which a reasonable man might be expected to consider before giving his consent."[227]

But it also extends to negligence as it relates to ethics review committees' responsibilities of ensuring that such reviews are carried out according to specified standards, the breach of which may lead to liability for ethics review

---

223 Linda Nielsen, "From Bioethics to Biolaw" in Cosimo Marco Mazzoni, ed., *A Legal Framework for Bioethics* (The Hague: Kluwer Law International, 1998) at 42.

224 *Ibid.* at 44.

225 See Cheluchi Onyemelukwe, "The Legal Framework for the Governance of Health Research Involving Humans in Nigeria" (2011) 11:2 Oxford University Commonwealth Law Journal 143.

226 See Cheluchi Onyemelukwe, "The Need for Comprehensive Domestic Legal Frameworks for Research Involving Humans in African Countries" (2008) 16:2 Afr J Intl & Comp L 152.

227 *Halushka v University of Saskatchewan*, (1965), 53 D.L.R. (2d) 436 (Sask. C.A.). See also *Grimes v Kennedy Krieger Institute Inc*, 782 A.2d 807. See Susan M Wolf, Jordan Paradise & Charlisse Caga-anan, "The Law of Incidental Findings in Human Subjects Research: Establishing Researchers' Duties" (2008) 36:2 J L Med Ethics 184.

committee members. An ethics review committee may also face legal liability on the grounds that the approval of a study was undertaken in a negligent way. In the Canadian case of *Weiss v Solomon*, the ethics review committee was found liable for non-disclosure of material information which caused harm to the research participant (the liability for which was to be borne by the hospital which established the ethics review committee).[228]

One question that may arise is what should well-conceived, comprehensive legislation contain? The Danish legislation on biomedical research *Act on a Biomedical Research Ethics Committee System and the Processing of Biomedical Research Projects*[229] is a good example of a law dedicated to biomedical research. Although it covers only biomedical research (thus not including other types of research covered in the wider umbrella of health research), it provides details of the organisation of the research governance system and the funding of the system but also addresses many other issues, including, for instance, conflicts of interest.[230] I must emphasise that this is just a broad sketch of what the legislation should contain. African countries may decide to expand the contents of such legislation, but the following requirements are, I suggest, basic requirements that should be contained in such legislation. Such legislation must also fit within the constitutional frameworks of such countries.

The basic requirements would include the requirement for all health research involving humans to undergo ethics review. It is necessary to make it explicit in law and even criminalise failure to seek such review, creating sanctions for such behaviour. In Denmark, for instance, it is illegal, and punishable by up to four months imprisonment or the imposition of a fine, to commence a biomedical research project without the approval of an ethics review committee or to implement substantial changes in the research project after commencement without the approval of an ethics review committee.[231]

Such legislation should require the establishment of ethics review committees. It should state which type of organisational structure, whether institutional or regional committees. It should state that research protocols must be submitted to these committees and elucidate general methods of operation. It should grant these committees power to review research, approve or reject research protocols, propose modifications to research protocols, monitor research, and order the discontinuation of research where it is found to be unethical or unsafe. The legislation should aim to provide consistency in the rules for the creation,

228 *Weiss v Solomon* (1989) 48 CCLT 280 (Quebec Supreme Court). See also Remigius Nwabueze, *Legal and Ethical Regulation of Biomedical Research in Developing Countries* (New York: Routledge, 2013); see Benjamin Freedman & Kathleen Cranley Glass, "*Weiss v Solomon:* A Case Study in Institutional Responsibility for Clinical Research" (1990) 18:4 L Med & Health Care 395. See also Jennifer L Gold, "Watching the Watchdogs: Negligence, Liability, and Research Ethics Boards" (2003) 11 Health L J 153.
229 *Act on a Biomedical Research Ethics Committee System and the Processing of Biomedical Research Projects* 2003 (as amended).
230 Section 14.
231 Section 29 of the Act.

organisation, composition, powers, and operation of the ethics committees[232] and to provide secure resources for ethics review committees by addressing sources of funding, particularly for a national ethics review committee. The provision of secure resources for ethics review committees in legislation is necessary to ensure the independence and sustainability of such committees. In Denmark, for instance, the costs of the regional committees are required to be paid by the county councils, which, in turn, can charge a fee payable by research sponsors and research institutions, thus providing a stable source of funding for the ethics review committees. The law even provides for the reimbursement of members who serve on the regional committees.[233] Payment for research review might raise ethical questions regarding whether such payment may undermine the independence of ethics review committees. But particularly in resource-constrained developing countries, there may be few viable alternatives.

Thus, in addition to making ethics review a legal requirement, such legislation could create or recognise other specific institutions, including national ethics committees and policymaking structures, and specify the powers of such committees, such as the power to create guidelines. Legislation should create national ethics review committees, which, as discussed earlier, are particularly helpful in easing bureaucratic issues such as those involved in multicentre research. The significance of empowering the national ethics review committees to make guidelines by law is that, depending on the manner in which this provision is couched, compliance with such guidelines may become mandatory, having a derivative force in law.[234] The establishment of these national guidelines would also be helpful in assuring uniformity of practice among the regional or institutional research ethics committees. Such committees should be required to provide public reports of their activities from time to time: for example, annually.

The law should also provide time limits within which ethics review committees must reach a decision about whether or not a research project can proceed. The Danish law has similar provisions.[235] This is obviously helpful for researchers and is one example of a situation in which the law undertakes a facilitative action. It should also provide a complaints mechanism through which researchers and research sponsors can present complaints, perhaps to a national committee where these limits are exceeded. Additionally, the law should delineate appeal processes for researchers who have submitted projects to ethics review committees.

It should also define clearly the relationship between the drug regulatory agency and the ethics review committees to ensure that there is harmony, no

---

232 Dannie Di Tillio-Gonzalez & Ruth L Fischbach, "Harmonizing Regulations for Biomedical Research: A Critical Analysis of the US and Venezuelan Systems" (2006) 8:3 Dev World Bioeth 167–177.

233 See Section 28 of the Act.

234 Bernard Starkman, *supra* Note 58 at 268. Commenting in respect of the legislative approach taken by the United States, Starkman argues that "[t]he legal basis of the regulations provided an important rationale for insisting on responsible cooperation with the research review process."

235 See Section 10.

unnecessary duplication of responsibilities or loopholes, and an understanding of where oversight functions lie, and to assist researchers and research sponsors in understanding what the requirements are.[236] Similarly, the proposed legislation should address the place of other existing guidelines, international or domestic, either by incorporating them or by explicitly recognising their application or non-application in the country. The legislation should also have a mandatory review period, for instance, every ten years, to take into consideration any changes in the area of health research involving humans.

With respect to substantive provisions, at minimum, I suggest that informed consent, widely recognised as mandatory for the ethical conduct of research, should be a statutory requirement. The basic details of how to obtain informed consent should, ideally, be a part of the legislation. It should also include how to obtain consent in less than ideal situations, such as in emergencies, and from persons who are incapable of providing consent, such as children. The law should also provide penal sanctions for non-compliance with informed consent provisions.

Such legal regulations should address such issues as legal capacity to participate in research; legal representation of minors; and the protections that must be available to such vulnerable groups as children, the mentally challenged, the developmentally disabled, and prisoners. The Pfizer incident, which I discuss in the following chapters, involved children. In the absence of clear legal rules regarding what constitutes informed consent in the case of children, and who can give such consent, the safety of children involved in such research may be jeopardised. Additional specific legal protections are needed for vulnerable groups, and these should be provided in legal regulations or legislation.[237] Also, the law should address the legality or otherwise of all biomedical research but particularly non-therapeutic biomedical research involving children and the mentally challenged, and other persons in vulnerable situations.[238] Other key issues would include privacy and access to information issues, adequate health insurance for research participants, and compensation for injury or harm to participants. Given the additional protection that research participants require and the fact that many developing countries lack effective public health insurance schemes, this is an area that ought to be addressed in legislation. Authors like Burris have also questioned whether a fault-based system would repeat the malpractice system's combination of under and over claiming and if a compensation scheme is worth the effort and cost, given that the research

---

236 See Section 15.
237 See G Dworkin, "Law and Medical Experimentation: Of Embryos, Children and Others with Limited Capacity" (1987) 13 Monash ULR 189, noting that "There seems to be a strong case for general legislative consideration, and clarification of the power to give proxy consent for the purposes of research on children."
238 Scott Burris, "Regulatory Innovation in the Governance of Human Subjects Research: A Cautionary Tale and Some Modest Proposals" (2008) 2:1 Regulation & Governance 65 at 82.

participants volunteered, and harm from research is arguably rare.[239] Conflict of interest issues should also be addressed in such legislation. It should be made statutorily mandatory for adverse events discovered over the course of research to be reported to participants, the drug regulatory authority, and the ethics review committee which approved the trial. Where this is a clear legal requirement, a research sponsor would be unable to legally insert a clause in a contract with an investigator or researcher not to provide such a report to the relevant persons. Whistle-blower protections should also be provided under these laws, so that an investigator or any person who makes a confidential report about unethical practices in research receives clear protection under the law. Beyond these, the law should provide for a mechanism that is increasingly accepted around the world as necessary in ensuring ethical conduct in health research, namely, registration of trials in clinical trial registries. The law should mandate the establishment of such a registry and make it compulsory for all clinical trials to be registered in such a registry to ensure that it is known at any given time what trials are ongoing in the country and be better able to monitor these trials.

Such legislation should also address issues that will begin to arise as ethics review becomes more entrenched in developing countries, including issues relating to the legal liability of ethics review committees and insurance for ethics review committees. In the absence of any law creating ethics review committees and defining their responsibilities and their legal liability, certain difficulties arise for research participants in establishing the liability of these committees.[240] Difficulties may also arise for members of these committees in defending themselves in the absence of any statutory limitations on the degree of possible liability. A system of liability created by legislation may be more appropriate, both for ethics review committees whose role is to protect research participants and for research participants who require protection.

The foregoing is, as stated at the outset, only a broad sketch of what such legislation should cover. Legislation on research governance in developing countries could therefore go beyond the matters proposed here. African countries must take into consideration their contexts and their peculiar challenges in enacting such legislation. Broad-based consultations with key stakeholders in which vigorous debate is permitted and an understanding of what other jurisdictions have done in these areas will obviously be necessary precursors to the successful enactment of legislation that has the potential to be effective in promoting health research and protecting research participants in such research. Enactment of such legislation would also have to fit within the framework of a country's constitutional distribution of powers and be consistent with other laws in place, including, for instance, human rights laws.[241] Several African countries have

---

239 *Ibid.*
240 See M Brazier, "Liability of Ethics Committee and Their Members" (1990) PN 186, quoted in Ian Kennedy & Andrew Grubb, *Medical Law,* 3d ed (New York: Oxford University Press, 2005) at 1702. These arise from difficulties in establishing the legal status of ethics review committees.
241 See Dickens, in the Canadian context, *supra* Note 50.

enacted laws. The case studies in this book include a consideration of the legislation for health research involving humans, where enacted.

Recognition of the relationship between the ethical, legal, and institutional frameworks

I have described generally many of the mechanisms within the ethical, institutional, and legal components employed in governing research in different countries and some of the systemic issues which may hinder health research governance. These systemic challenges may stem from the non-existence of the components; lack of proper use; lack of the mandate or authority to operate more broadly; or the challenging context in which they have to operate, particularly in African countries. None of the components, it seems, can work by itself to achieve effective governance of health research involving humans.

It is important to recognise that each of the components brings something important to the governance of health research involving humans – ethics lays the value foundation and gives the reason for governance, the legal framework regulates behaviour and lends the "punch" of legal force, and the institutional framework actuates both the legal and the ethical frameworks. It seems to me, then, that to put the different components of research governance in silos, whether in scholarship or in the actual operation of these components in different jurisdictions, without realising that they may be more effective when they work together, is counterproductive. For instance, the issue of ethics review committees, which I have categorised under the institutional framework, has received so much attention in the literature that such committees may therefore be mistakenly considered *the* governance system.[242] The literature has tended to focus mainly on the work of ethics review committees. However, for scholars interested in the governance of health research, researchers involved in health research, research sponsors, and perhaps most importantly research regulators, to see the linkages between the different components of governance is to take a view of the big picture. These frameworks have to work together to effectively achieve the objectives of research governance.

Recognition of these components assists in identifying instances in which some issues may not be addressed effectively or do not fall within the ambit of any legal, policy, or institutional framework, or inadequacies in sponsor requirements (such as the reporting of adverse events within a clinical trial or disseminating research findings). Such identification helps then to find the appropriate mechanisms to deal with such matters.

An acknowledgement of the possible relationship and the interactions between these components allows us to not only identify possible gaps and weaknesses in a particular framework but determine if such gaps or weaknesses can be remedied within that framework or whether a better remedy can be found in

---

242 McDonald, *supra* Note 68 at 9. See also Susan V Zimmerman, "Translating Ethics into Law: Duties of Care in Health Research Involving Humans" (2005) 13 Health L Rev 13 at 13.

the context of another framework, where appropriate. In the foregoing sections, I have discussed the systemic issues affecting different mechanisms of the institutional component and the limitations of law in a developing country context. A specific issue in the governance of research may therefore be more effectively dealt with by addressing it in the context of that particular component or in the context of all three components. For instance, the issues of conflict of interest or reporting adverse events may be dealt with not only in the domestic ethics policy but in legislation, with researchers and ethics review committees then required to carry out their obligations under both the ethical and legal framework. A funding mechanism may be mandated in legislation to ensure that ethics review committees have the necessary resources to effectively carry out their functions. Employed appropriately, the work of civil society organisations may be helpful in articulating community concerns and in promoting the enforcement of legislation.

Moreover, legislation is particularly well suited to establishing the connections between the frameworks (including other parts of the legal framework, such as tort) and to facilitating collaborative functioning between the components. It is by its nature a "meta-governance" tool. It can, however, only be deployed in this way if it is designed in new governance ways, with much consultation, and with the need for responsiveness and effectiveness at the forefront of legislators' minds.

Finally, the recognition of the possible relationships between these frameworks may help streamline the legislation, policies, and guidelines, and assist in defining the sources of authority for governing the ethical conduct of health research, which, especially in the case of the African countries, may be myriad and yet insufficient. In doing this, an investigation of the relationships between the institutions which conduct research and the relationships between the institutions which regulate research would become possible. This would, in turn, help researchers in navigating the regulatory requirements and ultimately result in better governance of health research. A systematic approach that recognises the relationships between all three frameworks, both in scholarship and in the actual operation of these frameworks, would be beneficial.

4 Health research needs in African countries

A prelude to the case studies

A prelude

The previous two chapters have examined the concept of governance and the components that actuate this governance. However, it is important and appropriate to provide broad background and information on the research and research governance context prior to the analysis of specific case study countries. First, the colonial backgrounds of many African countries is a necessary background issue to consider. Much research took place in the colonial era, a significant portion of which provided significant improvements to existing treatments or helped develop the eventual treatments. In Nigeria, for example, yellow fever and leprosy were studied extensively,[1] with research participants drawn from the general populace. Some of the research practices in research conducted in colonial Africa left fears amongst the peoples, which, several have argued, persist to this day. Some of these fears included the fears of research involving blood collection, as has been examined in the Kenyan setting.[2] The asymmetry of power between colonial researchers and the subjects of the research raises key questions on consent and autonomy. It is no surprise then that rumours of blood stealing, forced sterilisation, amongst others trailed past research.[3] The more recent ethical issues in HIV research, some of which were described in Chapter 1, reiterate the point that health research can raise problematic issues. Even now issues related to "helicopter science" continue to be raised about research where tissue samples, blood, spit, and other human specimens are collected without due consent, and the lack of access to benefits of the research. Thus, trust in the research process is an expensive commodity in African countries, necessitating the need for good research governance in these contexts. Understanding the

---

1 See, for example, John Manton, "Testing a New Drug for Leprosy: Clofazimine and Its Precursors in Ireland and Nigeria, 1944–1966" in P Geissler & C Molyneux, eds, *Evidence, Ethos and Experiment: The Anthropology and History of Medical Research in Africa* (New York: Berghahn Books 2011). See generally H Tilley, "Medicine, Empire and Ethics in Colonial Africa" (2016) 7 AMA J Ethics 743.

2 See, for instance, P Wenzel Geissler, "'*Kachinja* Are Coming!' Encounters around Medical Research Work in a Kenyan Village" (2005) 75:2 Africa 173; K Peeters Grietens et al, "Doctors and Vampires in Sub-Saharan Africa: Ethical Challenges in Clinical Trial Research" (2014) 91:2 Am J Trop Med Hyg 213–215. doi:10.4269/ajtmh.13-0630.

3 Grietens et al, *supra* Note 2 at 213.

colonial precedents of research in Africa also foreshadows some of the key ethical issues, such as the importance of making available the results of research to the communities where the research has taken place,[4] clarifying the research agenda and who determines it, and the need for research governance from a local perspective.

Second, the need for research in African countries (which was touched upon briefly in the first chapter) remains a key factor to consider in any discussion of research governance. Endemic conditions such as malaria, epidemics of infectious diseases such as meningitis, the problematic challenge of carrying the world's heaviest HIV rates, emergent concerns of non-communicable disease, and the need for evidence-based approaches for meeting the Sustainable Development Goals (SDGs), amongst other things, emphasise the need for universal health coverage, curative interventions, and research interventions. Such research interventions will be focussed not only on developing better curative interventions and vaccines but also on the best methods of delivery to people. However, there is broad agreement that there is a clear need for clinical trials and other forms of health research to address the disease burden in African countries.

Available research suggests that "as little as 1% of all funding for health R&D is allocated to diseases that are predominantly incident in developing countries, such as malaria, TB and NTDs, despite these diseases accounting for more than 12.5% of the global burden of disease,"[5] further lending credence to the 10/90 gap position.[6] At present, there are 352 times more researchers in the developed world than in the developing world.[7] While information on expenditures on health research are generally not standardised,[8] data is more available for the developed world.[9] As noted in much of the literature, developing countries, in general, spend much less than developed countries on health research. However, an appreciable increase has been noted in Asian countries' expenditures on health research,[10] and even African countries have seen some increase in research funding[11] and research publication.[12]

4 See generally T Warikandwa, "Double Victimisation? Law, Decoloniality and Research Ethics in Post-colonial Africa" (2017) 10 Africology: The J Pan Afr Stud 64.

5 WHO, *World Health Statistics 2017: Monitoring Health for the SDGs* (Geneva: WHO, 2017) online: <http://apps.who.int/iris/bitstream/10665/255336/1/9789241565486-eng.pdf?ua=1>.

6 Global Forum for Health Research, *The 10/90 Report on Health Research, 2003–2004* (Geneva: Global Forum for Health Research, 2004).

7 WHO, Global Observatory on Health R&D.

8 Robert F Terry, "Mapping Global Health Research Investments, Time for New Thinking – A Babel Fish for Research Data" (2012) 10 Health Res Pol'y Syst 28, online: <https://health-policy-systems.biomedcentral.com/articles/10.1186/1478-4505-10-28>.

9 See, for example, Hamilton Moses et al, "The Anatomy of Medical Research: US and International Comparisons" (2015) 313 JAMA 174–189.

10 See, for example, Justin Chakma et al, "Asia's Accent – Global Trends in Biomedical R&D Expenditures" (2014) 370:3 N Engl J Med 2451; Sala Sariolla, "Big-Pharmaceuticalisation: Clinical Trials and Contract Research Organisations in India" (2015) 131 Soc Sci & Med 239–246.

11 Francis Collins et al, "A Database on Global Health Research in Africa" (2013) 1:2 Lancet Glob Health e64–e65.

12 Joses Kirigia et al, "National Health Research Systems in the WHO African Region: Current Status and the Way Forward" (2015) 13:61 Health Res Pol'y & Syst 1 at 8.

By some accounts, clinical trials, a type of health research, have increased significantly in developing countries, with a significant number of trials taking place in emerging economies, particularly in Asian countries.[13] Some reports even suggest that clinical trials in sub-Saharan Africa now surpass those in South Asia.[14] This is an oxymoronic situation that exists alongside limited research in African countries on neglected diseases, raising questions about agenda and priority setting. From one perspective, the burgeoning of clinical trials on the continent has been argued to be a continuation of "Africa as site of experimentation," which has long existed. Indeed experimentation has formed part of the provision of healthcare. In this regard, Geissler notes that

> In the near-absence of government health care, experimental formations have become vital for people's survival and well- being; this includes experimentation sensu stricto, clinical trials, which provide health care and treatment. Medical experimentation has thus a particular place in contemporary Africa, referencing a wider spectrum of novel biopolitical forms between nation- state and medical science, which can be discerned more clearly and earlier in Africa than elsewhere.[15]

This assertion raises valid concerns about the importance of clinical trials as part of healthcare in resource-constrained settings. The protection of persons involved in such trials becomes of particular importance, given their vulnerability and the heightened risk of misunderstanding of the primary purpose of trials. The lack of access to basic healthcare, a key thrust of universal health coverage campaigns in countries around the world but particularly in resource-poor countries, also emphasises the need for protections in health research. Further, there is often little integration of research work into healthcare provision, referral systems, public health programs, or national academic institutions.[16]

Increasing the levels of research and research funding is not only for the benefit of African countries. The 2014 Ebola epidemic drew more attention to the need for global health research focussed on developing countries, particularly African countries. The global village terminology is no more appropriate than in the context of infectious disease in a globalised world. Indigenous or domestically sponsored research is also essential. However, research indicates that this remains much less than required, and the systems for ensuring such research remain weak.[17] Large funding organisations like the Bill and Melinda Gates Foundation do support research in African countries.

13 Remigius Nwabueze, *Legal and Ethical Regulation of Biomedical Research in Developing Countries* (London: Routledge, 2013).
14 See ARIANNE, Why You Should Be Conducting Clinical Trials in Sub-Saharan Africa Citing Clinicaltrials.gov (2016), online: <www.ariannecorp.com/arianne-ressources/brochure-sub-saharan-africa/>.
15 See also Wemos, "The Clinical Trials Industry in South Africa: Ethics, Rules and Realities" (2013) describing primary care centres offering clinical trials.
16 P Wenzel Geissler, A Life Science in Its African Para-State at 12.
17 See P Mbondji et al, Overview of National Health Research Systems.

Recent research suggests that the most important methods of funding research were international organisations, followed by government taxation.[18] But there is clearly a need for more. As has been noted, while there exist international, multilateral funds for health delivery, particularly in developing countries, such as Unitaid, the Global Fund to Fight AIDS, Tuberculosis and Malaria; and the Global Alliance Vaccines and Immunisation (GAVI), there is no similar large pooled funding mechanism for research on infectious diseases or non-communicable diseases.[19] Health research expenditures by African countries remain too low.[20] In short, health research is not on top of the health agenda in many African countries. One of the suggestions that has been made in this regard is equitable collaboration between African countries in research, harnessing existing resources and forming synergies that would achieve goals that may be impossible for lone countries.[21] This has yet to take firm root, particularly with regard to equity.[22]

Even where research is taking place it is often difficult to obtain information on health research in African countries.[23] This is critical for addressing issues of prioritisation; setting research agendas; and knowing who is conducting research, where, why, and what remains unexplored. Clinical trials registration may be one way of obtaining existing information, helping to map health research in Africa[24] (or, more specifically, clinical trials research), and providing information on current priorities, funders and remaining gaps. Data from the Pan African Clinical Trials Registry, a regional registry for registering clinical trials conducted in African countries, show an appreciable increase in registration, from 5 registered trials in 2008 to 273 registered trials in 2016.[25] It is not foolproof, however. Registration may not necessarily indicate all the trials that were conducted, especially where it has not been made mandatory by African countries that clinical trials must be registered. Further, clinical trials are only one type of health research involving humans. The establishment of the Global Observatory on Health Research and Development in 2013, following a World

---

18 Kirigia et al, *supra* Note 12 at 1.
19 A Global Biomedical R&D.
20 Kirigia et al, *supra* Note 10 at 12.
21 Jimmy Volmnick & Lola Dare, "Addressing Inequalities in Research Capacity in Africa" (2005) 331 BMJ 705.
22 See, for instance, Gregorio Gonzalez-Alcaide, "Dominance and Leadership in Research Activities: Collaboration between Countries of Differing Human Development Is Reflected through Authorship Order and Designation as Corresponding Authors in Scientific Publications" (2017) PLOS One. doi:10.1371/journal.pone.0182513.
23 Roderick Viergever et al, "Use of Data from Registered Clinical Trials to Identify Gaps in Health Research and Development" (2013) 91 Bull World Health Organ 416–425.
24 Ignacio Atal et al, "Automatic Classification of Registered Clinical Trials towards the Global Burden of Diseases Taxonomy of Diseases and Injuries" (2016) 17 BMC Bioinformatics 392.
25 See EDCTP, Pan African Clinical Trials Registry, online: <www.edctp.org/pan-african-clinical-trials-registry/> (August 15, 2017).

Health Assembly Resolution,[26] is one major step towards making such information available. Contribution to the Observatory, like clinical trial registries in some countries, is, however, not mandatory.

The need for health research in African countries has certain connections with the necessity of better research governance. On the one hand, as already described in foregoing chapters, trust is a key requirement: for increased research, there must be willing participants. On the other hand, while the challenges of prioritisation and coordination may be said to be separate from the issues of regulating research such that participants are protected, research ethics and regulation cannot be divorced from economic realities.[27] The governance of health research has to take into account the contextual challenges of research funders/sponsors and priorities. Ethics review committees cannot but be concerned with these issues. This may draw them from outside the strict issue of protecting research participants to broader social and contextual challenges that may also have an impact on research participants' protection.[28] Questions will continue to be raised with regard to who determines research priorities, who funds the research, and what the potential challenges are of having funders determine research priorities in African countries.[29] When the research does take place, the issues of who leads the research team, picks the members of the research team, and determines when and how outcomes are provided to the public, are key questions of power. Who is understood to be in charge by the public, members of the research team, and the government, and who is responsible for the long-term effects of the research, sometimes long after it is over, are both questions which raise the issue of power differential between research sponsors and funders, and research recipients (typically African countries).[30] Questions of publication in top journals and access to information about research conducted in African countries are also relevant concerns.[31] Do ethics review committees who review protocols ask questions about these issues when they review research protocols?

Furthermore, if health research is not on the top of the list of health priorities generally in African countries, given the paucity of resources, amongst other challenges, can health research governance and the resources required be a priority? Do African ethics review committees have the requisite resources that would allow them the independence to ask these and other pertinent questions?

---

26 World Health Assembly, *Follow Up of the Report of the Consultative Expert Working Group on Research and Development: Financing and Coordination*, WHA66.22, online <http://apps.who.int/iris/bitstream/10665/150173/1/A66_R22-en.pdf?ua=1&ua=1&ua=1>.

27 Global Research in an Unequal World (2016), at 230.

28 Bob Simpson et al, "Pharmaceuticalisation and Ethical Review in South Asia: Issues of Scope and Authority for Practitioners and Policy Makers" (2015) 131 Soc Sci & Med 247–254.

29 Viergever, et al.

30 See P Wenzel Geissler, A Life Science in Its African Para-State at 13.

31 "Kenyan Doctors Win Landmark Discrimination Case" Nature (2014), online: <www.nature.com/news/kenyan-doctors-win-landmark-discrimination-case-1.15594>.

Do emerging laws and the national codes on research governance in these countries take these concerns into consideration? What, if anything, does it mean for the sustainability of research governance in Africa if clinical trials registries are established through the initiative of foreign funders and with foreign funding? The Pan African Trials Registry, which started its life as the HIV/AIDS, Tuberculosis (TB), and Malaria (ATM) Clinical Trials Registry in the Medical Research Council in Cape Town, South Africa, was established, for instance, with initial funding from the European & Developing Countries Clinical Trials Partnership (EDCTP).[32] The Fogarty Institute of the United States National Institutes of Health have put much funding towards training members of ethics review committees in several African countries, and there is some evidence that it has had a positive impact on research ethics.[33] Thus, support from external sources is not negative in and of itself – improving regulatory systems, generally speaking, and providing protections for research participants in Africa. But it does raise at least the questions of sustainability and ownership.

Ownership is particularly crucial in the African context, especially given the origins of research governance in many African countries. In this respect, it has been noted that

> The history of colonialism, as well as the internationalisation of research over the past decades, have significantly influenced research ethics standards in African countries. Some African countries have either established, or have remodelled their research oversight systems and committees on the US institutional review boards system, or in accordance with the World Health Organisation (WHO) guidelines on the operations of research ethics committees (RECs) research ethics in Africa.[34]

The history of research governance in some African countries also indicates an origin that owes much to research scandals and foreign research funding for health challenges such as HIV/AIDS; malaria; and, more recently, the Ebola epidemic, which served as impetus for vaccine trials in several African countries. Projects such as the now-concluded HapMap Project and the Human Heredity and Health in Africa (H3Africa) Consortium project also bring in research funding from the West. The specifics of these are discussed in the context of the case study countries. However, there are indications that things are moving in the direction of sustainable ownership – from legislative requirements for mandatory ethics review in different countries to harmonisation of medicines regulations. Thus, for example, the African Medicines Agency commencing operations in 2018, is a harmonisation effort for regulating medicines registration,

32 PanAfricanClinicalTrialsRegistry,online:<www.edctp.org/pan-african-clinical-trials-registry/>.
33 Paul Ndebele et al, "Research Ethics Capacity Building in Sub-Saharan Africa: A Review of NIH Fogarty-Funded Programs 2000–2012" (2014) 9:2 J Empir Res Hum Res Ethics 24–40.
34 Mariana Kruger, P Ndebele & L Horn, eds, *Research Ethics in Africa: A Resource for Research Ethics Committees* (Stellenbosch: Sun Press, 2014) at 6.

including clinical trials requirements under the NEPAD umbrella, the adoption of the African Union Model Law on Medical Product Regulation, based largely on the work of the African Medicines Regulatory Harmonisation Programme.[35] The newly established West African Network of Ethics Committees, consisting of ethics committees in West Africa, established to manage ethical challenges peculiar to research in the West African region, is another example.

Even so, previous studies in several African countries have noted, for example, that ethics review committees have challenges of resources, lack of multidisciplinary membership, lack of capacity, etc.[36] It is critical to continue to check whether these challenges remain and suggest what can be done within the broad framework of governance. In 2016, the Ebola Panel, for instance, made recommendations including the need for facilitation of capacity for rapid ethics review, development of legal agreements, including memoranda of understanding to facilitate data sharing, and the incorporation of health research in the agenda of national health systems.[37] In addition, emerging studies show an increase in novel subjects of research in African countries, including genomic and bio-banking research, and experimental medicines. Some studies have engaged in analyses of the guidelines, finding that they often fall short in regulating these areas of research.[38]

In essence, the unequal power differential, the scarcity of resources, the prioritisation or lack thereof of research, and research governance are relevant factors in discussing the effectiveness and sustainability of the governance frameworks in African countries.

Governance through the various means that will be discussed in subsequent chapters takes place against the background of the tension between the possibilities of health research and the risks which are compounded by the realities of economic constraints and political challenges. There is likely to continue to be a push and pull between the research priorities, research funding, and research ethics in African countries.

35 Kevin Fisher, P Bahati & B Thyagarajan, "A Review of Regulatory Capacity Strengthening in Africa in HIV Research: The Need for a New Paradigm" (2017) BMJ Global Health, online: <http://gh.bmj.com/content/2/Suppl_2/A44.3>.

36 See, for example, A Nyika, "Composition, Training Needs and Independence of Ethics Review Committees across Africa: Are the Gate-Keepers Rising to the Emerging Challenges?" (2009) 35:3 BMJ, online: <http://jme.bmj.com/content/35/3/189.long?utm_source=TrendMD&utm_medium=cpc&utm_campaign=J_Med_Ethics_TrendMD-0>.

37 United States National Academies of Sciences, Engineering, and Medicine. Committee on Clinical Trials during the 2014–2015 Ebola Outbreak. *Integrating Clinical Research into Epidemic Response: The Ebola Experience* (Washington, DC: The National Academies Press, 2017), online: <https://www.nap.edu/catalog/24739/integrating-clinical-research-into-epidemic-response-the-ebolaexperience>.

38 See, for example, Cheluchi Onyemelukwe, "Access to Experimental Medicines, Fundamental Rights and Clinical Trials Regulation" (2017) 10:2 Asia Pac J Health L & Ethics 81; Jantina de Vries et al, "Regulation of Genomic and Biobanking Research in Africa: A Content Analysis of Ethics Guidelines, Policies and Procedures from 22 African Countries" (2017) BMC Med Ethics, online: <https://bmcmedethics.biomedcentral.com/articles/10.1186/s12910-016-0165-6>.

One key goal of this book is a comprehensive analysis of the research ethics governance contexts of developing countries. Thus, apart from the research policy context, as described earlier, the components of research governance need to be assessed in line with the research governance goals of adequacy, effectiveness, and comprehensiveness, amongst others, as developed in Chapter 2. In line with the components of research governance discussed in the previous chapter, I will examine the context and the components of research governance in each country under consideration: the ethical, institutional, and legal frameworks.

The case studies: South Africa, Nigeria, Kenya, and Egypt

The following chapters engage in detailed case studies of research governance contexts and arrangements in four African countries: South Africa, Nigeria, Kenya, and Egypt. The countries have been chosen on several grounds – geographical spread (north, south, east, and west). They have also been chosen on the basis of their history of health research, each of these countries having been involved in health research for many years. Several of them have had some research scandals which have impacted their direction in research governance. They have taken active steps in research governance in recent years, thus providing room for analysis of the directions they have chosen to go in and potential lessons for other African countries. Finally, availability of information was also a factor in the choice of these case studies.

5 Health research governance in South Africa

Introduction

South Africa is a middle-income developing country with a population of almost 55 million people,[1] often recognised as the most developed country in Africa.[2] It has been a democracy since 1994, when it rejected apartheid. While it has more wealth than many African countries, it is also a country with great economic disparity and a large population of poor people. Its health profile includes a much lower life expectancy than in developed countries, 59 for men and 66 for women, and a total healthcare expenditure of 1,148 dollars.[3] It has a significant incidence of HIV/AIDS, being the country with the highest rates of HIV infection in the world (about 7 million persons),[4] and a significant burden of tuberculosis (1 out of every 100) (including a significant incidence of multi-drug-resistant tuberculosis), high maternal mortality rates, and significant rates of non-communicable diseases[5] and gender-based violence. HIV/AIDS causes the most deaths, followed by interpersonal violence.[6] Almost 20 years ago, South Africa's health system was ranked 182 out of 191 countries by the World Health Organisation.[7] Much has happened since then, including the more conscientious tackling of the HIV/AIDS epidemic, after a period of denial, but inequalities persist in the health system and in the health outcomes of white and black, rich and poor,

1 World Bank Data, online: <https://data.worldbank.org/country/south-africa>.
2 Keymantri Moodley & Landon Myer, "Health Research Ethics Committees in South Africa 12 Years into Democracy" (2007), online: <https://bmcmedethics.biomedcentral.com/articles/10.1186/1472-6939-8-1>.
3 WHO, online: <www.who.int/countries/zaf/en/>.
4 UNAIDS, AIDSInfo, online: <http://aidsinfo.unaids.org>.
5 See WHO, Country Profiles: South Africa, 2012; Cancer Association of South Africa, "Fact Sheet on a Health Profile of South Africa and Related Information" (2016), online: <https://www.cansa.org.za/files/2016/01/Fact-Sheet-Health-Profile-South-Africa-Related-Information-Jan-2016.pdf>.
6 Global Burden of Disease, 2015 – South Africa.
7 WHO, *Improving Health Systems: World Health Report* (Geneva: World Health Organisation, 2000).

from the legacies of systemic racism, ongoing issues of corruption, and inadequate human resources.[8]

With a history of apartheid, and ongoing efforts to ensure racial harmony, South Africa presents an interesting context within which to study research governance and regulation. This is especially so in light of its early and fraught history with HIV/AIDS, which helped spawn activist civil society groups in the rea of healthcare and the progressive nature of the country's constitution. The Constitution of South Africa states that it is a democratic state founded on the values of human dignity, the achievement of equality, and the advancement of human rights and freedoms. It contains a bill of rights, which is stated in the Constitution to be a cornerstone of democracy in South Africa, enshrining the rights of all people in the country and affirming the values of human dignity, equality, and freedom. The bill of rights contains both civil and political rights on the one hand and social and economic rights on the other. Both sets of rights are enforceable in South Africa, subject to any limitations stated in the Constitution. Because of the recognition of the interdependence of civil, political, and socio-economic rights, the South African Constitution is regarded as one of the more progressive constitutions which exists today. One of the socio-economic rights included in the Constitution is the right to health.[9] This right has been the subject of court decisions reiterating the entitlement of citizens, especially with regard to HIV/AIDS treatment.[10]

Outside of this general context, South Africa's research infrastructure is sophisticated, including well-recognised academic institutions, good laboratories, and a sizeable number of well-trained research scientists, all providing an enabling environment for health research.[11] The research infrastructure, in addition to a significant burden of disease, including a high prevalence of HIV/AIDS (a developed world research infrastructure alongside a developing world burden of disease) and a growing burden of non-communicable disease,[12] provides both rationale and fertile ground for local and international research. The clinical trials industry is bigger than in any other African country and is estimated to bring in over 250 million dollars a year. Many clinical trials are currently being undertaken for such conditions as HIV/AIDS, asthma, schizophrenia, and

---

8 Bongani M Mayosi & Solomon R Benatar "Health and Health Care in South Africa — 20 Years after Mandela" (2014) 371 NEJM 1344; Bongani Mayosi et al, "Health in South Africa: Changes and Challenges since 2009" (2012) 308:9858 Lancet 2029–2043; A Dhai, "A Health System That Violates Patients' Rights to Access Health Care" (2012) 5:1 S Afr J Bioeth & L, online: <www.sajbl.org.za/index.php/sajbl/article/view/216/194>.

9 Section 27 (1) of the Constitution states that "Everyone has the right to have access to health care services, including reproductive health care."

10 *Soobramoney v Minister of Health, KwaZulu-Natal*, 1998 (1) SALR 765 (Constitutional Court and *Treatment Action Campaign v South Africa (Minister of Health)*, 2002 (10) BCLR 1033 (Constitutional Court).

11 Regulations 2015. See also Christa Van Wyk, "South Africa Report: Clinical Trials, Medical Research and Cloning in South Africa" (2004) J Roman & Dutch L.

12 South African AIDS Initiative, online: <www.saavi.org.za/index.htm>.

rheumatoid arthritis.[13] Recruitment for clinical trial participants is relatively easy compared to that in other African countries. However, this has been attributed to poverty and limited access to healthcare.[14] What this means, therefore, is that attention must be paid to the protection of research participants in the country.

Moreover, South Africa has a long history of efforts towards implementing research governance mechanisms and has been noted to be the only country in the world[15] where informed consent in research is a constitutional requirement.[16] Many of its innovations and regulatory requirements have been adopted by other African countries, and thus it provides a good starting point for examining health research ethics, regulation, and governance in Africa.

Health research in South Africa

A history of health research in South Africa takes off in the second half of the 20th century, when research units and centres were established, and mining industries supported research into disease. However, prior to that period, South African Institute for Medical Research (SAIMR) was established in 1912, funded in part by the Chamber of Mines[17] and subsequently by the Council for Scientific and Industrial Research (CSIR), a more general research entity. From this latter body, the Medical Research Council (MRC) was established in 1969. Research priorities followed funders' priorities. The focus of much research was on asbestosis, pneumococcal pneumonia, tuberculosis, and silicosis, diseases that were relevant for the mining industry, which also provided much funding for such research. With the entrenchment of apartheid, researchers and persons who entered the medical professions were almost entirely white, the funders' priorities and agendas were racialised, the result was a skewing of the research towards racial explanations for disease conditions.[18]

South Africa has been the site of the development of several vaccines, including for yellow fever and polio, and, in the past, discoveries of connections between conditions such as nutrition, heart disease, and liver cancer as well as

---

13 *The Clinical Trials Industry in South Africa: Ethics, Rules and Realities* (Wemos, 2013), online: <https://www.wemos.nl/wp-content/uploads/2016/06/Clinical_Trials_Industry_South_Africa_2013.pdf>.

14 *Ibid.*

15 P Cleaton Jones & Doug Wassenar, "Protection of Human Participants in Health Research – A Comparison of Some US Federal Regulations and South African Research Ethics Guidelines" (2011) 100:11 S Afr Med J 710 at 710.

16 Section 12 of the Constitution of the Republic of South Africa (Act no 108 of the 1996).

17 S Meiring-Naudé & AC Brown, "The Growth of Scientific Institutions in South Africa" in AC Brown, ed, *A History of Scientific Endeavour in South Africa* (Cape Town, Royal Society of South Africa: Rustica Press, 1977) at 60–85.

18 For this history, see Academy of Science of South Africa, *Consensus Report on Revitalising Clinical Research in South Africa: A Study on Clinical Research and Related Training in South Africa* (Academy of Science of South Africa, 2009). See also Lundy Braun, "Structuring Silence: Asbestos and Biomedical Research in Britain and South Africa" (2008) 50:1 Race & Class 59–78.

important research in genetics.[19] However, as became apparent during the Truth and Reconciliation Commission hearing, researchers and health professionals were implicated in some major malpractices founded on racism.[20] Much of the research also focussed on diseases of the rich, and when focussed on black people, research agendas tended to slant results, fostering a distrust of medical science among blacks.

Researchers have noted substantial state support for health research and evidence-based medicine in South Africa over the years.[21] Many clinical trials are ongoing for various disease conditions, including HIV, and the South African AIDS Vaccine Initiative (SAAVI), a programme of the MRC, is a prominent initiative. In regard to its attractiveness for clinical trials specifically, it has been noted that

> South Africa is an attractive location for clinical trials, inter alia because it has a good clinical infrastructure, low levels of litigation, a credible regulatory environment, and a full spectrum of health problems. Recruitment for clinical trials has been relatively easy in South Africa due to a large treatment-naïve urban population, who experience high unemployment and difficulty accessing expensive drugs.[22]

As in many African countries, health research priorities in South Africa today remains opaque. As has been noted, health research was not conducted in an equitable manner for much of the 20th century as a result of apartheid, with much research being done for the benefit of the white minority.[23] Recent studies have shown a weak link between research conducted and research priorities based on the burden of disease.[24] Studies have also shown that government funding of research remains much lower than foreign funding, with South Africa spending less that 1 per cent of its gross domestic product (GDP) on health research.[25] (The situation is possibly better in South Africa, given its sophisticated research infrastructure and income status.) Of the foreign funding, pharmaceutical investment in drug trials is substantial, while the international donors focus on the areas of tuberculosis and HIV/AIDS.[26] However, the National Health Act establishes

19 See Academy of Science of South Africa, *supra* Note 18 at 27–35.
20 Academy of Science of South Africa, *ibid.*
21 *Ibid.*
22 Academy of Science of South Africa, *supra* Note 46 at 88.
23 Academy of Science of South Africa, *supra* Note 18 at 22.
24 See, for instance, Leslie London et al, "Health Research in the Western Cape Province, South Africa: Lessons and Challenges" (2014) 6:1 Afr J Prim Health Care Fam Med 698, noting the relative lack of research on trauma, mental health, and non-drug trials for non-communicable diseases (NCDs) in the Western Cape Province, relative to the significant burden of these conditions.
25 *Ibid.* Academy of Science of South Africa, *supra* Note 18. Cf with earlier research: Michelle Sneider, *The Setting of Health Research Priorities in South Africa* (Medical Research Council, 2001).
26 Academy of Science of South Africa, *ibid.* at xvi.

an institutional framework for health research through the National Health Research Council, a key function of which is to identify research priorities in South Africa. A National Health Research Database was first established in 2009 and revised in 2017.[27] The National Health Research Database "serves as a repository of health-related research which has been and is currently being conducted in South Africa."[28] Amongst other things, this database helps to identify research priorities, both past and present, and assists in the monitoring of research.

In the sections that follow, I consider and analyse the context of health research governance more closely.

Health research governance in South Africa

South Africa's research governance system has moved from a largely voluntary system to a more regulated system. This is a very valuable tool, given the concerns raised in the previous chapter about who dictates the research agenda and priorities in African countries.

The timeline for research governance has been traced by Cleaton-Jones and Wassenar.[29] The ethics review system dates back to October 1966, when the first ethical review committee was established at the University of Witwatersrand. This made it one of the first ethics review committees in the world.[30] This followed the revelations of Henry Beecher in the *New England Journal of Medicines* of cases of unethical clinical research in June 1966.[31] However, it was not until 1977 that universities and the MRC established ethics review committees. The MRC developed a set of ethics guidelines in 1979: "Guidelines on Ethics for Medical Research," the first ethics guidelines in the country. Several ethics guidelines were issued thereafter, including the Guidelines on Good Clinical Practice by the National Department of Health, which was an adaptation of the ICH-GCP Good Clinical Practice Guidelines.[32] In 2015, the National Guidelines were revised. The South Africa Medical Association established an ethics review committee in 1992. There are now ethics review committees in all tertiary institutions and independent ethics review committees in the private sector and the state departments of health. The Constitution also established informed consent as a constitutional requirement in 1996 and the 2003 National Health Act, which established the ethics review as mandatory in research involving human participants.[33]

27 National Health Research Database, (2017), online: <http://nhrd.hst.org.za/>.
28 National Health Research Database, 'About,' online: <http://nhrd.hst.org.za/Home/About>.
29 Cleaton-Jones & Wassenar, *supra* Note 23 at 711.
30 Peter Cleaton-Jones, "Research Ethics in South Africa: Putting the Mpumalanga Case into Context" in J Lavery et al, eds, *Ethical Issues in International Biomedical Research* (Oxford: Oxford University Press, 2007) at 240.
31 Henry K Beecher, "Ethics and Clinical Research (1966) 274 N Engl J Med 1354–1360.
32 Cleaton, *supra* Note 57 at 241.
33 Cleaton-Jones & Wassenar, *ibid.*

South Africa has had a few research scandals, the most prominent of which was the Bezowda Breast Cancer Trials scandal. In that case, Dr Bezowda presented a paper on the treatment of breast cancer with a high-dose chemotherapy at the American Society of Clinical Oncologists in 1999 on trials conducted between 1995 and 1999. His findings had the potential to provide a viable, effective alternative to the treatments available at the time. To conduct similar trials among a wider cohort of participants, some American scientists sought to audit his records. The verification exercise showed a marked difference between Dr Bezowda's reported findings and the obtainable data. It turned out that the scientist provided false accounts of his research methodology and kept poor records, and it was also alleged that proper informed consent was not obtained from research participants, given the falsification of the methodology. The high-dose chemotherapy regimen may also have caused harm to the research participants.[34] One of the key questions that arose was the role of any ethics review committee in monitoring the research. Investigations revealed, however, that the research protocol had not been submitted for ethics review.[35] This was prior to the enactment of the National Health Act, which now makes ethics review mandatory. Even so, legally, the requirement for informed consent under the Constitution of South Africa was not adequately met.

Other studies have raised controversy. In 2000, the government stopped the FTC 302 trial, a drug trial for HIV drugs, after several participants died due to liver toxicity.[36] In another study on HIV-positive patients' surgical outcomes, the ethics committee "considered the clinical implications of the study important enough to waive patients' right to informed consent."[37] This raised a flurry of arguments on the pages of a prominent journal, with one author comparing it to the unethical experiments at Nuremberg and the spectre of apartheid.[38] As in most African countries, care and treatment are integrated to a significant degree, rendering the vulnerability of research participants almost palpable. This is heightened by the history and legacy of apartheid.[39] The identification of vulnerability

34 Raymond B Weiss et al, "High-Dose Chemotherapy for High-Risk Primary Breast Cancer: An on-site Review of the Bezwoda Study" (2000) 351 Lancet 999; George W Sledge, "Why Big Lies Matter: Lessons from the Bezwoda Affair" (2000) Medscape, online: <www.medscape.com/viewarticle/408908>.

35 Peter Cleaton-Jones, "Scientific Misconduct in a Breast-Cancer Chemotherapy Trial: Response of University of the Witwatersrand" (2000) 355 Lancet 1011.

36 Pat Sidley, "South Africa to Tighten Control on Drug Trials after Five Deaths" (2000) 320 BMJ 1028; M Danetshalab, "Emtricitabine (Emory University/Glaxo Wellcome/Triangle Pharmaceuticals)" (2000) 3:8 IDrugs 940.

37 Satish Bhagwanjee et al, "Does HIV Status Influence the Outcome of Patients Admitted to a Surgical Intensive Care Unit? A Prospective Double Blind Study" (1997) 314 BMJ 1077, online: <www.bmj.com/content/314/7087/1077>.

38 See JN Ana, "South African Study Raises the Ghosts of Nuremberg and Apartheid" (1997) 314 BMJ 1482; Wendy Holmes, "Minimum Ethical Standards Should not Vary among Countries" (1997) 314 BMJ 1481.

39 See Keymanthri Moodley. See also Gavin H Mooney & Diane E McIntyre, "South Africa: A 21st Century Apartheid in Health and Health Care?" (2008) 180:11 Med J Aust 637–640.

also raises questions of research agenda, who dictates the research agenda in South Africa, and how this affects (or does not affect) research governance.[40]

In 1997, the controversial placebo trials conducted on HIV drugs, referred to in Chapter 1 of this book, that took place in South Africa (and other developing countries) had raised furore about the ethics of internationally sponsored research in African countries. As noted in that chapter, Lurie and Wolfe's arguments about the ethics of conducting trials in developing countries such as South Africa catalysed further arguments about internationally sponsored trials in resource constrained settings and changes to important international ethical guidelines, including the Helsinki Declaration and the CIOMS Guidelines, and raised key issues about domestic governance of research: could the structures in place manage the conflicts between ethical relativism and universalism? These issues, alongside South Africa's more sophisticated research infrastructure, indicate that South Africa is an interesting context within which to learn about research governance.

Legal framework

South Africa has a mixed or a hybrid legal system – consisting of both the civil law inherited from the Dutch and the English law inherited from English colonisers and statutes. However, the Constitution[41] is supreme. It specifically includes a right to bodily integrity which explicitly includes the right "not to be subjected to medical or scientific experiments without their informed consent,"[42] making it the only constitution in the world with such a provision.[43] This requirement is further developed in the National Health Act, the key legislation for health research ethics governance. Legislation such as the Health Professions Act, 1974, which confers power on the Health Professional Council of South Africa to regulate health professionals, is also part of the legal framework as are the Children's Act, 2005, and the Protection of Personal Information Act.[44] Case law on consent, insurance for research participants, and other matters are also part of the legal framework for research in South Africa.

The National Health Act[45] is the key legislation for health research and research ethics governance in South Africa. Enacted in 2003, it contains requirements on informed consent, ethics review, and research priorities, amongst other

---

40 See Marcelle C Dawson, "Ethical Challenges in Social Movement Research: Lessons from South Africa" in Kevin Gillan & Jenny Pickerill, eds, *Research Ethics and Social Movements* (New York: Routledge, 2016) at 48.

41 Constitution of the Republic of South Africa, 1996 (Act No. 108 of 1996).

42 Section 12 (2) (c) of the *Constitution of South Africa, 1996* (Act No.108 of 1996).

43 P Cleaton Jones & D Wassenar, "Protection of Human Participants in Health Research – A Comparison of Some US Federal Regulations and South African Research Ethics Guidelines" (2010) 100:11 S Afr Med J 710 at 710, online: <www.samj.org.za/index.php/samj/article/viewFile/4525/2993>.

44 Protection of Personal Information Act 4 of 2013 (Act No. 4 of 2013).

45 *National Health Act*, 2003, as amended by *the National Health Amendment Act* 12 of 2013.

things. The Act also defines key terms for health research governance. Its definition of health research is broad and encompasses the categories identified in
Chapter 1. Hence it defines "health research" as including

> any research which contributes to knowledge of
>   (a) the biological, clinical, psychological or social processes in human
> beings;
>   (b) improved methods for the provision of health services;
>   (c) human pathology;
>   (d) the causes of disease;
>   (e) the effects of the environment on the human body;
>   (f) the development or new application of pharmaceuticals, medicines and
> related substances; and
>   (g) the development of new applications of health technology.[46]

In essence, then, the law applies to all health research involving humans, a key
strength of the South African legal framework. This may be contrasted with
situations in Canada (no general law);[47] the United States (research which falls
under the Common Rule);[48] or Denmark (biomedical research),[49] where some
but not all research is covered by law. In addition, where health services are to
be provided as an experiment, the user of such health services must be informed,
and the head of the institution as well as an ethics review committee must give
approval.[50] This requirement is considered a weakness by some commentators
because of its potential for over-bureaucratisation, its incongruence with current
norms internationally, and the fact that such services provide direct benefit to
users of the health services.[51] However, these criticisms do not address the key
concern in all research involving humans, which is the possibility of harm in
experimentation. If there may be risk of harm, there must be a way to manage it.
An approval by the head of the health institution cannot be said to be overreach-
ing and may be said to be basic. The risk of overregulation in this instance would
therefore come from the requirement for ethics approval. This can be addressed
by ensuring speedier approval times within guidelines and regulations for health
services research specifically.

---

46 Section 1 of the National Health Act.
47 The Tri-Council Policy Statement operates as the main research regulatory framework. But
    some provinces have laws on research governance, such as Newfoundland's *Health Research
    Ethics Authority Act* (2006) came into force (2011); Article 21 of the Quebec Civil Code, reg-
    ulates research involving incompetent minors or adults in that province.
48 45 CFR 46.101.
49 *The Act on a Biomedical Research Ethics Committee System and the Processing of Biomedical
    Research Projects Act.*
50 Section 11 of the National Health Act.
51 AE Strode, "The Parameters of the Current Legal Framework for Health Research: Forms of
    Health Research Which Are Regulated and Obligations Imposed on Researchers" (2013) 6:3 S
    Afr J Bioeth & L, online: <www.sajbl.org.za/index.php/sajbl/article/view/284/318>.

The Act provides a legal and institutional framework for health research priorities, a key challenge already identified in foregoing pages and chapters. In this regard, the Act empowers the Minister of Health, after consultation with the National Health Council, to establish the National Health Research Committee.[52] This is a committee of 15 persons which has the functions of determining the health research to be carried out by public health authorities, ensuring that health research agendas and research resources focus on priority health problems, and developing and advising the Minister on a national strategy for health research and coordination of the research activities of public health authorities. The factors to be taken into consideration in identifying research priorities include the burden of disease; the cost effectiveness of interventions; the health needs of vulnerable groups, including women, the elderly, and persons with disabilities; and the health needs of communities.[53] Members of the Committee are, by the provisions of the Act, to be remunerated.

It must be noted that the focus of the Committee is on health research conducted by public authorities.[54] Thus the priorities, the health research agenda, the strategy, and the coordination of research activities are all limited to a focus on government/public agencies. It logically follows that the Committee is concerned with what is clearly and primarily within government control. A clear research agenda allows for an intensification of efforts towards increasing government expenditure on health research and ensuring that such expenditure is in fact geared towards what the government considers to be research priorities in the country. From a new governance perspective, it would also be important to get the perspectives of the private sector and to seek to the extent possible to encourage private expenditures towards the identified research priorities. More research would be needed to address the extent to which such collaboration between public and private sectors is occurring in health research in South Africa.

With respect to research ethics, regulation, and governance, the Act makes provisions for informed consent and ethics review structures. In this regard, it mandates that research or experimentation on a living person may only be conducted in the prescribed manner, and with the written and informed consent of the prospective participant. Information to be provided consists of the objects of the research and the positive or negative consequences of such participation on his or her health.[55]

The Act also contains legal safeguards for research involving children (defined under the Children's Act as persons under the age of 18). It provides the criteria that must be present for health research involving children. Such research has to be in the best interest of the child, has to be in accordance with the prescribed condition, and has to be accompanied by the consent of the parent or guardian of the child

---

52 Section 69.
53 Section 70.
54 Section 69 (3).
55 Section 71 (a).

and the consent of the child if they are capable of understanding the information.[56] If the research is for non-therapeutic purposes, in addition to obtaining the consent of the parents and the child (where they are capable of understanding), the consent of the Minister must also be obtained. The Minister cannot give consent under the Act in certain circumstances, for example, where the same research can be conducted with adults, the research poses a risk to the health of the child, and the benefits of the research do not outweigh any risk posed to the child's health.[57]

On ethics review, the National Health Act requires that every institution, health agency, and health establishment at which health research is conducted must establish or have access to a health research ethics committee. Such health research ethics committee (HREC):

> must (a) review research proposals and protocols in order to ensure that research conducted by the relevant institution, agency or establishment will promote health, contribute to the prevention of communicable or non-communicable diseases or disability or result in cures for communicable or non-communicable diseases; and (b) grant approval for research by the relevant institution, agency or establishment in instances where research proposals and protocol meet the ethical standards of that health research ethics committee.

The Act also establishes the National Health Research Ethics Council (NHREC).[58] The NHREC is composed of 15 members who are appointed for an initial term of three years. The functions of the NHREC are to

(a) determine guidelines for the functioning of health research ethics committees;

(b) register and audit health research ethics committees;

(c) set norms and standards for conducting research on humans and animals, including norms and standards for conducting clinical trials;

(d) adjudicate complaints about the functioning of health research ethics committees and hear any complaint by a researcher who believes that he or she has been discriminated against by a health research ethics committee;

(e) refer to the relevant statutory health professional council matters involving the violation or potential violation of an ethical or professional rule by a health care provider;

(f) institute such disciplinary action as may be prescribed against any person found to be in violation of any norms and standards, or guidelines, set for the conducting of research in terms of this Act; and

(g) advise the national department and provincial departments on any ethical issues concerning research.

---

56 Section 71 (2).
57 Section 71 (3).
58 Section 72.

The functions of the NHREC are thus wide-ranging in the governance of health research. Specifically, it is required by law to set guidelines for the ethical conduct of research. It has set these guidelines, *Ethics in Health Research: Principles, Processes and Structures – 2015* (which replaces the 2004 edition), and this constitutes the principal ethics guidance for health research. This will be considered in more detail under the ethics framework. Another key function is the regulation of ethics review committees (called health research ethics committees) through registration and auditing. With respect to health research ethics committees (HRECs), the Act requires that every institution at which health research is conducted establish a HREC, which must be registered with the NHREC. The functions of the NHREC include the reviewing of research proposals and protocols in order to ensure that research conducted "will promote health, contribute to the prevention of communicable or non-communicable diseases or disability or result in cures for communicable or non-communicable diseases" and the registering of the committees.[59] HRECs are also required to grant approval for research to the relevant institution, agency, or establishment in instances where research proposals and protocol meet the ethical standards.

In 2014, the Minister passed some regulations under powers granted to him by the Act to operationalise some sections of the Act. These regulations included those dealing with research: *Regulations Relating to Research with Human Participants.*[60] Originally issued in 2004 by the Department of Health, the NHREC revised them, and they were reissued in 2015 by the Department of Health: *Ethics in Health Research: Principles, Processes and Structures – 2015* (the Ethics Guidelines).[61] They emphasise, amongst other things, that health research must comply with the Ethics Guidelines, thereby imbuing the guidelines with legal authority. The Ethics Guidelines can therefore be invoked in legal action by research participants. Further, the Regulations require that research be responsive to the health needs of the population being researched, echoing the CIOMS Guidelines,[62] and valid scientific methodology must be employed for the research. The Regulations also require that participants' rights to dignity, privacy, bodily integrity, and equality, amongst other things, be respected. In addition, they require that researchers pay compensation for research-related injuries[63] and consult with the communities in which research will take place and other governmental or institutional authorities.[64] The Regulations also provide guidance for researchers when the participants are dependent in some manner,

---

59 Section 73.
60 *National Health Act (61/2003): Regulations Relating to Research with Human Participants* R.719, no 4 Gazette no 38000, online: <http://research.ukzn.ac.za/Libraries/Research_ Document/National_Regulations_Relating_to_Research_With_Human_Participants_ R719_of_2014.sflb.ashx>.
61 Department of Health, Republic of South Africa, *Ethics in Health Research: Principles, Processes and Structures – 2015*, 2nd ed (Pretoria: Department of Health, 2015).
62 See the CIOMS Guidelines.
63 Section 2 of the Regulations.
64 Section 3 of the Regulations.

such as when they are persons who lack capacity as a result of mental illness, prisoners, or persons in dependent or hierarchical relationships.[65]

The requirement of informed consent is reiterated with an obligation on the researchers to obtain the same with appropriate consent processes.[66] The Regulations provide the information that must be given to the prospective participant – the purpose of the research; the methods and procedures, including possible randomisation; alternatives to participation in the research; the potential harms and risks of harm posed by the research; the expected benefits of the research; the freedom to choose to participate or not, or to withdraw from the research without penalty or reason; the extent to which confidentiality and privacy will be maintained; the details of the contact person in the event of a query or research-related injury; reimbursement and/or incentives given for participation; information about the sponsor; any potential conflicts of interest; information about approval from the health research ethics committee or the Medicines Control Council, where relevant; insurance in the event of research-related injury for more than minimal risk research; and the availability of beneficial products or interventions post-research.[67] The modalities for obtaining the Minister's consent for non-therapeutic research[68] with children are also provided in the Regulations.[69]

Under the Regulations, health research involving humans is required to undergo independent ethics review, thus making ethics review a legal requirement. Thus, while the Act establishes the HRECs, the Regulations make submission of health research protocols to the committees a legal obligation.[70] In addition, the researcher is required to submit the protocol to other requisite bodies, such as the Medicines Control Committee, replaced in June 2017[71] by the South African Health Products Regulatory Authority (SAHPRA), South Africa's drug regulatory authority. Clinical trials are thus required by law to obtain approval from both the SAHPRA and the HREC, and to adhere to the Regulations. As previously stated, one of the requirements of the Regulations is that researchers must adhere to the Ethics Guidelines.

Another important feature of the Regulations is its requirement for the registration of trials with the South African National Clinical Trials Register.[72] As discussed in Chapter 4, clinical trial registry is one key way to manage research priorities and develop a cohesive, responsive national health research agenda, especially in resource-constrained settings. While not every country mandates

65 Section 4 of the Regulations.
66 Section 2 of the Regulations.
67 Section 5 of the Regulations.
68 Defined in the Regulations as "research that does not hold out the prospect of direct benefit but holds out the prospect of generalizable knowledge" (application form to the Minister for consent).
69 See Section 7 of the Regulations.
70 See Section 2(c) and Section 3 of the Regulations.
71 Proclamation No 20 of 2017: Commencement of Medicines and Related Substances Act, 2008.
72 Section 3 of the Regulations, online: <www.sanctr.gov.za>.

this by law, South Africa has now done so through the 2014 Regulations. The registry is specifically for clinical trials. This leaves open the question of the need for a database for other kinds of health research. There is a coordinated system of registration through the NHREC, the steps of which are provided on a website and which include obtaining an NHREC registration number, obtaining ethics approval, uploading the trial information, and eventually obtaining a Department of Health number – the National Register Number.[73]

In essence, South Africa's legal framework for research provides a legal foundation for the ethical framework (which is discussed later). It provides the force of law to the ethical requirement by incorporating ethics guidelines into legislation and regulations. Its reach is far, encompassing many aspects of the health research enterprise. The key question that this broad legal framework raises is the extent of its implementation and the protection of participants in health research. Some of the answers may lie in the functioning of the institutions which it establishes, such as the NHREC and the HRECs, or the implementation of the ethical framework for which it provides legal backing. These matters are considered in the following sections.

Ethical framework

The ethical framework for research in South Africa is contained primarily in the Department of Health's *Ethics in Health Research: Principles, Processes and Structures – 2015* (the Ethics Guidelines),[74] which replaced the first edition from 2004. Apart from this, the ethical framework also consists of other guidelines, such as the Health Professions Council of South Africa's Ethical and Professional Rules.[75]

The Ethics Guidelines contain the national policy on health research governance. Among other things, the Ethics Guidelines are developed to provide guidance to every researcher or research organisation involved in research in South Africa. They derive from the National Health Act, having been developed by the National Health Research Ethics Council established by the Act and given the norm-setting function of making guidelines on ethics.[76] The Ethics Guidelines do not, however, provide guidance on clinical trials (except for research-related bodily injury insurance and compensation which covers clinical trials) – guidance for clinical trials is provided in the Good Clinical Practice, which is discussed later, as part of the ethical framework. The Guidelines draw from and endorse several national and international ethics guidelines, several of

---

73 <www.ethicsapp.co.za/>.

74 Department of Health, Republic of South Africa, *supra* Note 61 (hereafter, Ethics Guidelines).

75 Ethical and Professional Rules of the Health Professions Council of South Africa as promulgated by the Health Professions Council of South Africa as promulgated in Government Gazette R717/2006, online: <www.hpcsa.co.za/downloads/conduct_ethics/rules/generic_ethical_rules/booklet_2_generic_ethical_rules_with_anexures.pdf>.

76 Section 72 of the National Health Act.

which were highlighted earlier in the book, including the Belmont Report, the Declaration of Helsinki 2013, the CIOMS Guidelines, South Africa's MRC, the Guidelines on Ethics for Medical Research: HIV Preventive Vaccine Research, the Singapore Statement on Research Integrity, Human Heredity and Health in Africa (H3Africa) Initiative, and the ICH-GCP Guidelines.

Amongst its provisions, it emphasises the requirement of independent ethics review for health research and the requirement for ethics committees to ensure that protocols stand up to scientific and ethics inquiry, and meet the health needs and priorities of the people as required under Section 73 of the National Health Act. Ethics review, as observed in the Ethics Guidelines, is not meant to merely present an obstacle to research and innovation. Instead ethics review is "to ensure a comprehensive and frank assessment of the ethical implications of proposals so that participants (and researchers) can be protected appropriately."[77] This is often a key concern for researchers who are concerned that many of the burdens of ethics review are merely part of a bureaucratic process that adds little to the protection of participants in research. The review, according to the Ethics Guidelines, is to ensure the protection of participants from harm by weighing risk/benefit (including impact on society and future beneficiaries) and ensuring the minimisation of harm, holding researchers accountable, and promoting important social and ethical values.[78] It is important to note in this regard that the Ethics Guidelines outline research projects which do not need to pass through ethics review. These include researching using exclusively publicly available information or information obtainable through legislation or regulation, research involving observation of people in public spaces and natural environments (that meet certain specified criteria), quality assurance, or improvement studies.

The Ethics Guidelines provide the 'core ethical principles' that must be applied in research involving human participants and research involving the use of human biological materials and data collected from living or deceased persons, including human embryos, foetuses, foetal tissue, reproductive materials, and stem cells. These core principles are drawn from the principlism approach: beneficence and maleficence, distributive justice, respect for persons. These principles are to be applied by HRECs in their reviews of research.

In addition, the Ethics Guidelines identify key norms of standards that must guide HRECs in their review. These are relevance and value; scientific integrity; role player engagement; fair selection of participants; fair balance of risks and benefits; informed consent; ongoing respect for participants, including privacy and confidentiality; and researcher competence and expertise.[79] Relevance and value require that the research be of value to the South African people, be responsive to their needs, and have the potential to be translated into products that will be available to the South African people. As has been highlighted in

---

77 Section 1.6.6 of the Ethics Guidelines.
78 Section 1.6.7 of the Ethics Guidelines.
79 Section 2 of the Ethics Guidelines.

different sections in this book, this is a key concern. Another key norm is the requirement for role player engagement. This includes engagement of the communities in which research is to be conducted. Ongoing respect for participants includes respect for their privacy and the establishment of measures to maintain the confidentiality of any information obtained from or through them during the research.[80] These norms are further distilled into a deeper analysis of the substantive norms and how they apply to research in different contexts.[81] The Ethics Guidelines also list several pieces of legislation that researchers must be cognisant of in conducting research in the country, including the Mental Health Care Act and the Children's Act, and which may provide other norms that HRECs must be aware of in evaluating research proposals.

Among the interesting discussion of the norms, a key contemporary concern in a resource-constrained setting, is the question of inducements for research participants, which may have a significant effect on informed consent. The guidance on reimbursements and inducements in the Ethics Guidelines recommends the use of the Time, Inconvenience, and Expenses (TIE) method, which costs expenses at the current hourly rate for unskilled labour in the market place, regardless of whether the participant is employed. A more detailed analysis of this is contained in an earlier document developed by the NHREC, which is incorporated into the Ethics Guidelines: NHREC (2012) *Payment of trial participants in South Africa: Ethical Considerations for Research Ethics Committees.*[82] The Ethics Guidelines recognise that inducements can affect participation but note that justification for providing inducement should be made by researchers to the ethics committee and that the inducement provided must not be such as to "unduly influence" an informed choice about participation or more importantly jeopardise a potential participant's assessment of risk of harm.[83]

Privacy and confidentiality are also key ethical issues provided for by the Ethics Guidelines. Researchers are to ensure the privacy and confidentiality of the participants' data and must also provide information about how they will deal with notifiable information such as child abuse or notifiable diseases. Researchers must also provide information to prospective participants about situations in which confidentiality cannot be guaranteed, for example, where focus groups are employed for obtaining information. The following information must be provided to prospective participants: the information to be collected and why, what will happen to it, how long it will be retained, if it will identify the participant, if it will be shared with others and why, and if it will be sent outside South Africa and why. The prospective participant should agree to these terms. The Guidelines make reference to the Protection of Personal Information Act 4 of 2013.

Informed consent and related procedures also receive comprehensive coverage in the Ethics Guidelines. The Guidelines provide a list of matters that must be

---

80 Section 2 of the Ethics Guidelines.
81 See Section 3.
82 Section 3.1.7.
83 *Ibid.*

addressed in informed consent procedures, including the information that must be provided, such as that participation is voluntary, that consent can be withdrawn, the purpose of the research, the anticipated risks of harm or discomfort, measures to minimise risk of harm, provisions for confidentiality, duration of participation, the responsibilities of researcher and participant, and information on reimbursement of expenses.[84] The environment within which consent is sought must be conducive. Also the information must be provided in a simple, easy to understand manner, free of jargon, translated into a language that the prospective participant will understand and make it clear that they can ask questions and provide requisite information in this regard. Given the difficulties of ensuring that participants understand that the proposed project is indeed research, especially in the African context, the Ethics Guidelines also require that "a measure to probe understanding and comprehension of the information is planned and how it proposes to do so especially for very vulnerable potential participants" be provided. For clinical trials, further information is required under the *Guidelines for Good Practice in the Conduct of Clinical Trials with Human Participants in South Africa*,[85] discussed in the following.

The Ethics Guidelines note that by comparison to participants in Western countries, many participants in South Africa may be considered "vulnerable," thus requiring researchers to provide extra protections. Such vulnerability may be in regard to environmental factors, like extreme poverty and ordinarily poor access to healthcare or low levels of formal education and literacy, or personal circumstances, like mental or intellectual impairment, acute illness, advanced age, or pregnancy and childbirth. The Ethics Guidelines require that particular care be taken where vulnerability is established and provide some steps in this regard, noting that research ethics committees may impose further measures to protect the prospective participants. The committee may withdraw the approval given where researchers fail to comply with the additional measures or where the risk of harm is great. The Guidelines emphasise the need for research ethics committees to not be patronising and to recognise that poverty, for example, may not make a community or participant less able to understand the risks and benefits of participation.[86] In the African context, this is a tricky balance – recognising vulnerability yet upholding personhood and respect.

The Guidelines focus on children as well, articulating "minimum conditions" for research involving children. It builds on the provisions of the National Health Act, requiring appropriate review of the research and elaborating on the issues that a research ethics committee must consider, including the scientific indispensability of involving children in the research, equipoise, prioritising the best interests of the child, written permission from the parents or guardians, written assent from the child, and the requirement that the research ethics committees

---

84 Section 3.1.9.
85 Department of Health, *Guidelines for Good Practice in the Conduct of Clinical Trials with Human Participants in South Africa* (2001).
86 Section 3.2.

include members with appropriate paediatric research experience.[87] The Guidelines also touch upon the researcher's legal obligation to report sexual abuse, informed consent requirements attached to this, and the arising privacy and confidentiality challenges.

The inclusion of women, which has been noted as a key ethical challenge in research, with the historic exclusion of women leading to insufficient data about women's health, is also considered in the Ethics Guidelines.[88] So, too, is research involving persons with reduced capacity and persons in dependent relationships, prisoners, persons needing ongoing medical care, persons with physical disabilities, and persons participating in research as a group.[89]

The Ethics Guidelines also provide guidance on research involving human biological materials and specimen, which is becoming a big issue with increased research in these areas. It specifies the necessity for informed consent, the nature of the consent, the possible need for re-consent, and the types of consent (narrow, tiered, and broad). It makes specific reference to the H3Africa Initiative, noting its recommendation that informed consent must be broad enough to allow for future and secondary uses, and appropriate for the context. It calls for attention to be paid to anonymisation and instances in which hereditary material remains, making it possible, despite anonymisation, for identification of donors to be ascertained.[90] The Guidelines also provide for the use of databanks, including tissue banks, which act as a repository for tissues, and the basic requirements for such banks, such as informed consent, ethics committee oversight, and privacy and confidentiality.[91]

Interestingly, the Ethics Guidelines also consider research related to traditional medicines. Traditional medicines remain a key part of healthcare in many African countries but are not always amenable to scientific methods of inquiry. Traditional medicines research under the Guidelines require that research participants receive the same protections available under other Western medicines research. Research ethics committees are required to pay attention to the intellectual property rights which may be sought by non-South Africans over the course of such research. This is clearly a sensitive issue that has given rise to problems in the past, including the issues around benefit sharing and biodiversity.

Finally, the Ethics Guidelines deal with a myriad of other issues, including insurance for research-related injury[92] and research ethics operations.[93] The legislative framework for, composition of, and other requirements for research ethics committees are considered extensively in the Ethics Guidelines. It will be recalled that the National Health Act requires every institution that conducts

---

87 Section 3.2.2.1.
88 Section 3.2.2.2.
89 See generally Section 3.2.
90 Section 3.3.6.
91 Section 3.5.2.
92 Section 3.5.3.
93 Section 4.3.

research to establish a research ethics committee.[94] The Act also establishes the National Health Research Ethics Council to oversee research ethics committees in institutions. A further look at the research ethics committees alongside some of the issues that have arisen in practice will be the main crux of the following section.

The institutional framework

We turn our attention now to the institutional framework which actually implements the ethical and legal frameworks. Following the outline already set out, we consider ethics review committees, the drug regulatory authority, policymaking structures, and non-governmental organisations as well as their functioning and the systemic issues that have affected such functioning, such as composition, structure and organisation, and capacity and funding issues. In general, adequate resources, training, and understaffing have been some of the challenges for these institutions in African countries.[95] These affect the quality, regularity, consistency, and consequently the research governance role of these institutions, particularly with respect to research participants' protection. Here, we consider South Africa's implementing institutions and their challenges.

Ethics review committees

The fundamental prerequisite of ethics review for health research involving humans has been noted, and ethics review is long-standing in South Africa, with the first such committee being established over 50 years ago. Many types of health research involving humans in South Africa are required by law under the National Health Act and under the Ethics Guidelines to obtain ethics review approval before commencement.

The major function of ethics review committees in South Africa, as in many countries around the world, is to approve research which meets ethical standards and disapprove research which does not meet such standards. In addition, the Ethics Guidelines specify that health research ethics committees have the right to monitor the research that they have approved. The degree of monitoring should be based on the specific research, the risks, and the potential harm. It may be by spot-checking or impromptu visits, or, at the minimum, annual checks.[96] It will be recalled that this was a major gap in the Bezowda Case discussed earlier.

At the top of the hierarchy for ethics review in South Africa, the NHREC has the responsibility under the National Health Act and the Ethics Guidelines to provide general oversight of HRECs in South Africa and to register and audit them. In addition, the NHREC manages complaints about HRECs through

---

94 Section 72.
95 See generally Mariana Kruger, Paul Ndebele & Lyn Horn, *Research Ethics in Africa: A Resource for Research Ethics Committees* (Stellenbosch: SUN MeDIA, 2014).
96 Section 4.5.1.10.

its Complaints and Advisory Disciplinary Committee (CADC). HRECs must report to the NHRECs annually on their activities at a specified date, providing information on membership and changes in membership, number of meetings held, participation by required categories of members, number of protocols presented, and number approved and rejected.[97] The NHREC is required to meet at least four times annually and to submit annual reports to the Minister of Health.[98] The hierarchy for ethics review in South Africa is thus clear.

All HRECs are required to register with the NHREC. Outside of the required registration and reporting requirements, HRECs are expected to be independent and have a terms of reference; Standard Operating Procedures (SOPs), which should be available to members via the internet or intranet; and a code of conduct provided by the host institution. Even with the use of SOPs, the Guidelines note that ethics must not become "mechanical" but must undergo a case-by-case analysis.[99] They are also required to review research according to the level of accreditation given to them by the NHREC.

The composition of ethics review committees is a key matter in effectiveness and functionality. Research ethics committees are required to be, amongst other things, "independent, multi-disciplinary, multi-sectoral and pluralistic."[100] Membership of research ethics committees in South Africa is defined by the Guidelines – there is a requirement of at least nine members, a simple majority of whom can constitute a quorum; at least one layperson; and at least one member with knowledge of, and current experience in, the professional care, counselling, or health-related treatment of people. Such a member might be a medical practitioner, psychologist, social worker, or nurse; there must also be at least one member with professional training and experience in qualitative research methodologies, a member with expertise in biostatistics, a member with expertise in research ethics, and at least one member who is legally qualified. Research ethics committees are required to have a chairperson. Members of ethics committees are required to have research ethics training, with a refresher undertaken at least once during the membership of the committee. The Guidelines do not specify where the training may take place and if it should be accompanied by certification.

While much-deserved focus is placed on the functioning of health research ethics committees in terms of logistics, resources, composition, and independence, all crucial aspects of their work, not much has been said in the literature about the interplay between law and ethics in the implementation of ethics oversight in African countries. Certainly, the training of members of HRECs must include training on the legal framework: in South Africa's case, relevant provisions of the National Health Act. However, legal issues such as the understanding of the legal framework for health research and scrutiny of agreements

---

97 Section 4.6.
98 Section 5.2.3.
99 See generally Section 4 and Section 4.5.
100 Section 4.3.2.

between communities and researchers, and between researchers and participants have not yet received much attention. Interestingly, the Guidelines makes reference to key cases that have been decided in South African courts on legal issues such as insurance. They also provide for a Legal and Regulatory Working Group as part of the working groups under the NHREC. The research on other African countries shows that this is not often the case and is therefore an innovative aspect that is well worth emulating, given the legal issues that arise in the context of health research and health research regulation.

Drug regulatory body

With respect to clinical trials, in addition to ethics review, approval must also be obtained from the SAHPRA. The SAHPRA began work in 2017 and replaced the Medicines Control Council (MCC), which previously regulated drug clinical trials in the country. The MCC was established as an oversight body for the regulation of medicines by the Medical Registration and Related Substances Act of 1965,[101] amended most recently in 2008[102] and 2015.[103] The 2008 amendment brought into existence the SAHPRA[104] which was operationalised in June 2017. In pursuance of its responsibilities under the Act, it established the Guidelines for Good Clinical Practice (GCP).[105] One of the key reasons for this replacement was to reduce the workload of the MCC which also included the regulation of the supply and distribution of medicines, and which led to significant delays in the approval of clinical trials. Studies conducted on the approval times for clinical trials by the MCC showed significant variability and unpredictability, and took much longer than ethics review approval by HRECs.[106]

A look at the pre-existing framework is thus relevant. Prior to the change, the MCC was responsible for reviewing all applications for the clinical trials of new drugs, including Phases I to IV, prior to the marketing of such drugs for consumption. Clinical trials are required to have MCC approval before commencement. Each application was passed through the Clinical Trial Committee of the MCC. This Committee considers the application from medical, scientific, and ethical perspectives in order to ensure the suitability, safety, quality, and efficacy of the investigational drug.[107] The basis for this consideration is primarily the GCP, first established in 2000 and revised in 2006.[108] They provide for the basic ethical requirements of informed consent, justice, study rationale, a balance of

---

101 *Medicines and Related Substances Act* 101 of 1965.
102 Medicines and Related Substances Amendment Act, No 72 of 2008.
103 Medicines and Related Substances Amendment Act, No 14 of 2015.
104 Section 1, Medicines and Related Substances Amendment Act, No 72 of 2008.
105 Section 15, Medicines and Related Substances Amendment Act, No 72 of 2008.
106 H Geldenhuys et al, "Analysis of Time to Regulatory and Ethical Approval of SATVI TB Vaccine Trials in South Africa" (2012) 103:2 S Afr Med J 85–88.
107 NIAIDS ClinRegs: South Africa.
108 Department of Health, *Guidelines for Good Practice in the Conduct of Clinical Trials with Human Participants in South Africa* (Pretoria, South Africa: Department of Health, 2006).

harm and benefit, transparency, and privacy. The GCP recognise the fundamental place of ethics review. Apart from the role of the HRECs and the NHREC, the Data and Safety Monitoring Committees are recognised as important in the ethics review of clinical trials. These committees provide oversight in regard to overseeing ongoing clinical trials, managing issues such as safety and adverse events. SAHPRA which replaces the MCC is also part of the ethics review infrastructure of clinical trials in South Africa. It reviews ethical issues as part of its overall oversight function.[109]

The GCP emphasises the requirement for clinical trials registration by the principal investigator in the South Africa Clinical Trials Registry (SANCTR) prior to trial commencement. Other key actors and their responsibilities are identified – principal investigator (who should be a South African-based scientist), sponsor, contract research organisations monitor, auditor, and inspector. These last actors are required to ensure that the trials are conducted according to the GCP and other relevant guidelines. Amongst other requirements, the GCP provides that innovative research which involves therapy for one or more patients requires extra attention from the research ethics committee, which should ensure that proper provisions are made for the long-term care and observation of participants, and for maintenance and security. It also provides specific requirements for emergency research, research involving vulnerable persons, and research with collectives, in the latter case requiring the trial to be relevant to such groups and an engagement of such groups in all aspects of the research, including the planning phase.

The GCP is compulsory for clinical trials conduct in South Africa; however legal requirements under the National Health Act supersede the requirements of the GCP in the event of a conflict. The Ethics Guidelines are also a bedrock for the ethical conduct of clinical trials in South Africa. HRECs are required to conduct ethics reviews in line with the Ethics Guidelines.

With respect to the transition to SAPHRA it has been noted that:

> The transition process is a complex one, involving, among others, the constitution of a new authority in terms of the Public Finance Management Act, the appointment of a Board, and the transfer of existing MCC secretariat staff to the new authority. In order to effect a seamless transition, the Council will continue to perform its current functions, and its decisions, procedures and activities will be deemed to be those of the new authority, until the latter comes into existence.[110]

Given how recent the change to the SAHPRA is, it is too early to evaluate its work. The remit of SAHPRA has been expanded to include both approval of medicines (including complementary medicines) and medical devices. More importantly, it is expected to build on the existing regulatory framework for clinical

---

109 Section 1.2 of the Good Clinical Practice Guidelines.
110 Andy Gray & Yousouf Vawda, "Health Policy and Legislation" in *South Africa Health Review* (2016) 3–15 at 15.

trials in South Africa but most probably in a more efficient fashion that will allow for quicker reviews of new drugs and devices.

Health professional bodies

In South Africa, the umbrella professional body for health professionals has recently made ethical guidelines for health researchers: *General Ethical Guidelines for Health Researchers 2016*.[111] The Health Professional Council of South Africa is established by the Health Professions Act to regulate the conduct of health professionals in the country.[112]

In general, these guidelines align with the National Health Act to which it makes specific reference. It is instructive that the Guidelines do not specifically mention the Ethics Guidelines or the GCP. However, it does require that health professionals "observe and keep up to date with the ethical and regulatory frameworks that affect health research."[113] It also requires that researchers comply with the law. Where, however, the ethical standard is higher than the legal standards, health professionals involved in research must conform with the higher standard.[114] Researchers are also expected to comply with the requirements of the regulatory bodies such as the MCC (now SAPPHRA).[115]

Following from this, health professionals who are involved in research must submit protocols for ethics review as required under the National Health Act. The HRECs to whom they submit their protocols must be registered by the NHREC.[116] Health professionals involved in research are required to report any "inadequate or inappropriate reviews of research protocols" to the Council.[117] This is an interesting requirement which raises the question about what the Council is empowered to do in that situation: does the Council report to the NHREC which has authority over HRECs? Or does it take any action over such HRECs?

Health professionals must also ensure that their research is relevant to the community. Key principles such as the principles of beneficence, justice, and non-maleficence, and the necessary actions flowing from these – informed consent, privacy, and confidentiality. It emphasises non-discrimination by researchers, including in the selection of participants and communities in which research

---

111 Health Professions Council of South Africa, Ethical and Professional Rules of the Health Professions Council of South Africa as Promulgated in Government Gazette R717/2006 – *General Ethical Guidelines for Health Researchers* (Booklet 13). Pretoria: Health Professions Council of South Africa, 2016.
112 Health Professions Act.
113 Section 8.1.2.3.
114 Section 9.4.
115 Section 10.
116 Section 10.1.3.
117 Section 10.1.5.

is to place. It addresses the thorny ethical issues largely in line with the Ethics Guidelines. For example, the use of placebos is only permitted in the absence of proven effective treatment. Research participants are to have access to the best proven prophylactic, diagnostic, and therapeutic methods identified by the research.[118] There is an emphasis on ensuring that the health professional provides information to the participant, clearly distinguishing for such participants what is healthcare and what is health research in the procedures undertaken. Further, health professionals should "Ensure that research participants understand that the health researcher's role as a researcher differs from their role as health care practitioners."[119] In addition, health professionals should provide access to healthcare over the course of research and, where this is not possible, direct participants to another healthcare practitioner or healthcare centre. These are very important responsibilities conferred on health professionals. However, while they may be helpful guidelines, they may not be easy to implement in practice. There are also guidelines relating to relationships with other researchers, such as not making disparaging comments about fellow health professionals to research participants and not hindering other colleagues who want to pursue research in similar fields.

In multinational research, the Principal Investigator is required to be permanently based in South Africa; this stops just short of saying that such an investigator must be South African. The Investigator must also be registered with the Health Professionals Council of South Africa.[120]

Discipline is one key component of the regulatory functions of health professional bodies. The Guidelines require that scientific misconduct be reported to the Council. Scientific misconduct is defined broadly to include "fabrication, falsification, or plagiarism in proposing, performing, or reviewing research, or in reporting research results"[121] but also failure to obtain informed consent, inappropriate disclosure of research participant data, deviation from approved protocol, falsification of credentials, and deception in the research proposal.[122] The Guidelines do not specifically state what would happen if such a report were made. To determine this, resort must be had to general parts of the Guidelines which provide the sanctions for misconduct.[123]

The Guidelines are quite recent, and research for this book did not reveal whether scientific misconduct in the course of research has been brought before the Council since the Guidelines for researchers were established in 2016.

---

118 Section 6.6.2.
119 Section 6.6.5.
120 Section 8.
121 Section 9.2.
122 Section 9.2.
123 Health Professions Council of South Africa, Ethical and Professional Rules of the Health Professions Council of South Africa as Promulgated in Government Gazette R717/2006 – *Guidelines for Good Practice in the Health Care Professions* (Booklet 2). Pretoria: Health Professions Council of South Africa, 2008.

However, failure to obtain informed consent before medical procedures has attracted sanctions under earlier guidelines for ethical conduct in healthcare practice.[124] Under the Guidelines, sanctions can range from the application of fines against a practitioner to the removal of a practitioner's name from the register.

Civil society organisations

It may be recalled that during the HIV/AIDS crisis in South Africa in the 1990s, with skyrocketing rates of HIV infections and high prices of patented antiretroviral drugs, worsened by government denialism, civil society organisations like Treatment Access Campaign (TAC) eventually pushed the government into action to tackle the problems. An umbrella group – People Living with Cancer – also advocates for people living with cancer in South Africa. Groups supporting persons living with HIV/AIDS also exist. Each of these groups may also advocate for the interests of research participants who are living with these conditions, including research-related interests. However, at the present time, there does not appear to be an advocacy group dedicated to the support of research participants.[125]

Analysis and assessment of current governance arrangements

South Africa's research regulatory landscape, as described in the foregoing pages, is sophisticated and arguably one of the most organised in Africa. The country's long experience with clinical trials and research review provides a head start in matters of research governance, especially when compared with other African countries. The Ethics Guidelines and the GCP address key regulatory and ethical concerns that have been the subject of controversy in the globalisation of health research debate.

With respect to substantive ethics, placebo-controlled trials are allowed under the GCP when there is no effective treatment. This position is aligned with the Helsinki Declaration on this issue and clarifies what had hitherto been a controversial issue. More generally, the Ethics Guidelines 2015 specifically endorse the Helsinki Declaration (2013), aligning South Africa's ethical framework with the international and most authoritative guideline for ethical research, and other international guidelines, such as the CIOMS Guidelines.

Informed consent for research participation is a constitutional requirement, underscoring the importance conferred on the concept in South Africa. Furthermore, the adoption of a legal framework as a key component of research governance provides the necessary legal force to the governance arrangements,

124 Earlier analyses indicate application of sanctions for other types of medical malpractice; see Willem A Hoffman & Nick Nortje, "Patterns of unprofessional conduct by medical practitioners in South Africa (2007–2013)" (2016) 58 S Afr Fam Prac 108–113.
125 See Wemos, *supra* Note 13.

providing protections for all who are involved in the research enterprise, researchers, and research participants. The establishment of a Clinical Trials Registry which is mandated by law makes it possible to obtain data on how many clinical trials are being undertaken and even to trace issues such as the relevance of such clinical trials.

Experimental medicines are becoming an important consideration with public health emergencies in Africa and around the world. The Ethics Guidelines discuss unproven or experimental medicines and technologies, a growing issue in the era of epidemics and pandemics where cures may not be available, such as in the recent Ebola Virus Disease epidemic in West Africa. The Guidelines require the enforcement of the right to health as articulated in the Constitution of South Africa,[126] the National Health Act's provision for experimental health research,[127] the necessity of ethics review approval prior to the research and use in a patient, and the provisions of the Helsinki Declaration requiring expert advice, appropriate informed consent, and subsequent formal research of the experimental therapy.[128] There is therefore reasonable clarity about how to manage access to experimental medicines in the context of research governance.

In addition, ethics review is a legal requirement. Moreover, the ethics review process is streamlined. The hierarchy of ethics review is clear – from the NHREC to accredited HRECs. So, too, are the powers conferred on HRECs to approve and monitor research. The requirement of registration and accreditation provides some assurance of quality. The law plays a crucial role, providing a legal foundation for this.

The recent Guidelines for health researchers developed by the Health Professions Council of South Africa, the regulatory body for all health professionals in South Africa, lends much support to the existing legal and ethical framework. It provides another channel for regulating the conduct of researchers and ensuring accountability. Its requirement that health professionals abide by existing legal and ethical rules of conduct relating to research in South Africa ensures the coordination of the guidance received by researchers and eliminates confusion.

However, the current framework has not eliminated all challenges with research governance. In the area of ethics review, as some of the challenges indicate, for example with the Bezowda case and with the placebo-controlled trials, problems arise with both implementation and substantial ethical understanding. From a substantive ethics perspective, there remain issues, for instance, around matters such as placebo-controlled trials and research with children. Research shows that despite strict provisions on the use of placebos in the GCP, South Africa appears to have a high rate of placebo-controlled trials, including, in some cases, where there is effective treatment.[129] Some of these trials also include children. Research with children is a tricky terrain in research ethics generally and even more so with

---

126 Section 27 of the Constitution.
127 Section 11 of the National Health Act.
128 Article 37 of the Helsinki Declaration.
129 Wemos, at 12–18.

non-therapeutic research where children do not stand to benefit directly from the research. Here, the legal framework contributes significantly to clarifying the requirements. The provisions of the National Health Act, which took effect from 2012, especially the provision requiring the Minister's consent for non-therapeutic research involving children, has been argued to be overly broad and restrictive, which may preclude much-needed research. This is especially because the Act provides a broad definition of "health research," and it does not except minimal-risk research.[130] However, this criticism must be balanced against the possibility of harm to children in research, especially when they do not stand to gain direct medical benefits. Regulations drawn up under the Act in 2014 emphasise this point and define "significant" risk as provided under the Act. The regulations also allow a delegated authority to consent on the Minister's behalf.[131] There remain disparities between the Ethical Guidelines (broad types of consent in different scenarios) and the law (requiring parental and child consent) with respect to how and from whom consent should be obtained, which may prove problematic to ethics review committees.[132] What is evident, however, is that there is ongoing interest and discussion on the subject of research with children, the ethical considerations and legal safeguards of which, when compared with other countries to be considered in this book, must be seen as clearly positive.

With regard to implementation, studies have noted that health research ethics committees in South Africa are typically well organised.[133] The requirements for registration and accreditation of HRECs are now clear and underpinned by law. However, while the requirements are clear, they have not always been practiced seamlessly. HRECs face conflict of interest issues and a lack of empowerment to enforce their decisions in some instances. A 2012 audit by the NHREC revealed some issues of concern: for example, several of the RECs approved all the research protocols presented to them, and overall only 1 per cent of all submitted protocols did not get approved, giving the impression that protocols were rubberstamped. A significant number of RECs, 45 per cent of them, were not sure if the approved protocols were adhered to, raising the issue of monitoring and the effective protection of research participants.[134] While the Ethics Guidelines require the monitoring of clinical trials and other research involving

130 See Ann E Strode et al, "One Step Forward, Two Steps Back – Requiring Ministerial Approval for All 'Non-Therapeutic' Health Research Involving Minors" (2007) 97:3 S Afr Med J 200; Ann E Strode et al, "Failing the Vulnerable: Three New Consent Norms That Will Undermine Health Research with Children" (2014) 15:2 S Afr J HIV Med 46–49.

131 South African Government, *Regulations Relating to Research with Human Participants*. Government Gazette No. R 719 of September19, 2014, online: <http://research.ukzn. ac.za/Libraries/Research_Document/National_Regulations_Relating_to_Research_With_ Human_Participants_R719_of_2014.sflb.ashx> (February 25, 2015).

132 AE Strode & CM Slack, "Child Research in South Africa: How Do the New Regulations Help?" (2015) 105:11 SAMJ 899.

133 Keymanthri Moodley & Landon Myers, "Health Research Ethics Committees in South Africa 12 Years into Democracy" (2007) 8:1 BMC Med Ethics 1.

134 Wemos, at 8–9.

humans, there are challenges related to resources. Monitoring obviously requires resources, as do other aspects of research review. Institutions are required to fund the HRECs, and this is not always done.[135]

MCC reviews for clinical trials have often suffered delays. It is hoped that with the coming in of the SAPPHRA, these delays will be a thing of the past. After trials are approved, it is the responsibility of monitors to report any problems under the GCP. But the monitoring process can be convoluted, with Clinical Research Organisations (CROs) hiring the monitors, and then reporting to the pharmaceutical companies who have employed such CROs to undertake the trials. Although the principal investigator remains primarily responsible for what occurs, a convoluted monitoring process and limited resources for monitoring by RECs can mean that research participants are not properly protected.[136]

Apart from resources for monitoring, providing resources for persons working on ethics review committees is also a challenge. Chairpersons in South Africa do not work full time in their positions on ethics review committees, nor do they appear to have special resources at their disposal to carry out their work. Indeed, besides other responsibilities, they are also required to liaise with the NHREC. Whether the position of chair can be a full-time position with appropriate remuneration or be supported with other resources is an issue that requires closer attention because other demands on their time may affect the quality of ethics review.[137] Remuneration, no matter how little, for members of ethics review committees is also worth paying attention to. Further, resourcing for ethics review committees is a serious challenge. Even so, South Africa's health research ethics committees likely have more resources than in other countries, given that many have dedicated offices, and a functioning clinical trials registry exists, amongst other indicators of provision of resources.

HRECs also face challenges related to complying with the composition requirements of the Guidelines. These challenges have included gender and racial imbalance in the composition of ethics review committees and the resource differences between the richer, usually white universities and the historically disadvantaged black universities. Some of these are a result of South Africa's racial history[138] but remain critical precisely because of the need to overcome this history. The imbalance also extended to disciplines, with the health sciences and clinicians in the majority. In addition to not allowing sufficient diversity of views, the imbalance also raises the possibility of undue pressure if members submitted their protocols to their institutional health research ethics committees.

---

135 *Ibid.*
136 Wemos, *ibid.* at 12. See also M van Huijstee & I Schipper, *Putting Contract Research Organisations on the Radar. An Exploratory Study on the Outsourcing of Clinical Trials by Pharmaceutical Companies to Contract Research Organizations in Non-Traditional Regions* (2011).
137 For a similar view, see Mary Kasule et al, "Silent Voices: Current and Future Roles of African Research Ethics Committee Administrators" (2016) 38:1 IRB: Ethics and Human Research 13.
138 See Moodley & Myers.

Finally, there are hardly any advocacy organisations that focus on research participants' protections in South Africa.[139] The implication of this is that, outside individual advocacy, there are few organisations that work on ensuring that other stakeholders in the governance process are adhering to legal rules and ethics guidelines. This is a gap, therefore, that requires addressing.

Conclusion

South Africa is a much sought-after destination for health research in Africa. Over the past two decades, it has developed a sophisticated research governance infrastructure. In sum, the research governance framework of South Africa is extensive and continues to be developed. While many of the ethical issues have received attention, and while there is a legal framework for research governance, there are challenges in the effective implementation of the policies. Even so, there is certainly much that other African countries can learn from the research governance infrastructure of South Africa.

139 See Wemos, *supra* Note 13.

6 Health research governance in Nigeria

Introduction

Nigeria is a lower-middle-income developing country in sub-Saharan Africa. It is Africa's most populous country, with an estimated population of over a 190 million people, approximately a quarter of Africa's population.[1] A former British colony, Nigeria is a democratic federal republic with a multiparty political system. After 29 years spent under intermittent bouts of military rule, in 1999, it became a democracy. Although blessed with many resources, including oil, solid minerals, and human resources, it has been besieged by political instability, weak leadership, military rule, human rights abuses, ethnic and tribal conflicts, corruption, mismanagement, and many squandered opportunities to effectively utilise its relatively vast resources to provide a high standard of living for its many citizens. Notwithstanding these weaknesses Nigeria remains a regional force, the continent's most populous country, and one of its largest economies.

Nigeria's health profile is a mixture of high rates of infectious diseases, a growing non-communicable diseases (NCD) challenge, and relatively low life expectancy rates. The life expectancy in Nigeria is estimated at 56 years for females and 53 years for males. There are high prevalence rates of malaria and HIV, and meningitis is endemic in some parts of the country. Over three million people are infected with HIV,[2] one of the highest numbers in the world. Infectious diseases such as Lassa fever, cholera, cerebrospinal meningitis, measles, tuberculosis, and yellow fever are prevalent in certain parts of the country and remain a significant cause of morbidity and mortality.[3] In addition, there are high rates of maternal and infant mortality. NCDs such as hypertension, cardiovascular problems, diabetes, and cancer are growing issues of concern, with few coordinated efforts to address the rising prevalence. While there are significant prevalence rates of mental health challenges, with estimates of about 30 per cent prevalence,[4] this

---

1 World Bank, Wrld BankOpen Data, 2017 <https://data.worldbank.org/country/nigeria>
2 UNAIDS, AIDS Info, online: <http://aidsinfo.unaids.org/>.
3 National Bureau of Statistics, Nigeria Health Profile, online: <http://nso.nigeria.opendataforafrica. org/tzpws/nigeria-health-profile>.
4 Mental Health Leadership and Advocacy Program, Mental Health Situation Analysis in Nigeria, (2012), online: <www.mhlap.org/jdownloads/.../mental_health_situation_analysis_ in_nigeria.doc>.

remains largely neglected. Nigeria's healthcare system was ranked 187th out of 191 members of the World Health Organisation (WHO) in 2000, making it one of the worst healthcare systems in the world. The lack of coordinated efforts by the different levels of governments and development agencies in the execution of health programmes has seriously impeded improvements in healthcare delivery in Nigeria and led to a duplication of efforts and waste of resources. More recently, a high rate of medical error and patient safety concerns has been noted in research – Nigeria received an aggregate score of 39 out of a possible 100 on the Health Care Quality Index, which measures Health Access Quality (HAQ) globally on the indicator of adverse medical treatment in the period between 1999 and 2015.[5] But this remains a back-burner issue. Gender-based violence is considerable, with an estimated one in three women suffering violence on account of their gender.[6] This is similar to rates of violence against children, where six out of ten children, by the age of 18, have been noted to suffer physical, sexual, or emotional violence, with the attendant health consequences.[7] Health status is often dependent on income status, with Nigeria ranking low on the equity index.[8] Health expenditures are low, even by comparison with other African countries, with the latest health budget representing 3.8 per cent of the 2018 budget, much less than the 10–15 per cent recommended by the WHO to be devoted to health[9] or the 15 per cent of the annual budget to which Nigeria committed itself in the *Abuja Declaration on HIV/AIDS, Tuberculosis and Other Related Diseases.*[10] However, although Nigeria faces many challenges in health, its decisive and effective management of the Ebola crisis in 2014 indicated that, with sufficient political will, the country has the potential to improve its health system and improve its health profile.

The country provides an interesting context within which to study research governance in the African context – its large population provides a significant pool of potential research participants and a significant and growing number of potential researchers. It also has a significant burden of disease and thus a great need for health research. In this regard, it has a relatively long history of being a

---

5　GBD 2015 Healthcare Access and Quality Collaborators, "Healthcare Access and Quality Index Based on Mortality from Causes Amenable to Personal Health Care in 195 Countries and Territories, 1990–2015: A Novel Analysis from the Global Burden of Disease Study 2015" (2017) Lancet, online: <http://thelancet.com/pdfs/journals/lancet/PIIS0140-6736(17)30818-8.pdf>.

6　National Population Commission and ICF International, Nigeria Demographic and Health Survey, 2013.

7　National Population Commission, Violence against Children Survey, 2014.

8　WHO, Global Health Observatory, Equity Country Profiles: Nigeria, online: <who.int/gho/health_equity/countries/en/>

9　WHO, "Proposal on Innovative Sources of Funding to Stimulate Research and Development Related to Diseases that Disproportionately Affect Developing Countries," online: <www.who.int/phi/Nigeria.pdf> (March 23, 2010). A study has also pointed out that all the research funding provided by the government to Nigerian universities did not exceed 0.03 per cent of the GDP. See Donwa, *supra* Note 93 at 3.

10　*Abuja Declaration on HIV/AIDS, Tuberculosis and Other Related Diseases* OAU/SPS/ABUJA 3.

site of medical research, beginning in colonial times. The significant burden of HIV, malaria, etc. continues to provide fertile ground for research. Nigeria has the third highest burden of HIV in absolute terms, providing room for a lot of clinical research. Public health diseases such as Lassa fever, polio, and meningitis continue to present challenges and have received attention from a research perspective. A research study conducted by Pfizer on meningitis in the 1990s has received much attention in the literature and is often cited as an example of the room for exploitation that exists in many African countries. Still research remains at a relatively rudimentary stage, with relatively little government attention. A significant amount of research is funded by international bodies.

Research governance in Nigeria is underpinned by the National Health Act enacted in 2014 and other policies examined in this chapter.

Health research in Nigeria

Health research in Nigeria has a long history which predates Nigeria's independence from the British colonial regime in 1960.[11] Although recent by Western standards, medical research has been undertaken in Nigeria for many decades, beginning with the establishment of the Rockefeller Foundation Yellow Fever Commission in 1920. The Yellow Fever Foundation, as it was popularly called, built a Research Unit in Yaba, Lagos, in 1925, where research on yellow fever was conducted. It is not clear from available sources whether this was meant to benefit Nigerians. But this is unlikely.[12] From about 1932, the Uzuakoli Leprosy Research Unit became operational, first as a clinic which treated Nigerians but eventually also as a hub of research on leprosy.[13]

In 1952, the British government established the University College Hospital (UCH) at the University College Ibadan. The UCH had been a campus of the University of London since 1948. The UCH was mandated under the *University College Hospital Act, Laws of the Federation of Nigeria and Lagos, 1958*, amongst other things, to conduct medical research.[14] In 1957, a facility for clinical research was commissioned at the University of Ibadan.

In 1954, the British colonial government made provisions for research funding in colonial territories, leading to the formation of the West African Council

---

11 Olajide Ajayi, "Health Research in Nigeria," Online: Oxford Research Forum. See also Adetokunbo O Lucas, "Health Research in Africa: Priorities, Promise, and Performance" (1989) 569:1 Ann N Y Acad Sci 1 at 17. See also Remigius N Nwabueze, "Ethical Review of Research Involving Human Subjects in Nigeria: Legal and Policy Issues" (2003–2004) 14 Ind Intl & Comp L Rev 87.

12 Moses Ochonu, "'Native Habits are Difficult to Change': British Medics and the Dilemmas of Biomedical Discourses and Practice in Early Colonial Northern Nigeria" (2004) 5:1 J Colonialism & Colonial Hist, noting that "Colonial medicine was about keeping British colonial personnel healthy."

13 Uzuakoli Leprosy Research Unit, online: <http://leprosyhistory.org/database/archive1015>.

14 Chapter 215, Section 3. As Nwabueze observes, other teaching hospitals established subsequently have been mandated similarly. Nwabueze, *supra* Note 11.

for Medical Research for the West African territories of Nigeria, Ghana, Gambia, and Sierra Leone.[15] According to the Ordinance which established it,[16] its functions included organising medical research in the territories and providing information obtained therewith to the British government. The West African Council for Medical Research consisted of four research units dedicated to helminthiasis, virology, hot climate physiology, and haematological research. With the establishment of universities in Nigeria like the University of Ibadan and the University of Lagos, the West African Council for Medical Research, whose activities had previously extended to other West African British colonies like Ghana, was dismantled in 1962.

The Medical Research Council of Nigeria, established by military decree in 1972,[17] took over the responsibilities of the West African Council for Health Research. In 1977, the *National Science and Technology Development Agency Decree* repealed the decree which established the Medical Research Council of Nigeria and instituted the National Science and Technology Development Agency. The Agency's mandate was to advise the federal government on matters relating to scientific research and development. The responsibilities and assets of the Medical Research Council of Nigeria were subsequently transferred to the National Institute for Medical Research established by the *Research Institute's Order of 1977.*[18] Mabey notes that many examples exist of trials in developing countries like Nigeria which have influenced clinical and public health practice, even in the developed world.[19] One of the examples he cites is of a trial of chloramphenicol sponsored by the United Kingdom Medical Research Council in Zaria, Northern Nigeria, in 1973 and carried out by researchers at the Ahmadu Bello University, Zaria. This trial showed that, for the treatment of Group A meningococcal meningitis, a single therapy of chloramphenicol was more effective than sulphonamides. It was also as effective, simpler to use, and much cheaper than large and frequent doses of penicillin, the standard drug at the time.[20] This was at a time when combination therapy was the norm in many industrialised countries.[21]

It is clear from the brief history provided here that interest in health research has existed for a long time in Nigeria and even predates Nigeria as an independent country. Today, there remains a clear need for health research, perhaps best

---

15 Ajayi, *supra* Note 11.

16 *West African Council for Medical Research Ordinance,* Laws of the Federation of Nigeria and Lagos, Cap. 215 (1958).

17 Medical Research Council, Decree No 1.

18 *Research Institute's (Establishment etc) Order of 1977,* Annual Volume of the Laws of the Federal Republic of Nigeria (1977). See The Nigerian Institute of Medical Research, "About NIMR" online: <www.nimr.gov.ng/aboutus.php?page=an> (February 22, 2010).

19 David Mabey, "Importance of Clinical Trials in Developing Countries" (1996) 348 Lancet 1113.

20 HC Whittle et al, "Trial of Chloramphenicol for Meningitis in Northern Savanna of Africa" (1973)3 BMJ 379.

21 Mabey, Note 20.

exemplified by the low rates of life expectancy. In the context of Nigeria, the HIV/AIDS epidemic is a significant threat, and it has attracted a lot of research, some of which has been on social issues like stigma. Research continues to be required on problems like cancer, mental health stigma, health consequences, prevention of sexual and domestic violence, and the impact of vehicular accidents and road safety. Other common diseases in Nigeria, like malaria (which continues to be the most significant health issue in the country), and infectious diseases, such as trypanosomiasis (sleeping sickness), require further research to provide more effective, less drug-resistant, less expensive treatments and vaccines. Non-infectious diseases such as diabetes, cancer, and heart disease, which are affecting an increasing number of Nigerians, also need to be studied. Apart from treatments, research needs to be undertaken to provide better disease prevention behaviours and methods (some of which might be established from studies on environmental and genetic determinants of non-infectious diseases) and more cost-effective devices. These diseases could be studied in other countries. However, genetic differences, such as among the Yorubas of Nigeria, who have a high twinning rate, may make Nigeria not only attractive to researchers but perhaps even necessary for the development of some interventions. For instance, Nigeria is part of a six-country consortium involved in the HapMap project, which is significant because of the potential information it could provide about the human genome and the effect it could have on the rest of the world. Yorubas from Ibadan, Nigeria, were recruited for the project.[22] Further research is necessary to provide cost-effective interventions and interventions that can be easily utilised in a resource-constrained setting like Nigeria. The potential benefits of health research could include other related gains to the country, such as the improvement of the quality of healthcare services offered to the population and an increase in the country's capacity to participate in the international research enterprise. This may also include possible contribution to economic development and growth by providing employment, equipment, training, and income to local researchers and their institutions; transferring skills; and ensuring the retention of talented individuals who may otherwise be lost to the country.

Nigeria's National Health Policy, 2016, notes the existence of research structures such as the National Institutes of Medical Research (NIMR) and the National Institute for Pharmaceutical Research and Development. However, it also notes that research is underfunded, that there is insufficient research, and that the results of research are often not used effectively in policy implementation.[23] Given the clear need for health research in Nigeria, what is the current policy for health research? The current policy on health research in Nigeria is embodied in several policies, including the *National Health Policy*; the *National Drug*

---

22 See The International HapMap Consortium, "The International HapMap Project" (2003) 426 Nature 789. Elizabeth G Phimister, "Genomic Cartography—Presenting the HapMap" (2005) 353:17 N Engl J Med 1766. See A Akinboro, MA Azeez, & AA Bakare, "Frequency of Twinning in Southwest Nigeria" (2008) 14:2 Indian J Hum Genet 41.

23 Federal Ministry of Health, National Health Policy, 2016.

Policy,[24] most recently revised in 2005; and the *National Child Health Policy*, 2006.[25] The most important policy on research, however, is embedded in the National Policy on Health Research, 2016.

The National Policy on Health Research provides the criteria for identifying the key priority areas for research: severity of the health problem, magnitude of the problem, socio-economic importance, feasibility, availability of funding, and emerging health issues. Such prioritisation is required every five years. The Policy identifies the current priorities for health research in the country: namely, communicable diseases such as malaria, HIV/AIDS, sexually transmitted infections (STIs), tuberculosis, diarrhoeal diseases, acute respiratory infections, neglected diseases, other notifiable diseases, and emerging and re-emerging infections; non-communicable diseases, including nutrition-related diseases, smoking-related diseases, cardiovascular diseases and other systemic diseases, haemoglobinopathies, mental health including substance abuse, cancers, and diabetes mellitus; improved diagnosis, treatment, and prevention; accidents and injuries; reproductive health, including determinants of and prevention of maternal mortality, cervical cancer prevention, gender-based violence, unsafe abortions, and sexual dysfunction; child health and adolescent health (childhood nutrition, sexuality, sexual violence, aggressive/violent behaviour, cultism, peer pressure, youth-friendly health services, etc.); occupational health; sociocultural factors in health such as perceptions and reactions to STIs, HIV/AIDS, female genital mutilation (FGM), early marriage, health beliefs, and healthcare-seeking behaviours; medical products development; traditional medicine; health systems; healthcare financing; health sector reform; and transdisciplinary research to support national health priorities. One of the functions of the National Health Research Committee, a creation of the National Health Act,[26] is to ensure that the health research agenda is focussed on priority health problems. The focus of the National Policy on Health Research closely reflects the challenges that are currently significant parts of Nigeria's health profile.

In addition, the National Child Health Policy requires the Federal Ministry of Health to initiate and support research relevant to child development in collaboration with different organisations. It also requires that ministries of health and other institutions be supported in order to enhance their capability to undertake relevant research in child survival, development, protection, and participation.[27]

Health research in Nigeria, as in many developing countries, is a complex issue with different angles. These angles include the fact that Nigeria needs health research, but not enough is currently taking place. Another angle is that the

---

24 Federal Ministry of Health, *National Drug Policy* (Abuja, Federal Ministry of Health, 2005).
25 The Federal Ministry of Health, *National Child Health Policy* (Abuja, Federal Ministry of Health, 2006).
26 Section 31 of the National Health Act.
27 Sections 3.5 and 4.16 of the Child Health Policy, at 14 and 46. Local government councils have a similar mandate under the policy.

government has directed insufficient resources for health research in Nigeria. Yet another angle is that external sponsors, as in many developing countries, support a significant amount of health research. Further, there is the challenge of setting national health research priorities and ensuring that those priorities are met and that all of the research that does take place is effectively regulated. I address these different angles in explaining the current state of health research in Nigeria briefly in the following.

With about 129 universities and over 40 medicals schools, several of which have public health programmes, there is a significant (though underutilised) number of avenues for health research, including research involving humans.[28] University lecturers, who also typically practise as clinicians, make up research teams.[29] Health research is conducted in all the medical schools (which have affiliated teaching hospitals) in Nigeria, with the more cosmopolitan schools in cities attracting the most research funding, including from external sources. Generally speaking, the government provides much of the funding for different kinds of research that takes place in Nigerian universities, including health research.[30]

The Federal Government also funds some research through research institutes, such as the Nigerian Institute of Medical Research, a parastatal of the Federal Ministry of Health, which carries out research on parasitic, infectious, and non-infectious diseases.[31] The National Institute for Pharmaceutical Research and Development was established by the government principally to advance indigenous pharmaceutical research and development, and enhance the development and commercialisation of pharmaceutical raw materials, drugs, and biological products.[32] The Institute has produced and is currently marketing a drug for the treatment of sickle cell disease, Niprisan.[33] Another is the National Institute for Trypanosomiasis Research, which conducts research into the pathology, immunology, and methods of treatment of trypanosomiasis or sleeping sickness. Twenty research institutes operate as parastatals under the umbrella of the Federal Ministry of Science and Technology. Also involved in research is the

---

28 D Olaleye et al, "Enhancement of Health Research Capacity in Nigeria through North-South and In-Country Partnerships" (2014) 89:8 Acad Med S93–S97. Dianne Miller et al, "Knowledge Dissemination and Evaluation in a Cervical Cancer Screening Implementation Program in Nigeria" (2007) 107 Gynecol Oncol S196 at S197.

29 Patrick Okonta, "Ethics of Clinical Trials in Nigeria" (2014) 55:3 Niger Med J 188.

30 See PA Donwa, "Funding of Academic Research in Nigerian Universities," online: <http://portal.unesco.org/education/en/files/51642/11634301905Donwa-EN.pdf/Donwa-EN.pdf>.

31 Established by the Federal Government under the *Research Institute (Establishment etc) Order 1977*, pursuant to the *National Science and Technology Development Agency Decree* (No 5) of 1977, it succeeded the Medical Research Council of Nigeria created in 1972. The *National Science and Technology Development Agency Decree* repealed the *Medical Research Council Decree of 1972*. The Clinical Science division of the NIMR has the mandate to conduct research into "human health problems in Nigeria."

32 National Institute for Pharmaceutical Research and Development, online: <www.niprd.org/niprd>.

33 "May & Baker to Signs Sickle Cell Production Deal" The National Online, June 17, 2018, online: <thenationonlineng.net/may-baker-signs-sickle-cell-drug-production-deal/>.

Nigerian Natural Medicine Development Agency, a parastatal under the Federal Ministry of Science and Technology[34] whose main mission is to collate, document, research, preserve, develop, and promote traditional medicine practices and products in Nigeria.[35]

However, as acknowledged by the National Health Policy and the National Policy on Health Research, there is still an inadequate level of health research in Nigeria. This may, as some commentators suggest, be partly a result of potential participants' scepticism and mistrust, and limited technical knowledge and expertise.[36] But this has also largely been attributed to lack of government commitment to health research, even given the limited resources available.[37] In 2006, African governments in a High Level Ministerial Meeting on Health Research in Africa convened by the Federal Ministry of Health in Nigeria and the Ministry of Health in Ghana, through their Ministers of Health and Heads of Delegation, agreed, amongst other things, "To strive to ensure the allocation of 2% of the national health budget and to further mobilize other resources from national and international sources for health research."[38] This has not been implemented. The healthcare budget as a whole is minimal, as already noted (less than 4 per cent of the budget, much of which is spent primarily on salaries, compensation, and emolument, leaving very little for health research). The lack of a health research council, whose mandate would include funding health research in the country, is also evidence of insufficient understanding by the government of the necessity for health research in the Nigerian context. It has been argued that, despite infrastructural and personnel limitations, Nigeria remains an attractive venue for health research, including clinical trials. Ikeme, for instance, notes that

> Because of relative lack of access to medical treatment and medications, participating in a clinical trial is a unique and beneficial opportunity for many patients. Rapid recruitment is thus an advantage for conducting a clinical trial in Nigeria when compared to the Western countries. Despite these compelling qualities, a lot of myths still exist about the country's capacity for trials.[39]

34   It is mandated by statute to formulate, promote, administer, monitor, coordinate, and review science and technology policies and activities, including research in the health sciences.

35   Nigerian Natural Medicine Development Agency, "About NNMDA," online: <http://nignature med.net/index.php> (February 10, 2010). Some but not all of these institutes require human participants in carrying out their areas of research: for instance, the Nigerian Natural Medicine Development Agency does not carry out research involving humans.

36   See, for example, Darren Roblyer et al, "Objective Screening for Cervical Cancer in Developing Nations: Lessons from Nigeria" (2007) 107 Gynecol Oncol S94 at S96.

37   See also Christina Scott & Abiose Adelaja, "Key African Countries 'Not Keeping Health Research Promises'" (November 18, 2008), SciDev.net, online: <www.scidev.net/en/news/key-african-countries-not-keeping-health-research-.html> (February 22, 2014).

38   See Communique, High Level Ministerial Meeting on Health Research in Africa, Abuja, Nigeria, March 8–10, 2006, online: <http://whocc.who.ch/countries/nga/reports/Health_ Research_meeting_Communique.pdf> (March 2, 2017).

39   Anthony C Ikeme, "Nigeria's Clinical Trials Scene" (2008) App Clin Trials, online: <http:// appliedclinicaltrialsonline.findpharma.com/appliedclinicaltrials/CRO%2FSponsor+Articles/

Thus, there is both need and ample room for growth in health research to provide the necessary knowledge to improve health in Nigeria. Apart from the small and inadequate proportion of health research funded domestically, a significant amount of health research is, as in most African countries, funded by foreign sponsors, including multinational pharmaceutical companies, foreign governments, and foreign-based non-governmental organisations.[40] Several studies, including clinical trials, epidemiological studies, and social science health-related studies are, and continue to be, funded by external sponsors, such as the WHO Special Programme for Research and Training in Tropical Diseases and the United States National Institutes of Health (NIH).[41] Other foreign development initiatives which partner with developing countries, such as the European and Developing Countries Clinical Trials Partnership, have been very active in promoting clinical trials in Nigeria and other developing countries. The Family Health International, a non-governmental organisation, has sponsored many HIV prevention trials, including microbicides trials.

Additionally, although the level of drug research in developing countries is much lower than necessary, multinational pharmaceutical companies have conducted, and continue to sponsor, clinical trials for the purpose of testing new drug interventions in Nigeria.[42] A recent example is GlaxoSmithKline's Ebola vaccine trials.[43] Clinical trials are essential to understanding the peculiarities of certain disease conditions in Nigeria. But not as many occur as are needed.[44] Clinicaltrials.gov, a United States NIH database of clinical trials,

---

Nigerias-Clinical-Trial-Scene/ArticleStandard/Article/detail/522051> (February 2, 2010).

40 See Temidayo O Ogundiran, "Enhancing the African Bioethics Initiative" (2004) 4 BMC Med Educ 21.

  See the National Institute for Medical Research, online: <www.nimr-ng.org/> (October 4, 2008).

41 Among some of the studies funded by external sources are the NIH-sponsored studies of the social, environmental, and genetic determinants of hypertension in African populations; studies in breast cancer genetics; and studies in the genetic and environmental determinants of diabetes type 2. Patricia Marshall, "The Relevance of Culture and Informed Consent in U.S-Funded International Health Research" in NBAC, *Ethical and Policy Issues in International Research: Clinical Trials in Developing Countries*, Volume II (Commissioned Papers and Staff Analysis) (Bethesda, Maryland, 2001) at C-11.

42 See, for instance, BN Okeahialam et al, "Lacidipine in the Treatment of Hypertension in Black African People: Antihypertensive, Biochemical and Haematological Effects" (2000) 16:3 Curr Med Res & Opin 184.

43 This trial is registered in the National Clinical Trials Registry <www.nhrec,net/nctr>. It is also listed on Clinicaltrials.gov. In 2008 the government commissioned the first centre dedicated solely to clinical trials, donated by the multinational pharmaceutical company, GlaxoSmith-Kline, at the Lagos State University College of Medicine. See Zakariyya Adaramola, "Nigeria: Country Gets its First Clinical Trial Site," *Daily Trust*, (2 November 2008).

44 See, for instance, Osaro Erhabor et al, "Randomised Clinical Trials on Breast Cancer in Nigeria and Other Developing Countries: Challenges and Constraints" in Michael W Retsky & Ramono Demicheli, eds, *Perioperative Inflammation as Triggering Origin of Metastatis Development* (Cham: Springer International Publishing, 2017), 123–159. Clinical Trials: Omolara A Fatiregun, "A Key Tools in Improving Breast Cancer Survival in Nigeria" (2017) 35:15 J Clin

for example, has records of 123 studies compared to South Africa's 2,448 and Egypt's 2,090. Reportedly, Nigeria's drug regulatory agency, NAFDAC, had approved 50 Clinical Trials over a five-year period.[45] A Clinical Trials Registry was established in 2012 by the National Health Research Ethics Committee.[46]

Health research governance in Nigeria[47]

The history of research governance in Nigeria can be roughly divided into two broad stages: pre-2006, before the establishment of the National Code on Health Research Ethics, and post-2006, when the most recent and more concerted efforts were made to formalise governance arrangements in a national and country-wide manner. Many of the allegations of unethical research fall into the pre-2006 era. While health research was conducted during the colonial era, pre-1960, there are no documented attempts to establish mechanisms for research governance in Nigeria during colonial times.[48] An attempt was made to institutional health research, though not specifically its regulation, first through the establishment of the Medical Research Council of Nigeria by a decree of the Federal Government.[49] This decree was later amended to bring the Council under the National Science and Technology Development Agency Decree.[50] Nor were there any other documented efforts to establish such mechanisms in the post-independence era, until 1980, when the first attempts to create a formal regulatory structure began.

In a 1980 article,[51] Ajayi proposed a three-tier structure for research governance in Nigeria. This would consist of a National Ethical Committee, comprising biomedical researchers and social scientists, which would determine the relevance of proposals for research on large populations, articulate national health research priorities, and ensure that the source and funding of such programmes did not conflict with political goals and policies. The second tier was to be peer-review committees, to be situated in a hospital, communities, or

---

Oncol e18198Se. Onnaedi Okar, "Set Up More Clinical Trials in Nigeria – Health Stakeholders Urge," *Pulse* Nigeria (9 June 2015).

45 Onnaedi Okar, "Set Up More Clinical Trials in Nigeria – Health Stakeholders Urge," (9 June 2015) *Pulse*, Nigeria.

46 Nigeria Clinical Trials Registry - nhrec.net/nctr.

47 Excerpts from this chapter were previously published in Cheluchi Onyemelukwe, "The Legal Framework for Health Research Governance in Nigeria" (2011) 11: 2 Oxford Univ Commonw L J 143–170.

48 See Nwabueze, *supra* Note 11.

49 Decree No. 1 of 1972.

50 Decree No. 5 in 1977. See A Yakubu & A Adebamowo, "Implementing National System of Health Research Ethics Regulations: The Nigerian Experience" (2012) 1:1 BEOnline 4–15.

51 OO Ajayi, "Taboos and Clinical Research in West Africa" (1980) 6 J Med Ethics 61 at 62.

research institutes, which would review research proposals according to ethics standards. The third tier would be a subcommittee, situated in individual research departments or laboratories to determine scientific validity and technical competence. These suggestions appear to have been adopted to some degree. A national ethics review committee was established sometime afterwards in 1980. However, it became non-functioning as a result of lack of funding and lack of political interest.[52]

There appear to have been no significant activities with respect to research governance at the national level until 2002. Until 2002, there was no functioning national ethics review committee. Any reviews conducted at the national level were done through the Directorate of Clinical Services, Research, and Training in the Federal Ministry of Health.[53] At the institutional level, there were several ethics review committees in different institutions, particularly the teaching hospitals attached to some federal universities. Some of them had been established in the 1980s and had functioned sporadically over the years.[54] In the University of Ibadan, for instance, although the Ethics Board had existed since 1980, it became inactive, was poorly organised, had no standard operating procedures (SOPs), met infrequently, and had no funding from the university; furthermore, not many faculty knew about the board.[55] This is particularly interesting because the University College Hospital, Ibadan, is a pioneer medical establishment in Nigeria, and much of the externally sponsored health research which occurs in the country is conducted there. Researchers and staff at the University did not know of the existence of an ethics review committee in the institution, and the public had a negative perception of research practices in the hospital. The situation was unlikely to have been different in other institutions with even less research than the University of Ibadan. Indeed, it appeared that the few Nigerian institutions with ethics review committees which functioned at all provided ethics review of mainly collaborative studies (especially those conducted in collaboration with United States-based institutions).[56] Apart from any other reservations that one might have to this ad hoc manner of functioning, it could be argued, as Nwabueze argues, that research participants were likely to be denied "the protections afforded by the existence of a regular, functional, and competent ethics committee."[57]

---

52 EDCTP, "Support for Ethics Review Boards: Strengthening the National Health Research Ethics Committee of Nigeria (NHREC)" on file with the author.

53 Adefolarin O Malomo et al, "The Nigeria Experience" (2009) 6:4 J Acad Ethics 305.

54 See "Networking for Ethics on Biomedical Research in Africa (NEBRA): Final Report," online: <http://elearning.trree.org/file.php/1/NebraReport/FinalReport-2006-english.pdf> at 69–70.

55 Adeyinka G Falusi, Olufunmilayo I Olopade & Christopher O Olapade, "Establishment of a Standing Ethics/Institutional Review Board in a Nigerian University: A Blueprint for Developing Countries" (2007) 2:1 J Emp Res on Hum Res Ethics 21 at 22.

56 A Yakubu & A Adebamowo, *supra* Note 50.

57 Nwabueze, *supra* Note 11 at 104.

According to a survey conducted between 2003 and 2005, there were 30 ethics review committees in institutions in Nigeria in the early 2000s.[58] These institutions were mainly in federal institutions, including the major teaching hospitals, some of the federal hospitals, and the major research centres like the NIMR. These ethics review committees were variously called the Institutional Review Board (as in the United States), the Institutional Review Committee, and the Ethical Review Committee.[59] However, many state hospitals did not have ethics review committees. As the Pfizer incident which occurred in 1996 shows, this did not mean that research never took place in them or that the possibility of research did not exist. Many of the existing committees, as described in the case of the ethics review committee at the University of Ibadan, were grossly underfunded and lacked the necessary expertise to carry out their duties.[60] Many of them had no significant activity.[61]

In 2002, the National Ethics Review Board was created.[62] Its mission was to promote "good ethical practice in Nigerian scientific research, safeguard the dignity, right, safety and well-being of all actual or potential research participants through the auditing and accreditation of ethics review committees, the training of ethics review members, and advising the government on ethical matters."[63] The Board was never recognised either legally or in a government policy, and it has now been by replaced by another national body.[64]

In 2005, another national committee, called the National Ethics Committee of Nigeria, was established by the Chairman of the National AIDS Control Agency. Its mandate was to coordinate and provide oversight for institutional ethics review committees. This national committee was also not legally recognised and had no financial support from the government. It existed for a time alongside another national committee, the National Health Research Ethics Committee, established by the Federal Ministry of Health, which is currently functioning.[65] This indicated the challenges of duplication of functions and the lack of clarity about which government department could legally establish a national ethics review committee.

There were also no national policies on research ethics and governance. Although the Federal Ministry of Health is the key health policymaker in Nigeria and had the mandate to policies, including research ethics policies, it did not

---

58 "Networking for Ethics on Biomedical Research in Africa (NEBRA): Final Report," online: <http://elearning.trree.org/file.php/1/NebraReport/FinalReport-2006-english.pdf>.

59 *Ibid.*

60 Ogundiran, *ibid.*

61 *Ibid.*

62 See Malomo et al, Note 55. See National Ethics Review Board, *Draft National Ethical and Operational Guidelines for Research on Human Subjects*, Nigeria.

63 *Ibid.*

64 It has been replaced by the National Health Research Ethics Committee created in 2006.

65 Information provided by Professor Femi Soyinka, the former chairman of the National Ethics Committee. See also WHO, "National Bioethics Committees in the African Region," online: <www.who.int/ethics/committees/afro/en/> (June 2, 2010).

make any general research ethics policies that applied in every situation and to all institutions. A draft national guideline, *Draft National Ethical and Operational Guidelines for Research on Human Subjects*,[66] was prepared but never took effect. Thus, prior to 2006, there were no national domestic ethics guidelines providing guidance, either in terms of substantive ethical standards or with regard to the procedures and composition of ethics review committees. Marshall, in a 1999 study commissioned by the United States National Bioethics Advisory Commission, noted that there was considerable variation in the implementation of the process of ethical review between institutions, especially in terms of their composition.[67]

For guidance on ethical standards, the defunct National Ethics Review Board described earlier relied on different documents, including the Constitution, the Helsinki Declaration, the CIOMS Guidelines, the WHO/TDR Guidelines, the ICH-GCP Guidelines, and the Council of Europe's *Convention for the Protection of Human Rights and Dignity of the Human Being with Regard to the Application of Biology and Medicine: Convention on Human Rights and Biomedicine*.[68] Some institutional ethics review committees employed the Helsinki Declaration as their main reference document, or the CIOMS Guidelines, while others used internal guidelines developed by the institutions.[69]

Apart from the ethics review structure, the National Agency for Food and Drug Administration and Control (NAFDAC) was established by the National Agency for Food And Drug Administration and Control Act in 1993. NAFDAC is a parastatal of the Federal Ministry of Health and is responsible for ensuring drug safety and compliance with approved specifications and quality, and regulates the importation, exportation, manufacture, registration, and marketing of drugs. Its functions also include the regulation of clinical trials for drugs. With regard to research for pharmaceutical production, NAFDAC drew up a set of guidelines around 2002 for the purposes of regulating clinical trials of drugs in Nigeria (NAFDAC Guidelines).[70] The application of the NAFDAC Guidelines was limited, however, to drug research and did not apply more generally to all health research involving humans. NAFDAC also drew up draft Clinical Trials Regulations in 2004,[71] which were never formally promulgated.

The Medical and Dental Council of Nigeria (MDCN) is the professional regulatory body, established by statute,[72] which determines the standards for

---

66 National Ethics Review Board, "Draft National Ethical and Operational Guidelines for Research on Human Subjects, Nigeria," online: <http://elearning.trrec.org/file.php/1/Nebra Report/nebra-Annex-15.pdf> (February 24, 2010).
67 Patricia Marshall, *supra* Note 41at C-11-C-12.
68 NERB, *supra* Note 58 at 15.
69 *Ibid.*
70 The Guidelines which I have on file are undated. However, according to a NAFDAC official from whom the document was obtained in 2004, at the time, the document had been prepared recently.
71 NAFDAC has now drawn up a new set of guidelines based on the ICH-GCP.
72 *Medical and Dental Practitioners' Act Cap 221 Laws of the Federation of Nigeria* (LFN) 1990.

educating medical and dental professionals, and makes rules for maintaining universally acceptable professional standards of practice and conduct. The MDCN took a formal step in research regulation in the 2004 revision of the Code of Ethics in Nigeria.[73] This edition of the Code provided, amongst other things, that, "Every Teaching Hospital or Medical Research Institute MUST constitute an Ethical Review Committee composed of competent individuals to examine the research protocol of every researcher in the institution."[74] However, there is no evidence that this was enforced by the Council.

Research governance appears to have proceeded in a very haphazard, fragmentary fashion, with little coordination between the various bodies involved in regulating health research involving humans. For instance, a cursory look at the different guidelines and regulations, including the NAFDAC Guidelines, the MDCN Code of Medical Ethics, National Ethics Review Board's *Draft National Ethical and Operational Guidelines for Research on Human Subjects*, showed that they provided varying requirements for the conduct of health research involving humans. There were different requirements for the composition and structure of ethics review committees and somewhat different substantive ethical standards. Moreover, ethics review committees, both nationally and institutionally, had been non-functional over the years.

In this inchoate state of research governance, there were several allegations of unethical research, many of them revolving around lack of informed consent and failure to obtain approval from an ethics review committee prior to marketing drugs. Some of these allegations were based on anecdotal evidence, and although not independently verified, they nevertheless affected public perception and trust in some cases. For example, Ajayi, in a 1999 paper, points out that

> [The] University College Hospital, Ibadan has not lived down the perception of the local population that unethical human experimentation went on in the hospital. The selection of cases for admission (often linked to the severity of illness and types that could not be handled outside a tertiary centre) were misunderstood to be related to research interests. Mortality in the very ill patient was often ascribed to injections given for research purposes.[75]

Similarly, Anya, a physician, detailed his experiences as a medical student in Nigeria in the 1990s, noting in the Lancet that

> Training to be a doctor in Nigeria a decade ago included little more than cursory attention to either clinical or research ethics: a single hour-long

---

73 The edition of the code which preceded the current edition was titled Rules of Professional Conduct for Medical and Dental Practitioners in Nigeria. The code of ethics was first put in place in 1963. The 2004 edition replaced the MCDN, *Rules of Professional Conduct for Medical and Dental Practitioners in Nigeria, 1995.*

74 Section 31 (C), Medical and Dental Council of Nigeria, Code of Medical Ethics, 2004.

75 Ajayi, *supra* Note 11.

lecture on ethics and professional practice, delivered close to the final examinations, sufficed. As a house officer at a major teaching hospital, it was not unusual to be instructed to take samples for a research project without any research protocols or consent forms being provided. Ethics committees were weak or non-existent at most hospitals.[76]

Another example, although not strictly about the conduct of research, was a 1999 controversy involving the marketing of a HIV/AIDS drug and vaccine, which highlighted the vacuum in Nigeria's regulatory procedures. In that incident, a Nigerian doctor, Dr Jeremiah Abalaka, claimed to have found the cure for HIV/AIDS as well as a vaccine to prevent the diseases.[77] At this time, there was very little access to antiretroviral treatment in Nigeria. Several infected persons received treatment from the doctor at exorbitant costs. The drug and vaccine received support from top army officers, who proceeded to make it available to soldiers suffering from AIDS.[78] Dr Abalaka claimed to have performed clinical trials (involving testing the drug on himself) before making the drug available to the general public. However, in 2000, after much opposition from different scientific bodies, including the Nigerian Medical Association (NMA) and the Nigerian Academy of Science, the Federal Ministry of Health banned the drug and vaccine.[79] The Nigerian Academy of Science had criticised the methods of Dr Abalaka on the grounds that the drug and vaccine had not passed through any clinical trials or ethics review procedures. They could not, however, refer to any domestic legislation or policy that required these steps because none existed at this time.[80] Accusations of political machinations were made by the doctor and his supporters against the government and different associations of medical doctors. The lack of clear regulatory procedures meant that there was no impartial domestic standard against which to judge such claims.[81] A recent court case was decided in favour of Dr Abalaka, indicating that not even judges understand the research governance regime, including the requirement for clinical trials.[82]

Beyond the anecdotal evidence described earlier, studies have noted that many research projects were conducted in Nigeria without ethical review.[83] The Pfizer

---

76 Ike Anya & Rosalind Raine, "Strengthening Clinical and Research Ethics in Nigeria—An Agenda for Change" (2008) 372 Lancet 1594.

77 Barnaby Phillips, "Nigerian Doctor finds HIV Cure," *BBC News* (8 May 2000), online: BBC News <http://news.bbc.co.uk/1/hi/world/africa/740523.stm> (April 3, 2010).

78 *Ibid*. See also "Nigeria-AIDS: Nigerian Army Again Backs Claims of HIV/AIDS Cure," *Agence-France Press* (4 July 2000), online: Agence-France <www.aegis.com/news/afp/2000/AF000713.html> (April 3, 2010).

79 Khabir Ahmad, "Public Protests as Nigeria Bans Use of Untested HIV Vaccine" (2000) 356 Lancet 493.

80 *Ibid*.

81 Lumumba C Achilonu, "The Politics of Abalaka's Vaccines," *Thisday* (9 February 2001), online: <www.thisdayonline.com/archive/2001/02/09/20010209com01.html> . Barnaby Phillips, "Nigerian Doctor Finds HIV 'Cure,'" *BBC News* (8 May 2000) online: <http://news.bbc.co.uk/2/hi/africa/740523.stm>.

82 I discuss this case in further detail later.

83 NEBRA, *supra* Note 58 at 72.

incident which occurred in 1996 is a prime example. That incident encapsulates many of the problematic issues in research governance in Nigeria in the past, underscores Nigeria's challenging context, and has had consequences beyond the arena of health research. An account of the history of research governance in Nigeria is thus incomplete without a discussion of the Pfizer incident.

In 1996, there was an outbreak of a meningitis epidemic in Kano, a state in the northern part of Nigeria. About 250,000 people were infected during the epidemic, and about 15,000 people died.[84] Humanitarian organisations such as Medicins Sans Frontier went to Kano and began providing the cheap and effective antibiotic chloramphenicol (which interestingly had been tested in the northern part of Nigeria about 20 years earlier).[85] At the same time, Pfizer, an American multinational pharmaceutical company, sent in staff to conduct a trial of the antibiotic Trovafloxacin (commonly called Trovan).[86] The Kano Infectious Diseases Hospital, where the trials took place, was reported to be at the time an ill-equipped hospital with few beds, poor power supply, and no clean water.[87]

Pfizer's main reason for conducting the clinical trials in Kano was to obtain approval for the drug from the United States Food and Drug Agency.[88] The trial was to investigate whether the oral form of Trovan was more effective and efficient in treating children infected with meningitis than other existing treatments, including Ceftriaxone, the gold standard treatment. Later, when charges of unethical conduct were made, Pfizer also alleged that another major reason for conducting the trials was to provide humanitarian services to the infected victims who were obviously in need of medical assistance at the time.[89] Sometime after the trial had ended, several allegations were made regarding the unethical manner in which Pfizer conducted the trials. These were first publicised by the *Washington Post* in a series of investigative articles on the conduct of clinical trials by developed country researchers in developing countries.[90]

Pfizer's Trovan had not previously been tested in children. However, about 200 children, aged between 1 and 13, and infected with meningitis, were

---

84   Emmanuel R Ezeome & Christian Simon, "Ethical Problems in Conducting Research in Acute Epidemics: The Pfizer Meningitis Study in Nigeria" (2010) 10 Dev World Bioethics 1. Other sources put the death toll at 15,000. The BBC has a figure of 15,000 people. "Nigerians Sue Pfizer Over Test Deaths" *BBC News* (30 August 2001).

85   See Whittle, *supra* Note 20.

86   WHO, "Cerebral Meningitis in Nigeria- Update in Disease Outbreaks Reported" (7 March 1996).

87   Joe Stephens, "The Body Hunters (Part 1): As Drug Testing Spreads, Lives Hang in the Balance" *Washington Post* (17 December 2000) at A01.

88   *Ibid*.

89   See Remigius N Nwabueze, *supra* Note 11 at 98.

90   This was a series of six articles containing stories on clinical trials in developing countries. See, J Stephens, *supra* Note 88.

enrolled in the Kano trials. 100 of the children were thus put on the Trovan, while another 100 were put on the Ceftriaxone.[91] Out of the enrolled number, it was alleged that 11 died in the trials,[92] five of whom were on the experimental drug, Trovan, given orally, and the other six of whom were on injections of the standard drug Cetrifaxone.[93] It was also reported that other children involved in the trials suffered seizures or became paralysed.[94] It was also reported that at least one child was not taken off the experimental drug and given the standard drug when it was clear that her condition was not improving, which was clearly unethical.[95] The trials were conducted within three weeks, and Pfizer left Kano immediately.

The allegations made against Pfizer include that there was no informed consent and no follow-up with the children after the conclusion of the trial. The parents of the children alleged that they had not been adequately informed about the trial and would not have subjected their children to it had they been informed that their children were participating in a trial rather than simply receiving treatment. No written consent was obtained, although Pfizer had prepared an informed consent form. Due to the illiteracy of the parents, only verbal consent was obtained after oral explanations had been made to the parents of the children in English and Hausa (the language of the participants).[96] Also, there was no follow-up with the children partly because many of them did not show up after leaving the hospitals and because Pfizer reportedly did not send people to check up on them.[97] It is necessary to note that Nigeria had no direct policy on research involving children, although common sense suggests that obtaining informed consent from poor and illiterate parents, whose children were in danger of dying in an epidemic, would be a difficult matter.[98]

91 *Ibid.*

92 S Bosely, "New Drug 'Illegally Tested on Children': Pfizer Accused of Irregularities during Clinical Trials in Nigeria," *The Guardian* (London), (17 January 2001) at 19.

93 Stephens, *supra* Note 162.

94 *Ibid.*

95 *Washington Post, ibid.* See also Jacqui Wise, "Pfizer Accused of Testing New Drug without Ethical Approval" (2001) 322 BMJ 194, online: <www.bmj.com/cgi/content/full/322/7280/194> .

96 *Ibid.* Barnaby Phillips, "Nigeria's Drug Trial Fears" *BBC News* 14 March 2001.

97 As was alleged, many of the affected children were "rural people with no address." Stephens, *supra* Note 162.

98 See generally Ayodele S Jegede, "Understanding Informed Consent for Participation in International Health Research" (2009) 9:2 Dev World Bioethics 87. See also Ezeome & Thomson, pointing out that

> People may mistake research activities as compulsory elements of public health intervention being directed at the epidemic. Therapeutic misconception is almost inalienable from research endeavors in this setting. This may explain why the Pfizer study reported a one hundred percent participation rate among patients that were approached for enrollment.

A puzzling issue was why Pfizer would choose to conduct a trial during an epidemic in a poor area when other organisations were seeking to provide assistance. Was it ethically permissible to conduct tests for a drug that would, if things went well, yield huge profits for Pfizer during an epidemic? Was it ethically acceptable to conduct a trial in a developing country like Nigeria which had minimal chances of actually being used in that country due to its exorbitant costs?[99] Pfizer defended itself on the grounds that acute epidemics of meningitis are rare in developed countries, that drug response may differ from one setting or population to another, and that it is necessary to determine what kinds of drugs will be most effective in an epidemic situation.[100] According to a press statement it made in 2006,

> At the time of the epidemic - the largest in the country's history, according to health officials - Pfizer believed that Trovan would provide a life-saving treatment for meningococcal meningitis that was afflicting tens of thousands of Nigerians. The goal of the study was simple - to find an effective treatment for a disease that was having a devastating effect on the people of sub-Saharan Africa.[101]

Also, in its statement of defence in a case eventually filed against it by the Nigerian government, Pfizer stated that it had donated over 18 million naira to Kano State (about US$180,000) in medicine equipment and materials to fight the concurrent epidemics.[102]

There were also apparent procedural defects: for instance, proper records of the trials were not kept as required in such trials.[103] Further, there was no approval of the research protocol by an independent ethics review committee. Pfizer stated that it had obtained the necessary approvals from NAFDAC, the Federal Ministry of Health, and the Kano State Ministry of Health.[104] When the incident was publicised by the *Washington Post*, Pfizer also stated that it had received approvals from an ethics review committee in the hospital. But there

99 Hauke Goos, "Using Africans as Guinea Pigs: Nigeria Takes on Pfizer over Controversial Drug Test," *Spiegel Online International* (2008).

100 Ezeome & Thomson, *supra* Note 85 at 5.

101 Pfizer, "Pfizer Statement – 1996 Trovan Clinical Study in Nigeria" online: <www.pfizer.ca/ english/newsroom/press%20releases/default.asp?s=1&year=2006&releaseID=193> (March 14, 2010).

102 Pfizer Inc., *Trovan, Kano State Civil Case – Statement of Defense Summary* (New York: Pfizer Inc, March 2, 2010) online: <www.pfizer.com/files/news/trovan_statement_defense_ summary.pdf>. However, as Ezeome & Thomson rightly note, "research cannot be paraded as a form of emergency relief at the cost of taking appropriate steps to protect affected individuals." Ezeome and Thomson, *supra* Note 85.

103 Ruth Macklin, *Double Standards in Medical Research in Developing Countries* (Cambridge: Cambridge University Press, 2004) at 101.

104 Pfizer, "Summary: Trovan, Kano State Civil Case – Statement of Defense," online: <www. pfizer.com/files/news/trovan_statement_defense_summary.pdf>.

was no ethics committee in the hospital at the time of the trial,[105] and no evidence exists that any ethics review committee in Nigeria examined the research protocol before the trial commenced.[106] A purported letter of approval was not given at the time of the incident and was backdated by at least a year.[107] It may be stated, however, that there were no domestic regulations or guidelines in Nigeria at the time of the trials requiring Pfizer to obtain any such approval. Pfizer, in its statement of defence, sought to rely on this gap in Nigerian law and policy, stating,

> Pfizer contends that there was no regulation or law in Nigeria requiring ethical committee approval before conducting a clinical trial or investigative study. Therefore, there was no need to obtain what the law did not require. In addition, there was no formal ethics committee sitting at either Kano's IDH or at the nearby Bayero Teaching Hospital. There were, however, numerous other forms of approval by local physicians and government officials authorizing the study to go forward including, but not limited to, the head of the IDH and Dr. Idris Mohammed. At no time was patient care compromised in any way.[108]

However, the requirement for ethics review approval was also a requirement of international ethical guidelines, such as the Helsinki Declaration. There were also questions as to whether the foreign physicians used by Pfizer in the study were licensed by the Medical and Dental Council of Nigeria to treat patients in Nigeria.[109]

The drug was approved by the US Food and Drug Administration (FDA) in 1997, a year after the trials in Nigeria. One of the grounds of the approval was the beneficial impact of the drug as manifested in the clinical trials conducted in Kano.[110] Later, in 1999, the FDA issued a public health advisory limiting the use of the drug to certain categories of patients and restricting its use because it was shown to cause fatal liver damage.[111] The European Union also withdrew the drug from the market in 1999 because of liver problems.[112] The drug was

---

105 See also Phillips, *supra* Note 97.
106 B Ukwuoma, "Pfizer Official, Others Summoned to Kano over Drug," *The Guardian* (12 January 2001).
107 See also Joe Stephens, "Doctors Say Drug Trial's Approval Was Backdated," *Washington Post* (17 December 2000) at A01.
108 Pfizer Statement of Defense, *supra* Note 105.
109 T Soniyi. "Pfizer's Drug Trial Illegal – FG Panel," *Punch* (Lagos, Nigeria) (22 October 2007).
110 Sonia Shah, "Globalization of Clinical Research in the Pharmaceutical Industry" 33:1 Int J Health Serv 29 at 33.
111 US Food and Drug Administration/Centre for Drug Evaluation and Research, Public Health Advisory: Trovan (Trovafloxacin/Alatrofloxacin Mesylate): Interim Recommendations 09 June 1999.
112 Tinker Ready, "Pfizer in Unethical Trial Suit" (2001) 7 Nat Med 1077.

not registered or marketed in Nigeria since it was too expensive and therefore not affordable.[113]

The parents of the children involved in the trials brought action in the Federal High Court in Nigeria, alleging lack of informed consent and seeking compensation from Pfizer.[114] This case was dismissed in 2002. Another suit was filed by 30 families in a District Court in the United States in August 2001 while the case filed in Nigeria was pending, seeking punitive damages against Pfizer under the United States *Aliens' Tort Claims Act*,[115] alleging that Pfizer had violated the law of nations due to its alleged nonconformity with international ethical standards for research.[116] The plaintiffs in this case sought to rely on the internationally recognised guidelines for ethical clinical research, the Helsinki Declaration, the Nuremberg Code, and the International Convention on Civil and Political Rights (ICCPR). The suit was later dismissed by the District Court on the grounds of *non forum conveniens*, finding that, despite acknowledged problems of corruption and bias, Nigerian law recognises medical malpractice, negligence, and personal injury claims, and Nigerian courts thus afforded an adequate forum for trying the matter.[117] The plaintiffs appealed. The suit was remanded to the District Court by the Court of Appeals in October 2003.[118] This appeal was also dismissed in August 2005 on similar grounds, with the court stating that Nigeria was the proper forum for action.[119] In that case, the judge noted that language used in the instruments relied on by the plaintiffs was merely 'aspirational' language which could not be characterised as creating well-defined and universally accepted legal obligations under international law to sustain an action under the *Aliens Tort Claims Act*.[120] However, in January 2009, the Court of Appeals for the Second Circuit, in a decision remarkable for its potential impact not only on United States law but on international law and multinational companies' liability, held that the District Court had jurisdiction under the *Alien Torts Claims Act* for a violation of the norm of customary international law prohibiting medical experimentation on non-consenting human participants.[121] In June 2010, the United States Supreme Court dismissed an

---

113 B Ukwuoma, *supra* Note 107.
114 *Zango v Pfizer Inc.* No. FHC/KCS/2001.
115 The *Aliens Tort Claims Act* 28 USC 1350 empowers the District Court in the United States to decide on any civilian action brought by non-citizens of the United States on allegations of violation of the law of nations or a treaty of the United States and was famously applied in the case of *Filartiga v Pen-Irala* 630 F.2d 876 (2d Cir. 1980). See a history of the Act in Marisa Anne Pagnattaro, "Enforcing International Labor Standards: The Potential of the Alien Torts Claims Act" (2004) 37 Vanderbilt J Transnat'l L 203 at 211–214.
116 *Abdullahi v Pfizer, Inc.*, 2002 WL 31082956 (S.D.N.Y. September 17, 2002).
117 *Ibid.*
118 *Abdullahi v Pfizer, Inc.* 77 Fed. Appx. C.A (2nd Cir. N.Y.), 2003, WL 22317923 October 8, 2003.
119 *Abdullahi, et al. v Pfizer Inc.*, No. 01 Civ. 8118, SDNY; 2005.
120 *Ibid.*
121 *Rabi Abdullahi v Pfizer, Inc* Docket Nos. 05-4863-cv (L), 05-6768-cv (CON), 2009 WL 214649 (2d Cir January 20, 2009).

appeal by Pfizer against the Court of Appeals ruling, effectively allowing the case to proceed further in the United States court system.[122]

The Nigerian government, now under a democratic regime, opened an inquiry of the incident in 2001, five years after the trial took place. The findings of the panel of inquiry were not made public until the *Washington Post* obtained a leaked copy in May 2006.[123] The panel found, among other things, that Pfizer had not obtained the informed consent of the participants in the trial since they were not informed that they were engaged in a trial and that no ethics approval was obtained.[124] The panel also criticised NAFDAC, the Nigerian drug regulatory agency, and the Federal Ministry of Health, for failure to take action after the chairman of the task force for the epidemic made complaints to them about the trial.[125]

In June 2007, the Kano State government and federal government instituted civil[126] and criminal proceedings against Pfizer, respectively.[127] These legal actions were settled out of court in 2009, with no admission of liability by Pfizer.[128] The settlement amounted to US$75 million in total. Under the terms of the settlement with Kano State, Pfizer agreed to establish a Healthcare/Meningitis Fund from which study participants can receive financial support. Pfizer also agreed to finance several healthcare initiatives selected by the Kano State government that benefit the people of Kano State, amounting to US$30 million over a period of two years, and to reimburse Kano State for the US$10 million in legal costs associated with the litigation. The Healthcare/Meningitis Fund would pay out a maximum of US$35 million, to be divided amongst persons who could show that they participated in the Trovan clinical trial.[129] The settlements do not, however, resolve the claims brought by the trial participants in the United States since the government actions were not brought on behalf of these participants.

The Pfizer incident raised questions about the motives of research sponsors, particularly pharmaceutical companies, in conducting research in developing countries like Nigeria; possible corruption in developing countries in the area

---

122 BBC, "US Supreme Court Rejects Pfizer Nigeria Lawsuit Appeal," *BBC News* (29 June 2010).

123 J Stephens, "Panel Faults Pfizer in '96 Clinical Trial In Nigeria Unapproved Drug Tested on Children," *Washington Post* (Sunday, 7 May 2006) A01.

124 The purported letter of approval was not given at the time of the incident and was backdated by at least a year. *Ibid.*

125 Soniyi Note 112.

126 *Attorney General of Kano State v Pfizer Inc and Others* SUIT No: K/233/2007. N Ugochukwu. "FG Makes N876.3bn Claims from Pfizer over Tests" *Businessday* Online (Lagos, Nigeria) (June 4) 1.

127 See Joe Stephens, "Pfizer Faces Criminal Charges in Nigeria," *Washington Post* (Wednesday 30 May, 2007) A10. Heidi Vogt, "Pfizer Facing 4 Court Cases in Nigeria" *Associated Press* (11 August 2007).

128 Pfizer, "Pfizer, Kano State Reach Settlement of Trovan Case" (2009) on file with author. (March 15, 2010). Joe Stephens, "Pfizer Reaches Settlement in Nigerian Drug-Trial Case," *Washington Post* (4 April 2009).

129 *Ibid.*

of health research; and the vulnerability of participants in these countries to exploitation. It also raised questions about the existence, and adequacy, of domestic legal, ethical, and policy requirements, and governance structures for the conduct of research in Nigeria. The incident further called into question the government's role in ensuring the protection of research participants in Nigeria.

Further, as some research has suggested, the trial was partly responsible for a boycott of polio vaccine immunisation from 2003 to 2004 in the northern part of Nigeria, where polio has been endemic.[130] This is particularly significant because Nigeria is one of only six countries in the world where polio has remained endemic.[131] The continued survival of the polio virus in Nigeria has been cited as potentially jeopardising the global efforts to eradicate polio.[132] Political and religious leaders in the northern states specifically alluded to the Pfizer incident in support of their stance against polio immunisation.[133,134]

Nigeria's history of health research and research governance includes instances of unethical conduct, some documented and others anecdotal. These instances, as the Pfizer incident shows, damage public trust in a context where health research is very much needed. These instances, particularly the Pfizer incident, also exposed the vacuum that existed in Nigeria's research governance arrangements prior to 2006.

The recent move towards a domestic ethical framework and a new national regulatory structure, as discussed earlier, began around 2002. The impetus for this move came from both domestic and international events. International interest in research governance in developing countries like Nigeria, the Pfizer incident, and growing domestic interest in health research and research ethics appear to have been contributory to increased national attention to research governance in Nigeria.

In 2000, the Fogarty International Centre of the National Institutes of Health in the United States, through the International Bioethics Education and Career Development Award, began to train several researchers in research ethics and ethics review.[135] These researchers have been influential in the recent developments in

---

130 Maryam Yayha, "Polio Vaccines – "No Thank You" Barriers to Polio Eradication in Northern Nigeria" (2007) 106:423 Afr Aff 185. See also Ebenezer Obadare, "A Crisis of Trust: History, Politics, Religion and the Polio Controversy in Northern Nigeria" (2005) 39:3 Patterns of Prejudice 265.

131 David L Heymann & Bruce Aylward, "Eradicating Polio" (2004) 351:13 N Engl J Med 1275. There is evidence more recently that progress is being made to eradicate polio in Nigeria. See Stephanie Nebehay, "Nigeria Makes Gains in Polio Eradication," *Reuters* (6 March 2010).

132 See Lancet, "Vaccine-Derived Poliomyelitis in Nigeria" (2007) 370 Lancet 1394.

133 Abiodun Raufu, "Polio Vaccine Plans may Run into Problems in Nigeria" (2004) 327 Br Med J 380.

134 See Bolu Olusanya, "Polio-Vaccination Boycott in Nigeria" (2004) 363 Lancet 1912. A S Jegede, "What Led to the Nigerian Boycott of the Polio Vaccination Campaign?" (2007) 4:3 PLoS Med e73.

135 See Adnan A Hyder et al, "A Case Study of Research Ethics Capacity Development in Africa" (2007) 82:7 Acad Med 675.

the ethics review infrastructure in Nigeria. According to Adebamowo and others, by 2004, several Nigerians had graduated from the Fogarty-funded training programme in the United States, Canada, and South Africa, and set out to assist their institutions in setting up ethics committees where none had previously existed, to strengthen existing ones, and to provide local bioethics training. [136] In addition, the need to meet the requirements of foreign sponsors, particularly government institutions in United States, was contributory.[137] Moreover, the Pfizer incident, as described, exposed the vacuum that existed in Nigeria's governance arrangements for health research involving humans.

The international interest (particularly from the United States) and the Pfizer incident generated a desire among local researchers to engage the government in efforts to develop a national structure for research governance. Several researchers advocated at the national level to encourage the federal government to develop a national structure. The government subsequently established the National Health Research Ethics Committee in 2005.[138]

Several key meetings in 2006 solidified the need to further formalise a research governance system for the country. Amongst these was the Technical Panel Meeting on Essential National Health Research (ENHR), held in February 2006.[139] Further, during a 2006 Presidential Retreat on the Health of Nigerians, the fact that Nigeria needed domestic regulatory structures to meet its Millennium Development Goals targets was strongly emphasised.[140] In addition, a High-level Ministerial Meeting on Health Research for Development was convened by the Nigerian Federal Ministry of Health and the Ghana Ministry of Health in March 2006, at which health research and the need for good systems for research participants' protection was discussed.[141]

The federal government through the Federal Ministry of Health then signed a technical cooperation agreement with the West African Bioethics Training Programme, a programme funded by the Fogarty International Centre. According to the agreement, the West African Bioethics Training Program was to provide training and support for members of the National Health Research Ethics Committee and several members of the staff of the Federal Ministry of Health. Adebamowo and others note that "Previous bioethics needs' assessment

---

136 Adebamowo, Note 64 at 18.
137 See for example, Falusi et al, Note 57, noting the importance of gaining the Federal Wide Agreement (FWA) in the University of Ibadan. For instance, the United States National Institutes of Health requires that any research institution in the world that receives United States government funds for research must have a certification known as the FWA, showing that the standards of current United States human subjects' regulation have been met.
138 Eyitayo Lambo, Address of the Federal Minister of Health, Prof. Eyitambo Lambo at the Inaugural Ceremony of the National Health Research Ethics Committee, Held at Conference Hall of the Federal Ministry of Health, Abuja on 5th October 2006, online: <http://nhrec.net/nhrec/news2.html> (March 2, 2010). See also the National Health Research Ethics Code at 3.
139 A Yakubu & A Adebamowo, *supra* Note 50.
140 Adebamowo, *supra* Note 64 at 18.
141 See Communique, Note 40, and see the Preface to the National Code on Health Research Ethics.

studies had indicated that the potential for bureaucratic delays, corruption and obstructionism were the most important concerns that biomedical researchers in Nigeria have about a national ethics committee."[142] The draft code was developed, taking into account international research ethics guidelines, the United States Code of Federal Regulations (CFR), guidelines from India and South Africa, the Nigerian Constitution, the federal structure of the country, relevant laws, the history of research, and research ethics in Nigeria as well as the needs of local and international researchers. It was submitted to the National Health Research Ethics Committee in 2006. It was adopted by the Federal Ministry of Health after consultations and amendments.[143]

Thus, in 2006, the National Council on Health approved the National Health Research Ethics Committee as well as a *National Code for Health Research Ethics* (the National Code) designed to provide oversight for research.[144] It "represents the collective concern of the government and the people of Nigeria to ensure the protection of human participants in scientific research to the highest ethical standard that is possible."[145] The National Code applies to "all health research involving human participants, conducted, supported or otherwise subject to regulation by any institution in Nigeria."[146] These developments have been given a legal foundation with the enactment of the National Health Act in 2014.

Overall, there is currently a formal, more comprehensive, national system of ethics review in Nigeria. There is also more clarity about research governance structures in Nigeria. Many of these developments can be attributed to the recent democratic regime in the country, increased international attention to health research and regulation, and to instances of unethical research in Nigeria. While these are positive developments, there remain gaps in implementation and enforcement. There are still claims today of cures which have not yet passed through clinical trials procedures or ethics review, and like the Abalaka case, Nigeria's newspapers still report cases of 'miracle' cures made by medical professionals and scientists.

Legal framework

Nigeria's legal framework for health research governance is a combination of legislation, subsidiary legislation, and common law derived from judicial precedents. These include the Constitution, the National Health Act, and related state law, and the laws regulating health professional bodies, in particular, medical doctors. The movement of health research into the legal domain indicates a role for the state which, as discussed in Chapter 2, is the main wielder of the weapon of law.

142 Adebamowo, *supra* Note 64 at 18.
143 National Health Research Ethics, National Code on Health Research Ethics, online: <www.nhrec.net/nhrec/> at 3.
144 National Code on Health Research Ethics, online: <www.nhrec.net/nhrec/>.
145 *Ibid*. See Preface.
146 Section B.

In Nigeria's federal system, the Constitution, aside from being the supreme law,[147] delineates the division of responsibilities for the Nigerian federation. This demarcation of authority has important consequences for research governance in Nigeria. Matters relating to drugs are within the exclusive powers of the federal legislative body, the National Assembly.[148] This would include the regulation of clinical trials of drugs, which, as I describe later, comes within the remit of NAFDAC, the federal drug regulatory agency. However, health and education are residual legislative matters, while scientific research falls under the concurrent list.[149] In essence, the governance of health research therefore comes within the powers of both federal and state governments. For concurrent matters, under the doctrine of "covering the field," the federal government can legislate on any matter on which it has legislative competence.[150] As emphasised by the Supreme Court in the 2002 case of *Attorney General of Abia State versus Attorney General of the Federation*,[151] and in other cases before it, under that doctrine, any state law which conflicts with a federal legislation on a subject matter on which both governments have concurrent legislative powers, on which the federal legislature has enacted a law, or on which law can be taken as evincing an intention to cover the field, shall to the extent of its inconsistency be void.[152] The state is thus subordinate to the federal government in any area of scientific research in which the federal government has made a law of general application. For residual matters such as health and education, the states can make their own laws without interference. On health, however, the states can make their own law.

What this means, then, is that the federal government can create a generally applicable law on research governance, as it has done (partially) with the

---

147 In *Daniel Orhiunu v Federal Republic of Nigeria*, Suleiman Galadima JCA said,

> The Constitution is what is called the grund norm and fundamental law of the land. All other legislations in the land take their hierarchy from the provision of the Constitution. By the provisions of the Constitution, the laws made by the National Assembly come next to the Constitution; followed by those made by the House of Assembly of a State. By virtue of section 1(1) of the Constitution, the provisions of the Constitution take precedence over any law enacted by the National Assembly even though the National Assembly has power to amend the Constitution itself.

> *Daniel Orhiunu v Federal Republic of Nigeria* (2005) 1 NWLR,
> Part 906 55 – 56, paragraphs H- B

148 Section 26, Schedule 2, Part I, of the CFRN.

149 See the *Constitution of the Federal Republic of Nigeria, 1999* (CFRN), Second Schedule. Section 21, 22, 27, and 28.

150 See Section 4(5) of the Constitution, which provides that

> If any Law enacted by the House of Assembly of a State is inconsistent with any law validly made by the National Assembly, the law made by the National Assembly shall prevail, and that other Law shall, to the extent of the inconsistency, be void.

151 *AG Abia State v Ag Federation* (2002) 6 NWLR (pt 763) 264.

152 See *AG Abia State v Ag Federation* (2002) 6 NWLR (pt 763) 264; *AG of Ogun State and Anor. v AG of the Federation* (1982) 1-2 SC 13, 1982 13 NSCC 1. See NA Inegbedion & E Omoregie, "Federalism in Nigeria: A Reappraisal" (2006) 4:1 J Commonw L & Leg Educ 69.

development of the National Health Act. The states may also make laws to regulate health research. Practically speaking, it is easier for the tier of government which has exclusive authority over drugs and related matters, such as clinical trials, and which has also enacted law to regulate professionals in the area of health research to make laws regarding all health research involving humans. Further, as rightly stated in the National Code,

> The Federal Government of Nigeria acting through any of its organs and establishments has the overall duty of protecting the welfare of the citizens of Nigeria. It may therefore exercise all the powers of protecting citizens according to the law, including citizens participating in research. In addition, some agencies of state in discharge of their duties according to law may also exercise regulatory functions within the research environment.[153]

An active role by the federal government offers the possibility of a uniform set of standards for health research involving humans for the country. A uniform set of standards, in turn, offers the same protections for research participants across the country. It permits clarity of responsibilities and roles for other actors in research governance, thus potentially promoting health research, which is needed in Nigeria.

Apart from the division of powers, there are specific matters that come within the umbrella of research governance, which may be covered generally under the Constitution. An example of such a matter is privacy. The right to privacy is a fundamental right protected under the Constitution. Section 37 of the Constitution provides that "The privacy of citizens, their homes, correspondence, telephone conversations and telegraphic communications is hereby guaranteed and protected." The phrase "the privacy of citizens" could be inferred to cover various aspects of a citizen's life. In *Medical and Dental Practitioners Disciplinary Tribunal v Okonkwo*, the Supreme Court, per Ayoola, JSC, noted that the constitutional right of privacy includes the right of a competent, mature adult to refuse life-prolonging treatment.[154] One could logically infer from this decision that a right to privacy includes the right to refuse to consent to participate in research (which is, essentially, a voluntary activity). Also, the protection of health information, and information collected in the process of health research, could reasonably come within the scope of that right, which would be applicable generally to all research.

In addition to the right of privacy, the Constitution also provides under Section 34 that "Every individual is entitled to respect for the dignity of his person."[155] Accordingly, the section continues, "No person shall be subjected to

---

153 Section M of the National Code.
154 *Medical and Dental Practitioners Disciplinary Tribunal v Okonkwo* (2001) 7 NWLR 206 at 245–246.
155 Section 34.

torture or to inhuman or degrading treatment."[156] A broad construction of this provision could be argued to include debasing or humiliating psychological treatments in pursuit of scientific knowledge, mental harm, or unnecessary bodily harm in the course of research.

The National Health Act provides a legal foundation for health research governance in Nigeria, including requirements related to ethics review structures, informed consent, and rule-making functions for governance. On health research governance, the Act has similar provisions as South Africa's National Health Act and highlights the ways in which African countries are replicating the steps that other African countries are taking in research governance. This also emphasises the need to critique the emergent systems for the benefit of other African countries. One of these similarities is in the establishment of two key institutions – the National Health Research Committee (similar to South Africa's National Health Research Council) and the National Health Research Ethics Committee (similar to South Africa's National Health Research Ethics Council) – with similar responsibilities and composition. As in South Africa, Nigeria's National Health Research Committee has the responsibility of developing the health research agenda and the resources available for research focus on priority health areas.[157] The Committee is composed of 13 persons and has the functions of promoting health research by public and private health authorities; as in South Africa, ensuring that health research agendas and research resources focus on priority health problems; and developing and advising the Minister on a national strategy for the health research and coordination of the research activities of public health authorities. However, the factors to be taken into consideration in identifying research priorities are not specified as they are in South Africa's legislation.[158] Members of the Committee are, by the provisions of the Act, to be remunerated.

The Act governs "research or experimentation on a living person" and states that such research can only be conducted as prescribed by the relevant authority and with the informed consent of the research subject.[159] Relevant authority is not defined. However, as I have noted, health research is not a matter on the Exclusive List. Indeed, it can be argued that it is on the residual list, which allows states to make their own laws with respect to health research, and thus to designate a "relevant authority." Informed consent is now a legal requirement by the provisions of the Act.

The provision also refers to all kinds of research involving living persons. This raises a key question: does it apply to social science research which involves humans but does not necessarily affect health, for example, the impact of domestic violence on the productivity of women in a particular location? At the moment,

156 Section 34(1).
157 Section 31 of the National Health Act.
158 Section 70.
159 Section 32.

the answer would appear to be "yes." A review of the responsibilities of the National Health Research Ethics Committee includes the setting of norms on "research involving humans and animals including clinical trials,"[160] seemingly reiterating the breadth of what the Act intends to govern. This may raise the sort of questions that have plagued social science research ethics, referred to in Chapter 3, including the creeping or overreach complained about in certain quarters.[161] Given the purpose of the Act, which is to provide for the health system, should its provisions apply out of its stated objects? The second question is what about research involving dead persons or tissues? Is the intention of the Act to exclude these matters? These questions require more in-depth analysis because of the impact they have on the governance of health research. A comparison with the South African National Health Act shows more specificity in South Africa, which limits what is governed to "health research," which is then specifically defined to determine what is governed.

The Act stipulates that research be carried out in the manner required by the relevant authority. It does not define "relevant authority," although this may be construed to refer to an ethics review committee or the authority of a research institution. Specificity would have been desirable. It is, however, more specific about informed consent, requiring that the person on whom the research is to be conducted provide written, informed consent prior to the research or experimentation's taking place. Such a person is to be informed of the purpose of the research and the possible effect on her health.[162] It makes further provision for research involving children. With respect to children, the research can only be conducted if it is in the best interest of the child in a manner prescribed by the Committee and with the written and informed consent of the parent or guardian.[163] For non-therapeutic research, research must be done in the manner prescribed by the Committee and with the written consent of the parents or guardians. It is not clear why the best interests of the child are not specifically provided for here, where there ought to be more stringent conditions. In any event, the Child Rights Act requires that all actions be in the best interests of the child. The Child Rights Act, enacted in 2003, does not have any direct provisions on the involvement of children in health research. But it does have certain provisions that may have implications for health research involving children. For instance, Section 1 of the Act provides that in any actions concerning a child undertaken by an individual, public or private body, institution or service, court of law, or administrative or legislative authority, the best interest of the child shall be the primary consideration. Thus, researchers, research sponsors, and ethics review committees must consider whether any research involving children would be in their best interest. Section 33 of the Act also provides that a person who exploits a child in any other form not already mentioned in the Act (which

---

160 Section 33.
161 See Chapter 3.
162 Section 32 of the National Health Act.
163 Section 32 of the National Health Act.

could be interpreted to include a research context) in a manner prejudicial to the welfare of the child commits an offence and is liable to a fine of 500,000 naira or imprisonment to a term of five years. Exploitative practices in the course of research arguably come within this provision.

The Act also confers power on the Minister of Health to establish the National Health Research Ethics Committee,[164] which is the main instrument of enforcing governance. Its functions are to:

a   Set norms and standards for conducting research on humans and animals, including clinical trials;
b   Determine the extent of health research to be carried out by public and private health authorities;
c   Adjudicate in complaints about the functioning of health research ethics committees and hear any complaint by a researcher who believes that he has been discriminated against by any of the health research ethics committees;
d   Register and audit the activities of health research ethics committees;
e   Refer to the relevant statutory health regulatory body matters involving the violation or potential violation of an ethical or professional rule by a health-care provider;
f   Recommend to the appropriate regulatory body such disciplinary action as may be prescribed or permissible by law against any person found to be in violation of any norms and standards, or guidelines, set for the conduct of research under this Bill; and
g   Advise the Federal Ministry of Health and State Ministries of Health on any ethical issues concerning research on health.[165]

The Act defines "clinical trials" to mean "a systematic study, involving human subjects that aims to answer specific questions about the safety or efficacy of a medicine or method of prevention and treatment." The National Health Research Ethics Committee (NHREC) has set norms and standards through the National Code on Health Research Ethics. It will be recalled that this instrument was established in 2006 and revised in 2007 prior to the enactment of the National Health Act. Several additions have been made to the Code since then. It now draws legal force from the National Health Act, which confers power on the NHREC to set norms and standards for conducting research on humans.

The Act also requires that every institution in which health research is conducted establish or have access to a health research ethics committee. The functions of the health research ethics committees in Nigeria include reviewing, approving of, or disapproving of health research protocols.[166] Surprisingly, however, it does not expressly state that all health research must pass through ethics review or provide penalties for failure to submit research projects for approval. In

---

164 Section 33 of the National Health Act.
165 Section 33(6) of the National Health Act.
166 Section 34 of the National Health Act.

view of the Pfizer incident, this is a crucial provision which should be expressly stated, not merely deciphered from other provisions in the Act or from subsidiary legislation. However, the National Code on Health Research Ethics contains that requirement and can be considered subsidiary legislation, having been made under powers given by the Act.

Clearly, the National Health Act provides a formal, legislative basis for the governance of all health research in Nigeria. It confers legal force on the National Code Health Research Ethics made under powers granted by the Act. However, there are gaps in the Act which should be remedied. For instance, the Act does not contain a requirement for ethics review. In a similar manner to the requirement for informed consent, this is so fundamental that it should be contained in the principal legislation. The symbolic force of this provision in the Act cannot be understated. But while the National Code contains such a requirement, there is no clearly defined sanction for failure to meet it, as suggested in the hybrid framework of governance. Furthermore, the Act does not establish a compensation scheme for research participants. Further, unlike in South Africa, it does not contain a mandatory requirement for the registration of a clinical trial in a clinical trial registry, nor does it mandate the creation of a clinical trials registry. No penal sanctions are provided for failure to comply with the Act.

There are also areas of potential conflict with existing legislation. In this respect, the Act confers power on the National Health Research Ethics Committee to make guidance for clinical trials. As described in the following, NAFDAC has powers under the NAFDAC Act to make regulations for drugs, including clinical trials. While the National Code requires that there should be compliance with both the NAFDAC regulations and the National Code,[167] it does not make it clear what would happen in the event of a conflict between any guidance promulgated by the National Health Research Ethics Committee, such as the National Code, and any regulations on clinical trials made by NAFDAC. It would have been helpful if the National Health Act included a provision stating that the guidance provided by the National Health Research Ethics Committee supersedes all other regulations in the event of a conflict.

Other aspects of the legal framework are discussed in the context of examining health professionals' regulation and the role of the drug regulatory authorities.

Ethical framework

Within a national context, however, there may be several domestic sources from which ethical values may be drawn. The Constitution of the Federal Republic of Nigeria, 1999, underscores the value of respect for human rights, with a chapter on fundamental rights.

In addition to the general values of the Nigerian state, as provided under the Constitution and documents such as the National Health Policy, the ethical

167 Section M (a).

framework of Nigeria can be deciphered more specifically from the provisions of the National Code for Health Research Ethics ("the National Code).[168] As noted in Chapter 3, national guidelines and policies, such as the National Code, which take into consideration the contexts and the values of different countries may be one way of resolving the existing ethical dilemmas of conducting research in developing countries, including African countries. As soft law, favoured under the new governance approach and adopted in the hybrid framework of governance, it offers greater potential for flexibility, responsiveness, and participation.

The National Code on Health Research Ethics (National Code) developed by the NHREC under powers given under the National Health Act provides the main ethical framework for health research involving humans. The NHREC has also developed policy statements to address some subjects not covered in the National Code, including policy statements on the enrolment of children in research in Nigeria and biobanking.

The National Code applies to all health research conducted in Nigeria. It states that "Health research that is conducted anywhere in Nigeria must comply with all sections of this code."[169] Thus, the National Code has broad coverage, both geographically and with regard to the types of health research covered. Its provisions, including the ethical principles contained therein, thus apply to all kinds of health research in Nigeria. It defines "health research" as a systematic investigation, including research development, testing, and evaluation, designed to develop or contribute to generalisable knowledge. Such investigation may consist of therapeutic procedures, including interventions administered with the intention of providing direct benefit to the research participant. It may also consist of non-therapeutic procedures and interventions only intended to answer scientific questions.[170] The definition of research in the National Code is therefore broad, encompassing clinical trials but also other types of health research. This is different from the ethical framework in South Africa, which specifically excludes clinical trials. The impact of this is discussed in the context of the drug regulatory framework in Nigeria. It must also be noted that the limitation of the matters on which ethics review must be sought is helpful to address the problems of mission creep mentioned in the previous section. In any event, the National Code emphasises its focus on health research rather than all "research involving humans."

However, as in South Africa, there are some types of research exempted from the requirements of the National Code, including ethics review. Exemptions are determined by health research ethics committees (HRECs).[171] These include research on the effectiveness of or comparison between teaching methods, curricula, or classroom management methods and research

---

168 National Health Research Ethics Committee, *The National Code for Health Research Ethics* (Abuja: Federal Ministry of Health, 2007).
169 Section A.
170 Section A.
171 Section B – Who Determines the Exemptions?

involving the evaluation of the outcomes of procedures, programmes, and services designed to produce information leading to improvement in delivery, clinical audits, and so on.[172] If these kinds of research can make human participants identifiable or expose them to criminal liability or harm, then the Code applies to them. Another exemption is innovative or non-validated medical treatment, in other words, experimental medicine. The Code defines this as treatment that is designed solely for the benefit of the patient but in which the ability of the treatment to result in the desired result is to some degree not proven. The National Code exempts such activities but recommends that such treatments be researched to generate information about their efficacy as soon as possible.[173] This particular exemption was tested during the Ebola epidemic of 2014. At this time, certain innovative products were proffered as cures for a disease for which there was as yet no definitive cure (such as Nanosilver and ZMapp). Ebola, as may be recalled, has a high rate of fatality. The NHREC attempted to clarify the provision on innovative or experimental treatment in 2014 as Nigeria dealt with the epidemic.[174] As the author observed in an article, innovative or experimental medicines raise ethical and legal dilemmas – weighing a patient's right to live by trying an innovative treatment and allowing an unproven treatment which may prove not only inefficacious but unsafe.[175] There is as yet little clarity on this issue. Nigeria's ethical framework as contained in the National Code does not address it in any depth, although it provides for the process of seeking an exemption from an HREC.[176] Should experimental treatment be exempt from informed consent, ethics review, and other kinds of protection? This question becomes even more urgent in view of the court decision in Abalaka's case, where the Federal High Court held that the banning of an experimental drug by the drug regulatory authority (NAFDAC) on the grounds of non-compliance with ethical guidelines which had not yet been developed was wrong because the guidelines had not yet been established. The only requirement in the view of the court was the requirement for informed consent from the prospective patient.[177] Around the world, access to such experimental medicines remains a keenly contested issue,[178] with some states in the United States enacting the

---

172 Section B.

173 Section B (f).

174 NHREC, "Statement on the Use of Innovative or Non-Validated Medical Treatment," online: http://nhrec.net/nhrec/statement-on-the-use-of-innovative-or-non-validated-medical-treatment-in-nigeria/ (October 2, 2015).

175 Cheluchi Onyemelukwe, Access to Experimental Drugs, Fundamental Rights and Clinical Trials Regulation in Nigeria (2017) 10:2 Asia Pacific J Health L & Ethics 81–114.

176 Section E (g).

177 *Abalaka and Anor v President of the Federal Republic of Nigeria and others* (Suit no. FHC/ABJ/CS/640/2010).

178 See cases such as *Abigail Alliance for Better Access to Developmental Drugs v von Eschenbach,* 495 F.3d 695, 696.
      (D.C. Cir. 2007) (en banc), cert. denied, 128 S. Ct. 1069 (2008) (US); Simms v Simms EWHC 2734 (2002).

so-called "right to try" laws.[179] At present, the National Code does not provide for a compassionate access programme. It does not state what an HREC must consider in granting an exemption for experimental treatment and what protections must be in place for the prospective receiver of such treatment. Reference to the South African *Ethics in Health Research: Principles, Processes and Structures – 2015*, which requires appropriate informed consent, ethics review, expert advice and subsequent formal research, and compassionate access guidelines in other countries, may be helpful in a future reconsideration of this exemption.

A substantial part of the National Code deals with the structure, process, and modalities of ethics review. This is considered in a subsequent section on Health Research Ethics Committees. The other part of the National Code distils the ethical principles that provide guidance for ethics review committees in reviewing research into ten principles.[180] The National Code does not reference the statutes or international ethics guidelines from which it draws inspiration, but there is no doubt that other ethics guidelines have some influence on the principles enunciated therein. However, while many of the principles might be considered to fit into, for instance, the Belmont framework of respect for persons, beneficence, and justice, a broader set of principles, as espoused by the Code, arguably allows for the capturing of many moral considerations. These include considerations that might have specific implications in a developing country context like Nigeria, particularly in the area of community engagement, and with respect to issues with implications for vulnerability in resource-challenged settings.

The first principle is that research must have social or scientific value to either participants, the population they represent, the local community, the host country, *or* the world in order to justify the use of finite resources and risk of harm to participants.[181] In view of the potential for exploitation, it would have been more helpful to specify that research undertaken in Nigeria should be relevant to local needs (*and* the world). Simply stating that research must have value for the

179 See A Bateman-House & Christopher T Robertson, "The Federal Right to Try Act of 2017: A Wrong Turn for Access to Investigational Drugs and the Path Forward" (2018) JAMA Intern Med, doi:10.1001/jamainternmed.2017.8167. Sam Adriance, "Fighting for the "Right to Try" Unapproved Drugs: Law as Persuasion," (2014) 124 Yale L J 148.

180 Under the section titled "Ethical Principles and Guidelines for HREC's Approval of Research," it states,

> In order to approve research covered by this code the HREC, shall determine a balance between the various principles guiding the ethical conduct of research, some of which are outlined below. Since some of these will inevitably conflict, judgement and consensus are essential in determining whether a research should be conducted.Researchers, research sponsors, and research institutions are thus not expressly required to ensure the application of these principles in health research. Instead, it is implied that these principles should guide the conduct of research by researchers due to the fact that all research must pass through ethics review as required under the Code, but this should have been made explicit.

181 Section F (a). (Emphasis mine).

host country *or* the world leaves room for the possibility of research which may have value for the rest of the world but perhaps not for Nigeria. An example is research on developing expensive medication that may not be affordable in Nigeria after the research. One could contrast this with a similar principle in South Africa's guidelines, which provides that

> Research should be relevant and responsive to the needs of the people of South Africa. The proposal should explain the anticipated contribution to knowledge generation and, ideally, how the findings might be translated into products, interventions, processes or services likely to improve living standards and well being of South Africans.[182]

This places on researchers in South Africa an ethical responsibility to ensure that their research is relevant to both the broad health and development needs of South Africans, encouraging researchers to ensure that findings are translatable into mechanisms for improving the health status of South Africans. The National Code does, however, require that, in international collaborative studies, research be accompanied by "comprehensive capacity building, technology transfer and health care delivery strategies that address significant local health problems and add value to local participants of research, including researchers, institutions, communities and the country."[183]

The second principle is the requirement for scientific validity.[184] Thus, health research involving humans must have clear scientific objectives; use valid methodology; have equipoise in the case of clinical trials; have adequate operationalising plans within the context of the environment in which the study is to take place; have a plausible data analysis plan, including a specific role for Data and Safety Monitoring Boards in clinical trials; and use correct measurements for outcomes. In the absence of these requirements, a research project is deemed unethical.

The third principle is that there must be fair selection of participants based on the scientific objective(s) of the research, while minimising any attendant risk.[185] However, it goes on to state that this should not be construed to allow the exclusion of groups such as women, children, groups of people disadvantaged

---

182 Section 2.3.1 of the National Health Research Ethics Council, *Ethics in Health Research: Principles, Structures and Processes Guidelines* (Pretoria: Department of Health, 2015). The Kenyan Guidelines contain similar provisions, requiring that "Externally sponsored research designed to develop a therapeutic, diagnostic or preventive product must be responsive to the health needs of Kenya. That means the research to be conducted must address health problems that are important in Kenya." National Council for Science and Technology (NSCT), *Guidelines for Ethical Conduct of Biomedical Research Involving Human Subjects in Kenya*, NCST no. 40 (Nairobi, NCST, 2004).

        3(hereafter, "Kenyan Guidelines"). Section F(a).

183 F (a).
184 Section F (b).
185 Section F (c).

in any way, and other vulnerable people, especially from research that would benefit them, without explicit reasons for doing so, but specific safeguards are required to protect the vulnerable. This is a very useful principle, especially in a context that remains to a large extent paternalistic. Further elaboration of this principle beyond the brief, general discussion contained in the National Code would have been helpful.[186] For instance, while it can be argued that under the National Code, pregnancy is not, by itself, a ground for exclusion from health research (as, for instance, in the Kenyan Guidelines),[187] the principle could have been couched in more specific terms with respect to pregnancy and reproductive capacity. Might these be considered sufficient reason for exclusion? What other grounds could constitute good reasons (or insufficient reasons) for excluding persons from participating in research? It would have been helpful if examples of reasonable grounds for any exclusion were provided in the National Code.

The fourth principle[188] requires there to be valid attempts to minimise risks and maximise health-related benefits for participants to ensure a favourable risk and benefit ratio. These benefits are distinguished from the risks and benefits of therapies that participants would be exposed to even if they were not participating in research or incidental risks or benefits. In the weighing of risks, the principle requires that risks and benefits be considered at the level of both individual participants and community. It does not delineate specifically how such risk should be weighted. (For instance, if the risk to the community is minimal, but the risk to the individual is higher, what happens?)

The fifth principle states that, for research to be ethical, it must undergo independent review. It states that independent review, through a system of ethical review and oversight of such systems, provides assurance that reasonable attempts have been made to minimise the potential impact of the conflicting interests of the different parties involved in health research, including participants, researchers, and sponsors of research, and ensures balanced judgement.

The sixth principle is informed consent. It states that informed consent is a prerequisite for the ethical conduct of research. It delineates the process for obtaining informed consent in Nigeria. Consent forms are to be no longer than eight pages and should not contain unnecessary jargon and legalisms. Importantly, it also requires that all consent activities be documented, and where written consent is not possible, witnessed thumb-printing or witnessed audio recording may be acceptable, if approved by the ethics review committee.[189] It permits verbal consent and states that information about the research is to be

---

186 See, for instance, a discussion of this principle in the Australian context: Angela J Ballantyne, Wendy A Rogers on behalf of the Australian Gender Equity in Health Research Group, "Fair Inclusion of Men and Women in Australian Clinical Research: Views from Ethics Committee Chairs" (2008) 188:11 Med J Aust. 653.

187 See, for instance, the Kenyan Guidelines, Section 14, which deals with research involving pregnant women.

188 Section K (d).

189 Section F (f) (9).

provided at an educational level no higher than for individuals with nine years of education in Nigeria. This is essential in the Nigerian context because of the considerable degree of illiteracy in certain parts of the country.[190] Translation of documents may be required in other situations. Consent in instances such as those involving persons with diminished autonomy or children and other extraordinary instances is to be provided in other guidance documents issued by the National Health Research Ethics Committee. These documents have yet to be produced but are clearly essential, especially in light of the Pfizer incident.

The National Code emphasises procedural requirements and the informed consent form. However, the focus on crucial substantive issues is, in my view, much less than desirable. For instance, it provides the size of the paper documenting informed consent (A4), the font, the font size, spacing, and margins.[191] Substantively speaking, it does require that "adequate information"[192] be provided to research participants, but it does not specifically state what constitutes adequate information. This is a matter that would have benefited from a clearer discussion in a country like Nigeria, with its diverse circumstances.[193] For instance, it has been noted that in some parts of Nigeria, a strict disclosure of all possible risks, as required in many developed countries, may unnecessarily frighten potential participants and cause huge difficulties in enrolling them.[194] This cannot be generalised, however, as many educated Nigerians would prefer to have as much information as possible. Although it requires a statement of all the risks and benefits in the discussion of another principle, clearly stating that in the section dealing with *informed consent* would have been very helpful. Fadare and Porteri note that it would also have been appropriate to discuss the dependent relationship between researchers (who are often physicians acting in the dual role of doctor and researcher) and research participants. They contend that, in a paternalistic context where doctors are still often regarded as having all the knowledge, it would have been appropriate for the National Code to emphasise or itemise the rights of research participants, even within such relationships.[195]

---

190 See UNESCO, *Education for All (EFA) Global Monitoring Report 2010: Reaching the Marginalised* (Oxford: Oxford University Press, 2010). Ben Chuks Okeke, "Literacy/Numeracy and Vocational Training among Rural Women in Nigeria for a Good Livelihood and Empowerment" (2004) 23:3 Int J Lifelong Educ 287.

191 Section K (f) (2) and 9.

192 Section K (f) (1).

193 Elsewhere, the Code requires the consent processes to include explicit information about the researchers and their affiliations, qualifications, and contact details that will allow research participants or ethics review committees to contact them. But this cannot be all the information required in the informed consent process. See Section S (1) (i).

194 Ezeome & Marshall, *supra* Note 85 at 3. Are there circumstances in which it could be ethically appropriate to withhold any information, and what effect would this have on the validity of any consent obtained for participation in the research project? This question would have been answered by a clearer definition of informed consent than is currently contained in the National Code.

195 Joseph O Fadare & Corinna Porteri, "Informed Consent in Human Subject Research: A Comparison of the International and Nigerian Guidelines" (2010) J Empir Res Hum Res Ethics 67 at 71.

In such a relationship, it may be best for the informed consent process to be conducted by a physician not directly in charge of the potential participant's care and treatment.[196]

Related to this point, although parts of informed consent issues are dealt with in the discussion of other principles (including respect for persons, maintaining of trust relationships), there is no clear definition of informed consent. Nor is there any discussion of related concepts, such as voluntariness, coercion, incentives, and undue inducement. There is, instead, a requirement that some of these matters be contained in the informed consent document. Presumably, it is assumed that everything contained in the informed consent document would be discussed by the ethics review committee. The committee may, however, focus exclusively and erroneously on the document rather than the process. Moreover, these issues are vital in health research involving humans and have particular relevance in a developing country context like Nigeria, as discussed in Chapter 1. They deserve to be articulated in fuller and clearer terms in the Code, especially in light of the circumstances of the Pfizer incident.[197] There is arguably room for elaborating further on informed consent in the Code.

The seventh ethical principle under the Code is that there must be respect for potential and enrolled research participants from the commencement to the end of the research project. According to the Code, this mandates that their right to privacy may not be compromised, that their involvement must be voluntary, and that they are able to withdraw at any time. However, it makes an exception to the ability to withdraw at any time, stating,

> However, data, samples, etc. already contributed to the research up to that point may not *needlessly* be withdrawn as this may jeopardise the scientific validity of the research, unjust to those who remain in the study and all or part of their sample or data may have been used or modified into different form(s), including presentation at meetings or publications by the researchers.[198]

This provision has particular significance in light of other research that has occurred in Nigeria, including the HapMap project, mentioned earlier. The use of the word "needlessly" is troubling, if not inappropriate. Who determines what is "needless" – the ethics review committee, the researcher, or the participant who submitted the sample or data and the community?

The current statement in the seventh ethical principle thus needs revision as it is tantamount to unduly limiting the rights of research participants and

---

196 This is required by the Helsinki Declaration and the Code of Medical Ethics, 2004, s.31.
197 The Kenyan Guidelines, for instance, state that undue inducement is not to be permitted. It will be recalled that one of the issues that arose in the Pfizer incident discussed earlier in this chapter was that the parents alleged that they had inadequate understanding of information because they assumed that the children would receive treatment.
198 Section F (g).

communities. What is required is clear guidance on when it would be possible or not permissible to withdraw data.[199] A revision is necessary, especially given that the National Code states elsewhere that a Materials Transfer Agreement required for samples and biological materials does "not vitiate the right of research participants or communities to request that their samples be withdrawn from research according to the terms of the informed consent process."[200] For instance, it would be better to state that data can be withdrawn at any time except when the data has been modified or is impossible to extricate from other data (such as when it has been anonymised).

In a similar manner, the requirement for privacy is treated rather cursorily, with the National Code stating that "Their right to privacy may not be needlessly compromised."[201] While it requires the informed consent document to contain a section on confidentiality,[202] the National Code does not address what might comprise "needless" interference with privacy or needful limitation of privacy. Nor does it address possible mechanisms for maintaining privacy.

Respect for participants also requires that they be informed of the progress of the research and any finding that may have a potential effect on their health and well-being, and their continued participation in the research. This would ostensibly include any adverse events. The respect principle also includes engagement with the community where the research is to take place. According to the National Code, community consultations or assent may have to precede research activities so as to ensure community acceptance and to respect the sociocultural values of the community and its institutions. The community "may" also be informed of the progress of the research, relevant findings that may influence their health and well-being, and the outcome of the research. The use of the word "may" indicates that this is not mandatory. It ought to be mandatory to inform communities of relevant findings that may influence their health and well-being. Further, although this is implied, there is no explicit emphasis on the continued importance of individual consent. The Kenyan Guidelines, for instance, note that for cultural reasons women in some rural areas may not be allowed to give their consent to participate without the expressed permission of their husbands. However, the Kenyan guidelines also emphasise that in such instances, the woman must still give her consent.[203] Such emphasis is also present in the Canadian guidelines with respect to Aboriginal participants in research.[204] The Nigerian context is pluralistic, making more direct guidance useful. In a study on informed consent practices in Nigeria, it was observed that "Nigeria, like most

---

199 For a discussion of this issue, see generally OECD, *Creation and Governance of Human Genetic Research Database* (Organisation for Economic Cooperation and Development, 2006) at 95.
200 Section N.
201 Section F (g).
202 Section K (f) 5 (x).
203 Kenyan guidelines, Section 6.
204 *CIHR Guidelines for Health Research Involving Aboriginal People* (Ottawa: CIHR, 2008), Article 4.

nations in Africa, is too pluralistic in its culture and social norms for any of the factors to uniformly apply, and most significant generalizable factors are shaping informed consent practices in Nigeria along a Western model."[205] Another study on informed consent to genetic epidemiological research on hypertension and breast cancer in Nigeria noted that women in rural areas in Nigeria were more likely to state that they needed spousal permission to participate in research than women in urban areas.[206] In Nigeria, where communities, particularly in rural areas, play crucial roles in the lives of their members; women in some areas require permission from their husbands; or parents seek the endorsement of adult children on important matters, an emphasis on the continued necessity of the individual's informed consent would have been appropriate. This would be in line with the fundamental value of each person in Nigeria, a value articulated in the Constitution.

The eighth principle in the National Code states that for research to be ethical, the trust relationship between researchers and research participants must in no way be undermined. This also requires a transparency between researchers, participants, and communities, including an explanation of goals, risks, and benefits.[207] Like the principle of respect for persons, the trust principle also encourages the engagement of individual participants and communities, respect for local sociocultural values, and the provision of relevant and timely feedback to communities.

The ninth principle[208] states that for research to be ethical, the interest of participants, researchers, sponsors, and communities must be protected. This principle requires the transfer of technology where appropriate, capacity building, and respect for sociocultural and other differences. It also requires that intellectual property, indigenous knowledge, and contributions of all parties must be taken into consideration, adequately protected, and compensated, particularly where research leads to tangible or intangible benefits. Satisfactory parameter(s) that shall determine sharing of commercial and other benefits should be clearly articulated. Where appropriate, benefit sharing agreements, materials transfer agreements, patent rights, intellectual property, and royalty distribution agreements should be signed before the commencement of the research project. In light of the controversy that has arisen with respect to the distribution of benefits in developing countries, this is an important principle. Unfortunately, it does not state what happens where the interests of participants and others conflict. It

---

205 Emmanuel R Ezeome & Patricia A Marshall, "Informed Consent Practices in Nigeria" (2009) 9:13 Dev World Bioethics 138 at 140.
206 Patricia A Marshall, "The Individual and the Community in International Genetic Research" (2004) 15:1 J Clin Ethics 76. See Anant Bhan, Mina Majd & Adebayo Adejumo, "Informed Consent in International Research: Perspectives from India, Iran and Nigeria" (2006) 3 Med Ethics 36.
207 It also includes explanations of and "alternatives to participation and voluntariness." The phrasing here is confusing.
208 Section K (i).

would have been appropriate to state explicitly that the interests of participants are paramount in the event of a conflict.[209]

The tenth principle[210] states that, for research to be ethical, it must be conducted according to the principles of good clinical and laboratory practices. Any clinical trial conducted in Nigeria has to be conducted according to the principles articulated in the National Code, relevant laws, the provisions of guidelines or regulations set periodically by the Federal Ministry of Health, the provisions of the current *Harmonized Tripartite Guideline for Good Clinical Practice* (ICH-GCP E6), and the provisions of the current ISO 14155-1, 14155-2 (2003): *Clinical Investigation of Medical Devices for Human Subjects.*

In addition to the ethical framework, the Code also provides for the specific responsibilities of the ethics review committees, sponsors, host institutions, and researchers.[211] The National Code also includes procedures for institutional ethics review committees to register with the National Health Research Ethics Committee.[212] I discuss these later.

The ethical framework provided in an instrument such as the National Code should provide an ethical foundation for the operation of the research governance system. This would include providing coherent guidance for ethics review committees reviewing research. It should also provide specific protections for research participants. The National Code attempts to meet these expectations. It articulates guidance for ethics review committees in Nigeria. It provides a ready reference source for researchers conducting research in Nigeria, thus covering the gap that previously existed. It applies to all health research conducted anywhere in Nigeria, thus providing broad protections for all research participants in Nigeria.[213]

Health research anywhere in Nigeria, according to the National Code, "*must* comply with all sections of this code."[214] It also uses mandatory words in describing several of the responsibilities of sponsors, researchers, and ethics review committees, thus making it clear that these cannot be waived. The use of strong language is commendable, as is the reach of the National Code, that is, health research conducted anywhere in Nigeria. The National Code thus creates not only ethical standards but also obligations. In so doing, it elevates protections for research participants while creating parameters for other parties involved in health research in Nigeria.

Moreover, the National Code addresses several issues that have much significance in the developing world, especially matters relating to distributive justice.

---

209 *Ibid.* In one of several confusing provisions, it also states, "Risks, benefits, and responsibilities of research must be shared during the development, planning, conduct, dissemination of *results.*"
210 Section K (f).
211 Section S.
212 Section C.
213 Section A.
214 Section A (emphasis is mine).

Thus the ethical framework provided by the National Code includes the principle of a trust relationship, which invokes the concept of fiduciary relationship not only between researchers and research participants but also between researchers, research sponsors, and communities. Issues such as conflicts of interest, which evoke divided loyalties, would be antithetical to such a relationship. Further, in many of the principles, the need to bring communities into the research process, a matter that is of great significance in a developing context like Nigeria's, is emphasised. Also, the need to ensure that research benefits the communities in which a project takes place is highlighted.[215]

However, there are important areas in the National Code that would benefit from fuller discussion, especially in view of the Nigerian context. These include the areas of informed consent and privacy. Particularly with regard to informed consent, the National Code leans towards procedural matters rather than substantive issues. For example, it lists what needs to be contained in the informed consent document but does not even define the concept. Nor does the National Code engage in a comprehensive discussion of issues arising in informed consent and how they should be addressed by researchers and ethics review committees in the Nigerian context. There are similar issues with the concept of privacy as dealt with in the National Code.

As stated, the use of words such as "Code"[216] and "must" throughout the National Code indicate that the responsibilities of researchers, sponsors, and ethics review committees are mandatory. However, what may have been sacrificed in the pursuit of such directness is the provision of guidance in areas that have proved controversial in research ethics in developing country contexts like Nigeria's. Thus, issues that have caused controversy in research in developing country settings, such as the use of placebos, standard of care, undue inducements, and paying research participants, do not, unfortunately, receive specific or significant attention in the Code.[217] These matters are very relevant in the Nigerian context. For instance, with regard to undue inducements and paying research participants, Marshall, in a study commissioned by the United States National Bioethics Advisory Commission, records the apparent limitations in choices that prospective research participants face as a result of poverty and lack of education. She reports a Nigerian physician as stating that

---

215 Section S(6) (iv) further provides that

> The investigator must provide assurances that reasonable efforts shall be made to ensure that the benefits of research is made available to the community where the research was conducted. Details of any arrangement to ensure this shall be worked out by the researchers, sponsors, HREC, community leaders and Community Advisory Committees.

216 The word 'Code' in some legal traditions indicates that a document is legally binding. See Bernard Dickens, "Codes of Conduct and Ethics Guidelines" in Lester Breslow ed, *Encyclopedia of Public Health* (New York: Macmillan Reference, 2002) at 226.

217 This contrasts with the provisions in other developing countries' guidelines, like South African and Kenyan research ethics guidelines. See, for example, Section 2.14 of the South African Guidelines.

Because of the scarcity of everything [in Nigeria], to be talking about a choice [is questionable]...in the United States, you can ask questions, you can ask for a second opinion, but that doesn't happen here. We are challenged by [our] culture, by poverty, by lack of literacy, by education of what basic rights a person has... [the] power [of these factors] is too awesome."[218]

Thus, the Nigerian context demands specific guidance as to what might constitute undue inducement. As Dickens and Cook suggest, payments to research participants may not be considered "undue inducement" in every instance, and in some circumstances payment may be ethically acceptable.[219] But specific guidance, as contained, for instance, would have been helpful.

In the case of the use of placebos and standard of care, old articles show that placebos have been used in trials in Nigeria when there was effective treatment.[220] Some recent trials have also been placebo-controlled.[221] The National Code provides that an investigator "must ensure that the investigational product and any comparator products are of appropriate quality and are subject to quality assurance procedures. This information must be accurate and adequate to justify the nature, scale, and duration of the clinical trial."[222] This does not, however, address whether the use of placebos is appropriate or in what circumstances. It could, of course, be argued that the use of placebos with respect to drug trials is addressed in the Code because the National Code requires compliance with the ICH-GCP, which allows the use of placebos under certain circumstances.[223] As some commentators[224] have pointed out, however, the ICP-GCP's stance on placebo use in drug trials is permissive by comparison to other international

---

218 Patricia Marshall, "The Relevance of Culture for Informed Consent in U.S.-Funded International Health Research" in National Bioethics Advisory Commission, *Ethical and Policy Issues in International Research: Clinical Trials in Developing Countries Volume1 - Report and Recommendations of the National Bioethics Advisory Commission* (Bethesda, Maryland: National Bioethics Advisory Commission, 2001) 212 at C-26 to C-27.

219 BM Dickens & RJ Cook, "Challenges of Ethical Research in Resource-Poor Settings" (2003) 80 Int J Gynecol & Obstet 79 at 80.

220 See, for instance, LA Salako, AO Falase & A Fadeke Aderounmu, "Placebo-Controlled, Double-Blind Clinical Trial of Alprenolol in African Hypertensive Patients" (1979) 6 Curr Med Res Opin 356.

221 "Placebo controlled trial of Amalar" in the Nigeria Cinical Trials Registry - Trial No: 61209749; Date registered: 2014-06-11; Trial Status: Pending online: <nhrec.net/nctr>. See also Paul Feldblum et al, "SAVVY Vaginal Gel (C31G) for Prevention of HIV Infection: A Randomized Controlled Trial in Nigeria" (2008) 3:1 PLoS ONE e1474. doi:10.1371/journal.pone.0001474.

222 Indian Council of Medical Research, *Ethical Guidelines for Biomedical Research on Human Subjects* (New Delhi: ICMR, 2000) at 21.

223 See International Conference on Harmonisation of Technical Requirements for Registration of Pharmaceuticals for Human Use, ICH Harmonised Tripartite Guideline: Choice of Control Group and Related Issues in Clinical Trials E-10 (Geneva: International Conference on Harmonisation of Technical Requirements for Registration of Pharmaceuticals for Human Use, 2000), online: <www.ich.org/LOB/media/MEDIA486.pdf> (April 1, 2010).

224 See Chapter 3.

guidelines such as the Helsinki Declaration (which has, as noted in Chapter 3, been revised severally on this point).[225] This suggests that this is an area which needs to be debated domestically and addressed in greater detail in domestic guidelines. A more detailed treatment would have been appropriate.

There are other matters, such as informed consent in studies involving children[226] and the mentally ill, which have been left out deliberately, and which the National Code states are to be tackled in other guidance.[227] These are important matters, especially in light of the Pfizer incident, which involved children. Sexual and reproductive health research involving adolescents is another area that is subject to ethical dilemmas.[228] To plug the gap in addressing health research involving children, the Federal Ministry of Health developed the *Guidelines for Young Persons' Participation in Research and Access to Sexual and Reproductive Health Services in Nigeria* in 2014.[229] These guidelines were provided as guidance but not policy as only the NHREC has the power to set norms for research by law. However, the NHREC has now issued an interim policy statement regarding the enrolment of children in research.[230] As defined by the Child Rights Act, a child is a person under the age of 18.[231] Under the policy statement, enrolment of children under the age of 12 requires the consent of both parents. In studies involving children between 12 and 18 years old, the child is required to assent to treatment, and parents must consent. The policy statement also states that children are a vulnerable group and adequate protections to prevent exploitation must be maintained. In essence, the interim policy only addresses the questions of assent, consent, and the appropriate ages for these requirements. There is as yet no policy dealing with gradations of risks for therapeutic and non-therapeutic research or the particulars of how HRECs should appraise research protocols involving children.

Other matters that raise substantial ethical issues, like biobanking, have also been the subject of policy statements by the NHREC. Biobanking raises the issues of third-party rights to donated samples; the uses to which such samples

---

225 *The ICH E-10 Guideline: Choice of Control Group and Related Issues in Clinical Trials* indicates that placebo use is permitted, except when there "is proven effective treatment [that] is life-saving or known to prevent irreversible morbidity." Thus the effective treatment need not be the "best" treatment, and apart from fatal diseases or extensive harm, no other exceptions appear to be made.

226 Other trials have included children in the past. See, for instance, HB Jibril, AS Ifere & DU Odumah, "An Open, Comparative Evaluation of Amoxicillin and Amoxicillin Plus Clavulanic Acid ('Augmentin') in the Treatment of Bacterial Pneumonia in Children" (1989) 11:9 Curr Med Res & Opin 585.

227 Section (f)13.

228 See, for example, Morenike O Folayan et al, "Ethical Issues in Adolescents Sexual and Reproductive Health Research in Nigeria" (2015) 15:3 Dev World Bioethics 191.

229 Federal Ministry of Health (FMoH), Guidelines for Young Persons' Participation in Research and Access to Sexual and Reproductive Health Services in Nigeria 2014.

230 NHREC, Policy Statement Regarding the Enrollment of Children in Research in Nigeria (PS2. 1016).

231 Section 277 of the Child Rights Act.

may be put, including genetic mapping; cultural sensitivities in certain contexts; potential commercial interests and the rights of patients in this and other regards; and the sort of consent which may be required for such usage. The anxieties for African countries in particular stem from anxieties about the potential friction between customary norms around the use of the body and the ownership of the body[232] as well as historical distrust stemming from issues such as slavery and colonialism. At present, there are biobanks in the country, the most prominent of which is the H3Africa biobank, established in 2009 and operated by the Institute of Human Virology of Nigeria (IHVN) Abuja which administers the operation of biorepositories in Jos and Zaria.[233] Prior to this, the International Haplotype Mapping Project, mentioned earlier, also collected Nigerians' samples. The National Code requires a Materials Transfer Agreement for the transfer of biological samples. There currently exists a prototype document for materials transfer. The current state of the Agreement has sometimes raised issues with foreign researchers on the grounds of conflicts with the laws of their countries or the policies of their institutions, for instance, on the grounds of intellectual property, as the current Agreement requires the two parties – the foreign recipient of samples and the Nigerian provider of samples – to apply for patents over any inventions developed as a result of samples provided to the foreign recipient. The reasoning behind this is simple, if not necessarily agreed upon by all analysts – Nigeria intends to benefit from samples taken from it, often free of charge. Otherwise, when cures or diagnostic tools are developed from the materials, they often become too expensive for resource-constrained African countries like Nigeria.

The Policy Statement issued by the NHREC further elaborates on the biobanking regulatory regime in Nigeria.[234] In accordance with the Policy Statement, the NHREC (not the institutional HRECs) registers biobanks in Nigeria and provides the ethics review required in regard to usage of biological samples. The policy also requires broad consent for use of samples, which covers the entire period of use of the samples and does not require re-consent, but not blanket consent, where the sample may be put to a different or another use. While the guidelines have been deemed generally appropriate by some authors, there are some gaps, for example with respect to permitting the sharing of samples amongst local researchers. There is more of a focus on the sharing of samples and biological materials internationally through the exportation of such samples.[235]

The National Code does not mandate registration of clinical trials in the clinical trials registry. Although a Clinical Trials Registry, managed jointly by

---

232 Simisola Akintola, "Ethical and Legal Issues in Biobanking for Genomic Research in Nigeria" (2012) 1:1 BeOnline J 16–25.
233 Obiajulu Nnamuchi, "Biobank/Genomic Research in Nigeria: Examining Relevant Privacy and Confidentiality Frameworks (2015) J L, Med & Ethics 776.
234 NHREC, *Policy Statement on Storage of Human Samples in Biobanks and Biorepositories in Nigeria* (PS1.02013).
235 Nnamuchi Note 249 at 784.

NHREC and NAFDAC, the drug regulatory agency, was created a few years ago, there is no mandatory requirement to register any trials. The benefits of a registry have been noted in previous chapters. In Nigeria, where there is little data on research, and there is an ongoing need to encourage the prioritisation of disease conditions that are prevalent in the country, the need for such a mandate cannot be overemphasised. Although a registry is in place, it is currently at least partly non-functional – it is difficult to find trials on the site indicating a need for ongoing maintenance.

Furthermore, the National Code does not expressly address the place of other guidelines, such as the Helsinki Declaration and the CIOMS Guidelines (with the exception of the ICH-GCP with respect to drug trials) in research governance in Nigeria. It does state, however, that all health research in Nigeria must comply with the National Code.[236] Thus, it would appear that the National Code would, at the very least, be the first reference point for health research involving humans in Nigeria. And, at the most, the National Code rules out the application of other guidelines. As will become clear shortly, this is problematic mainly because other instruments in Nigeria that provide guidance for health research involving humans essentially require compliance with the Helsinki Declaration. These include the Clinical Trial Guidelines[237] which currently provide guidelines for drug trials in Nigeria. This creates potential room for debate and confusion.

According to the provisions of the National Code, the National Health Research Ethics Committee is required to update, revise, edit, and modify the National Code in accordance with international research ethics and local laws, and at its discretion.[238] The National Health Research Ethics Committee may also provide additional guidelines in subcodes, although the National Code takes precedence when there is a conflict between it and a subcode. It is hoped that gaps in the discussion of the ethical principles will be addressed either in a revision of the National Code in the near future or in the development of additional guidelines. It can be argued that the supplementary policy statements are part of the standards-setting functions of the NHREC under the National Health Act. However, amending the National Code seems to be a more appropriate and clearer measure than interim notes, particularly in the absence of an emergency. As noted in the National Code itself, the National Code supersedes other guidance and subcodes, and is therefore the principal instrument for health research and other issues.[239] Consequently, any gap with respect to these and other issues in the National Code is problematic and potentially exposes participants to harm and researchers and research sponsors to confusion. Further, as I argued in Chapter 3, domestic ethical codes and guidance, such as the National Code, can have more positive impact than the international ethical guidelines if they go

236 Section A.
237 Section 3 (b) of the NAFDAC Regulations.
238 Section P.
239 See p. 68 of the National Code.

beyond such guidelines and address any problematic or controversial issues more clearly. They would thus create room for easier implementation in domestic contexts and offer greater protections to research participants. The National Code and subsequent policy statements have done this only partially.

The institutional framework

As in the previous chapter, we now consider the institutional framework through which Nigeria's ethical and legal frameworks are implemented. We consider the challenges that the various institutions face in carrying out their tasks in protecting research participants while promoting beneficial research, including matters relating to quality, regularity, and consistency.

Ethics review committees

The requirement to submit research protocols to ethics review was not a formal requirement under domestic instruments until 2004, when it was required for biomedical research in the Code of Medical Ethics. As the Pfizer incident showed, there were instances where research projects did not undergo ethics review. The early history of research governance included inconsistent and ad hoc operations, gross underfunding, lack of expertise, a lack of awareness by researchers of the existence of ethics review committees, and no SOPs. In terms of structure, there were non-functional national committees and, at certain points, two national committees in operation. Financial support, stability, and sustainability are therefore key concerns with respect to the functioning of ethics review committees in Nigeria. As the following discussion indicates, while some of these challenges have been addressed through the development of a research governance structure, the operational aspects of the structure remain challenges today.

The enactment of the National Health Act, which confers power on the Minister of Health to create the NHREC, has solved the problem of ad hoc operations and the mandatory requirement for all institutions of research to have an HREC, clarifying and legitimating a clear structure founded on law. [240] The NHREC, as already noted, has the responsibility of registering HRECs;[241] updating, revising, and editing the Code;[242] auditing HRECs;[243] and sanctioning erring researchers by referring them to the professional councils regulating the researchers.[244] All institutions that seek to conduct health research must now have an HREC, which must be registered with the NHREC,[245] renewable on

---

240 Sections 32 and 34.
241 Section C.
242 Section O of the National Code for Health Research Ethics.
243 Section L.
244 Section N.
245 Section C.

a biannual basis.[246] The last updated list on the NHREC website shows that 43 HRECs from various institutions have been registered with the NHREC.[247]

Registration requirements with the NHREC include an institutional guarantee of responsibility for members' actions; certificates of completion of research ethics training for members of HRECs in NHREC-approved programmes; and confirmation of the provision of necessary resources by the institution, including meeting space of sufficient quality, office and storage space, sufficient staff, and funds to support the HREC in its review and record-keeping duties. The line of reporting authority is required to be from the chairperson of the Health Research Ethics Committee to the chief executive of the institution, such as a Vice-Chancellor of a university underlining the importance of the HREC.[248] Institutions that lack an HREC may enter into an agreement with another institution that has such a committee to provide ethics review of proposed research.[249] Such an agreement may only exist between institutions in the same state or in the same geopolitical zone.[250] The NHREC reviews multisite research involving more than three sites.[251] HRECs may adopt the reviews of another HREC in international collaborative research, where such approvals comply with the requirements of the Code, and take account of local circumstances.[252] HRECs are also required to monitor already reviewed research at intervals appropriate to the degree of risk involved in participation in the research. They may initiate the oversight process in the event of the receipt of any complaints or information from any source.[253] Studies have indicated that a majority of the HRECs have SOPs in place.[254]

To promote efficiency, the National Code requires that HRECs review and provide decisions within three months. Where the HREC is unable to provide a decision in three months, it must refer the proposal to the NHREC, which may reallocate the review to another HREC. Where the HREC does not provide a decision within the specified period and does not refer it to the NHREC, the

246 Section C (b).
247 Registered Health Research Ethics Committee, online: <http://nhrec.net/registered-health-research-ethics-committees-in-nigeria-hrec/>.
248 Section C (a) (1) – (6). According to the website of the National Health Research Ethics Committee, there are currently 19 ethics review committees from various health institutions registered with the National Health Research Ethics Committee (NHREC). See NHREC, "Registered HREC Database," online: <www.nhrec.net/nhrec/hrec_db.php> (May 2, 2010).
249 Section C (f).
250 Section C (f). In the absence of an institution that has an ethics review committee in the same state or geopolitical zone, an institution is required to refer the national ethics review committee to for guidance.
251 Section C (n).
252 Section E (3) (b).
253 Section E (e).
254 A Yakubu et al, "Research Ethics Committees in Nigeria: A Survey of Operations, Functions, and Needs" (2017) 39:3 Hastings Center Report, online: <https://www.thehastingscenter.org/irb_article/research-ethics-committees-nigeria-survey-operations-functions-needs/>.

researcher may make a report to the NHREC which may sanction the HREC.[255] Further, among other procedural rules, HRECs are required to keep records of proceedings and maintain such records for ten years.[256]

In terms of composition, the NHREC is composed of a chair; a medical doctor; a lawyer; a pharmacist; a community health worker; a representative each of the Christian and Islamic faiths; a researcher in the medical field; a researcher in the pharmaceutical field; a radiographer; a physiotherapist; and three persons of integrity, one of whom must be a woman.[257] The members are appointed for an initial period of three years, with a possibility of renewal for another three years only.[258] HRECs, on the other hand, are required to have at least five members. The criteria for membership of HRECs are experience; expertise; and diversity of its members' ages, genders, sociocultural backgrounds, religions, and sensitivities to such issues as community attitudes to promote respect for its advice and counsel in safeguarding the rights and welfare of researchers and research participants. Members are also required to have varying academic and professional backgrounds to promote complete and adequate review of health research. The National Code also requires the membership of a lawyer, "whenever feasible." The National Code does not specifically require community membership, but it requires at least one scientific member and one non-scientific member. Further, if the HREC wishes to review research that involves vulnerable participants, such as children, prisoners, pregnant women, or physically and psychologically disabled persons, the HREC is to appoint one or more individuals knowledgeable about, and experienced in, working with such participants for the review process. However, these individuals are not allowed to vote.[259]

In order to ensure the independence and effectiveness of such a national committee, the membership of and the appointment process into the committee are key factors. There is currently a concentration of persons in the health field, which would reflect the focus of ethics review in Nigeria. But it also means that people with other backgrounds are very much in the minority and may not bring the necessary diversity and balance for proper consideration of the issues raised in ethics review. There is also no requirement for gender balance. In a country where women remain under-represented in many sectors, and where research participation raises key issues relating to gender equality,[260] the mandatory requirement for only one woman is insufficient. Further, while Muslims and Christians are in the majority, an argument could be made that other

---

255 Section E (d).
256 Section E (d).
257 Section 33 (2) (o) of the National Health Act.
258 Section 33 (3).
259 Section D.
260 Chity W Princewill et al, "Factors Affecting Women's Autonomous Decision Making in Research Participation Amongst Yoruba Women of Western Nigeria" (2017) 17:1 Dev World Bioethics 40–49.

religions, including traditional religions, are left out unjustifiably. At any rate, a recent study shows that this requirement is not often complied with by many HRECs.[261]

Moreover, drawing from a new governance approach in the proposed hybrid framework of governance, participation by those on behalf of whom regulation is undertaken is essential. Surprisingly, with the emphasis on community participation in the ethical framework outlined in the National Code, there is no specific requirement for a community member or a requirement for the inclusion of research participants. Nor does the National Code expressly require that the institution in which the HREC operates seek members from outside the institution. An institution could reasonably argue substantial compliance with the National Code, even if all members are institutional employees. A survey of several African countries, including Nigeria, showed that before 2002, all committee members were full-time employees of the institution, except in South Africa.[262] There has therefore been a propensity for using only institutional employees in these committees. A recent study of HREC composition in Nigeria also showed that there was no lay membership in 80 per cent of the HRECs surveyed.[263] Further, the requirement for consultation of someone familiar with working with vulnerable persons without an accompanying requirement that such persons be allowed to vote (as is the case in South Africa and the United States) seems incongruous and may adversely affect the protection of such persons as research participants. Perhaps this is because such persons with familiarity with vulnerable persons may not have undergone the training required for regular members. But this means that vulnerable persons, or a professional who is familiar with their situation, are effectively excluded from actual decision-making on the HRECs. Accountability, the need for balance and diversity, and the necessity to prevent inherent conflict of interest require that the compositional requirements of ethics review committees be revisited. Implementation is also essential as studies have noted that the composition of many HRECs is done in a "haphazard" manner.[264]

Another key systemic issue is the development of capacity for ethics review. This would include knowledge about the requirements of relevant policies and guidelines for the ethical conduct of health research in Nigeria.[265] The National Code's requirements for registration with the NHREC include a prereq-

---

261 A Yakubu et al, "Research Ethics Committees in Nigeria: A Survey of Operations, Functions, and Needs" (2017) 39:3 Hastings Center Report, online: <https://www.thehastingscenter.org/irb_article/research-ethics-committees-nigeria-survey-operations-functions-needs/>.

262 Jean-Paul Rwabihama, Catherine Girre & Anne-Marie Duguet, "Ethics Committees for Biomedical Research in Some African Emerging Countries: Which Establishment for which Independence? A Comparison with the USA and Canada" (2010) 36 J Med Ethics 243 at 244.

263 A Yakubu et al, Note 267.

264 AM Agunloye, "Current Role of Research Ethics Committees in Health Research in Three Geopolitical Zones in Nigeria: A Qualitative Study" (2014) 7:1 S Afr J BL 19–22.

265 See Jocelyn Downie, "The Canadian Agency for the Oversight of Research Involving Humans: A Reform Proposal" (2006) 13 Account Res 75 at 80.

uisite for the members of the HREC to undergo NHREC-approved training programmes. Research on capacity building on research ethics indicates that while training is now more common, knowledge gaps in terms of the provisions of the Code remain.[266] Another recent study on researchers in South-Western Nigeria indicated that the levels of awareness of the National Code and knowledge of its provisions are very low.[267] A study also noted a strong association between the committee members' training on research ethics and the degree of conformity with the requirements of the National Code; this was also associated with committee members' perceptions that ethics training was a strength in carrying out their duties effectively.[268] Lack of training has been reported as a significant challenge,[269] indicating a gap that exists in other sub-Saharan African countries.[270]

To conduct ethics review effectively, adequate financial support, including expenditures for documentation, administrative support and necessary office equipment, training, project monitoring, site visits, any honoraria for ethics review committee members, and other direct and indirect costs, is essential. In this respect, the National Code provides that HRECs may charge fees for any or all of their activities, at their discretion, and in consultation with the principal officers of the institution. The fees must be commensurate with the anticipated expenses required for adequate oversight of research.[271] The National Code further provides that as part of its oversight functions, the NHREC shall review the commitment of institution(s) to provide resources for the proper functioning of HRECs.[272] There are no provisions for remunerating members of either the NHREC or the HRECs (which is different from the National Health Research Committee). This is problematic because this is likely to affect the commitment of members who volunteer time out of otherwise busy schedules. Studies have noted that lack of remuneration or incentives are a key challenge for HRECs which may be related to irregular meetings.[273]

Although the National Code states that the NHREC may revoke the registration of HRECs which lack funding, past experience has shown that institutions have often failed to provide resources for ethics review committees.

266 O Adeyeye & T Ogundiran, "Knowledge of and Training in Research Ethics in an African Health Research Community" (2013) 4:2 AJOB Primary Res 44–50.

267 O Ogunrin et al, "Knowledge of the Nigerian Code of Health Research Ethics among Biomedical Researchers in Southern Nigeria" (2016)11:5 J Empir Res Hum Res Ethics.

268 A Yakubu et al Note 267.

269 *Ibid.*

270 C Zielienski et al, "Research Ethics Policies and Practices in Health Research Institutions in Sub-Saharan African Countries: Results of a Questionnaire-Based Survey" (2014) 107:1 J R Soc Med 70–76. Blessing Silaigwa & Douglas Wassenaar, "Biomedical Research Ethics Committees in Sub-Saharan Africa A Collective Review of Their Structure, Functioning, and Outcomes" (2015) 10:3 J Empir Res Hum Res Ethics.

271 Section E (r).

272 Section L (c).

273 Agunloye Note 285.

Governments, too, have failed to provide resources for ethics review commit-tees.[274] Nigeria's NHREC, for example, lacks dedicated funding for its legal obligations. It does not have a dedicated office space nor funding for regular meetings.[275] Many HRECs lack dedicated office space and staff for their opera-tions.[276] At present, university-based HRECs currently charge a fee to research-ers, mainly students, for research review.[277] In some cases, this has devolved into a fundraising scheme for universities and risks becoming a business, creating an incorrect impression of the main purpose of ethics review and potentially un-dermining HRECs' principal responsibility of protecting research participants.

Even though the National Code requires fees to research sponsors to be com-mensurate with the anticipated expenses of the review, charging fees raises the spectre of conflict of interest and regulatory capture in a resource-limited setting like Nigeria. Yet it may be difficult for institutions, which are already straining under the burden of limited funds to provide resources, independent of such fees, for ethics review committees. In addition, it may not be desirable to charge fees for all types of research, including research conducted by students, projects for expedited review, and non-funded research. Conflicts of interest and the related concomitant of regulatory capture are serious concerns for the govern-ance of health research in countries around the world. In a telling observation, a survey on ethics review in African countries observed that "No committee has rejected a research protocol."[278] Of course, this may be because each protocol reviewed met the requisite ethical standards. But it is also a reminder that many institutions in all countries, but especially institutions in the developing world and specifically in African countries like Nigeria, have many reasons to want to attract the resources represented by research, especially externally sponsored re-search. Ideally, a funding scheme, independent of the institutions, is necessary to provide resources while ensuring independence. Perhaps a better approach might be to establish a scheme through which ethics review committees in Nigeria, including the NHREC, are funded.

Related to this point, conflict of interest is addressed in different provisions of the National Code. These include provisions requiring that any conflict of interest of any members, including employment, ownership of stock, and re-ceipt of honoraria or grants from potential research sponsors, be indicated to the NHREC at the time of registration.[279] It also states that a member must not participate in the review of a project in which she has a conflicting interest.[280] Also, the director of a medical institution in which clinical trials are to be con-ducted must ensure that there is no conflict of interest in conducting the trial at the medical institution between the sponsoring company and the researcher who

274 Adeyinka G Falusi, Olufunmilayo I Olopade & Christopher O Olopade, *supra* Note 55 at 23.
275 The author is a member of Nigeria's National Health Research Ethics Committee.
276 A Yakubu et al, Note 286.
277 Agunloye Note 285.
278 Rwabihama et al, *supra* Note 189 at 244–245.
279 Section C.
280 Section D.

is an employee of the medical institution.[281] The informed consent form should also contain information on any apparent or actual conflicts of interest.[282] There are, however, no direct injunctions on what should happen in other cases. Instead, there is a requirement for any potential conflicts of interest to be indicated to the NHREC at the time of registration and for informed consent forms to contain an indication of any conflicts of interest. The National Code does not state what indicating such potential conflict of interest would mean for registration with the NHREC or what the ethics review committee should do if the informed consent form indicates that a researcher has a conflict of interest. More generally, the provisions do not address institutional conflicts of interest, that is, circumstances in which an institution would benefit from proposed research projects and therefore has an interest in ensuring that the project is approved. Presumably the establishment of an "independent" HREC would take care of this circumstance. Nevertheless, the potential for such conflict becomes even more significant, given the wording of the membership requirement in the National Code that allows members to be drawn solely from the institution. There is therefore an increased potential for perceived, if not actual, conflict of interest. Further, as already described, many institutions rely on foreign funding for maintaining ethics review committees. The peculiarities of the establishment of some of these committees in the past also contribute to a perceived lack of independence. As Rwabihama and others describe it, in the African context,

> fault may lie in the peculiarity of the origin of these committees. The establishment of the first African ethics committees is connected to the need of conducting Western research projects in developing countries. While African scientists are managing to conduct local research in order to solve some endemic or tropical diseases in the region, ethics committees are still working with the dependences of Western agencies. Committees are not independent enough, according to the history of their creation and the socioeconomic context.[283]

The creation of a national system of governance has the potential to deal with the problematic beginnings of ethics review, as described earlier. However, more specific guidance would have been helpful. Given its importance and the adoption of an institutional system, where members of ethics review committees could include members of the same department as a researcher or previous or potential collaborators on research projects, a specific section on conflicts of interest would have been helpful in the National Code. Such a section could include a detailed expatiation on what may constitute conflict of interest in different

---

281 Section O (8).
282 Section F (f).
283 Rwabihama, et al, *supra* Note 189 at 249.

circumstances and how institutions, ethics review committees, research sponsors, and researchers should deal with such conflicts.

After ethics review approval, there is need to ensure that the protocol is conducted as approved. Moreover, the National Code provides for access to the benefits of health research as well as post-trial access, and these require follow-up or monitoring. Monitoring has been identified in several pieces of research as an area of lacuna in the regulation of research. In effect once research is approved, monitoring often does not occur, leaving room for deviations from approved protocols and potentially impacting adversely on research participants' safety and welfare.[284] Lack of monitoring is attributable mainly to lack of finances for HRECs operations.[285]

Without means to ensure compliance, the provisions of the National Code would be mere words on paper. In international collaborative research, the NHREC is required to report its findings of misconduct against researchers, sponsors, and collaborators to the national ethics regulatory agency of the country of origin of the researcher.[286] The institution is not precluded from taking appropriate legal action against such researchers and their representatives in Nigeria. This provision has not been employed as yet. More generally, the NHREC has powers to undertake other punitive action against researchers found guilty of unethical practices, including barring them from conducting research for variable periods of time depending on the severity of findings of misconduct. The National Code also provides that NHREC shall recommend disciplinary action against researchers; report all cases of fraud, deception, infamous conduct, plagiarism, fabrication, and falsification to the appropriate regulatory authorities, including the police; and bar researchers from conducting research for variable periods of time depending on the severity of findings of misconduct.[287] Although there have been instances which could warrant such action as researchers advertising miracle drugs which have not been adequately tested or reviewed by any authorities, these sanctions have not been imposed by the NHREC.

The sanctions which the NHREC can impose in the event of a breach by researchers include reporting to professional regulatory bodies. Particularly in relation to external researchers, it may be argued that the sanctions in the National Code are insufficient since these researchers may not face any direct penalties for unethical conduct. This would be different, however, if there were penalties, especially for basic infractions, such as failure to obtain informed consent or failure to submit projects for ethics review.

In sum, there has been significant progress in the development of a uniform ethics review system in Nigeria. But the history of research governance in Nigeria

---

284 Bridget G Haire et al, "Development of Guidelines for the Conduct of HIV Research Monitoring by Ethics Committees in Nigeria" (2014) 18:3 (Special Edition) Afr J Reprod Health 70.

285 Agunloye, Note 285 at 21.

286 Section N (f).

287 Section N (a) to (f).

shows that sustainability is crucial and has been lacking in the past. Funding challenges, lack of monitoring capacity, other basic resources, irregular meetings, and gaps in the standards set out by the National Code remain challenges for effective ethics review in Nigeria.

Drug regulatory authority: NAFDAC

Established in 1993, NAFDAC is the principal regulator of drugs in Nigeria.[288] I have already discussed the guidelines that NAFDAC has developed and the regulations it is currently developing, pursuant to its powers under the NAFDAC Act. [289] *National Agency for Food And Drug Administration And Control Act 1993* (the NAFDAC Act) and the *Drug and Related Products (Registration, Etc.) Act 1993*,[290] are both federal laws, drugs and poisons being matters on the Exclusive List.

The NAFDAC Act establishes NAFDAC, which regulates food and drugs in Nigeria. It is primarily responsible for clinical trials regulation by virtue of the *Drug and Related Products (Registration, Etc.) Act 1993*, which provides that clinical trials for the importation, manufacture, or supply of a sample of drug, or a drug product, can only be undertaken after a permit has been granted by NAFDAC, which would issue a valid clinical trial certificate for that purpose.[291] Applications for a clinical trial certificate are to be made as prescribed by regulations provided by NAFDAC, and clinical trials are to be conducted under regulations made by NAFDAC.[292] Pursuant to powers conferred on it by the NAFDAC Act, NAFDAC has established the NAFDAC Good Clinical Practice Guidelines, 2016 (NAFDAC Guidelines).[293] Under the Guidelines, the basic ethical principles of justice, respect for persons, beneficence, and non-maleficence must be adopted by researchers.[294] The protection of research participants is the paramount consideration, and trial investigators are required to ensure that informed consent is obtained, the privacy and confidentiality of participants are maintained, and the rights of the participants to physical and mental integrity are maintained, amongst other things. A trial should not commence unless the Agency and an ethics committee are of the view that the therapeutic and public health benefits justify the risks.[295] The Agency can also prohibit, suspend, or terminate a trial if it believes that the conditions in the initial authorisation permitting the trial have not been met, or the safety or scientific validity of the trial

---

288 Section 5 of the *NAFDAC Act*.
289 Section 29 *NAFDAC Act*.
290 Section 1, *National Agency for Food and Drug Administration and Control Act 1993 (NAFDAC Act)*, Cap N1.
291 Section 1(2) and 5 of *Drug and Related Products (Registration, Etc.) Act 1993*.
292 Section 5(2) of the *Drug and Related Products (Registration, Etc.) Act 1993*.
293 NAFDAC, NAFDAC Good Clinical Practice Guidelines. See also NAFDAC (Regulatory and Registration Directorate), Documentation Guidelines for Clinical Trial in Nigeria.
294 Section 1.16 of the NAFDAC Guidelines.
295 Chapter 2; Section 1.1 of the NAFDAC Guidelines.

is in question.[296] There are also extensive provisions about the responsibilities of sponsors and investigators, monitoring, report requirements, and archiving, amongst other things.

The NAFDAC Guidelines require that the current version of the Helsinki Declaration be followed in carrying out clinical trials. There is no mention of the National Code or the NHREC. Even so, there are many similarities between the provisions of these instruments. However, there are also some differences between the National Code and supplementary policy statements, and the NAFDAC Guidelines, including, for example, the requirements for informed consent in children, the use of investigational drugs in the absence of proven interventions, and placebo use. The NAFDAC Guidelines requires that "The current revision of the Declaration of Helsinki is the accepted basis for clinical trial ethics, which must be fully known and followed by all engaged in research on human beings."[297] These requirements essentially indicate that the Helsinki Declaration is the standard for the conduct of clinical trials of drugs currently in Nigeria. As described earlier, there are areas of potential conflict, particularly with respect to matters like the use of placebos in clinical trials between the National Code (which endorses the ICH-GCP's arguably less strict stance on placebo use) and the Helsinki Declaration (which is stricter on placebo use). While the National Code does not mandate registration in a clinical trials registry, the NAFDAC Guidelines list "Evidence of registration in a WHO Clinical Trial Primary Registry" as one of the required documents that the Agency may inspect.[298] The two organisations also collaborated on a clinical trials registry, the Nigeria Clinical Trials Registry (NCTR) (www.nhrec.nt/nctr), but this is not yet a WHO clinical trial primary registry[299] and is, in any case, not recognised in the NAFDAC Guidelines. Investigators would be in a better position if they register with the Pan African Clinical Trial Registry (PACTR), which is recognised as a WHO Clinical Trial Primary Registry.

These points suggest a lack of coordination between the key bodies that govern research in Nigeria. From a legal standpoint, the law is clear that no one may import any material into the country for investigation without obtaining a clinical trial study authorisation.[300] But the NHREC also has powers under the National Health Act to set norms and standards for research involving humans, including clinical trials. The legal framework for both are creations of the National Assembly. Both bodies have created standards which

---

296 Section 4.102 of the NAFDAC Guidelines.
297 Section 1 of the NAFDAC Guidelines.
298 Section 7; 70 NAFDAC Guidelines.
299 WHO Primary Register, online: <www.who.int/ictrp/network/primary/en/>. The WHO recognises clinical trial registers and registry after ensuring that they meet certain criteria regarding Content, Quality and Validity, Accessibility, Unambiguous Identification, Technical Capacity, Administration, and Governance. See WHO Registry Criteria, online: <www.who.int/ictrp/network/criteria_summary/en/>.
300 <www.pactr.org/>.

are different in some respects. This could lead to confusion for investigators and researchers.

There is limited publicly available analysis of NAFDAC's role in clinical research, including the analysis of effectiveness, outcomes, and turnround times. However, it is clear that NAFDAC's regulatory role must be coordinated properly with other actors, including national and institutional review committees, in order to provide comprehensive protections for participants in health research and to prevent potential confusion for research sponsors. Greater uniformity in the provisions of the regulations provided by NAFDAC and other documents, such as the National Code, is desirable. Further, as the Pfizer incident indicates, NAFDAC must take its role as a regulator of clinical trials of drugs in Nigeria seriously. Moreover, efforts need to continue to be made to address systemic issues that have been previously identified: inadequately trained staff and a lack of conflict of interest guidelines. An adequate number of trained staff members is necessary to monitor trial sites and review documentation, among other things. Investment of resources by the Nigerian government is clearly necessary to assist NAFDAC in its regulatory functions. Thus, with respect to NAFDAC, adequacy of resources and implementation, accountability, and uniformity of regulatory requirements are key issues as research governance develops.

Health professional bodies

There are several health professional bodies. Each has its own regulatory body, established by statutes. Since professional regulation is a matter under the Exclusive Legislative Lists, it is a federal matter, and the laws made in that regard are national laws governing all professionals in that discipline. The *Medical and Dental Practitioners' Act*[301] is key in this respect. It establishes the Medical and Dental Council of Nigeria as a statutory body[302] and confers the power of determining entry requirements and standards on it. Medical and dental practitioners who wish to practice in Nigeria are required to register with the Medical and Dental Council of Nigeria.[303] The Act also establishes the Medical and Dental Practitioners Disciplinary Tribunal, which tries cases brought by the Medical and Dental Practitioners Investigation Panel, also established under the Act.[304]

A primary responsibility of the Medical and Dental Council of Nigeria (the Council), as provided in the Act, is to establish a conduct of conduct for medical and dental practitioners in the country.[305] The most recent edition of the rules is *The Code of Medical Ethics in Nigeria*, (hereafter *Code of Medical Ethics*) drawn

---

301 *Medical and Dental Practitioners' Act* Cap M8, Laws of the Federation of Nigeria, 1990, as amended.
302 Section 1 of the *Medical and Dental Practitioners' Act*.
303 Section 6 of the MDCN, *Code of Medical Ethics in Nigeria*, 2004.
304 Section 15 of the *Medical and Dental Practitioners' Act*.
305 Section 1 (c) of the *Medical and Dental Practitioners' Act*.

up in 2008.[306] The Code has indirect legal force as subsidiary legislation, having been drawn up under powers given by the Medical and Dental Practitioners Act.[307] The legal status of the *Code of Medical Ethics* has significant implications for research governance in Nigeria. First, it moves medical and dental practice, and research from merely professional self-regulation to the domain of legal regulation. The provisions of the Code of Medical Ethics have legal force to the extent that they do not go beyond the remit permitted under the enabling statute under which the rules were made.[308] Any requirements regarding biomedical research involving medical practitioners and dental practitioners are therefore legal requirements which can provide grounds for legal actions in Nigerian courts.[309]

This does not, of course, mean a complete displacement of self-regulation since the professional disciplinary bodies are still the primary custodians of authority, except when a medical or dental practitioner's activities are a criminal offence.[310] Self-regulation thus remains a central reality for medical and dental practitioners in Nigeria, including in the area of biomedical research. In the hybrid framework of governance, such self-regulation is an important piece of the puzzle of research governance, and is complementary to other types of regulation, including legal regulation. In this regard the *Code of Medical Ethics*, like many professional codes, provides certain legal protections for medical and dental practitioners who act within its boundaries,[311] thus facilitating research

---

306 Medical and Dental Council of Nigeria, *Code of Medical Ethics in Nigeria*, 2004.

307 Section 37 of the *Interpretation Act, 1964*. The Interpretation Act defines subsidiary legislation as "any order, rules, regulations, rules of court or bye-laws made either before or after the commencement of this Act in the exercise of powers conferred by an Act." Similar rules, such as the Rules of Professional Conduct in the Legal Profession made pursuant to the Legal Practitioners' Act, have been ruled by the Supreme Court in Fawehinmi v Nigerian Bar Association (No.2), *Fawehinmi v Nigerian Bar Association (No.2)* (1989) 2 NWLR (pt. 105) 558. The significance of this is that, as decided by the Supreme Court in *Abubakar v Bebeji Oil and Allied Products Ltd.*, subsidiary legislation, such as the *Code of Medical Ethics*, has the force of law *Abubakar v Bebeji Oil and Allied Products Ltd.*, (2007) NWLR (pt. 1066) 319, at 385, Paragraph E. However, as decided in *Olarenwaju v Oyeyemi*, as subsidiary legislation, its scope, validity, and authority cannot go beyond the scope of the enabling statute from which it derives its authority: in this instance, the *Medical and Dental Practitioners Act Olarenwaju v Oyeyemi and Others* (2001) 2:697 NWLR 229 at 255–256. *Din v A G Federation* (1988)4:413 NWLR 292.

308 See *ibid*. See also *Ishola v Ajiboye* (1994) 6:352 NWLR at 506. *Governor of Oyo v Folayan* (1995) 8:413 NWLR 292.

309 See, for instance, *Okatta v The Registered Trustees of Onitsha Sports Club* (2008) 13:1105 NWLR 632, decided on the basis of the Legal Practitioners Rules.

310 The Supreme Court ruled in *Denloye v Medical and Dental Practitioners' Disciplinary Committee* that the disciplinary body of the Medical and Dental Council of Nigeria cannot decide upon criminal matters. Such matters are dealt with through the normal venues for criminal matters: namely, the courts. *Denloye v Medical and Dental Practitioners' Disciplinary Committee* (1968) 1 All NLR 306.

311 See Angela Campbell & Kathleen Cranley Glass, "The Legal Status of Clinical and Ethics Policies, Codes, and Guidelines in Medical Practice and Research" (2001) 46 McGill L J 473 at 477.

within professionally agreed-upon confines. But it also, if employed effectively, protects the interests of patients and research participants who can hold medical and dental practitioners to the standards articulated in the code.

The Code of Medical Ethics incorporates the National Code requirements with respect to health research and requires medical and dental practitioners to comply with them.[312] However, it observes that the Council was not duly consulted in the process of making the National Code. It also goes on to highlight the specific provisions regarding "biomedical research involving human subjects."[313] Biomedical research, which the Code of Medical Ethics governs, is a subset of health research involving humans, and thus the application of the *Code of Medical Ethics* is more limited than the National Code. The rules provided by the Code of Medical Ethics state that only a registered doctor can legally conduct research involving human subjects. The application of this is doubtful as it excludes social science researchers and even other health professionals. It is rooted in a very narrow definition of the terms "research involving human subjects." Other rules concerning the mandatory requirement of informed consent, provision of effective treatment where available, privacy, balance of risk-benefit ratio, use of the best proven treatment, and placebo use only in the absence of that are more widely accepted rules. The latter reflects the principle on placebo use as laid out in the Helsinki Declaration of 1996. Following from this point, it is important to emphasise that the Code of Medical Ethics does not indicate that the Helsinki Declaration, as amended, should be followed. Instead, it lists the principles culled verbatim from the 1996 version, in effect making them the standard for all medical and dental practitioners to follow in research. One principle requires that informed consent be obtained from research participants. It requires that every subject of biomedical research be informed of the aims, methods, potential benefits, and hazards of the research. Where the research is conducted by the physician treating the subject, informed consent must be obtained by another physician.

Also, in medical research combined with medical treatment, the Code of Medical Ethics states that the potential benefits and hazards of a new method should be weighed against the advantages of the best diagnostic and therapeutic methods.

Since the principles are drawn verbatim from the 1996 version of the Helsinki Declaration, it states that "The patient must be assured of the best-proven diagnostic and therapeutic method. This does not exclude the use of placebo in studies where no proven diagnostic or therapeutic methods exist." As I discussed briefly in Chapter 1, this is an area that has caused much controversy. This particular provision has been revised severally since the 1997 controversy surrounding the placebo-controlled trials of AZT in several developing countries. Further, the standard of the "best-proven diagnostic or therapeutic

312 Appendix 6, The Code of Medical Ethics, 2008.
313 Section 31.

method" is not the standard required under the National Code which requires compliance with the ICH-GCP in clinical trials of drugs. There could, therefore, potentially be conflict between the two codes with respect to what the standard of care should obtain in biomedical research. It must be noted, however, that the Code of Medical Ethics requires medical practitioners to comply with the National Code but does not state the effect of a conflict between the two Codes.[314]

The Code of Medical Ethics is an important component of the legal framework for research governance, including elements of both self-regulation and legal regulation. However, there are gaps, weaknesses, and problems that limit its usefulness as an instrument for the governance of research. Its applicability is limited to medical and dental practitioners in Nigeria.[315] Thus, it would not apply to other researchers, such as social scientists, or to domestic entities who may sponsor research or external research sponsors. Second, the *Code of Medical Ethics* does not provide specific penalties for failure to comply with its requirements. It must be recalled that the functions of the NHREC include referring erring professionals who violate the requirement for research ethics to their professional regulatory bodies. Presumably, if the practitioner is negligent in the treatment of a patient who is also involved in research or fails to comply with the requirements of the National Code which are now incorporated into the Code of Medical Ethics, the practitioner may be disciplined by the Tribunal established under the Medical and Dental Practitioners Act.[316] At present, there are no reported cases of disciplining a researcher for non-compliance with the rules for biomedical research involving humans. However, neither the Medical and Dental Council of Nigeria nor the Nigerian Medical Association have, in my view, been sufficiently active in ensuring proper research governance in Nigeria. There is, for instance, no evidence that either has tried to push for the establishment of ethics review committees at the institutional and state levels, as required in the Code of Medical Ethics.

As another example, neither body publicly condemned or took any actions against the doctor who reportedly provided a backdated letter to Pfizer in the 1996 trial. Interestingly, one of the sanctions that the National Health Research Ethics Committee can apply against an erring researcher is reporting her to the appropriate professional council.[317] If the professional council shows no interest in disciplining erring members, this sanction becomes merely illusory. Such inadequate professional interest is, as I discussed in Chapter 3, one of the systemic

---

314 Section 32 of the Code of Medical Ethics.
315 This would include medical and dental practitioners from other countries, who are required by the Code of Medical Ethics to register with the Medical and Dental Council of Nigeria in order to practise in Nigeria. See Section 6 of the *Code of Medical Ethics*.
316 Section 15.
317 National Health Bill, Section 33.

issues that adversely affects research governance in many countries.[318] Although the discussion here focusses on doctors, they are by no means the only professionals who are, or should be, a part of research governance.

Civil society organisations

Civil society organisations (CSOs), in particular, non-governmental organisations (NGOs) have provided many services in Nigeria, including in the areas of democratic governance, public participation, civil liberties and human rights, and health.[319] As in many developing countries where the state may not always meet the expectations of the people, CSOs often attempt to fill the gap or advocate for changes in the state's actions, policies, or proposals. While their achievements in some respects may only be modest, their impact in Nigeria has been significant. In the health sector, NGOs have been actively involved in different aspects of health delivery, gender issues, advocacy, and education.[320] For instance, CSOs have been closely involved with advocating for the health rights, assisting the development of policies for HIV/AIDS prevention and treatment in Nigeria, soliciting support from other countries and international organisations, and educating the public about health matters.[321] CSOs could also play such roles in the context of research governance by promoting awareness of issues surrounding health research and research governance, and by participating in related policymaking. Many of them work at the grass-roots level, allowing them significant access to, and opportunities in, communities in which research may take place.[322]

Currently, there are few CSOs which provide different services with respect to research governance. These include the Association for Good Clinical Practices in Nigeria (AGCPN) and The New HIV Vaccine and Microbicide Advocacy Society. The AGCPN was founded in 2006 and convenes an annual summit on clinical trials where issues of regulation and governance are discussed. Its goal is to build up the infrastructure for biomedical research in Nigeria by increasing the number of physicians and institutions capable of conducting clinical research. It also trains researchers in good clinical practices for clinical research. The New HIV Vaccine and Microbicide Advocacy Society advocates for the use

318 Henry Dinsdale, "Professional Responsibility and the Protection of Human Subjects of Research in Canada" (2005) 2 and 3 Health L Rev 80 at 82.
319 Matthew Todd Bradley "Civil Society and Democratic Progression in Postcolonial Nigeria: The Role of Non-Governmental Organizations" (2005) 1:1 J Civil Soc 61.
320 Kenneth L Leonard, "When Both States and Markets Fail: Asymmetric Information and the Role of NGOs in African Health Care" (2002) 22 Int Rev L & Econ 61.
321 Davidson Umeh & Florence Ejike, "The Role of NGOs in HIV/AIDS Prevention in Nigeria" (2004) 28:3–4 Dialectical Anthropol 339. Eudora Chikwendu, "When the State Fails: NGOs in Grassroots AIDS Care" (2004) 28: 3–4 Dialectical Anthropol 245.
322 MG Olujide, "Non-Govermental Organisations Self-Evaluation: Issue of Concern in Nigeria" (2005) 11:1 J Agri Educ & Ext 63.

and availability of new prevention technologies such as microbicide in Nigeria.[323] The work of these organisations touches on research ethics and governance but is also focussed on research promotion. While vital, research facilitation, or promotion sometimes conflicts with research regulation aimed principally at protecting research participants. There is, however, no CSO currently whose work focusses solely on research governance and on the rights, safety, and welfare of research participants. Such an organisation would be a welcome addition to the research governance landscape of Nigeria. The Pfizer incident, for example, would have benefited from the presence of such an organisation. CSOs are nevertheless not completely free of systemic problems that may limit their positive impact on research governance. Concerns about accountability, legitimacy, lack of autonomy, utility, and efficacy, of CSOs in Nigeria and other African countries.[324] Many of them actively seek and receive funding from the private sector and the donor community leading to questions about their effectiveness as watchdogs and the potential hampering factor of conflict of interests. This does not completely divest them of the capacity to advocate for issues such as research participants' protection or the benefits of research.

Assessing Nigeria's research governance arrangements

Health research governance in Nigeria prior to 2006 consisted of a spectrum of formal and informal mechanisms with little formal or comprehensive engagement with, and oversight of the conduct of, health research involving humans on a national level. Existing regulations were hardly implemented, as the Pfizer incident shows. As described, this state of affairs allowed much room for exploitation and unethical practices, and left participants with minimal options for legal redress. Research governance efforts, particularly with respect to the development of ethics review structures at the national and institutional levels, have long been in the making, beginning in 1980. There have been many fits and starts along the way, with ethics review committees at all levels failing and being re-established over the years. The issues of sustainability and political commitment are therefore matters that have great relevance in the Nigerian context. Now founded on legislation, issues of sustainability for research governance efforts have been partially addressed. But in view of resource constraints, sustainability and political commitment remain ongoing challenges for research governance.

Regarding uniformity and adequacy, the National Code provides a considerable degree of uniformity in terms of the ethical standards its sets. The potential

---

323 *Ibid.*
324 See Ebenezer Obadare, "Religious NGOs, Civil Society and the Quest for a Public Sphere in Nigeria" (2007) 1 Afr Identities 135. Julie Hearn, "African NGOs: The New Compradors?" (2007) 38:6 Dev & Change 1095. Daniel Jordan Smith, "AIDS NGOS and Corruption in Nigeria" (2012) 18:3 Health Place 475-480; Daniel Jordan Smith, "Corruption, NGOs, and Development in Nigeria" (2010) 31:2 Third World Quarterly, online: <https://www.ncbi.nlm. nih.gov/pmc/articles/PMC3832995/pdf/nihms524535.pdf>

consistency that the National Code represents is, to my mind, the strongest feature of the emerging governance system in Nigeria. However, current regulatory requirements are also inconsistent and confusing in some respects. There are varying requirements in different instruments with legal force, including the Code of Medical Ethics and the NAFDAC Guidelines. If all existing instruments and standards are enforced strictly, there is a potential confusion for researchers which will impede rather than facilitate research and hinder the protection of research participants. Although coordination may exist in practice, uniformity in provisions would be more ideal.

To promote efficiency, the matter of resources will require close attention and practical solutions, given the history of research governance in Nigeria. Although there is not much publicly available information on the review processes of NAFDAC with respect to clinical trials, there is evidence that ethics review at national and institutional levels may not be as efficient as it could be as a result of minimal resources. An independent funding system mandated by law for all ethics review committees is a potential solution. Efficiency might also be best achieved by having fewer instead of more ethics review committees. This may limit costs, maintaining sustainability and consequently protecting research participants in the long term.

In terms of comprehensiveness, the current research governance arrangements as articulated in the National Code address all health research involving humans in Nigeria, regardless of the funding source and geographical location. There are, however, matters which do not receive consideration which remain important. These include ethical issues such as undue inducement, standard of care, and the consent of children and mentally challenged individuals; accountability issues, such as the creation of clinical trial registries; or legal issues, such as providing sanctions for infractions of certain basic requirements. Some of these are addressed in the context of clinical trials, but might they not arise in other kinds of health research? There are also ethical issues which require a rethink, as discussed earlier, including the approach to privacy, or which are insufficiently addressed, such as conflict of interest.

The legitimacy of governance efforts is crucial. As Issalys observes, legitimacy or the appropriate derivation of authority has obvious consequences for both the effectiveness and efficiency of any mechanism of public intervention.[325] In this respect, there are questions regarding public participation in the processes. At the moment, the National Code can be (and has been) revised by the National Health Research Ethics Committee at will and without any sort of public consultation or formal consultation with other institutions involved in research governance. The National Health Research Ethics Committee is chosen by the Minister, who has very wide latitude in doing so. There are currently no

---

325 Pierre Issalys, "Choosing among Forms of Public Action: A Question of Legitimacy" in Pearl Eliadas, Margaret Hill & Michael Howlett, eds, *Designing Government: from Instruments to Governance,* (Montreal & Kingston: McGill-Queens University Press, 2005) at 154.

provisions in any of the instruments requiring an accounting to the government (the National Assembly) of any activities relating to research governance.

With regard to effectiveness, other institutions, such as professional associations, research sponsors, and universities, ought to become active in regulating their spheres of authority. This would allow not only a top-down approach from the national level but also a bottom-up approach to the governance of research, allowing a hybrid framework which is potentially more effective. Unfortunately, this has not often been the case because many of these institutions have not been active in regulating research. Further, there are currently few or no CSOs, which might act as checks and thus encourage these institutions to remain accountable. These issues may adversely affect effectiveness. Beyond these matters, practical implementation is crucial for effectiveness. The history of research governance suggests that this, in addition to uniform policies, had been lacking in Nigeria and requires close attention now.

Conclusion

As explained in this chapter, health research is critical for an improved health profile, and there is a significant need for health research in Nigeria. With this need comes the responsibility to ensure that not only is health research promoted, but research participants, many of whom might be poor, illiterate, and vulnerable in other ways, are protected. The Pfizer incident shows that this is a responsibility that must be taken seriously by all actors in research governance in Nigeria.

A framework for research governance – legal, ethical, and institutional – has emerged over the past decade or so in Nigeria. There is increasing use of the emergent research governance framework. There are, however, still issues with respect to implementation/effectiveness, uniformity and adequacy of standards, comprehensiveness, and clarity, amongst other issues.

7 Health research governance in Kenya

Introduction

Kenya is a lower-middle-income country in East Africa. One of Africa's most popular tourist destinations, it is also an increasingly popular destination for clinical trials. The country is the main commercial hub in East Africa, and it has the largest economy there.[1] Although it has a growing middle class and some health facilities with sophisticated infrastructure, it also has significant rates of unemployment and poverty;[2] four out every ten persons are estimated to live below one dollar a day.[3]

Health is a constitutionally recognised priority. The Constitution of Kenya, 2010, provides that every person has the right to "the highest attainable standard of health, which includes the right to health care services, including reproductive health care."[4] Although the provision does not expressly include it, health research, including health systems research, is a key avenue for improving healthcare. In recent years, Kenya has developed policies which emphasise the importance of health research for development. From a health research perspective, in addition to a large number of treatment-naïve patients, Kenya also has a high burden of disease, a weak public healthcare system, and health-related issues that would benefit from research[5] as well as lower research costs that may be attractive to health researchers and pharmaceutical companies.[6]

With a population of over 50 million,[7] life expectancy is 61 and 66, respectively, for males and females.[8] There is a high infant mortality rate of about

---

1 CIA, World Fact Book: Kenya, online: <https://www.cia.gov/library/publications/the-world-factbook/geos/ke.html>.
2 *Ibid.*
3 *Ibid.*
4 Constitution of Kenya, 2010, Section 43.
5 The Clinical Trials Industries in Kenya Realities, Risks and Challenges (2014), Wemos, 5.
6 Destination Kenya: A New Horizon for Conducting Clinical Research (2016), Clinical Trials Arena, online: <www.clinicaltrialsarena.com/news/operations/destination-kenya-a-new-horizon-for-conducting-clinical-research-4982984>.
7 See <www.worldometers.info/world-population/kenya-population/>.
8 WHO: Kenya Profile, online: <www.who.int/countries/ken/en/>.

37.1 deaths per 1,000 live births[9] and high prevalence of malaria, tuberculosis, and HIV/AIDS. HIV/AIDS is the leading cause of death; about 1.4 million persons live with HIV,[10] making Kenya the country with the fourth-largest HIV epidemic in the world.[11] It also has the fifth-highest tuberculosis burden in Africa.[12] In its fight against HIV, Kenya has recorded some successes; its HIV prevalence, which stood at 10.5 per cent in 1996, dropped to 5.9 per cent by 2015.[13] During the 2017 World HIV day, the Kenyan Minister of Health declared that Kenya had reduced HIV incidence by 45 per cent.[14] As part of its HIV prevention efforts, Kenya, in 2016, issued full regulatory approval for the use of pre-exposure prophylaxis (PrEP), which involves giving people who are HIV negative (who have a high risk of getting HIV) antiretroviral drugs to protect them from the virus.[15] Research is underway to determine the impact of PrEP, specifically on young women and girls in high-incidence areas.[16] Beyond the burdens of malaria, HIV, and tuberculosis, Kenya is also faced with an increasing number of deaths arising from non-communicable diseases (NCDs). An increasing number of deaths are attributed to NCDs. They account for 27 per cent of deaths in Kenya of persons between the ages of 30 and 70; the probability of dying too young from an NCD in Kenya is estimated to be 18 per cent. In Kenya, NCDs contribute to over 50 per cent of inpatient admissions and 40 per cent of hospital deaths, which dominate healthcare budgets in Kenya.[17]

In addition to NCDs, violence and harmful traditional practices, which are not only human rights violations but public health challenges, affect the Kenyan population. Although the law outlawed the practice in 2011,[18] the harmful traditional practice of FGM continues to be undertaken in the country: 21 per cent or one in five women are estimated to have undergone the practice.[19] There are high rates of violence against both men and women, and about 39 per cent of ever-married women have experienced domestic violence (physical and sexual

9 <https://www.indexmundi.com/kenya/infant_mortality_rate.html>.

10 UNAIDS, Kenya: Country Factsheet (2016), online: <www.unaids.org/en/regionscountries/countries/kenya>.

11 <https://www.avert.org/professionals/hiv-around-world/sub-saharan-africa/kenya>.

12 Wemos, "Clinical Trials In Africa: The Cases Of Egypt, Kenya, Zimbabwe And South Africa" online: <https://www.wemos.nl/wp-content/uploads/2017/07/JH_Wemos_Clinical-Trials_v5_def.pdf>.

13 Kenya National AIDS Control Council (2014), "Kenya AIDS Strategic Framework 2014/2015–2018/2019" [pdf].

14 <https://diasporamessenger.com/2017/12/kenya-marks-world-aids-day-amid-reduction-new-hiv-infections/>.

15 <https://www.avert.org/professionals/hiv-around-world/sub-saharan-africa/kenya>.

16 UNAIDS (2016), "Prevention Gap Report" [pdf].

17 <www.who.int/nmh/events/2014/kenya-ncd-prevention/en/>.

18 *Prohibition of Female Genital Mutilation Act, 2011.*

19 Kenya National Bureau of Statistics, Ministry of Health, National AIDS Control Council, Kenya Medical Research Institute, National Council for Population and Development, The DHS Program, ICF International, (2015), Kenya Demographic Health Survey, 2014, Nairobi, Kenya, (hereafter, "Kenya Demographic Health Survey") at 331.

violence, usually at the hands of husbands, while 9 per cent of men aged 15–49 have experienced domestic violence,[20] and 14 per cent of women and 6 per cent of men aged 15–49 have experienced sexual violence).[21]

Kenya, like many African countries, struggles to provide an appreciable level of quality healthcare services for its citizens at minimal cost. Universal health coverage remains far-fetched. In view of significant rates of poverty, a high disease burden, a healthcare system ill-equipped to address the many health challenges of the Kenyan people, and corruption, alongside a sizeable pool of potential research participants,[22] the need for robust health research efforts alongside comprehensive research governance cannot be overstated.

Just as importantly, as described in the pages that follow, international and collaborative research forms a significant component of health research in Kenya, and this has been so for many years, before and after Kenya's independence. Given some of the critical ethical dilemmas that have attended such research in the past around the world, Kenya provides a good context for undertaking a study of health research governance and the manner in which such dilemmas have been addressed by a national governance regime. This chapter focusses on health research governance arrangements in Kenya.

Health research has a long history in Kenya. The British colonial government engaged in health research and established the Veterinary Research Laboratories in 1908 and the Medical Research Laboratory in 1958.[23] The Yellow Fever Control programme (which eventually became the Ministry of Health's Division of Insect Borne Diseases and later the Division of Vector Borne Diseases) was established in 1938 and (like in Nigeria[24]) is one of the early markers for medical research in Kenya. As Geissler describes, while its mandate was parasitic disease surveillance, the Division also engaged in research as conducted by the colonial researchers who were posted there from Britain. The results included discovering the liver stages of the malaria parasite and the ecology of the blackfly that is a vector for river blindness.[25] The East African Medical Research Council was also established in 1957 to provide funding and other support for research in countries of the East African Community – Kenya, Tanzania, and Uganda. The African Medical Research Foundation (AMREF) was also founded in 1957 to engage in health research. As in the areas in which British colonial authorities set up shop, medicine generally and health research were a "tool of empire" and did not have Kenyans as the focus. As Ombongi notes, "in most of its aspects,

---

20 *Ibid* at 291.
21 *Ibid.*
22 See Wemos (2014), The Clinical Trials Industries in Kenya Realities, Risks and Challenges, at 16.
23 National Commission for Science, Technology and Innovation, History, online: <https://www.nacosti.go.ke/about-us/history>.
24 See Chapter 6.
25 P Wenzel Geissler, "Parasite Lost: Remembering Modern Times with Kenyan Medical Scientists" in P Wenzel Geissler & Catherine Molyneaux, eds, *Evidence, Ethos and Experiment* (New York: Berghan Books, 2011) at 297–298.

medical research was tributary to the exceedingly hegemonic ascendancy of the state, and racial-cultural dominance. Indeed, in the moral matrix of imperial legitimacy 'tropical' medicine operated a less contradictory way to its historical and social context."[26]

Thus, in the 1930s scientists at the Nairobi Medical Research Laboratory studied the stage of cerebral development of Kenyans, reaching the conclusion that Kenyan adults had the brain development of seven or eight year old European boys, justifying closely held racial prejudices.[27]

Following independence, the state remained involved in health research policy, shaping that policy through the active indigenisation/Kenyanisation and decolonisation that marked the period immediately following colonialist rule. One of these policies resulted in the creation of the Nairobi Medical School in 1967 (behind the Medical School at Makere University in Uganda). The school produced many medical researchers who worked to "Africanise" research and humanise Kenyans in contrast to some of the research conducted by colonial researchers, and who worked to ensure that diseases common in Kenya were addressed through research, including malaria, tuberculosis, and bilharzia.[28] After the dissolution of the East African Community in 1977, the Science and Technology Act was enacted by the Kenyan Parliament in 1977. It was subsequently amended in 1979 to provide for the establishment of the Kenyan Medical Research Institute (KEMRI). Many postcolonial researchers worked at KEMRI on the common diseases mentioned earlier.

As in many African countries, while the government had devoted resources to health research and gave it attention through policy, funding, and other efforts in the 1960s and 1970s, political support for research waned with more difficult economic circumstances and the consequent introduction of austerity measures. International development organisations and non-state actors stepped into the void, funding collaborative research, especially in the wake of the HIV/AIDS epidemic. In partnership with various institutions from the United Kingdom, the United States, Denmark, and so on, such as the Wellcome Trust, KEMRI conducts health research, including clinical, biomedical, and behavioural research. The presence of many research institutions in Kenya provides fertile ground for research. KEMRI, AMREF, teaching hospitals, and universities are some of the key sites for health research in the country. HIV/AIDS has presented many opportunities for health research in Kenya. Studies such as those testing the effects of male circumcision have taken place in recent years.[29] There is also research

---

26 See generally Kenneth S Ombongi, "The Historical Interface between the State and Medical Science in Africa: The Case of Kenya" in P Wenzel Geissler & Catherine Molyneaux, eds, *Evidence, Ethos and Experiment* (New York: Berghan Books, 2011) at 355.

27 *Ibid* citing Vint, 48.

28 *Ibid* at 363.

29 N Westercamp et al, "Risk Compensation Following Male Circumcision: Results from a Two-Year Prospective Cohort Study of Recently Circumcised and Uncircumcised Men in Nyanza Province, Kenya" (2014) 18:9 AIDS & Behav 1764–1767.

on malaria, tuberculosis, and neglected tropical diseases. More recent studies have also been undertaken along the intersections of health and social science research.[30] Traditional medicines research has also been a focus at KEMRI, with the creation of the Traditional Medicines and Drugs Research Centre in 1984.[31]

The evolution of Kenya's health research has been undertaken in other literature, and that history emphasises how "domestic" health research agendas and priority setting remain mirages where government does not spend significantly on research and where the agenda remains largely set by outside forces. In this regard, Wenzel Geissler notes that

> post-millennial science, by contrast, has become focused on clinical trials that usually are designed transnationally, under the leadership of European and North American institutions, charities and corporations; such trials rely upon big sites with large populations under demographic surveillance, they need sophisticated, expensive and rapidly changing immunological and genetic laboratory equipment, and they are regulated by internationally agreed standards such as ISO or 'Good Clinical Practice'; they require highly controlled environments – both to produce internationally recognised science and to manage large funding flows and staff bodies; and their results are directed towards 'global health' policies rather than immediate utilisation by local public health authorities.[32]

Prioritisation and maintaining a voice in the kinds of research that occur thus remains an issue for health research in Kenya. The Kenya Health Policy 2014–2030 states that the country considers health research to be a priority, in particular, research necessary to inform improvements in health systems strengthening, health promotion, environmental health, disease prevention, and early diagnosis and treatment.[33] In line with this, the Policy notes that there will be efforts to develop a national health research agenda and effective dissemination of research findings, obtaining funds from different sources, including from government and development partners, to execute the health research agenda, ensuring that research is relevant to the needs of the Kenyan people and developing the capacity to conduct health research in institutions in the country.[34] The legal framework under the recent Health Act, 2017, also includes provisions in this regard, examined in the following section. It remains to be seen how effectively the implementation of this Policy and other policies on health research will be.

---

30 See, for example, "RA Bryant et al, "Effectiveness of a Brief Behavioural Intervention on Psychological Distress among Women with a History of Gender-Based Violence in Urban Kenya: A Randomized Clinical Trial" (2017) 14:8 PLoS Med e1002371. doi:10.1371/journal. pmed.1002371.
31 Ombongi, at 364.
32 Wenzel Geissler, at 299–230.
33 Article 4.3.8 of the Kenyan Health Policy.
34 *Ibid.*

At the present time, many research studies have been undertaken or are underway. Clinicaltrials.gov contains 403 studies in Kenya, which is significantly less than the over 2,000 studies in South Africa and Egypt but higher than the over 200 studies registered for Nigeria. Several of the studies consider aspects of HIV, malaria, glaucoma, tuberculosis, medical device testing, reproductive health, and various other conditions. Several are behavioural – handwashing, motivation for HIV testing and behaviour change, grief management, sexual assault prevention, alcohol use reduction, use of menstrual cups for reproductive hygiene, and so on.

Health research governance in Kenya

Regulation of health research has been undertaken since the early 1980s. Prior to that, there is little evidence of formal research regulation over health research in the country. The Science and Technology (Amendment) Act of 1979 established the National Council for Science and Technology (NCST), which had the responsibility of determining the government's technology and science research priorities. In addition, it created KEMRI. Although the NCST has powers to "ensure co-operation and co-ordination between the various agencies involved in the machinery for making the national science policy"[35] and advise government on research-related issues, ethics was not initially a major focus.[36]

Research clearance, however, preceded the creation of the NCST, having commenced in 1966. Like Nigeria and Egypt, Kenya recognised the importance of a formal system of ethics review in the 1980s, but unlike these two countries, it established a framework for such ethics review and made it mandatory, under powers granted by the 1979 Act. In 1984, the NCST established the guidelines "Research Clearance in Kenya: Procedures and Guidelines."[37] Under these, it was mandatory to obtain ethics approval prior to commencing research, amongst other procedures.

The NCST developed national ethics guidelines to provide guidance for research in 2004. While there were ethics review committees in different health institutions, only KEMRI has research ethics guidelines.[38] With the increase in HIV/AIDS research and ensuing drug and vaccine trials, it was imperative for there to be some national guidance on research ethics. The NCST thus developed the national guidelines in 2004. The Guidelines noted that while ethics approval was mandatory, the ethical clearance mechanism was weak and had many loopholes which were exploited by some researchers.[39] There was also

---

35　Section 4 (e) the *Science and Technology (Amendment) Act of 1979.*

36　See the Foreword to the Kenyan Guidelines for Ethical Conduct of Biomedical Research Involving Human Subjects (2004).

37　National Council on Science and Technology (1984), Research Clearance in Kenya: Procedures and Guidelines, NCST No. 15.

38　Kenya Medical Research Institute, Guidelines on the Conduct of Research (1998).

39　National Guidelines at 4.

a multiplicity of ethics review committees and a lack of a unifying standard prior to the 2004 Guidelines. It was also important for the Council to have the power to sanction researchers who conducted research in an unethical manner. It would appear that the Council had either not had or not utilised these powers of sanction at the time of the establishment of the Guidelines in 2004, despite many years of health research in Kenya. The NCST (the Council) has now been replaced by the National Commission for Science, Technology and Innovation (NACOSTI) after the repeal of the Science and Technology Act, 1979.

With its long history of health research, Kenya has had its share of research scandals and troubling ethical dilemmas. Some of these have originated from international research. Suspicions of "blood-stealing" that have accompanied health research, often attributable to poor community engagement/participation in research and the association of medical research and state power, have sometimes hampered research.[40] Other scandals have concerned alleged failure to obtain ethical approval.[41] Prior to the development of ethical guidelines for HIV/AIDS research, the Majengo sex workers' research study which aimed to develop a vaccine for HIV, highlighted gaps in guidance in benefit-sharing. This project followed women involved in sex work to determine why several of them appeared to have immunity to HIV-1. The women were not involved in negotiations related to the research studies, which were undertaken by European researchers. This raised the kinds of ethical questions around benefit-sharing that have afflicted research in resource-constrained settings: what should participants get from research, and was there undue inducement? Who should benefit – the participants only, the local institution or the entire country? What constitutes exploitation or vulnerability? What measures could have been taken to limit participants' exposure to HIV?[42] Some of these issues point to issues in the governance framework – for instance, what are the conditions for engaging in research? What agreements must be in place prior to a movement of biological samples outside the country?

Most recently, a case involving a Kenyan medical researcher, a Kenyan nurse, and two Dutch medical researchers has emphasised the need for continued attention to health research governance in Kenya. In this case, the researchers, working through a foundation established in the Netherlands, the AIDS Remedy Fund, embarked on a research study in 2006 to determine whether or not a homeopathic remedy, "Iquilai," was effective in improving the health of

---

40 See, for instance, P Wenzel Geissler, "'*Kachinja* are Coming!' Encounters around Medical Research Work in a Kenyan Village" (2005) 75:2 Africa 173. K Peeters Grietens et al, "Doctors and Vampires in Sub-Saharan Africa: Ethical Challenges in Clinical Trial Research" (2014) 91:2 Am J Trop Med 213–215. doi:10.4269/ajtmh.13–0630.

41 Simon Siringa, "British Scientists Face Law Suit" (2004) 4 Lancet Infect Dis at 389.

42 See Pamela Andanda & Julie Cook Lucas, *Majengo HIV/AIDS Research Case*. A Report for GenBenefit (2007), online: <www.uclan.ac.uk/genbenefit>. Pamela Andanda, "Vulnerability: Sex Workers in Nairobi's Majengo Slum" (2009) 18:2 Cambridge Health Ethics Q 138. JV Lavery, "'Relief of oppression': An Organizing Principle for Researchers' Obligations to Participants in Observational Studies in the Developing World" (2010) 10 BMC Public Health 384.

HIV/AIDS patients in Kenya. The remedy had been developed by one of the Dutch researchers. About 228 HIV/AIDS patients were recruited into this "study." According to the researchers in a report published in 2008, they found that about 90 per cent of the patients showed significant improvement in their health (increased weight, more energy, better appetite, and better CD4 counts) after ingesting this remedy. Along with improved health, the researchers touted other benefits of the remedy – low cost, ease of administration, short duration of treatment, and non-interference with antiretroviral treatment.[43] These positive results were also showcased in media reports in Kenya.[44]

The Dutch Health Inspection Unit instituted before the Medical Disciplinary Tribunal a case against the two Dutch medical researchers after an investigation into their practice. In 2017, the tribunal found that they had violated basic ethical requirements as contained in the Helsinki Declaration, including failure to develop a proper study protocol, lack of risk assessment, failure to obtain ethics approval for the study, not providing documentation of informed consent, and inconsistent data collection.[45] Other sources have noted that there was no control group, that there were no clear numbers of persons who were on antiretroviral drugs and those who were not, and that CD4 counts were not taken consistently for all those enrolled in the trials, amongst other issues. As penalty, the tribunal reprimanded the Dutch medical researchers for their unethical conduct.

As noted elsewhere, this case is remarkable for two key reasons: first, in that the tribunal ruled that it could intervene in cases where medical doctors behaved unethically outside the Netherlands. The case is also remarkable for the punishment meted out to these doctors – only a reprimand on the grounds that the two Dutch doctors only had good intentions in undertaking the research in Kenya; that there was informed consent, although the documents were missing; and that there were no health harms.[46] A reprimand for actions which could have seriously damaged the lives of these patients was nothing more than a tap on the wrist, and there are several grounds on which the decision of the tribunal can be disputed. For the purposes of this book, this case was considered in the Netherlands but not in Kenya. Would this matter have been dismissed so lightly if Dutch citizens were placed at risk in this study? Could the Dutch medical researchers have been held responsible in Kenya, and by what means could any sanctions in Kenya have been meted out to them? It is interesting, to put

---

43 JH Ombaka, L van Gelder, J Scholten & L Omole, (2008) "Iquilai: Homeopathic Therapy for HIV/AIDS," Aids Remedy Fund, Amsterdam, online: <www.webcitation.org/6spnZQiNI>.

44 Kepher Otieno, "Researchers Launch New HIV/Aids Drug" *The Standard*, (1 May 2008), online: <https://www.standardmedia.co.ke/business/article/1144013008/researchers-launch-new-hiv-aids-drug>.

45 See Joyce Browne et al, "Good Intentions Do Not Replace Ethical Conduct in Research" (2018) 395:10125 Lancet 1020–1021, doi:10.1016/S0140-6736(17)32413-3. The case may be found here in Dutch: Dutch Disciplinary Tribunal for Healthcare, Decisions in the Case C2017.044. <tuchtrecht.overheid.nl/nieuw/gezondheidszorg/uitspraak/2017/ECLI_NL_TGZCTG_2017_217>.

46 *Ibid.*

it mildly, that the Kenyan health professionals have not been called to account in Kenya.[47] If it had been tried in Kenya, would the researchers have received a more severe penalty?

From a governance perspective, it is instructive that such a study could take place in Kenya and not be detected. The effectiveness of extant regulatory requirements and their implementation are thus called into question. Furthermore, the decision of the tribunal underscores one of the major reasons why domestic regulation remains vital – African countries must take responsibility for ensuring that health research within them is safe, justified, and relevant, and that participants in this research are protected.

Outside issues directly relating to research participants' protection and other research governance issues, such as inequitable relations in collaborative research, have also been a persistent issue, a problem which was noted in our earlier discussion on health research agendas. In 2004, a leading Kenyan scientist brought legal action against scientists from Oxford University, claiming that they illegally took away blood samples for HIV research. Intellectual property rights and publication rights were at issue. Also full approvals were allegedly not received by the Oxford scientists for the research, including ethics approval from the National Council for Science and Technology (NCST).[48] Intellectual property rights have also presented challenges in the context of international collaborative research with foreign research institutes and countries. In one instance, an intellectual property rights dispute arose between University of Nairobi scientists and their partners at Oxford when the latter patented the HIV development process that both sets of scientists were collaboratively working on.[49]

Labour issues, including disparities between local and foreign scientists, have also presented challenges. In 2014, in a landmark ruling, some scientists won significant damages of over 300,000 US dollars on the grounds that they were discriminated against with regard to career advancement, research publication credits, and salaries, whilst their European counterparts enjoyed better working conditions in research projects at KEMRI, mostly funded by foreign entities.[50]

---

47 Some Kenyan professionals have called for an investigation against the Kenyan health professionals involved in the study. See Gathonye Gathura, "Unethical HIV Drug Test Triggers Experts Outrage" *The Standard*, (26 March 2018), online: <https://www.standardmedia.co.ke/health/article/2001274509/unethical-aids-cure-trial-triggers-outrage>.

48 See Anthony Barnett, "Oxford Scientists Accused of Stealing Aids Orphans' Blood for Illicit Research" *The Guardian* (30 May 2004), online: <https://www.theguardian.com/society/2004/may/30/health.aids>.

49 Pamela Andanda (2004) "A Golden Chance for Medical Ethics in Kenya" SciDev, online: <https://www.scidev.net/global/health/opinion/a-golden-chance-for-medical-ethics-in-kenya.html>.

50 *Dr. Samson Gwer & 5 others v Kenya Medical Research Institute (KEMRI) & 3others [2014]* eKLR, online: <kenyalaw.org/caselaw/cases/view/100279/>. See also "Kenyan Doctors Win Landmark Discrimination Case" (2014) Nature, online: <www.nature.com/news/kenyan-doctors-win-landmark-discrimination-case-1.15594>. See also Linda Nordling, "Research: Africa's Fight for Equality" (2015) 521 Nature 7550.

Locally, issues of unethical research practices, such as plagiarism, have also been identified as problems affecting research quality.[51]

Under the Kenya Health Policy 2014–2020, efforts are required to ensure "an ethical code of conduct for health research in Kenya in accordance with the Science, Technology and Innovation Act of 2013."[52] This re-emphasises the continuing responsibility to ensure a national code of conduct for research. The research issues, some of which are noted here, suggest that continuing efforts need to be made to guarantee that relevant research is undertaken and that guidelines are implemented.

In general, health research in Kenya has had legal, ethical, and institutional underpinnings for longer than in several other African countries, including the ones discussed in this book. Thus ethics review has been mandatory. While research governance is not new, it is clear from these discussions that it has not necessarily been hitch-free. In the sections that follow, I consider the legal, ethical, and institutional framework for research governance in Kenya and the continuing challenges.

The legal framework

There are various legal instruments that govern health research in Kenya, starting with the Constitution of the Republic of Kenya. The Kenyan Constitution provides for key fundamental rights that have implications for research participants and the research process. The Constitution provides for the right to health,[53] which could be broadly interpreted to include a right to the benefits of health research. It also provides for the right to life,[54] the right to dignity,[55] the right to privacy, freedom from discrimination[56] (which may be interpreted to include the right to freedom from exclusion from participation in research without adequate justification), and the right to freedom from inhuman and degrading treatment.[57] These rights, as discussed in other parts of this book, are rights that are implicitly part of every research governance framework and which researchers must abide by.

Outside the fundamental rights provisions of the Constitution, the law has long been part of the health research governance framework in Kenya. Under the Science and Technology Act, 1979 (the 1979 Act), the NCST, as already mentioned, had the responsibility of coordinating research and advising government. In this regard, it monitored the research clearance procedures and

---

51 Lois Maru et al, "Reflections on Research Ethics and Quality in Kenyan Universities and Research Institutions" (2015), online: African Population and Health Research Centre <aphrc. org/post/6472>.
52 *Ibid* at iv.
53 The Constitution of Kenya, Article 43.
54 The Constitution of Kenya, Article 26.
55 The Constitution of Kenya, Article 28.
56 The Constitution of Kenya, Article 31.
57 The Constitution of Kenya, Article 25 (a).

provided general guidance for health research. Kenya's foremost health research institute, KEMRI, was also created pursuant to this Act. It was under this regime that Kenya's *National Guidelines on the Conduct of Health Research, 2004* was developed. The 1979 Act also provided for a medical sciences committee. This was eventually converted into the Health Sciences Specialist Committee in 1983, which had the responsibility for research ethics policy and regulating institutional research ethics committees, including the ethics review committee at KEMRI. It also reviewed proposals from foreign researchers. Further, the National Bioethics Committee which standardised processes for ethics review in Kenya was subsequently created by the NCST under its mandate in 2005. The National Bioethics Committee replaced the Health Sciences Specialist Committee.[58]

Thus, Kenya has had a relatively organised framework for health research governance founded on law. However, as discussed under the ethics review, there have been several bodies, with the potential for duplication and confusion. Furthermore, there was no oversight mechanism over the work of research ethics committees. Such oversight mechanism would have required, for example, the accreditation and audit of these committees. The result of this gap is a lack of standardisation. Recent legislation have attempted to address these concerns.

The current legislation regulating health research is the Science, Technology and Innovation Act, 2013, as amended; the Health Act; and the Pharmacy and Poisons Act, 2012. The first two pieces of legislation regulate health research (and other kinds of research), while the latter regulates clinical trials specifically. The provisions of the Pharmacy and Poisons Act will be considered under Drug Regulatory Authority in a later subsection.

The Science, Technology and Innovation Act, 2013, replaced the National Science and Technology (Amendment) Act of 1979, which established KEMRI. The Act established three institutions: these are the National Commission for Science, Technology and Innovation; the Innovation Board; and the Research Fund Board. The National Commission for Science, Technology and Innovation (NACOSTI or the Commission) performs key roles in the oversight of research involving humans in Kenya, including health research. NACOSTI is the national body charged with the regulation and coordination of research in Kenya; it is the Kenyan national ethics committee. It is supervised by the Ministry of Education, Science and Technology. Established under Section 3, its key objective, as provided in the Act, is to "regulate and assure quality in the science, technology and innovation sector and advise the Government in matters related thereto."[59] One of its functions is to establish research priorities for the country, an important function, given the antecedents of health research in Kenya, as described earlier. Other functions include the accreditation of research institutions and

58 See Adele Langlois, "Contextualizing Bioethics: The Declarations in Kenya and South Africa" in *Negotiating Bioethics: The Governance of UNESCO's Bioethics Programme* (London and New York: Routledge, 2013).

59 Section 3.

approval of all scientific research in Kenya, an improvement over the previous regime, which did not specify an accreditation function. NACOSTI's functions also include the coordination, monitoring, and evaluation of activities relating to scientific research; development of technology; development and enforcement of codes, guidelines, and regulations; and undertaking of regular inspections, monitoring, and evaluation of research institutions.[60] NACOSTI has the sole authority to undertake these functions in Kenya.[61] This gives it the authority that national health research ethics committees have in Nigeria and South Africa but also the powers of the national health research committees (which typically have the power to determine research priorities for the country).

In view of the challenges of research, in particular international collaborative research, Kenya has for several years required that any foreign organisations or individuals, or private institutions seeking to conduct research in the country obtain a research permit. The objectives of the research clearance or licence were provided in an earlier iteration of the research permit guidelines:

> To examine research proposals and to make sure that permits are issued to projects, which are in the interest of the Government and people of Kenya; and to facilitate access to data from public institutions and officials as well as other sources. The purpose for affiliation to Kenyan public institutions places the researcher in contact with facilities and experts highly knowledge-able on Kenyan conditions and sources of data. These are enormous advantages, which make the tasks of the researcher considerably easier. Therefore research clearance in Kenya is to be seen both as a screening as well as a facilitating mechanism for research.[62]

It is now the responsibility of NACOSTI to grant the research permit as part of its regulatory functions under the law. In this regard, NACOSTI must licence a research project involving human subjects, including biomedical and social science research, before it is commenced. University research is exempted from this provision. In line with the provisions of the Act, a research licence shall not be granted where it may adversely affect the culture of any community in Kenya or the environment; where such licence may adversely affect the environment or result in the exploitation of the intellectual property rights of communities to their traditional knowledge; or where it may, in general, adversely affect the lives of Kenyans.[63] It is the responsibility of a researcher seeking to engage in research to obtain this licence.[64] It is an offense to violate this provision, which attracts a fine of up to USD 60,000 or five years in jail.[65]

---

60 Section 6 of the Act.
61 Section 6 (4).
62 National Council for Science and Technology (Ministry of Higher Education, Science and Technology), Procedures and Guidelines for Research Authorization in Kenya, November, 2009, online: <https://www.healthresearchweb.org/files/ResearchClearanceGuideline.pdf>.
63 Section 12.
64 Section 12.
65 Section 17.

Ethics approval, where indicated, is a prerequisite for making an application for the licence. Such ethics clearance or approval must be provided by an accredited Institutional Review Committee (IRC). The licence granted by NACOSTI is valid for the proposed research, site, and specified period. It is given on the grounds that both the licence and any rights thereunder are non-transferable; NACOSTI may monitor and evaluate the research; any licensee granted the permit is required to report to relevant government offices in the area of research before commencement; the excavation, filming, and collection of specimens, including human tissues, are subject to further permissions from relevant government agencies; and reports are to be made available to NACOSTI within a year after the research is completed. It is also important to note that NACOSTI retains the rights to modify the conditions under which the License was given or even to cancel it.[66] Required documents include letters of approval of the research from an ethics committee; indication of affiliation with a public research organisation in Kenya; a collaboration agreement with the research organisation; a materials transfer agreement (MTA) provided by NACOSTI; acceptance of the requirement for Kenyan collaborators to be credited on materials from the research project, including publications; and acknowledgement of the Kenyan research permit in all materials coming out of the research, amongst other things. The research permit may be terminated by NACOSTI without any compensation where there is ethical misconduct or violation of the guidelines.[67]

A key matter worthy of note is that the permit or licence does not, by itself, confer authority to transfer research materials. For this, an MTA must be signed between the entity providing the materials (tissue samples and other biological materials, for example) with the terms for such transfer stated in the MTA.

Institutions intending to engage in biomedical research must be accredited by NACOSTI. Regulations have been developed to provide the requirements for the registration and accreditation of institutions.[68] Some of the key requirements are that the institution must have the capacity to carry out scientific research and have the necessary financial and human resources. Also, half of the directors of such an institution must be Kenyan. The institution must also be able to show that it has complied with standards set out in the regulations relating to clarity of research goals; institutional resources and sustainability; leadership; governance and integrity; institutional assessment (requiring the institution to have an assessment tool); and, interestingly, an institutional database which requires that the institution show evidence of a research database containing the research that has been conducted in the institution.[69] Such an institute must by necessity form an IRC in line with standard operating procedures established by NACOSTI. It is the duty of such an IRC to approve protocols on behalf of NACOSTI, to

---

66 These requirements may be found on NACOSTI's website: <https://oris.nacosti.go.ke/guidelines.php>.

67 See Note 65.

68 The Science, Technology and Innovation Regulations (Registration and Accreditation of Research Institutions Regulations), (2014), Legal Notice No. 106.

69 Third Schedule of the Regulations.

monitor adherence of researchers to their protocols, and to submit an annual report of its activities to NACOSTI. All research that is to be carried out in Kenya must be approved by NACOSTI or by an ethics committee accredited or recognised by NACOSTI. In order to keep up with the increasing applications for approval, the National Bioethics Committee (NBC) established by NACOSTI, as mentioned earlier, has been given the duty of promoting and monitoring ethical practices and accrediting institutional ethics review committees (IERCs). Any of the IERCs approved and recognised by NACOSTI can give ethical clearance and approval for research. This is discussed further in the following pages.

In its role as regulator, NACOSTI has also prepared several guidelines that touch on the formation of an IRC, material transfer, animal care, and standard operating procedures. The latter document concerns itself with the formation of an IRC, processes for approval of research protocols, and monitoring and evaluation. The guidelines for approval of research protocols on their part are quite detailed. They require an applicant researcher to indicate institutional affiliation and co-researchers (if any); to provide a scientifically sound protocol, providing for informed consent, withdrawal from the study, lack of inducements, and sources of funding; aspects of benefits sharing with the community; and mitigation of adverse effects (if any). Further, various references are made to ethics compliance throughout the Act, requiring researchers to comply with the provision of standards and ethics by the Commission and other bodies.

In addition to the Science and Technology Act, the Health Act, 2017, provides more specifically for health research. "Research for health," as defined in the Act,

> includes but is not limited to research which seeks to contribute to the extension of knowledge in any health related field, such as that concerned with the biological, clinical, psychological or social processes in human beings improved methods for the provision of health services; or human pathology; or the causes of disease; or the effects of the environment on the human body; or the development or new application of pharmaceuticals, medicines and other preventative, therapeutic or curative agents; or the development of new applications of health technology;[70]

This is a broad-ranging definition that captures all the contours of health research involving humans and more. The Health Act emphasises the fundamental duty of the State to observe, respect, protect, promote, and fulfil the right to the highest attainable standard of health, including by ensuring the prioritisation of, and adequate investment in, research for health to promote technology and innovation in healthcare delivery.[71] The Act also emphasises the constitutional rights to the highest standard of health and rights to dignity, respect, and privacy.[72]

70 Kenya Health Act, 2017.
71 Section 4 of the Health Act.
72 Section 5 of the Health Act.

In terms of prioritisation of research, similar to legal provisions in South Africa and Nigeria, the Health Act establishes a National Health Research Committee.[73] This Committee is composed of the chairperson, who shall be a distinguished health researcher and renowned in a health discipline; one representative from KEMRI; a representative from NACOSTI; the head of the directorate of the Ministry of Health responsible for research and development; a representative from the Authority; two representatives from public universities; a representative from private universities; a research expert whose work focusses on traditional and alternative medicine; a research expert with a focus on clinical trials; and a distinguished biomedical science researcher. This composition is also expected to reflect ethnic, gender, county, and regional balance.[74] As in South Africa and Nigeria, the main function of the National Health Research Committee is to identify and make recommendations for health research priorities. Such priority setting is to be based on the following criteria: the burden of disease; the cost-effectiveness of interventions aimed at reducing the burden of disease; the availability of human and institutional resources for the implementation of an intervention at the level closest to the affected communities; the health needs of vulnerable groups, such as women, older persons, children, and people with disabilities; the health needs of communities; national security; and emerging issues on health.[75] The Committee is to ensure that resources are devoted to the priority research areas and that research conducted by domestic and international parties is focussed on the identified priority areas. This is especially important because of the significant levels of international and collaborative research that are undertaken in Kenya. The Health Act also requires that legislation be developed to ensure mental health research.[76]

The Act also provides that 30 per cent of the National Research Fund established under the Science and Technology Act shall be devoted to health research. This is an important provision because of the low amounts of domestic research sponsored by lower-income countries. As stated elsewhere in this book, lack of domestic funding of research may limit the voice and influence of the governments of these countries in research and research governance. This provision is therefore a welcome development, and it is hoped that this is fully implemented in Kenya and serves as an example to other African countries.

The Health Act includes provisions that draw the linkages between the regulatory regime for research under the Science and Technology Act, and the guidance of NACOSTI. For instance, KEMRI, as the government health research institute, is required to review its programme to "attune" itself to the health needs of the people and the research programme of the country.[77] The Health Act also specifically states that, for health research involving humans,

---

73 Section 93 of the Health Act.
74 Section 93 of the Health Act.
75 Section 96 of the Health Act.
76 Section 73 of the Health Act.
77 Section 97 of the Health Act.

the regulations of NACOSTI under the Science and Technology Act must be complied with.[78] The Committee is also to provide for informed consent procedures in the case of non-therapeutic research.[79] While it makes these connections between the regulatory regime under NACOSTI and the Science and Technology Act, and the regime under the Health Act, there is room for more clarification. For instance, does the research licence discussed earlier now include a requirement for prospective researchers or research teams to show that their proposed research aligns with the priority health research areas identified by the National Health Research Committee? At any rate, the Act was enacted in 2017, and it remains to be seen how its provisions will be integrated into the wider research governance framework.

In addition to the legislation discussed here, there are other legal instruments that form part of the legal framework for health research governance in Kenya. An example is the HIV/AIDS Prevention and Control Act 2006, amended in 2012, which in essence refers to and reinforces the application of the Act. It provides that

> No person shall undertake HIV or AIDS related human biomedical research on another person, or on any tissue or blood removed from such person unless such research conforms to the requirements under the Science and Technology Act (Cap. 250) or any other written law for the time in force.[80]

Written informed consent is required for research on a person or tissue or blood removed from such a person. Information to be provided to such a person includes the aims, methods, anticipated benefits, and potential hazards and discomforts of the research.[81] Failure to comply with these provisions is an offence.[82] Another example is the Children Act,[83] which provides that the best interests of the child must always be paramount. This would affect research involving children – all research involving children must then, by law, be in the best interests of the child.

Kenya's legal framework is of longer standing than in any of the countries discussed – South Africa, Nigeria, or Egypt, where ethics policies and ethics review systems preceded the intervention of law. However, the revival of interest in the ethics of research and the protection of research participants occurred at about the same time, with the ethical dilemmas of HIV/AIDS, the establishment of ethics guidelines in 2004, and several regulations discussed earlier. The legal framework discussed does not articulate specific provisions with respect to matters such as what constitutes health research, the specific modalities for

---

78 Section 99 of the Health Act.
79 Section 100 of the Health Act.
80 Section 39.
81 Section 40.
82 Section 41.
83 The Children Act, 2001 Laws of Kenya, Chapter 141.

non-therapeutic research involving children, biobanking, and other issues. This is in part because these pieces of legislation either apply generally to or specifically relate to particular issues. These matters are addressed to some degree in ethics guidelines made under the authority of legislation, in particular, the Science, Technology and Innovation Act.

The ethical framework for health research in Kenya

The ethical framework for carrying out biomedical research involving human subjects in Kenya is set out in the Kenyan *Guidelines for Ethical Conduct of Biomedical Research Involving Human Subjects*[84] (the Guidelines), issued by the National Council for Science and Technology. The Guidelines were issued in 2004. NACOSTI now has the authority to issue the Guidelines. It continues to use the 2004 Guidelines. Made pursuant to powers under legislation, they have the indirect force of law. In addition to these, there are some issue-specific guidelines, including the *National Reproductive Health Research Guidelines* issued by the Ministry of Health, Division of Reproductive Health, and the *National Guidelines for Research and Development of HIV/AIDS Vaccines*, 2005, promulgated by the Ministry of Health. KEMRI has also developed guidelines: *National Ethics Review Committee: Guidelines and Standard Operating Procedures*, 2004.[85]

The Guidelines acknowledge that in experimenting with human subjects for clinical research, participants are placed at risk of harm for the good of others, and this holds a possibility for the exploitation of such human subjects. Hence, there is a need for an ethical regulatory framework to minimise the risk of exploitation of human participants. The Guidelines set out several factors which form a systematic and coherent framework for determining whether a clinical research study is ethical: value; scientific validity (including the imperative of clinical equipoise); fair subject selection; favourable risk-benefit ratio; risks to individual subjects are minimised, the potential benefits to individual subjects are enhanced, and the potential benefits to individual subjects and society are proportionate to or outweigh the risks; independent review; informed consent; and respect for potential and enrolled subjects – respect for potential and enrolled subjects commences from the point when they are approached to when they are enrolled and even after their participation ends. It entails five broad duties –

- Managing enrolled subjects' personal information in accordance with confidentiality rules;
- Respecting enrolled subjects' decision to withdraw from the research at any time without penalty;

84 National Commission for Science, Technology and Innovation, *Guidelines for Ethical Conduct of Biomedical Research Involving Human Subjects in Kenya*, NCST no. 40 (Nairobi, NCST, 2004) (the Guidelines").

85 Kenya Medical Research Institute (KEMRI), *National Ethics Review Committee: Guidelines and Standard Operating Procedures*, 2004.

- Furnish enrolled subjects with information discovered during the research to enable such subjects to make a decision about their continued participation in the research;
- Closely monitoring the welfare of participants and providing treatment, and removing them from the research if the need arises; and
- Recognising the contribution of the subjects in the research by informing them of what was learnt during the research.

The Guidelines also set out the three ethical principles that must guide all research involving human subjects, ostensibly drawn from the Belmont Report. The first is Respect for Persons. This principle embodies two broad ethical considerations, which are respect for autonomy and respect for those with diminished autonomy. This ethical consideration emphasises the need to respect people's right to make decisions about their bodies, and where a person may not be able to personally make that decision because of diminished autonomy, it emphasises the duty to protect such a person from harm or exploitation. The second is Beneficence: this ethical obligation requires that the benefit of the research be maximised and the attendant risks of the research minimised. The third is Justice, which refers to the equitable distribution of the benefits and burdens of the research.

The Guidelines make elaborate provisions on the consent of a participant in research. They focus considerably more on the substantive underpinnings of informed consent than the more procedural thrust of the Nigerian Code on Health Research Ethics. The Guidelines emphasise that a prospective participant must be given certain information to enable her to make an informed decision on whether to partake in the research or not. The prospective participant must not be led to believe that she is signing up for some beneficial medical services. Amongst other things, the participant ought to be informed of the duration of the research and her participation in the research. Where there are benefits that could be enjoyed by the subject or other persons by participating in the research, he should be informed of those benefits as well as foreseeable risks and discomfort that she would be exposed to by participating in the research. The participant is to be informed of the extent to which the investigator would provide medical services if there was a need for this. The participant is also to be informed that he will be entitled to free medical services for injury or harm resulting from his participation in the research, and he or his family will be entitled to compensation in the event of disability or death arising from participation in the research. A person who consents to participate in research reserves the right to withdraw from the research at any time without penalty; this must also be communicated to the participant to enable him to make an informed decision about his participation in the research. The Guidelines provide that before any biomedical research involving humans is commenced, the investigator must obtain the informed consent of prospective participants. In a few circumstances, the need to obtain informed consent may be waived by the ethics clearance committee. One such instance is when the research involves a minimal risk, that is, a risk not greater than that attached to a routine medical or psychological examination, and where it would be impracticable to obtain consent. An example of this is accessing and using a patient's medical record for research without the patient's knowledge or consent. Where a researcher intends to carry out several epidemiological research projects, for which it might be impracticable to obtain the individual consent of participants, an application may be made to the ethical review committee to waive the need to obtain the individual consent of participants. The ethical review committee, in granting the waiver, would consider mechanisms put in place by the investigator to protect the safety and safeguard the privacy of the research subjects. When the research has an entire community as its focus, the investigator is required to seek the agreement and cooperation of the community leadership (referred to as the Provincial Administration in the guidelines); the investigator is also required to inform the Provincial Medical Officer of Health and the medical officer of the nearest health facility of the study. Where the research would require personal contact between the subjects and the investigator, the informed consent of the participants must equally be obtained in addition to the foregoing. An individual's informed consent, voluntarily given or withheld, supersedes the cooperation and agreement given by the community leadership; thus, when an individual refuses to consent to research, the agreement of the community leadership notwithstanding, he cannot be compelled to participate in the research.

As in other African countries, informed consent has been shown to be anything but straightforward in practice. Language barriers, the complicated roles of the fieldworkers, power differentials, understanding of scientific concepts, and differentiation of research from treatment are all critical matters that require identification and management not only at the ethics review level but also in practice, in the research field.[86] Studies suggest that obtaining truly informed and voluntary consent from research participants in Kenya continues to be a problematic issue. An understanding of the context (cultural, social, economic, health) and the interplay of these factors, alongside the key principle of autonomy and the right of the research participant to know, is important for the effective application of the Guidelines' informed consent requirements. The significance of informed consent can also present challenges. A 2012 research study which investigated the informed consent process as engaged in by postgraduate students, who form over 70 per cent of researchers in Kenya, suggested that the postgraduate researchers were more likely to describe the risk of physical harm than other kinds of harm, including mental harm (perhaps because existing guidelines emphasise physical harm); researchers were also less likely to provide information to prospective research participants about privacy, confidentiality, and compensation for harm, and concluded that the consent form was mainly used to satisfy

---

86 CS Molyneux et al, "Understanding of Informed Consent in a Low-Income Setting: Three Case Studies from the Kenyan Coast" (2004) 59 Soc Sci & Med 2547, 2551.

a college requirement and for the students' legal protection, and not primarily for the patients' benefit.[87] While these were student researchers, even aside from being postgraduates, this suggests that more needs to be done to ingrain true understanding of the significance of informed consent.

Special provisions are made in the Guidelines in relation to obtaining the consent of persons with diminished capacity, that is, persons who lack the capacity to give informed consent because of age or disease. Children, adults with severe mental or behavioural disorders, and adults unfamiliar with modern medical concepts fall into this group. Consent given by this class of people should not be acted on without the approval of the ethics clearance committee. The Guidelines further stipulate that it is best to obtain proxy consent from a legal guardian or an authorised representative of the prospective participant. The Guidelines do not prohibit children from being used in clinical research; however children can only participate subject to the existence of certain conditions. A researcher who seeks the participation of children in research must ensure that the research cannot be carried out in adults, the research is for the purpose of generating knowledge relevant to the health needs of children, and the consent of a parent or legal guardian is obtained on behalf of the child. However, where the child withholds consent, such refusal to participate must be respected, except where there is no alternative medical intervention from which the child can benefit. Where the research is not directly beneficial to the child, then the risk it poses to the child must be commensurate with the importance of the knowledge to be gained from the research. And the therapeutic benefit to the child should be as advantageous to them as any available alternative where the research is intended to provide therapeutic benefit. The rules laid down in the Guidelines for using children as research subjects are more robust than what is contained in the Health Act or the HIV/AIDS Prevention and Control Act, as discussed earlier. The provisions of the Guidelines have the object of preventing or minimising potential and unnecessary harm to children. As in other countries, the application of the Guidelines in practice is often more problematic than may be apparent from their wording. For instance, studies that have been done amongst communities in Kenya indicate that, for research involving children, communities felt that it was more appropriate to seek the parents' consent only as the children may be focussed only on the pain, without understanding the potential benefits of the research.[88] However, the Guidelines appear to attempt a balance with international standards on children's rights to some degree, the health benefits of research for children, and the natural rights of parents to make decisions on behalf of their children. Moreover, the Guidelines emphasise "dissent," which

---

87 Miriam CA Wagoro & Kirana M Bhatt, "An Audit of the Informed Consent Process in Postgraduate Dissertation Studies at the College of Health Sciences, University of Nairobi, Kenya" (2012) 5:1 SAJBL 45–50, online: <www.sajbl.org.za/index.php/sajbl/article/view/188/203>.

88 See CS Molyneux et al, "'Even If They Ask You to Stand by a Tree All Day, You Will Have To Do It (Laughter)…!': Community Voices on the Notion and Practice of Informed Consent for Biomedical Research in Developing Countries" (2005) 61 Soc Sci & Med 443–445, 450.

would forestall participation, but do not emphasise "assent." Non-dissent may be taken to be implied assent, but this is a stance that is clearly different from international standards on children's assent[89] (also compare the stance in South Africa and Nigeria). This has implications for how the Guidelines are applied in practice, where parents and community leaders may engage children differently from the requirements in the Guidelines.[90]

In addition to children, persons with behavioural disorders have special protections under the Guidelines. The researcher must ensure that persons with mental or behavioural disorders are not used as the subjects of any research that can be done with persons who have no mental or behavioural disorder. Also, the knowledge to be gained from the research should be such that would be relevant to the specific health needs of people with mental or behavioural disorders. Moreover, the consent of the prospective subject is obtained to the extent of her capabilities, and where the prospective subject withholds her consent, her decision should be respected. Further, where the prospective subject lacks the ability to give informed consent, consent must be obtained from a legal guardian or any duly authorised person. In addition, where the research is not directly beneficial to the subject, the risk it poses to the subject must be commensurate with the importance of the knowledge to be gained from the research. Finally, the therapeutic benefit to the subject should be as advantageous to the subject as any available alternative where the research is intended to provide therapeutic benefit.

The Kenyan Guidelines take into consideration the peculiar cultural context with regard to the informed consent of potential female participants. Thus, they provide that in some rural communities, women may refuse to give their informed consent unless their husbands approve. In such cases, the investigator is cautioned to still obtain the woman's individual consent. Where the husband gives his consent for his wife to be enrolled into a clinical research programme, and the women withholds her consent, her withheld consent should be respected and should take precedence over her husband's consent. This nuanced approach may diverge from the direct understanding of a woman's right to consent or dissent to research participation, which understanding may vary in different cultures. This approach however provides an approach that is not a direct attack on cultural mores while not denying a woman's entitlement to decide for herself. Another recognition of the gender dynamics of clinical research may be located in the Guidelines' approach to the inclusion of women in research, an often problematic ethical issue. The Guidelines note that women should be included in

89 Heather L Mullins-Owens et al, "Protecting a Vulnerable Population with Little Regulatory Framework: A Comparative Analysis of International Guidelines for Pediatric Research Ethics" (2012) 29:5 J Contemp Health L & Pol'y 36. R Vreeman, W Nyandiko & E Meslin, "Pediatric Assent for a Study of Antiretroviral Therapy Dosing for Children in Western Kenya: A Case Study in International Research Collaboration" (2009) 4:1 J Empir Res Hum Res Ethics 3–16.
90 See CS Molyneux, N Peshua, & K Marsh, Understanding of Informed Consent in a Low-Income Setting: Three Case Studies from the Kenyan Coast (2004) 59 Soc Sci & Med 2547, 2551.

research as part of the principle of fairness.[91] However, the guidelines lay down a general rule prohibiting the use of pregnant or nursing women as subjects of clinical research, with some exceptions: for example, where the research carries no more than minimal risk to the foetuses or nursing infants; where the object of the research is to obtain new knowledge about pregnancy or lactation; or where the object of the research is to protect or advance the health of the pregnant or nursing women, foetuses, or nursing infants.

Amongst other things, the Guidelines also provide for the right to compensation, which is an entitlement that cannot be waived by the researcher or the research participant. The compensation is for physical injury, that is, temporary or permanent impairment, or disability resulting from research participation. One of the questions that this raises is why the focus is only on physical injury – what about mental or emotional harms? What about social harms, such as ostracism in a community as penalty? This indicates a gap that needs to be addressed. While it may be more difficult to identify or assess such injury, or easier to identify physical injury in biomedical research, this does not preclude the need to make provisions for this to serve as guidance for the ethics review committee in assessing issues relating to potential harm and compensation.

Externally sponsored research is expected to meet the scientific and ethical standards in the sponsoring country and in Kenya. The Guidelines emphasise that externally sponsored research engaged in for the purpose of developing any therapeutic, diagnostic, or preventive product must be responsive to the health needs of Kenya, reinforcing a recurring theme, as described earlier. It is a requirement under the Kenyan guidelines that scientific and ethical clearance is first gotten in the sponsoring country. The research protocol must be submitted for scientific and ethical review in the sponsoring country, and the standards to be applied should not be below the regular standard applied to research that is conducted in that country. When ethical clearance for the research is obtained in the sponsoring country, an application may be made to the relevant ethics clearance committee in Kenya for approval to commence the research in Kenya. In granting approval for externally sponsored research to be carried out in Kenya, the committee would only give approval if the research would address prevalent health problems in the country. In other words, the research must be designed to develop a therapeutic, diagnostic, or preventive treatment to Kenyans. It is also a requirement that, before approval is given, the sponsoring agency shall agree to make any product successfully developed through the research reasonably available to the members of the community where the research was done or the country as a whole. The Guidelines enjoin the committee to give consideration to a sponsoring agency that agrees to maintain health services and faculties for the purpose of the study at the conclusion of the research as this could build a capacity for further research.

There are several gaps in the Guidelines. For one thing, they focus on biomedical research. The description of Kenya's health landscape indicates several issues

---

91 See page 4 of the Guidelines.

that would benefit from social science and behavioural. It will be recalled that the Health Act defines research for health as including social science research and psychological research. An expansion of focus to include other kinds of health research is therefore appropriate. For another, the Guidelines' key ethical standards, including the provisions on standard of care debate, access to benefits etc. are not discussed in an in-depth manner and may not provide the needed guidance. And yet these ethical standards have been a source of concern (see, for example, the Majengo study, discussed in earlier where benefit-sharing was a concern). In addition, the Guidelines do not address contemporary dilemmas such as biobanking, MTAs, access to experimental drugs, etc. With respect to the usage of tissues and samples from research, the Guidelines provide for the need to obtain informed consent at the start of the research project, including for "anonymous left-over" samples, but there is little guidance on informed consent for samples of identifiable persons, storage of samples, reuse of samples, subsequent use, exportation, importation, ownership, intellectual property rights, etc. Some of these issues are, however, addressed in other guidance in the country.[92] There have been attempts to revise the guidelines,[93] but a new set of guidelines has yet to be developed. We consider the Guidelines' specific provisions on clinical trials and on ethics review under the section on institutional framework below.

Other guidelines have been established, such as the *Guidelines for Applications to Conduct Clinical Trials in Kenya*, 2016, issued by the Pharmacy and Poisons Board; *National Reproductive Health Research Guidelines* issued by the Ministry of Health, Division of Reproductive Health; and the *National Guidelines for Research and Development of HIV/AIDS Vaccines*, 2005, promulgated by the Ministry of Health. KEMRI has also developed guidelines: *National Ethics Review Committee: Guidelines and Standard Operating Procedures*, 2004,[94] and the *Guidelines for Conducting Adolescents Sexual and Reproductive Health Research in Kenya*, 2015, developed by the National AIDS and STI Control Programme (NASCOP).

These guidelines focus on specific areas of research and provide more in-depth guidance on those areas of research. For instance, the *Guidelines for Applications to Conduct Clinical Trials in Kenya*, 2016 (the Clinical Trials Guidelines) provide a legal and ethical framework for clinical trials in Kenya. They reference the ICH-GCP as the standard in Kenya. The implications of this include that the ICH-GCP provides the standards for determining some of the ethical dilemmas

---

92 See Francis Barchi & Madison T Little, "National Ethics Guidance in Sub-Saharan Africa on the Collection and Use of Human Biological Specimens: A Systematic Review" (2016)17 BMC Med Ethics 64. "Laws, Regulations and Guidelines of Developed Countries, Developing Countries in Africa, and BRICS Regions Pertaining to the Use of Human Biological Material (HBM) in Research" (2012) 5:1 SABJL 51–54.

93 Langlois, Note 49.

94 Kenya Medical Research Institute (KEMRI), *National Ethics Review Committee: Guidelines and Standard Operating Procedures*, 2004.

earlier discussed, such as the dilemmas around the best standard of care, the use of placebos, and follow-up treatment.

Consent remains a crucial aspect of clinical trials as in all health research. According to the 2016 Guidelines, not only should the consent of a participant be sought before a clinical trial is commenced, but it should be obtained, and it must be informed and voluntary consent. In this respect, a researcher or investigator is required to comply with accredited ethics committee requirements on consent and the Good Clinical Practice (GCP) and the ICH-GCP guidelines. Consent forms are to be written in English or Kiswahili and in the local language spoken within the area, without using technical language, to facilitate proper understanding and put the participant in a position to give informed consent.

The mode of recruitment has been identified as one of the problematic areas of clinical research in Kenya. In general, researchers are precluded from coercing or unduly influencing any person to participate or continue to participate in the research. However, in Kenya, it is common practice to recruit trial participants through local healthcare facilities, medical practitioners, trial participants, and community outreach workers. Headhunters are sent to hospitals and clinics within a particular location and are instructed to identify patients waiting for medical attention with certain symptoms for the purpose of enrolling them in the research. Medical doctors and other caregivers in hospitals are also used to enrol subjects under the guise of better treatment opportunities. Participants are also often asked to help identify persons in their community who have similar health conditions and recruit them into the programme. It has been suggested that the recruitment of patients in a context lacking universal health coverage, as in Kenya, threatens a patient's ability to give voluntary informed consent. In several cases patients may think that they are being offered a treatment option rather than being recruited into research.

Long-term care and follow-up are also ethical issues that raise concerns in practice. Under the Clinical Trials Guidelines, the investigator has a duty to ensure that adequate medical care is provided to a subject for any adverse event during and following the subject's participation in the clinical trial. The investigator also has an obligation to inform the subject when there is need for medical care for any other illness which the investigator becomes aware of following the subject's participation in the clinical trial. The Guidelines place a duty on the sponsor to provide insurance coverage for all trial subjects for clinical trial-related injury.[95] The insurance policy is required to cover compensation for all injury that can be linked to the clinical trial; it must not exclude the liability of the investigator and sponsor for negligence which results in harm or injury to the participant over the course of the clinical trial but must cover it. External sponsors also have an ethical obligation to provide healthcare services for subjects who suffer injury as a result of their participation in the research. Nevertheless,

95 Article 8 of the Clinical Trials Guidelines, 2016.

a recent study of clinical trial insurance indicates that a majority of the clinical trial protocols reviewed did not have insurance, that informed consent documents did not include if and how compensation would be provided in the event of harm, and that a significant percentage of the research participants were not aware of clinical trial insurance.[96]

In addition, some studies have shown that despite the provision in the guidelines requiring an investigator to provide adequate medical care for clinical trial subjects for injury that can be linked to their participation in the clinical trial, even after its conclusion, this requirement is rarely ever complied with by researchers in practice.[97] The Clinical Trials Guidelines do not provide a mechanism for enforcing this obligation, nor do they provide a platform through which an aggrieved participant may seek redress outside of the court system. Some clinical trial participants are unaware of their right to post-trial access to treatment.[98] Similar concerns have been raised about the benefits that are typically enjoyed during clinical trials – new equipment and infrastructure, in some cases more staff, reduced healthcare costs, better salaries for staff involved in the trials, and better service delivery. These inputs may create unhealthy dynamics that weaken instead of strengthen health systems: for example by demotivating staff that are not involved in trials and who therefore do not benefit from salary increments. In general, there is no guidance on post-trial obligations for researchers. It has, however, been suggested that drafting agreements, such as memoranda of understanding, would be helpful prior to starting such trials.[99] NACOSTI may provide a template for such agreements, which could be adjusted as needed by the host institution.

Other ethics guidance includes the Guidelines for Conducting Adolescents Sexual and Reproductive Health Research in Kenya, 2015. These guidelines focus on adolescents specifically and highlight key ethical issues that arise in sexual and reproductive health with children, including complexities arising from sexual and gender-based violation, which is significantly higher amongst adolescents than in any other group in Kenya;[100] early sexual debut; and sexually transmitted infections. These ethical issues include confidentiality in research, on which issue the guidelines require that any matters uncovered during the research must be kept confidential, even from the parents who may have given consent for the research. It also notes that researchers are to exercise caution in obtaining parental consent where such consent may worsen matters for the adolescent: for

96 Simon K Wahome (2015), *Insurance and Indemnity Coverage for Clinical Trials of Medicines in Kenya*, Unpublished Thesis, University of Nairobi.
97 See Somo, Post-Trial Access to Treatment Corporate Best Practices (2015).
98 *Ibid.*
99 Vibian Angwenyi et al, "Health Providers' Perceptions of Clinical Trials: Lessons from Ghana, Kenya and Burkina Faso" (2015) 10:5 PLoS One at e0124554.
100 National AIDS and STI Control Programme (NASCOP), Ministry of Health Government of Kenya and KEMRI, *Guidelines for Conducting Adolescents Sexual and Reproductive Health Research in Kenya* at 2.

instance, where the adolescent is kept in a safe space after abuse from the parents. Interestingly, in a seeming divergence from the 2004 Guidelines, adolescents are required to give assent (if under the age of 18) in addition to the parents' consent.[101] This is different from the guidance of the 2004 Guidelines, which require only dissent, but accords with the provisions of the Clinical Trials Guidelines, which provides for assent, requiring that "the agreement (assent) of the child has been obtained to the extent of the child's capabilities,"[102] signalling perhaps a shift in thinking around research involving children.

Under the Guidelines for Conducting Adolescents Sexual and Reproductive Health Research in Kenya, parental consent may be waived in certain circumstances: for example, in cases of child abuse; where the adolescent is determined to be a mature minor; or where it might be inappropriate to call on the parent to consent, such as where the adolescent is a prostitute. This waiver raises further ethical and legal questions. For example, where harm comes to an adolescent over the course of research, is the parent disentitled from raising this issue in view of their having been precluded from exercising the natural authority allowed parents under the law? Given some of the earlier discussion on community views, how do these guidelines take into account current cultural realities? Moreover, under the Clinical Trials Guidelines, there are no exceptions to the requirement for parental consent.[103] Which Guidelines take precedence in clinical research involving an adolescent who is still a child under the Children Act?

Furthermore, harm "is defined to include physical, psychological, social or financial, as well as harms that may affect individuals or communities,"[104] different from the emphasis on physical harms in the 2004 Guidelines. Providing information to adolescents on the findings of a study is also important and can be done via traditional and new media, the latter because adolescents are more likely to engage with that mode of communication. It is interesting to note that the 2004 Guidelines are referred to only minimally, and other guidelines are not mentioned. It is therefore not clear whether these guidelines are building on those guidelines, a broader interpretation of the guidelines, or (more likely) simply a different approach that does not take into account the original 2004 guidelines.

Another set of guidelines, the *National Reproductive Health Research Guidelines*, are stated to be the guide for any researcher conducting research on reproductive health in Kenya.[105] Researchers are also required to comply with NSCT (now NACOSTI) Guidelines, that is, the 2004 Guidelines. The need to obtain research clearance as discussed earlier and other basic regulatory requirements are outlined.[106] Under the Reproductive Health Research Guidelines,

---

101 See Article 2.2 r.
102 Paragraph 7.4.
103 *Ibid.*
104 Section 4 at XIII.
105 See Foreword to *National Reproductive Health Research Guidelines* at 3–4, 13.
106 See National Council for Science and Technology Regulations on Research Clearance and Implementation at 45.

researchers on reproductive health are required to submit a concept paper and final report, amongst other documents, to the Division of Reproductive Health of the Ministry of Health in order to help track reproductive health research being undertaken in the country and identify existing gaps.[107] The Reproductive Health Research Guidelines identify priority areas of reproductive health research, including safe motherhood and child survival, eclampsia, abortion, adolescent reproductive health, gender and reproductive health rights, family planning, STIs and HIV/AIDS, community reproductive health (including issues around child marriage), infertility, and cancers of the reproductive system. With respect to the ethics of adolescent research, the Reproductive Health Research Guidelines and the Adolescents Sexual and Reproductive Health Guidelines agree substantially on the key issues of informed consent and confidentiality. Beyond adolescents, the Reproductive Health Research Guidelines provide basic ethical guidance for research in reproductive health.

Like the legal framework for health research in Kenya, the ethics framework is quite significant, comprising several guidelines, with the 2004 Guidelines being the primary guidance. There are, however, matters that would benefit from more attention, having become topical since the promulgation of the guidelines in 2004. There are also other guidelines on other issues. From a regulatory perspective, the multiplicity of guidelines may be helpful where they address specific issues not clearly addressed in the main guidance document – the 2004 Guidelines. However, where they are in conflict in key respects, as they are in some respects, this may be confusing to researchers and obscure rather than clarify ethical dilemmas. Furthermore, from a legal perspective, where there is conflict between the guidelines, and these issue from different authorities, it becomes a key question as to which authority has the legal power to make guidelines and which guidelines should take precedence. Although this has not been addressed in the literature, it is an issue that merits further research as it has a clear impact on health research governance.

Institutional framework

The institutional framework for health research in Kenya comprises several Ministries, government agencies, and institutions that are charged with the regulation of research in the country. For health research, two ministries stand out: the Ministry of Education, Science and Technology (MOEST) and the Ministry of Health. These ministries exercise oversight functions over most of the agencies, with the authority to issue clearance for the conduct of research. In addition, ethics review committees based in several institutions oversee the ethics review of research projects. In general, Kenya has a robust regulatory framework, but sometimes there exists duplicity and a lack of clarity on the roles of some of the regulatory agencies. This can sometimes lead to uncertainty about the procedure for obtaining approval for research.

107 See 5, 12–13.

Ethics review committees

As described in the discussions of the legal and ethical frameworks, it is a pre-requisite in Kenya to obtain ethics approval for all research involving human subjects. Ethics review had early beginnings in Kenya relative to other African countries (except South Africa) – the first ethics review committee, the Kenyatta National Hospital-University of Nairobi Ethics and Research Committee (KNH-UoN- ERC), was established in 1974. The Health Sciences Specialist Committee was created by the NCST after it was established by law in 1977, as described earlier. Finding itself overwhelmed, KEMRI, the government-established health research institute, was asked to establish an ethics committee. Eventually, as more universities, such as the Moi University, established their own ethics committees, the NCST shifted more into regulatory, policy, and advisory roles, leaving the institutions to review protocols. The HIV/AIDS pandemic in the 1980s and 1990s brought with it much research and helped to ensure that ethics review committees were established in other hospitals and universities. The National Bioethics Committee was created within the NCST in 2009 to focus on health research-related matters – the development of guidelines, accreditation, arbitration, and other policy matters.[108]

Unlike in South Africa, where ethics review is a clear legal requirement, legal underpinning for ethics review is implied. In this regard, ethics approval has been required since the early 1980s under guidelines made by the NCST (now NACOSTI). Ethics review, as already discussed, is one of the prerequisites for obtaining a research licence as legally required prior to the commencement of research in Kenya under Section 12 of the Science, Technology and Innovation Act. The Act does not directly provide for the requirement for ethics review as obtains, for example, under South Africa's National Health Act. Instead, NA-COSTI requires ethics review to grant a research permit. Thus, failure to obtain ethics review does not by itself provoke a sanction under the law. However, failure to obtain a research licence is an offence accompanied by sanctions of five million shillings or four years' imprisonment.[109]

Ethics review committees are located in several institutions in the country. Ethics review clearance may be obtained from any institutional ethical clearance committees. Most of the major research institutes and the hospitals, like the KEMRI, Kenyatta National Hospital, Eldoret Referral Hospital, and Aga Khan Hospital, have institutional ethics committees. HIV vaccine research also undergoes additional review by the HIV Vaccine Subcommittee in the Ministry of Health. Above the institutional ethics review committees is NACOSTI, which acts as the national ethics committee in much the same way as the National Health Research Ethics Committees in South Africa and Nigeria.

As a national ethics committee, NACOSTI performs a number of functions, including oversight functions. It also reviews multisite research and research of

108 SK Langat, "A Quarter Century of Research Ethics in Kenya" (2015) 1:1 BSK News 9 at 9–10.
109 Section 14 of the National Commission on Science Technology and Innovation Act.

national importance. Where an institution does not have an ethics committee, NACOSTI will review the research prior to the commencement of the study. Further, it can provide a forum for appeal where researchers feel that proposals rejected by an institutional ethics committee deserve a chance.

In addition, NACOSTI accredits ethics committees for various institutions through the National Bioethics Committee (NBC). Accreditation is defined as "giving approval and delegated authority to an ethics committee to conduct ethics review on behalf of the NBC."[110] The objectives of accreditation are to maintain the standards of ethics review in the country, cultivate public confidence and trust for the national research system, help facilitate equitable access to research records in health facilities, ensure the standardisation of the composition and operations of ethics review committees, support coordination and collaboration in ethics review, identify areas of weakness and provide necessary support, and so on.[111] To be accredited, each institution must comply with the requirements set out by NACOSTI. The current requirements include membership requirements; annual reports to be made to NACOSTI; and the provision of standard operating procedures, which may require amendment as directed by the NBC. The accreditation expires after three years and must thereafter be renewed. Failure to renew accreditation or meet the requirements for accreditation has the consequence of termination of the powers of the committee to continue operating as an institutional ethics review committee.[112] A list of currently accredited ethics committees are provided on NACOSTI's website,[113] with the areas for which they have received accreditation – health sciences, biomedical sciences, research protocols involving humans, social sciences, and the environment. There are currently 24 accredited institutions listed on the website.

For an ethics committee in an institution to be accredited by NACOSTI, it must have the required composition. Membership of ethics committees as required by the accreditation guidelines consists of at least seven members, which must include the chairperson; a member with knowledge of Kenyan law; ; at least one member from outside the institution; at least two members with research expertise and experience, one of whom should be in the health field; at least one lay member; and at least two clinicians, one of whom must be currently in active practice or clinical research, where the research being reviewed is a clinical research., and other members (a third of whom must be of either gender)[114] A lay member is defined as a person who is "not a registered health practitioner, such

110 NACOSTI, *Guidelines for Accreditation of Ethics Review Committees in Kenya*, Section 1.1.1, online: <www.nacosti.ke> (hereafter, Accreditation Guidelines). This is different from the Science, Technology and Innovation Regulations (Registration and Accreditation of Research Institutions Regulations) (2014), Legal Notice No.106 which is focussed on the accreditation of "research institutions." Research institutions host ethics review committees.
111 Accreditation Guidelines.
112 Accreditation Guidelines.
113 <www.nacosti.go.ke/research-license>.
114 Section 2.2 Accreditation Guidelines.

as a doctor, nurse, midwife, dentist, or pharmacist; an officer or employee of a health board, a health authority, the Ministry of Health, or a medical school; a health researcher or employee of a health research agency; or a person construed by virtue of their employment, profession, or relationship to have a potential conflict or professional bias in a majority of protocols reviewed."[115] This is a broad definition that seeks to exclude any person who is a health researcher or health professional, a problem experienced in other countries where lay members are often members of the health professions. Interestingly, there is no requirement for community members, and yet some of the challenges that have been faced in health research indicate that community members would be a beneficial addition. Thus, community members should not only be a part of the discussion on research design and implementation (as has been argued regarding the Majengo study) but should, in a hybrid governance framework, also be a part of the discussions on the ethics and acceptability of research as part of the ethics committee.

The chair must have some basic training and/or experience in bioethics and leadership. Appointments of the members of ethics committees must be made by the administrative head of the institution. This is no doubt to provide both authority and legitimacy to the committee but also to provide a direct reporting line to the highest authority in the institution. In addition to the accreditation guidelines, the 2004 Guidelines also make provisions for the operation of ethics review committees. The 2004 Guidelines, for example, provide that

> [c]lear procedures for identifying or recruiting potential EC members should be established. A statement should be drawn up of the requirements for candidacy that includes an outline of the duties and responsibilities of EC members.[116]

The composition of Kenyan ethics committees thus bears much resemblance to the countries already studied and is fairly clear, except on certain issues, for instance, the requirements on gender. If one-third of the members can be of either gender, this may mean that we can have an all-male committee, with the attendant disadvantages of such composition – a lack of balance and a lack of recognition of the different perspectives that females and males can bring to the consideration of research protocols.

Aside from that, there is an emphasis on clinical research but none on social science or behavioural and humanities research. This also reflects much of what we have in Kenya in terms of research – a clear bias for biomedical research, including in the existing guidance and in the composition of the ethics committees. A review of the studies registered on Clinicaltrials.gov shows that behavioural research is a significant part of the research conducted in Kenya. Yet the guidance

---

115 Section 1.1.1Accreditation Guidelines.
116 See "Constituting an Ethics Review" 2004 Guidelines.

and composition of ethics committees are clearly skewed towards clinical or biomedical research. While not much research has been done on the burdens that this may place on social science and humanities researchers, this is an issue that requires attention, not only in Kenya but in other African countries as well.

The 2004 Guidelines also emphasise the importance of an office space, quorum requirements, and the need for the continuing education of members. The institution is required to provide office space for the secretariat of the committee. Where the committee serves more than one institution, the provider of the office space will be responsible for the committee. Analysts in this area note that there are serious challenges with operational infrastructure, like the office spaces, furniture, stationery, and equipment such as computers and scanners. Use of equipment from the institutions and other facilities often means that the confidentiality of the work of the committees cannot be guaranteed. In the same vein, the host institutions typically do not provide budgetary allocations to support the work of ethics review committees with the attendant challenges.

Further, problems that have been noted in other countries, such as lack of training for members of ethics review committees, especially on ethics; lack of monitoring of research once approved; and lack of monitoring and evaluation of the work of such committees are also challenges for ethics review committees in Kenya.[117]

The accreditation of ethics committees is a laudable idea which, if implemented vigorously, will promote high ethical standards as well as standardisation. For instance, if the requirements on training for ethics review members are enforced, this will raise the knowledge of the members of ethics committees across Kenya. While there may be few issues with the provisions of the requirements of ethics committees on paper, in practice there are outstanding issues to be overcome, including, for instance, failure to seek accreditation; ethics shopping; and over-concentration of accredited ethics committees in Nairobi, the capital city.[118] At the moment, nothing prevents researchers from presenting research protocols to other ethics committees after a rejection by another ethics committee. To prevent this occurrence, a database of all submitted protocols has been recommended by some to determine what protocols have been submitted at any time and to which ethics committee.[119] This is a good suggestion. In addition, researchers could also be required to provide information on previous submissions to ethics committees, identifying any amendments made, should they choose to resubmit a previously rejected protocol. Some studies also noted that most accredited committees were based in the cities, thus excluding the rural areas, increasing workload, and logistical difficulties for researchers.

117 Adiel Magana, "Challenges IERCs Face in Reviewing Research Proposals in the Biological and Social Sciences" (2015) 1:1 Bioethics Society of Kenya News 11–12. G Omosa-Manyonyi et al, "Enhancing Capacity of Research Ethics Review Committees in Developing Countries: The Kenyan Example" (2014) 7:2 SAJBL 59.

118 G Omosa-Manyonyi et al, "Enhancing Capacity of Research Ethics Review Committees in Developing Countries: The Kenyan Example" (2014) 7:2 SAJBL 59.

119 *Ibid.*

Independence is a key issue for ethics committees around the world. The 2004 Guidelines require that ethics committees "provide independent, competent and timely review of the ethics of proposed studies. In their composition, procedures and decision making, ECs need to have independence from political, institutional, professional and market influences."[120] However, they do not provide concrete steps for avoiding conflicts of interest.

Clarity on sanctions for lack of ethics review is also lacking. The 2004 Guidelines provide that "ECs should be established in accordance with the applicable laws and regulations of Kenya and in accordance with the values and principles of the communities they serve."[121] The current law – the National Commission on Science, Technology and Innovation Act, 2013 – does not specifically provide that there should be ethics review. But it does require that the Act give the Commission power to establish the ethics, guidelines, and regulations of the Commission. This arises by implication; NACOSTI has the power to make regulations and guidelines. These guidelines state that there must be ethics approval, giving it the indirect force of law. The indirect force of law underpinning ethics review appears not to be clear to many researchers and even ethics committees.[122] While research permits cannot be obtained without ethics approval, it would have been clearer to make ethics review a legal requirement, accompanied by sanctions. The problematic research incidents, discussed earlier in this chapter, suggest that ethics approval may still not be obtained in all research, despite all the regulatory requirements in place. Peer pressure, publication in a journal, "naming and shaming," and other methods of suasion are available.[123] However, the lack of clear legal sanctions also means limits in accountability and enforcement in Kenya.

Finally, for a country with a relatively long history of ethics review, not much research appears to have been done on the effectiveness of ethics review or the challenges of ethics review in Kenya by comparison with the other African countries studied in this book.

Drug regulatory authority

The Kenyan Pharmacy and Poisons Board is established under the Pharmacy and Poisons Act.[124] The Minister of Health is empowered by the Act to appoint members of the board. The board is the national drug regulatory authority. An agency under the Ministry of Health, it is semi-autonomous. It is responsible for

---

120 "Constituting an Ethics Review Committee" (2004) Guidelines.

121 *Ibid*, 8.

122 See, for instance, Caroline Kithinji, "Ethics Review Committees in Kenya" (2013) Interview, online: <www.peopleandperspectives.org/story/interview-kithinji>.

123 See, for example, Pamela Andanda, "A Golden Chance for Medical Ethics in Kenya" (2004) SciDev, online: <https://www.scidev.net/global/health/opinion/a-golden-chance-for-medical-ethics-in-kenya.html>.

124 Pharmacy and Poisons Act Cap 244, as amended, Section 3.

monitoring and granting approvals for the clinical trials of drugs in Kenya under powers given by the Pharmacy and Poisons (Registration of Drugs) Rules, which provide that "Any person wishing to carry out a clinical trial in the country shall apply to the Board for approval before engaging in such study involving investigational products."[125] In 2012, the Board appointed the Expert Committee on Clinical Trials (ECCT) to review all matters relating to clinical trials in the country.

As part of its powers, the Board has issued guidelines developed by the ECCT for the conducting of clinical trials in Kenya. The guidelines were issued and became effective first in 2011 and were revised and updated in 2016: *Guidelines for Applications to Conduct Clinical Trials in Kenya*, 2016 (the 2016 Guidelines).[126] The 2016 Guidelines contain a statement of the legal and ethical framework within which a researcher may carry out clinical trials in the country, and they set out the conditions under which clinical trials are to be conducted in order to satisfy ethical and scientific quality standards. In addition to these guidelines, the *National Guidelines for Research and Development of HIV/AIDS Vaccine* regulate clinical drug trials relating to HIV/AIDS. As required under the Guidelines, all HIV/AIDS-related clinical trials must obtain the approval of the Kenyan HIV/AIDs Vaccine Subcommittee.

It is mandatory to obtain the approval of the Pharmacy and Poison Board for all clinical trials involving humans, including for the testing of unregistered medicines, vaccines, medical devices, unregistered medicines, and registered medicines where the proposed clinical trials are beyond the approved use.[127] One application is required for a multisite trial; however, there must be a primary investigator (PI) who shall be responsible for each of the sites. The application to carry out a multisite trial should set out the details of available infrastructure and staff capability to conduct the study. The decision of the Board is expected to be communicated within 30 working days of receipt of a complete and valid application. The 30-day working period within which the Board communicates its decision on an application and its rules to prevent a conflict of interest or the biased review of an application accord with its declaration to provide a regulatory environment that avoids unnecessary delays in the clinical trial authorisation process, at the same time safeguarding the quality, efficacy, and public health of Kenyans.

Amongst other accountability requirements, such as record-keeping requirements by investigators,[128] the Board is obliged to visit clinical trial sites and trial sponsors to ensure compliance with generally accepted principles of good clinical practice, ensure that clinical trial participants are not subjected and exposed to undue risks, validate the quality of data generated, or investigate complaints.[129]

---

125 Section 1A of the Rules.
126 *Pharmacy and Poisons Board: Guidelines for Applications to Conduct Clinical Trials in Kenya*, 2016.
127 Paragraph 1 of the Guideline.
128 Paragraph 26.7.
129 Paragraph 26.

The Board also has the power to terminate a clinical trial with the withdrawal of the Board's approval: for example where the safety of the study participants in the trial is compromised, or the scientific reasons for conducting the trial have changed from that for which the approval was initially granted. A summary of the result of the clinical trial is also expected to be submitted to the Board, irrespective of the result of the trial; this should be prepared in accordance with the ICH guidelines.[130] All clinical trials taking place in Kenya are to be registered in the Kenyan Clinical Trials Registry.[131] At present, a total of 187 studies are listed on the Board's website in various stages.

The Board, as the regulatory body for the conducting of clinical trials in Kenya, may impose sanctions against the sponsor and/or principal investigator for non-compliance with the Clinical Trials Guidelines, including blacklisting a non-compliant sponsor or principal investigator, making public a list of sponsors or principal investigators found to be seriously or persistently non-compliant, denial of import permit of the study medications for non-compliance, suspending the study, stopping the study, or imposing a fine for non-compliance with the regulation.

As in some African countries, the Board has benefited from external support for much of its work, including its oversight function over clinical trials. Thus, for example, the Clinical Trials Registry and the Clinical Trials Guidelines were established with the support of international donors such as the WHO and European Commission.[132] The influence of non-state actors, including private-sector pharmaceutical companies, in shaping policy is a reality of life in many African countries and is arguably part of a hybrid framework of governance. Nevertheless, the need to ensure the interests of the State (Kenya) and, more importantly, of the research participants remains paramount. Regulatory capture is of critical concern, as is an agenda that does not place the safety and well-being of research participants in the centre. Devoting domestic resources to regulatory bodies such as the Board is therefore a necessity.[133] The lack of full autonomy from the

---

130 Paragraph 27.9.
131 Article 22. The Kenya Clinical Trials Register is provided here, online: <www.ctr.pharmacy-boardkenya.org/>.
132 Kathy Moscou & Jillian C Kohler, "Matching Safety to Access: Global Actors and Pharmacogovernance in Kenya- A Case Study" (2017) 13:20 Global Health, online: <https://pdfs.semanticscholar.org/5c84/19bf21398e4618540a19bdf18b2849fc0b28.pdf> at 11. See also WHO, *Experience with Supporting Pharmaceutical Policies and Systems in Kenya: Progress, Lessons and the Role of WHO* (2010) WHO/EMP/MPC/2010.2, online: <apps.who.int/medicinedocs/documents/s17551en/s17551en.pdf> See Annex 3 at 43.
133 In this regard, in the context of pharmacovigilance, Moscou and Kohler note that

> The research results [of their study] suggest that caution is warranted regarding the sole use of exogenous actors to fill a deficit in capacity for pharmacovigilance. It leaves Kenya vulnerable to: 1) a fragmented pharmacovigilance system; 2) ad hoc, drug specific pharmacosurveillance; 3) cross purpose interests; and 4) exogenous actors' shifting priorities. For although exogenous actors are likely to continue to advocate for pharmacovigilance while interests align, Kenya is already experiencing the effect of shifting priorities that have reduced donor funding.
>
> Moscou and Kohler at 14

Ministry of Health has also been described as a challenge to the full delivery of the Board's mandate in the regulation of medicines in Kenya generally,[134] although this is not apparent from the operations of the ECCT and the Board in the regulation of clinical trials in Kenya.

Regulation of health and other professionals

The Medical Practitioners and Dentists Board (the Board) is the regulatory body of the medical profession in Kenya. It was established by the Medical Practitioners and Dentists Act.[135] It is composed of only medical practitioners, including members representing universities which grant medical or dental degrees.[136] The Board licences and registers persons eligible to practice as medical practitioners in the country. The Act also gives the Board authority to inquire into a criminal act or conduct considered to be "infamous conduct in a professional respect" and to make rules with regard to discipline.[137] One such rule is the Medical Practitioners and Dentists (Disciplinary Proceedings) (Procedure) Rules. As part of its regulation of the profession, the Board has issued the Code of Professional Conduct and Discipline, 2012,[138] which sets out standards of conduct and regulates the profession. Specifically, it articulates the kinds of conduct that may warrant professional discipline. From time to time, the Board also establishes supplementary rules that must be complied with by professionals, in addition to the requirements of the Code. The Code is required to be complied with by all medical and dental practitioners, and all medical institutions registered in Kenya.

The Code has several provisions related to research and research governance. One of these provisions highlights the role of the Board – it states that one of its "core functions," as stated in the Code, is to provide advice to the Minister of Health on research involving humans.[139] The core functions of the Board also include conducting inquiries into the professional conduct of medical practitioners and dentists.

The importance of health professionals in Kenya is further emphasised by the provisions of the *Clinical Trials Guidelines*, which require that a qualified medical practitioner be responsible for all medically related decisions in a clinical trial.[140] The qualified medical practitioner must be one licenced with the Kenya Medical Practitioner and Dentists Board. The medical care given to clinical trial subjects and medical decisions made over the course of a clinical trial on behalf

---

134 Grace N Thoithi & Faith A Okalebo, "Country Case Study: Kenya" International Pharmaceutical Federation, online: <https://www.fip.org/files/fip/HR/2009/2009%20GPWR%20Part%205.4%20Kenya.pdf>.

135 Medical and Dental Practitioners Act Cap 253, Section 4.

136 Section 3 of the Medical and Dental Practitioners Act.

137 Section 20.

138 Medical Practitioners and Dentists Board, *The Code of Professional Conduct and Discipline, 2012* (6th Edition) (Republic of Kenya, 2012).

139 Article 7 (4) of the Code.

140 Article 4.7 of the Clinical Trials Guidelines 2016.

of a clinical trial subject must always be given by a qualified medical practitioner registered with the Board.

The Code also provides that a medical practitioner practising in Kenya shall be bound by all relevant international declarations which are in conformity with the laws of Kenya, including but not limited to the Declaration of Helsinki on Human Experimentation of 1964. The Code recognises that some medical practitioners might be involved in medical research and restates the key principles of the Helsinki Declaration on Human Experimentation of 1964, like Nigeria, as comprising the obligations and ethical duties of a medical practitioner involved in human experimentation under the Code.[141] Although the Code has subsidiary rules on certain subject matters, such as the payment of practising fees, referral of patients abroad, and advertising, it has no other rules on research outside of the provisions of the Code.

The Code lists several kinds of misconduct for which a professional may be found guilty in a professional respect. Complaints against a medical practitioner may be brought by different persons and bodies, including patients or their relatives, other healthcare professionals, health institutions, and other professional associations. Although clinical trial participants and participants in other kinds of health research are not specified, there is nothing precluding them from bringing a complaint against a medical practitioner. However, health research is not specifically provided as one of the grounds for bringing a complaint against a medical practitioner. Still, the ground of professional misconduct may be considered, broadly speaking, as possible ground on which a research participant or even a regulatory body can bring a complaint. For instance, failure to obtain a research permit, which is a criminal offence, is arguably grounds for the Tribunal to consider disciplinary action against a medical practitioner. Failure to obtain informed consent for research as required by the Declaration of Helsinki, which is an integral part of the Code, should also be grounds to consider whether a medical practitioner is guilty of "infamous conduct in a professional respect."

There are several sanctions that can be meted out by the Full Board acting as a Tribunal to a practitioner who engages in professional misconduct, including admonishment, probation, suspension, and removal from the register of medical practitioners. There are no special sanctions provided in the Code for non-compliance with any of the ethical obligations over the course of carrying out or participating in clinical research involving humans; the sanctions applicable to a medical practitioner involved in clinical research are those which may also be applied to a medical practitioner involved in regular medical practice.

Apart from the medical profession, which is directly involved in clinical trials and other types of health research, there appears to be no precedent for the regulation of other professionals involved in health research. Nursing, which is also a regulated profession, has a code of conduct, but this not address research involving humans in any specific manner. The largest association of nurses in Kenya,

---

141 Chapter V, no. 3(a) of the Code of Professional Conduct and Discipline.

the National Association of Nurses of Kenya (NNAK), has drawn up a code of conduct[142] but this does not address the nurse's role in the research process or the ethics of research involving human participants.

In sum, as in many African countries, professional regulatory bodies do not feature strongly as part of Kenya's health research governance arrangements. There appears to be no precedent for the type of disciplinary intervention discussed here with respect to research misconduct by medical practitioners. The Kenyan professional regulatory bodies would have been one way to address the HIV supplement trial referred to earlier, where a pharmacist and a nurse were involved in a trial declared unethical in the Netherlands. Given the number of clinical trials that are conducted in the country, it is surprising that the professional regulatory bodies have seemingly not shown a special interest in regulating the conduct of their members in those circumstances.

Civil society organisations

There are many civil society organisations in Kenya. Several of them do extensive work in health, especially in the areas of advocacy, provoking discussions, and putting pressure on government regarding issues of concern. Issues such as HIV, sexual and reproductive health, palliative care, patients' rights, advocacy on the constitutional right to health, and access to healthcare have been championed by these organisations and strategic litigation. Several legal actions have been filed by the civil society organisations (CSOs), including cases of the forced sterilisation of HIV-infected women. The organisations include the Centre of Patients Rights, Kenya Hospices and Palliative Association, Kenya Legal and Ethical Issues Network (KELIN), and the Bioethics Society of Kenya.

The Bioethics Society of Kenya is a relatively new organisation (it was founded in 2013).[143] Amongst other roles, it engages in public education on bioethics generally, including on research ethics. At this time, it is not a key part of the regulatory arrangements in Kenya, not being actively involved in advocacy.

Thus, as in other African countries, the current civil society organisations are not yet significantly engaged with advocacy or other support of health research ethics and governance.

Assessment of Kenya's research governance arrangements

Kenya has a long history of health research and research governance. At present, there are several pieces of legislation, several guidelines, and several institutions that govern health research involving humans presenting what is in many respects a robust framework. At first glance, there would appear to be a myriad

---

142 National Nurses' Association of Kenya, Code of Conduct and Ethics, 2009, online: <www.eacc.go.ke/docs/NNAK-CODE.pdf>.

143 <www.bioethicskenya.org/>.

of guidance on health research regulation and related matters, although, with careful attention, it can be seen how they may be aligned. Yet, despite the broad guidance, some key issues may not be addressed in any depth: for example, bi-obanking, access to experimental medicines, or the management of conflict of interest. Beyond that, researchers would have to be careful to compare and contrast guidelines in their area to ensure that there are no conflicts. Where there are conflicts, it is not always easy to be sure which guideline should take precedence. To that extent, uniformity and clarity remain works in progress. Legislation such as the Health Act is recent (2017), and it remains to be seen how its provisions on research governance will be integrated into the existing framework.

One of the unique features of its history was the early introduction of law into its research regulation and governance arrangements, introducing a hallmark of legitimacy. Interestingly, however, the law remains only indirectly connected to ethics review. Because of the indirect way in which ethics review is provided for, there is no direct government funding for ethics review committees, nor are they clearly permitted to charge for ethics review (with the attendant issues that this may bring). Institutions are expected to fund them, but there is no mechanism for compelling the institutions to do so.

Ethics review, while entrenched in the research governance system, is by no means without challenges. As in other African countries, resources for sustaining these committees have been described as insufficient, as have operating infrastructure. In particular, even where there is proper ethics review, lack of resources is a likely impediment to proper, ongoing monitoring or oversight of approved research.

Finally, in terms of comprehensiveness, amongst other challenges, the divide between social and biomedical research is markedly clear in the research governance arrangements. The various guidelines in place currently do not provide adequately (or even, it could be argued, acknowledge) the differences between such research. With the broad definition of "research for health" in the Health Act, it will be interesting to see how governance arrangements change. Similar to this, the active role of professional regulatory bodies in health research is yet to come, as is the engagement of civil society organisations in issues of health research governance.

8 Health research governance in Egypt

Introduction

The Arab Republic of Egypt, commonly referred to as Egypt, is a democratic republic located in the North-Eastern corner of Africa. A transcontinental country, it is geographically located in Africa and Asia, facing Europe.[1] In its Constitution, it is described as a part of the Arab nation, a part of the Islamic world, which belongs to the African continent and which cherishes its Asian dimensions.[2]

The current population of Egypt is over 96 million.[3] There are significant rates of poverty, with 14 per cent of people living below the poverty line.[4] Life expectancy at birth currently stands at 69 years for males and 73 years for females,[5] some of the highest in Africa. A low-income developing country, it has adopted a universal healthcare system in which health services are provided to all citizens freely, with the government subsidising the costs. Egypt's health system is a mixture of public health insurance through the Health Insurance Organisation, which oversees the social health insurance system. The Health Insurance Organisation is a parastatal but is connected to the Ministry of Health, which remains the main provider of healthcare in the country. Government spending on health remains low.[6] The public health system runs alongside the private health system; however, close to 30 million citizens have no private health insurance. Although Egypt seeks to implement universal health coverage, only about 57 per cent of the people are covered by public health insurance, and out-of-pocket payments have increased significantly.[7]

---

1 A Ghanaam & E Elazazy, Health Governance System Assessment: An Explanatory Methodology – Egypt (2015) at 10.
2 Article 1 of the Amended Constitution of the Arab Republic of Egypt 2014.
3 <www.capmas.gov.eg/HomePage.aspx>.
4 UNDP, Human Development Index, 2014.
5 WHO, Global Health Observatory Data Repository.
6 Ahmed Shoukry Rashad & Mesbah Fathy Sharaf, "Who Benefits from Public Healthcare Subsidies in Egypt?" (2015) 4 Soc Sci 1162.
7 *Ibid.*

Moreover, while the government remains committed to providing healthcare for the significant population who live in poverty, the subsidies provided have been shown to benefit the rich more.[8] A new health law is passing through the legislative process. The proposed law is intended to improve health coverage, including through mandatory enrolment and the inclusion of catastrophic health conditions.[9]

The main health and population challenges are increasing population rates; endemic and infectious diseases; maternal, infant, and childhood mortality; chronic diseases, renal failure and cancer; injuries and accidents; smoking, other addictions, and their complications; disabilities; and congenital anomalies. HIV and malaria prevalence are low. Several neglected tropical diseases, including worm-related diseases, persist.[10] Despite Egypt's impressive life expectancy compared to those of other African countries, it has a high prevalence of non-communicable diseases (NCDs), including cardiovascular diseases, diabetes, cancer, and chronic respiratory diseases.[11] This is reflective of the situation in other African countries, including those considered in this book: infectious diseases alongside a growing incidence of NCDs. Egypt also has the highest prevalence of the Hepatitis C Virus (HCV) in the world.[12] This has been attributed to 'medical procedures involving unsafe medical devices, repetitive injections, contaminated blood transfusions and female genital mutilation' during a government intervention to manage an epidemic of schistosomiasis decades before.[13] The result of the high prevalence is a high incidence of liver cancer, one of the highest in the world.[14] The high incidence of HCV has resulted in much research on the disease in Egypt.[15] In order to address the HCV challenge, Egyptian pharmaceutical companies began local production of HCV drugs.[16] A lot of clinical research is ongoing in respect to this disease, including on liver cancer and liver transplantation.

8 *Ibid.*

9 Sharmila Devi, "Universal Health Coverage Law Approved in Egypt" (2017) 391 Lancet 194.

10 WHO, Egypt: Health Profile, (2015). WHO, Health Systems Profile: Egypt (WHO, EMRO, 2006). World Bank, A Roadmap to Achieve Social Justice in Health Care in Egypt (2015), online: <www.worldbank.org/content/dam/Worldbank/Feature%20Story/mena/Egypt/Egypt-Doc/egy-roadmap-sj-health.pdf>. See generally, Nesreen M Kamal Elden et al, "Improving Health System in Egypt: Perspectives of Physicians" (2016) 34:1 Egypt J Community Med 45.

11 WHO, Egypt: Non-Communicable Diseases, online: <www.emro.who.int/egy/programmes/noncommunicable-diseases.html>.

12 Blach S, Zeuzem S, Manns M et al, Global Prevalence and Genotype Distribution of Hepatitis C Virus Infection in 2015: A Modelling Study (2016) 2:3 Lancet Gastroenterol Hepatol 161–176.

13 *Ibid* Fn.1 at 26.

14 WHO.

15 D Iskander, "The Right to Health: Case study on Hepatitis C in Egypt" (2013), online:

16 <https://www.egypttoday.com/Article/1/14537/Fighting-Hepatitis-C-Egypt-treats-1-8M-since-2014>. Accessed on 16 February 2018.

Female genital mutilation (FGM) is another health and behavioural issue that demands research. Egypt has one of the world's highest prevalence rates of FGM.[17] Although it was criminalised in 2008,[18] the rates of FGM remain high, with estimates of 88 per cent prevalence amongst adolescents in 2014 (down from 94 per cent in 2008).[19] Studies are ongoing with respect to reducing FGM and changing social attitudes towards the practice.

Egypt is the second-biggest destination country for clinical trials in Africa after South Africa.[20] This is despite the fact that Egypt has experienced tumultuous political upheavals since the Arab Spring of 2010. Egypt is a choice state for transnational pharmaceutical companies because of its attractive research infrastructure, its fast-growing and largely treatment-naïve population, its comparatively lower costs, its large numbers of trained scientists, and its peculiar location in the Middle East and Northern Africa (MENA) region, which make it a most preferred destination for clinical drug testing.[21] Its rates of biomedical research have increased significantly in recent years.[22] Further, Egypt's context is reflective of other North African countries, which have large Arab populations and may serve as an example for the development of research and research ethics infrastructure for those countries. The existence of a fast-growing, uninsured population; a high cost of healthcare; and the absence of a national law on health research[23] make Egypt even more attractive for clinical testing.

Egypt's transcontinental geographical location, health profile, relatively high rate of clinical trials, and recent revitalisation of research ethics committees make it a compelling case study for governance and regulation. Furthermore, the continuing high levels of clinical trials and other kinds of health research amidst political turbulence raise questions about how effective extant regulations have been. Recent studies have also shown that there appear to be ethical problems in relation to clinical trials conducted in Egypt.[24] All of these make Egypt relevant for the study of health research governance.

---

17 RefWorld, "FGM in Egypt: Findings," online: <www.refworld.org/pdfid/5a17eee44.pdf> April 2017.

18 Law No. 126 of 2008, amending Law No. 58 of 1937, also amended in 2016 to increase the penalty from three months to two years to between five and seven years.

19 Duna Alkhalaileh et al, "Prevalence and Attitudes on Female Genital Mutilation/Cutting in Egypt since Criminalisation in 2008" (2017) 20:2 Cult & Sex at 173–182.

20 "Clinical Trials on the Rise amid Ethical and Legal Concerns," online: <https://egyptianstreets.com/2016/10/19/in-egypt-clinical-trials-on-the-rise-amid-ethical-and-legal-concerns/>.

21 P Durisch, A den Boer, I Schipper & A Kohli, Industry-Sponsored Clinical Drug Trials in Egypt: Ethical Questions in a Challenging Context at 3, online: <https://www.somo.nl/wp-content/uploads/2016/06/Public_Eye_Report_Clinical_Drug_Trials_Egypt_12-2016.pdf>.

22 Between 2008 and 2011, Egypt's clinical research rates tripled (Matar and Silverman, 2013).

23 Wemos, Clinical trials in Africa, The cases of Egypt, Kenya, Zimbabwe and South Africa (Wemos Health Unlimited, 2017 at 7).

24 Industry-Sponsored Clinical Drug Trials in Egypt: Ethical Questions in a Challenging Context, Note 22.

Health research in Egypt

As in South Africa, there is, in relative terms, extensive health research in Egypt. This is not surprising, especially in light of the significant population, well-trained researchers, and considerable numbers of avenues for health research: 41 universities which have attached to them 94 health-related medical schools and 24 faculties of medicine, with about 34 departments in each. As noted in studies, bachelor's and postgraduate degrees require an element of clinical research, as does faculty promotion in faculties of medicine, where publication of clinical research is a critical element[25] There are also many pharmaceutical companies, including domestic and international pharmaceutical companies and biotechnology companies.

At the present time, there has been no comprehensive articulation of health research priorities by the government. Studies take place for academic purposes, but a significant number of clinical trials are also conducted by the pharmaceutical industry. There is therefore a possibility that health research is not conducted in line with the priority issues of the country, one of the key challenges of health research in African countries. There is no national database of health research taking place within the country, which is also a concern as there is little knowledge about who is doing what and where. However, a quick review of Clinicaltrials.gov indicated a total of 2,090 clinical trials in Egypt on a variety of health conditions, including various cancers, organ transplantation (especially liver transplants), diabetes, brain injury, various reproductive health issues, renal disease in particular HCV-related issues, and FGM. These are taking place in various locations in Egypt, from medical schools to maternity hospitals.

The upshot is that health research, including health research involving humans, is not uncommon and is on the rise in Egypt, and to some extent appears aligned to the priority health concerns identified in the Introduction. Cancer trials are disproportionately high, with other concerns taking up a smaller share. However, infectious diseases and social health concerns lag far behind in the trials that are ongoing, suggesting some mismatch of priorities. The lack of a process and policy identifying health priorities and ensuring that health research conducted in the country aligns with such priorities is nonetheless a significant vacuum. There is also little government funding for health research,[26] with the consequence that the government may dictate only little on health research priorities.

Clinical trials conducted in Egypt cost considerably less than they do in Western countries. It is estimated that they cost about half of what they cost in the United States, which is around 300 million dollars. In addition, with the large numbers of scientists and well-equipped medical centres, the attractiveness of

---

25 Sherif Shehata, Nehal M ElMashad & Azza M Hassan, "Current Review of Medical Research in Developing Countries: A Case Study from Egypt" (2017) at 43.
26 Industry-Sponsored Clinical Drug Trials in Egypt: Ethical Questions in a Challenging Context, at 20.

Egypt for pharmaceutical companies is hardly surprising, even in the face of a challenging political context.[27]

Health research governance in Egypt

The legal and ethical challenges posed for the governance of health research in Egypt include a weak legal and regulatory framework for monitoring and conducting health research, and limited regulatory protections for research participants, even as health research continues to increase. As discussed later, the Egyptian context differs in key policy respects from several other African countries' contexts in terms of a lack of national ethical guidance and thus continued reliance on international ethical instruments, and a lack of national law on health research generally and clinical trials.

Yet studies have suggested a significant level of vulnerability in relation to research participants who participate in clinical drug trials in Egypt. The reasons research participants are likely to be considered vulnerable include the lack of access to health insurance, identified in earlier discussions, and the inability of a significant portion of the population to afford many drugs, especially for catastrophic illnesses.[28] The result is likely to be challenges in obtaining truly informed consent. As noted in one study, "it may lead to the unwanted and unethical situation that vulnerable people are joining a clinical trial just to have access to treatment, even though the results are uncertain. This kind of environment exposes vulnerable people to exploitation as trial participants."[29]

Legal framework

The legal framework of research governance in Nigeria, though inchoate, is grounded in part by the Constitution of Egypt, 2014. The Constitution (like the South African Constitution) mandatorily requires informed consent. It provides that "The human body is inviolable… and it is not permissible to perform any medical or scientific experiment thereon without a certified free consent according to established principles in medical sciences and as regulated by Law."[30] Informed consent is therefore, as in South Africa, protected by the Constitution. Obtaining consent is to be governed by principles provided in medicine and is to be regulated by law.

With respect to law, Egypt has no national, comprehensive legislation on research governance. However, such a law has been under consideration. There is no law requiring the compulsory registration of a research ethics committee with a national committee, such as we now have in both South Africa and Nigeria. However, with regard to "established principles in medical sciences," as provided

27 *Ibid.*
28 *Ibid.*
29 *Ibid* at 19.
30 Constitution of Egypt, Article 60.

by the Constitution, the Professional Ethics Regulations 2003, issued by the Ministry of Health,[31] provides some framework for informed consent. The requirement for informed consent is emphasised, and the necessary information to be provided to those volunteering for research is detailed. These are:

i   The targets of the research;
ii The research approaches which will be adopted;
iii The expected benefits;
iv The probable risks and the extent of their effect on the volunteers;
v   Financing sources for the research;
vi The identity of the researcher in charge and his institutional belonging;
vii The right of the research participant to withdraw from research without sustaining any negative consequences;[32] and
viii The consent must be written.[33]

The Regulations also have some provisions that provide a regulatory framework for research ethics. The Egyptian Ministry of Health is charged with the responsibility of formulating health policy for the country and regulating the health sector. Regulation and governance of health research falls within the scope of its broad responsibilities under the Constitution.

The Regulations require that medical research and experiments on human beings, and clinical trials for drugs are prohibited unless they are endorsed by competent quarters, and a detailed analysis of the risks and benefits of the research are provided. Researchers are also required to submit a detailed and clear research targets report, which must provide justifications for conducting research on humans to the competent quarters for approval. "Competent quarters" is not defined but may be argued to mean the research ethics committee of an institution. The Regulations also require the official, written consent of the person to being involved in the research or the approval of the person's official guardian. Persons volunteering for research have the right to withdraw at any time.[34] We discuss the Regulations further in this chapter.

These Regulations would appear to apply only to physicians or medical researchers. This would leave other kinds of health researchers and health research, including social and humanities research and professionals, outside the umbrella of the Regulations. This also means that not all kinds of health research are regulated, with consequences for protections for research participants or clear parameters for researchers who are not medical doctors. Matters such as the kinds of research which require ethics review approval, requirements for research ethics committees, the mandatory registration of clinical trials, and other key

---

31 Egyptian Medical Syndicate. The Egyptian Medical Code of Conduct issued by Ministerial Decree 238/2003, 2003 Ministry of Health, Professional Ethics Regulations No. 238/2003, Part 4.
32 Section 55.
33 Section 56.
34 Sections 52–54.

requirements that could be captured in a legal framework are currently not addressed. While the Regulations make reference to matters "legally competent quarters" (an apparent reference to research ethics committees), there is at present no legislation that establishes these committees or mandates them to operate in any specific manner. Finally, these Regulations lack legal force.[35]

The challenges related to the lack of a proper legal framework of health research governance in Egypt are encapsulated in the statement of Sherifa et al, noting that

> Since there is no robust legislative constraints and clear guidance to charge entities or stakeholders involved in overseeing or executing clinical trials, concerns are increasingly being raised, whether ethical pitfalls of clinical research are adequately addressed, and whether the safety and the rights of subjects are constantly prioritized and maintained, leaving room for different interpretations and making it more difficult to identify violations and impose sanctions.[36]

Others have noted that the legal and policy vacuum, including with respect to developing new drugs within Egypt, is also an impediment for the pharmaceutical companies.[37] Further, it has been observed with regard to the need for law in relation to research injuries that "The procedures for obtaining compensation in Egypt are sometimes formidable, and local legislation is needed for extra protection and timely compensation."[38]

Efforts have been made to address the existing vacuum in the legal framework since 2011. A clinical trials law was drafted in 2016 but has not been enacted.

Ethical framework

Egypt does not have a comprehensive domestic local guidance. Several studies have noted gaps in its ethical framework.[39] There are no national guidelines which specify the considerations that must be taken into account in conducting health research. Health research as a concept is not defined nor does it receive specific

35　Mohamed Abdelgawad, Fadila Safwat & Sharkawy & Sarhan, "Medicinal Product Regulation and Product Liability in Egypt: Overview" in Practical Law (Thomson Reuter, 2017) online: <https://uk.practicallaw.thomsonreuters.com/w-008-4310?transitionType=Default&context Data=(sc.Default)&firstPage=true&bhcp=1>.

36　Sherif Shehata, Nehal M ElMashad & Azza M Hassan, "Current Review of Medical Research in Developing Countries: A Case Study from Egypt" in Seth Appiah-Opoku, International Development (Intech Open, 2017) at 43.

37　Dina Iskander, "TRIPS and Access to Medicines in Egypt" in Hans Lofgren & O Williams, eds, *The New Political Economy of Pharmaceuticals: Production, Innovation and TRIPS in the Global South* (Palgrave MacMillan, 2016) at 105.

38　Inas M Younis, "Overview of Research Committees Status in Egypt: Challenges Aspirations and Current Situation" (2015) 22 Acc Res 222 at 227.

39　See, for example, Ghiath Alahmad et al. Review of National Research Ethics Regulations and Guidelines in Middle Eastern Arab Countries (2012) 13 BMC Medical Ethics 34.

guidance. All of these corroborate the fact that, while medical ethics has been recognised for a long time in the country, "research ethics is a new concept."[40]

The current ethical framework consists of the earlier-mentioned Professional Ethics Regulations 2003 and international ethical guidelines. The Professional Ethics Regulations is the code of ethics for medical professionals, with a specific section focussed on medical research (as in South Africa and Nigeria). At the present time it covers certain specific matters. These include physician requirements: to comply with "moral criteria and guidelines as well as the social and religious values laid down by the competent authority for conducting medical research on human beings;"[41] to obtain approval from the "competent quarters"[42] (which suggests a mandatory requirement for ethics review; however this may also be construed to mean regulatory approval from a drug regulatory body or approval by the Ministry of Health); a mandatory requirement to obtain a report on the risk-benefit ratio of the proposed research;[43] and justification for the research.[44]

Where the research involves children, the consent of the parent or guardian must be obtained. The Regulations also states that the research must be therapeutic research; in other words, it rules out the participation of children in non-therapeutic research. It does not cover other matters, however. These include specific protections for children and rules relating to biobanking.

Research ethics committees in Egypt have been noted by studies to indicate that their functioning is hampered by a lack of national research ethics guidance. A survey of research ethics committees indicated that 92 per cent of these committees specified a need for national research ethics guidelines.[45] Other studies considering ethics guidance in the Middle East, including Egypt, point out with respect to clinical research that

> These deficiencies will have an effect on clinical research—especially experimental trials—in the region. Fewer protections mean less strict guidelines, which, in addition to good medical facilities and a suitable research environment, will prove attractive to many pharmaceutical companies who may wish to transfer their research activities to such a region [7]. The many deficiencies observed in these guidelines will leave a question mark as to their adequacy in offering the necessary protections to research subjects in the region.[46]

40 Inas M Younis, *supra* Note 38 at 222.
41 Section 52.
42 Section 53.
43 Section 54.
44 Section 55.
45 Hany Sleem, Samer S El-Kamary & Henry J Silverman, "Identifying Structures, Processes, Resources and Needs of Research Ethics Committees in Egypt" (2010) 11:12 BMC Med Ethics 1.
46 Ghiath Alahmad, Mohammad Al-Jumah & Kris Dierick, "Review of National Research Ethics Regulations and Guidelines in Middle Eastern Arab Countries" (2012) 13:34 BMC Med Ethics, online <https://bmcmedethics.biomedcentral.com/articles/10.1186/1472-6939-13-34>.

Apart from the ethical framework provided by the Regulations, the research ethics committees in Egypt, as indicated in the following section, use international ethical guidelines such as the Helsinki Declaration in the process of ethics review. There is no mandatory requirement, however, to rely on any of the international guidelines. Further, the challenge with this approach is that, as discussed extensively in the foregoing chapters, the international guidelines may not always provide a solution for some of the challenging ethical questions that arise in the African or the Egyptian context. Studies conducted in Egypt have raised ethical questions relating to failure to use the best proven treatments, testing medicines not yet registered in developed countries, or failure to ensure that the research is such that it is beneficial or will produce affordable interventions that can be applied to the local populations. Ethical issues such as informed consent in cancer trials, provision of effective treatment to control the arms of trials, and post-trial benefits remain key questions in the Egyptian context, especially in view of the significant number of cancer clinical trials. Furthermore, questions around compensation for research participants, biobanking, materials transfer agreements, privacy and confidentiality, research related to traditional medicines, research-related injuries, and compensation, amongst other things, are not clearly answered in the domestic context of South Africa.

Institutional framework

Here we consider the institutions established for the implementation of governance in Egypt. In view of the fact that a legal framework is still in the process of being developed, and the ethical framework remains inchoate, the functions institutions – ethics review committees, drug regulatory bodies, and non-governmental organisations – are perhaps even more crucial than they might be in other countries. The research indicates, however, that they face similar challenges to those described in relation to the other examined countries.

Ethics review committees

In the absence of legislation, ethics review is the key protective mechanism and the main governance instrument for research in Egypt. The Ministry of Health has established the scientific research and research ethics committee, which is registered with the United States Office of Human Research Protections. The Minister of Health also promulgated Ministerial Decree #95 in 2005, which prohibits the conduct of a clinical trial without obtaining the approval of the committee. The Care of Mentally Ill Patients Law provides that any clinical trial must be approved by the Research Ethics Committee.[47] The Central Directorate

---

47 Article 36 of Law no. 71/2009 regarding The Care of Mentally Ill Patients Law.

of Researches & Health Development (CDRHD) of the Ministry of Health is also, ostensibly, required to regulate the conduct of research and research ethics committees in the country.[48]

Ethics review is long-standing in Egypt, with some placing the origins of research ethics committees in the country in the 1960s.[49] Similar to Nigeria, it has an institutional ethics review system, and ethics review committees were established in some institutions in the 1980s.[50] Institutional research ethics committees are established in many schools and research institutes around the country. As noted elsewhere, research ethics committees are distributed around the country, mainly in universities and research centres.[51] The Ministry of Health and Population also has its own research ethics committee. However, not all institutions have such committees.

Although long-standing, research ethics committees have suffered from many problems, including the lack of capacity of members, lack of independence, and lack of resources.[52] A recent revitalisation of research ethics committees has occurred in Egypt. Key institutions have recently established research ethics committees, such as the National Research Centre (2003),[53] National Hepatology and Tropical Medicine Research Institute (2005), and Faculty of Medicine at Ain Shams University Research Ethics Committee (2007).[54] Many research ethics committees have been established for the purpose of meeting with foreign standards, in particular standards required for the Federal Wide Assurance. The Egyptian Network of Research Ethics has 45 research ethics committees listed on the directory on its website.[55] In 2011, Egypt had 45 ethics review committees registered with the United States Office of Human Protections. Other studies put the number of registered research ethics committees at 56.[56]

Research ethics committees (RECs) in Egypt are now part of a network established in part to address some of the challenges mentioned earlier. The Egyptian Network of Research Ethics Committees (ENREC) was established in 2008.[57] ENREC is operating under the auspices of an NGO (Egyptian Society for Healthcare Development). It is composed of about 30 members (research ethics committees representing different universities and institutions). It aims at

---

48 Azzah Saleh, "Research Ethics Governance in the Arab Region: Egypt" in H Silverman, ed, *Research Ethics in the Arab Region. Research Ethics Forum*, 5 (Springer, 2018), 237–243.

49 Younis, at 231.

50 Diaa Marzouk et al, "Overview on Health Research Ethics in Egypt and North Africa" (2014) 24:1 Eur J Public Health 87–91.

51 Marzouk et al, at 88.

52 Younis, at 223.

53 Abdel-Aal et al, "Research Ethics Committee NRC of Egypt" (2013) 29:10 Curr Med Res & Opin 1411–1417, 1411.

54 Marzouk et al, *supra* Note 18 at 86.

55 <www.enrec.org/directory/>.

56 Sherif Shehata, Nehal M ElMashad & Azza M Hassan, *supra* Note 25.

57 Egyptian Network of Research Ethics Committees, online: <www.enrec.org/>.

facilitating more uniform ethical review and simplifying REC procedures.[58] The mission and objectives of ENREC are wide-ranging and are listed on its website:

a   Vision: To be the reference and supporter of Egyptian RECs to help them to be consistent with the international quality standards of research.
b   Mission and Objectives:

    i   Strengthen coordination between the ethics committees of scientific research.
    ii   Enhance improvement in the quality of scientific research review.
    iii   Enhance the protection of participants in research.
    iv   Disseminate awareness of ethics of research to researchers and citizens.
    v   Enhance the current quality of Egyptian RECs performance.
    vi   Provide online training to REC members: www.menareti.net

These address some of the issues, including creating awareness of ethics of research to researchers and citizens, and promoting research participant protection. Furthermore, the purpose of establishing this network is to encourage the harmonisation between research ethics committees in "reviewing research proposals and to increase exchange of information and intellectual resources, policies and review strategies. The eventual aim is to create improved processes for protecting research subjects."[59] Harmonisation is a key issue especially where there are no uniform guidelines, leaving room for wide variations in the results that ethics review can bring. In this regard, the concerns have been captured by Sleem et al, noting that

> it is important to note that our survey shows variability among the respondent RECs in many of the structural and operating processes, including member composition, existence of written SOPs and conflict of interest policies, access to adequate financial and material resources, and processes of protocol review. The existence of variability in structure and processes probably equates to variability in functioning between the different RECs that might not offer a consistent protection mechanism for research participants across the country. These results strongly advocate the promotion of national operating standards for RECs, as well as the establishment of monitoring and oversight mechanisms for RECs.[60]

ENREC has provided model standard operating procedures (SOPs) for research ethics committees and a self-assessment tool for research ethics committees to employ in assessing how well they are functioning.[61] It must be noted that

58 *Ibid.*
59 *Ibid.*
60 Sleem et al, at 6.
61 <www.enrec.org/guidingdocuments/>.

ENREC is not a body established by law. It is therefore not mandatory that research ethics committees become members or adopt the tools that ENREC has provided.

Analyses of some research ethics committees in Egypt have been published in peer-reviewed journals[62] and provide some insight into their operations. At the present time, there is a lack of clarity on the structure of ethics review. Although there is an understanding that there are national, institutional, and local levels of ethics review, and research ethics committees, there is no policy defining which committee represents a specific level of review or the exact remit of each level, including policymaking. For example, the Egyptian National Bioethics Committee (NBC) was established in 1996. It has issued reports on aspects of research, including research ethics. However, as mentioned earlier, the Ministry of Health and Population also established an ethics review committee which is also considered to be the national ethics review committee. Younis notes that "Many other ethical committees hold similar claims; therefore, a higher re-search council to define the ethical committees' scope of function, roles, and responsibilities has become an imperative need."[63] There is no mechanism for cooperation or coordination, or the alignment of policies between the committees. There are no mechanisms for the registration, audit, and oversight of research ethics committees. ENREC, as earlier mentioned, strives to be the instrument for such coordination, but because it is not a statutory body with such a mandate, not all committees are members or align with its goals, nor can they provide the requisite oversight without such a mandate.

There is also a significant variability with regard to substantive ethics issues. This may stem in part from the use of different international ethics guidelines. While some committees rely on the Helsinki Declaration, others rely on the CI-OMS Guidelines or the ICH-GCP, amongst others. The result may be different approaches to the same ethical issues, depending on which committee and which ethics guidelines. As one commentator points out,

> It seems quite pointless to have many local RECs if no effective national or regional policies exist to uniformly guide them. The fact that a protocol may be rejected by one committee and then be accepted by another in view of the lack of standardization actually creates a state of chaos that is no more accepted in the world of today.[64]

Research ethics committees have been noted to have a composition that to some degree reflects international standards for health research ethics committees, with males and females, and persons from a variety of disciplines.[65] However, the absence of legislation or domestic policies dictating and enforcing specific

---

62 Abdel-Aal et al, *supra* Note 53.
63 Younis at 224.
64 *Ibid* at 232.
65 Marzouk *supra* Note 50.

guidelines on composition also means that such committees can function without certain requirements in composition. As one study has noted, "The current lack of legislation leads to a random composition of members in different IRBs in Egypt, with a heavy reliance on elderly members and alarmingly non-transparent processes and outputs."[66] The penalty may be lack of confidence in such committees by foreign agencies, which is not a minor consequence by any means. This vacuum also indicates a failure to have a nationwide, comprehensive domestic research governance system that affords the same protections to every Egyptian or resident who takes part in health research.

Although studies have noted some diversity in the membership of research ethics committees in Egypt, other studies have observed a concentration of members from the scientific and medical communities and a lack of community membership.[67] Others have noted that about 90 per cent of members are physicians, reflecting a non-adherence with international trends[68] and creating a bias that may not be favourable to research participants. As recalled, this is a challenge in other African countries. The lack of community membership is a failure from the perspective of the hybrid framework of governance and the new governance approach because it fails to engage the persons who carry the most burdens in governance: the research participants themselves and the communities from which they are drawn. However, research ethics committees typically lack a standard way of changing membership and even chairmanship, with the same persons remaining in place for years.[69]

Beyond the membership challenges, existing research committees display certain strengths, such as regular meetings, the previous research ethics training of committee members, and the written policies of committees.[70] However, capacity building for members of ethics review committees has also been noted to be a challenge. A study noted that 82 per cent of surveyed research ethics committees indicated that they were not provided with ongoing training.[71] From 2005 onwards, several research ethics workshops have been held in various universities, a step which led to the development of research ethics committees in various universities in the country.[72] Previous work had also highlighted the limited numbers of ethics experts able to provide necessary capacity building.[73] In some cases, only the chairs of committees and some members were offered training.[74] However, several research centres now have health research ethics curriculums for undergraduates and postgraduates in health disciplines. Even so, many research ethics committee members have not received sufficient, ongoing

66 Wemos and SOMO at 55.
67 Sleem et al.
68 Younis, at 225.
69 *Ibid.*
70 Sleem et al.
71 *Ibid.*
72 Marzouk et al.
73 *Ibid* at 90.
74 Younis et al, at 228.

training and certification in research ethics. This is in part attributed to resource challenges. In addition, in certain cases, members simply fail to attend required training courses. The ENREC has attempted to fill the gap through its training programmes. The lack of a framework (policy or legal) that mandates ongoing capacity development for research ethics committee members must therefore also be considered a challenge. As in the Nigerian context, a policy mandate on research ethics could include a requirement that universities and centres of research provide funding for ethics review capacity building and a requirement that each institution to obtain registration must show proof of training for research ethics committee members.

As in many African countries, members of research ethics committees are not remunerated, that is, compensated for their time.[75] The committees, though established by their institutions, typically do not have a budget and lack funding for carrying out their responsibilities. Remuneration for research ethics committee members encourages commitment and possibly improves the quality of ethics review.

Monitoring post-review has also proved challenging. A study showed that 90 per cent of surveyed research ethics committees in Egypt indicated that the monitoring and oversight of trials was very important. Nevertheless, 91 per cent stated that they had inadequate ability to monitor trials. The reasons for this are not clear from the study.[76]

Other challenges that have been noted come from researchers' or investigators. There is limited awareness of the work of research ethics committees. Again, a legal mandate may be helpful in this regard. Other issues have their origins in research ethics committee members. Some members have been noted to fail to attend courses as required for capacity building. Others have displayed "lack of knowledge, contact with the funding drug companies without committee permission and some filling the protocol review checklist without adequate consideration."[77]

Finally, as in other African countries, financial constraints abound amongst research ethics committees in Egypt. Many institutions do not have a set budget for ethics review or to meet the logistical and other needs of the committees. Lack of dedicated office space, spare administrative personnel, and other basic necessities.[78]

Drug regulatory body

The Egyptian Drug Authority, a department of the Ministry of Health and Population, acts as the drug regulatory body in Egypt. It determines the approval processes for clinical trials. The Ministry has made decrees in relation to

75 Younis, *ibid.*
76 Sleem et al.
77 Marzouk et al, at 89.
78 Sleem et al.

good manufacturing practices which are in use but are not yet underpinned by law, the latest of which is Decree no. 734/2016, which articulates the National Guidelines and Regulations for Good Clinical Practice (GCP Guidelines). All drugs for sale in Egypt are required to be registered by the Drug Authority in accordance with the Pharmacy Act.[79] All clinical trials have been required by the Ministry to be registered in a database since 2007.[80] But this is not a publicly accessible database as it contains confidential information.[81] The Ministry's Central Administration for Research and Health Development scrutinises proposed trials within 60 days of submission and provides a decision to applicants.[82]

The GCP Guidelines require clinical trials to go through an ethics review by research ethics committees. Amongst other requirements, the GCP Guidelines require written informed consent, that a sponsor provide insurance to cover trial-related injury or the death of research participants, and indemnity for the investigator.

There are proposals to develop an independent drug authority, but a law to this effect is yet to be enacted.[83] The lack of law regulating the conduct of clinical trials also means that many issues are not regulated. For example, registration of clinical trials occurs but is not mandated by law. There is a rule of the Drug Authority which requires clinical trial of drugs to take place only after the drugs have gone through approval processes and registered in other countries. Recruitment of patients is also not governed by law. Some studies have noted the use of 'patient brokers' who serve as middlemen who help health professionals recruit patients for trials in hospitals for a fee.[84]

Monitoring of clinical trials by research ethics committees has been noted to be weak as a result of resource and budgetary constraints. Supervision by the Ministry is also limited.[85] Monitoring is further hampered by the lack of mandatory registration of all clinical trials. Although clinical trials registration is not mandated by any regulation, clinical trials registry was established in Egypt out of necessity. It currently includes information on clinical trials, mainly from pharmaceutical industry-sponsored trials submitted to the Ministry of Health and Population for scientific and ethics approval.[86] However, it is not a full registry system: it is not mandated by law, so not all trials are registered in it. The information it contains is not disclosed to the public as it contains confidential information. It is restricted to information on trials submitted only to the Ministry of Health and Population, and does not include some information, even

79 Law no.127/1955 on the Regulation of Pharmacies (Pharmacy Law).
80 Decree no. 539/2007 on the Egyptian code for good manufacturing practices for pharmaceuticals.
81 Nadia Ragab, "The Role of MOHP in Clinical Trials Boosting: Clinical Trials Law" online: <nci. cu.edu.eg/App_Files/RecenciFiles/images/784136865.pdf> (March 12, 2018).
82 Wemos and SOMO, at 23.
83 Mohamed Abdelgawad, Fadila Safwat & Sharkawy & Sarhan, *supra* Note 35.
84 Wemos and SOMO at 24.
85 *Ibid* at 26.
86 Nadia Ragab, *supra* Note 81.

within centres controlled by the Ministry.[87] Studies have noted the low contribution of trial information to clinical trials registries, including the Pan African Clinical Trials Registry. This may be attributed in part to the lack of a domestic clinical trials registry, lack of knowledge about the benefits of registration and registration requirements,[88] and the lack of a legal mandate requiring such registration. The result is a mismatch between health priorities and registered research[89] without a clear understanding of why this is so: whether it is because research is not being conducted as required on priority diseases based on Egypt's health profile (there is no policy on research priorities at this time) or because the trials are not being registered. However, in 2015, the research ethics review committee in the Ministry of Health developed a process for monitoring the approved protocol compliance of Contract Research Organisations (CROs).[90] It remains to be seen how effective this is, but it at least demonstrates an understanding of the need for monitoring.

Conflicts of interest appear rampant, especially in relation to industry-sponsored trials. In this regard, a researcher notes that "trials provide income to support the budgets of the Faculty of Medicine and the hospital serving all patients, in addition to the educational value, which also places Egypt on the scientific map."[91] Research coordinators also get paid monies. All of these raise the spectre of conflicts of interest, and the monitoring and supervision roles of research ethics committees and the Ministry of Health are therefore essential. The arising ethical questions of effective (best proven) treatments to control arms, compensation for trial participants, and post-trial benefits are yet to be answered adequately from an Egyptian perspective. Studies have shown that trials have been conducted in Egypt for the purpose of meeting drug approval requirements in developed countries, and placebo-controlled trials are not unusual. Many medicines developed are also unaffordable to the average Egyptian due to high costs.[92] It is open to discussion how beneficial such trials ultimately are to the people of Egypt. At the present time, the Drug Regulatory Authority does not appear to be equipped to deal with these issues, especially in light of lack of clear guidance.

Professional regulatory bodies

A study estimates that there are over 42,000 faculty members and 344,000 postgraduate students, 140,000 physicians, 18,200 dentists, 37,500 pharmacists,

---

87 *Ibid.*
88 AA Zeeneldin & FM Taha, "The Egyptian Clinical Trials' Registry Profile: Analysis of Three Trial Registries (International Clinical Trials Registry Platform, Pan-African Clinical Trials Registry and clinicaltrials.gov)" (2016) 7:1 J Adv Res 37–45.
89 *Ibid.*
90 Younis, at 227–228.
91 Industry-Sponsored Clinical Drug Trials in Egypt: Ethical Questions in a Challenging Context, at 29.
92 *Ibid* at 31.

176,000 nurses, and 35,000 physical therapists in Egypt.[93] Amongst doctors, the majority, at least 60 per cent, practise in the private health system.[94] In addition, there are likely many other social scientists and persons working in the humanities involved in health-related research. For the discussion in this section, as we have done with other countries, we will focus on medical doctors because they appear to be more regulated in Egypt and have some guiding principles that touch on health research.

Regulation of doctors in Egypt is undertaken by the Ministry of Health and Population; the Egyptian Medical Syndicate (EMS); and, to some degree, the medical schools. It has been observed that there is no clear demarcation of lines of authority and remits between these entities, with the result that standard-setting is "patchy."[95] On the one hand, Law 54 provided for the establishment of the EMS, with the objective of providing regulation for the medical profession in Egypt. The EMS is the largest professional association of doctors. It also administers the Medical Union, a large-scale health insurance organisation, which includes syndicates of pharmacists, veterinarians, and dentists in addition to doctors. It registers doctors and administers continuous professional education. The Law also requires that members keep the traditions and honour of their profession in mind while performing their medical duties. They are also required to swear by God Almighty to keep the secrets of the profession and comply with the code of ethics. This brings in religion as part of the regulatory framework for medical professionals.

The Ministry of Health and Population, on the other hand, amongst various functions, such as quality assurance of health facilities, drug registration, and clinical trials regulation, as described earlier, also licenses all doctors in Egypt, creating an overlap with the remit of the EMS. However, doctors cannot register with the Ministry until they have registered with the EMS, making the EMS a key regulator of doctors. Earlier discussion had reviewed the provisions of the Professional Ethics Regulations developed by the EMS and issued by the Ministry of Health and Population. The Regulations contain four segments: the first part is an oath made to God to do all in the physician's ability to keep the patient's secrets and provide care to all without discrimination, amongst other things. The second and third parts consist of the ethical requirements of all physicians and address matters such as working for the benefit of the community; notifying the relevant authorities about public health concerns, including diseases of an epidemic nature; participating in solving the problems of the profession, including through supporting the development of health policy and providing necessary data; refraining from giving permission to use one's name

93 Sherif Shehata, Nehal M ElMashad and Azza M Hassan, *supra* Note 25. An older study placed the number of doctors at about 200,000. See Han de Vries et al, International Comparison of Ten Medical Regulatory Systems – Egypt, Germany, Greece, India, Italy, Nigeria, Pakistan, Poland, South Africa and Spain: Technical Report prepared for the General Medical Council, UK (Rand Europe, 2009) at 25.
94 International Comparison of Ten Medical Regulatory Systems at 25.
95 *Ibid* at 26.

in promoting drugs or treatments; using third parties to solicit from patients; and refraining from participating in teleconsulting. It also emphasises informed consent and patient education, amongst other things.

For the purposes of research, with regard to novel treatments, the physician is not allowed, under the Professional Regulations, to engage in providing such treatments, except under certain conditions:

> The physician may not apply a new way for diagnosis or treatment if he had not completed its testing by the right scientific and moral method, published in accredited medical fields, its validity proven and licensed by the competent medical quarters. He may not also unduly attribute to himself any scientific discovery or allege it to be his own.[96]

The fourth part of the Regulations details provisions regarding "Conducting Medical Research & Experiments On Human Beings." These Regulations have been addressed in the previous section on Ethical Framework, and they will not be repeated here except to state that physicians are required to comply with, observe, and implement "all moral criteria and guidelines as well as the social and religious values laid down by the competent authority for conducting medical research on human beings." The "competent authority" is not defined but would appear to mean the research ethics committee. Amongst other things, it provides for informed consent; substitute consent for children and mentally and otherwise disabled persons (in which case the research must have a therapeutic purpose); and prior approval by a research ethics committee ("competent authority"), ensuring a balance of risk and benefits, and the privacy of participants. Research which may involve mixing lineages or cloning are prohibited.[97] A physician is required to ensure that effective treatment is provided by the sponsor until the end of the project.[98] It does not address follow-up or what happens after the trial or research is completed.

Unlike the Nigerian Code of Medical Ethics, the Regulations do not refer to the Helsinki Declaration or indeed any other international ethical guidelines. Should there be a conflict between a provision of the Helsinki Declaration and the Regulations, which should a physician abide by? The use of placebo and the provision of effective treatment is one area where such a problem might arise. For instance, "effective treatment" differs from "best proven treatment," as is currently required by the Helsinki Declaration. Ostensibly, the doctor may have to rely on the research ethics committee's judgement in that case (it will be recalled that the research ethics committees follow the international ethics guidelines in the absence of local legislation and guidance). Also, as mentioned earlier, there are several other potentially problematic ethical issues not addressed by the Code.

---

96 Article 9 of the Professional Medical Regulations.
97 Article 60.
98 Article 61.

Further, there is no provision for review in the Regulations. While this does not mean that a review cannot take place, it does mean that there is little certainty about when that review might occur. This is important because of the evolving understanding of the health professional with regard to the protection of research participants. The Regulations also do not address the penalties for failing to comply with the provisions. There are, however, penal sanctions meted out by the EMS where a doctor is reported to have failed in her duties. These sanctions include notice, warning, public statement of blame, fines, suspension for a year or less, or loss of registration with the EMS, alongside revocation of license to practise by the Ministry.[99]

Apart from these weaknesses, it appears that there is limited knowledge of the provisions of the Regulations amongst physicians.[100] Some studies have shown limited knowledge of research ethics amongst health professionals – nursing, dentists, pharmacists, and doctors – highlighting the need for research ethics education amongst health professionals.[101] Such limited knowledge is likely to be more exacerbated amongst the lay population and potential research participants. This does not augur well for the research governance and the protection of research participants.

Civil society organisations

There are no organisations specifically focussed on research governance and regulation or aspects of it, such as the protection of persons involved in clinical trials. Given the level of development of health research governance in Egypt, this is not surprising. There are other organisations, such as Egyptian Initiative for Personal Rights and Cancer Patients Aid Association, however, that work in the area of health rights and that ostensibly may become involved in acting as watchdogs for the health research that takes place in the country,[102] if awareness improves.

Analysis and assessment of current governance arrangements in Egypt

Egypt's governance arrangements are not quite as sophisticated or organised as in some African countries. This is interesting in part because of Egypt's history of medical experimentation and the significant amounts of research that have

---

99 International Comparison of Ten Medical Regulatory Systems at 30.
100 International Comparison of Ten Medical Regulatory Systems. See also Susan Kamal et al, "Perceptions and Attitudes of Egyptian Health Professionals and Policy-Makers towards Pharmaceutical Sales Representatives and Other Promotional Activities" (2015) 10:10 PLoS ONE e0140457. doi:10.1371/journal.pone.0140457, making a similar point about knowledge of pharmaceutical advertisement regulations. "The interviewed Egyptian physicians admitted that information provided to them by the industry often favored a particular company's products over their competitors' and that they only received independent original information on clinical trials if they asked for them specifically."
101 N Kandeel, A Multicenter Study of the Awareness and Attitudes of Egyptian Faculty Towards Research Ethics: A Pilot Study (2011) 6:4 J Empir Res Hum Res Ethics 99.
102 Wemos and SOMO et al, at 29.

been conducted in the country for many years. One reason for this may be that no serious scandal appears to have occurred in relation to health research in the country, such as, for instance, the Pfizer scandal in Nigeria. However, this in itself may not mean that there are no ethical challenges to the safety and welfare of research participants. Indeed, recent research suggests that there is cause for concern with respect to substantive ethical issues such as the use of placebos and provision of effective treatments to persons involved in clinical trials. Little information was available regarding issues relating to health research involving the social sciences and the humanities; thus it is not known how serious the ethical challenges faced in these areas might be.

At the present time, there is no law governing health research in the country as is available in South Africa and Nigeria. There is, however, an ongoing effort to enact such law. In the absence of law, the ethical framework becomes even more important. But the existing ethical framework is less than robust – with no domestic consideration of issues, or even a formal and comprehensive uptake of the international ethical guidelines, it would appear that the ethics of health research in Egypt is a mere afterthought.

Institutional mechanisms – the ethics review committees – while long-standing, suffer many of the challenges of resources, staffing, and coordination faced in other countries. While a coordinating mechanism has been developed through ENREC, this is by no means mandatory. The structure of ethics review remains inchoate. There is need for clarity on the structure of ethics review committees and possibly a national ethics review committee who will develop and oversee the implementation of national ethics standards and address matters like the composition of research ethics committees. There are no clear compositional requirements; capacity building in research ethics, which is still a relatively new concept, is limited. In the face of a lack of national guidelines, the implementation of international ethics guidance suffers from variability. In short, standardisation remains problematic. The drug regulatory authority appears to lack adequate resources for monitoring and supervision. For professional regulatory bodies, the code of conduct for medical doctors provides a foundation for ethical conduct in research, yet it does not cover many items and may not be well known. It is not clear how well the professional regulatory body for medical doctors enforces the standards with their members.

It would also appear that the social aspects of health research have received little attention, with much of the focus on clinical trials. However, with issues such as FGM and mental health being significant health concerns with underlying social foundations, an understanding of the potential social harms and research ethics review committee composition that reflect this, as well as research on these aspects, seems necessary at this time.

Comprehensiveness, clarity, uniformity, and other key goals of governance are clearly lacking in Egypt's current research governance arrangements. The effectiveness of several of the implementing institutions is hampered by various factors. In the presence of high rates of persons of low income, who may be illiterate, and relatively high rates of research and low costs to researchers, the lack of robust protections and a seamless, comprehensive, considered, clear, and uniform research governance framework is problematic.

Conclusion

Egypt is one of Africa's most popular destinations for clinical trials. With a high population, a considerable portion of whom are poor and lack health insurance coverage, the imperative of comprehensive, effective, and efficient health research governance systems would appear to be overwhelming. At present, there appears to be room for much improvement in developing and strengthening all aspects of such governance systems. It is expected that some of the necessary changes will be made as the political climate becomes more settled.

9 Health research governance in Africa

Here to stay but how best?

Key findings

Debates around the ethics of externally sponsored research in developing countries, including countries in Africa, amid increase in such research, has brought a renewed attention to the way in which health research is conducted in these countries. Similar attention also continues to be drawn to the health research disparities between developed and developing countries. As noted in Chapter 1, it also raises questions about the governance of health research by developing countries, including African countries. Health research involving humans in African countries is likely to continue to increase as improvement in infrastructure occurs and the recognition of other key factors (such as the need to study infectious diseases that are a danger to the world) increases. Instances of unethical practices detailed in the case studies also indicate the need for research governance. Failure to obtain ethics approval, falsifying of research data, use of placebos under inappropriate circumstances, and perceived exploitation are research ethics challenges that have presented themselves in African countries. The governance of such research is likely, therefore, to remain a topical, relevant, and engaging matter for years to come. The focus of this book, as noted in Chapter 1, has been to provide systematic analysis, from a governance perspective, on how health research is currently governed within the domestic contexts of African countries.

The countries studied in this book present an interesting picture in terms of where they are with research governance. Similar health challenges face these countries (battling infectious diseases alongside rising incidence of NCDs; health systems challenges, including lack of universal health coverage; significant levels of income and gender inequality), with important differences (constitutionally protected right to health, different income levels and thus economic resources to prioritise research, and research governance arrangements). The history of research governance in each country indicates the propelling factors, which in some cases included allegations of unethical practices, but also indicated an increase in HIV research and a growing engagement internationally with research ethics in resource-constrained settings. The components of health research have generated analysis in each country, adopting the macro-perspective set out in

Chapter 2. Brief assessments using the governance criteria, including clarity, comprehensiveness, uniformity, and so set out in Chapter 2, have accompanied each case study.

In general, Kenya and South Africa have very robust governance frameworks for research involving humans. The reason may not be far-fetched. Both countries have had a long experience of research. Early research in both countries was tinged with racial and colonial prejudice, which rendered at least some of it unethical. In Kenya, with the long-standing experience of health research starting in colonial times and an indigenisation process that extended to research structures, health research has been governed by law and other institutional structures for a long time. Other reasons may also have drawn external sponsors, including political history and even geography and climate. South Africa has adopted legal regulation and a formal structure more recently with the enactment of the National Health Act but has had ethics review committees for a longer period of time. Egypt, though much research is conducted in it, has not had much formal intervention through regulation and governance. Nigeria is somewhere in the middle, having had a long history of research; formalisation of research governance can be said to have begun about a decade ago. Egypt, on the other hand, has very little in terms of a formalised system, using the tool of ethics review primarily. There is a move towards legislation, but the most significant guidance is a professional regulatory code which does not contain extensive provisions. At any rate, the ethics review committees in Egypt rely on the international ethical guidelines, while the drug regulatory authority uses the International Country Harmonisation's Good Clinical Practice (ICH-GCP) guidelines, raising questions about how ethics review committees reconcile the differences between the two. African countries such as The Gambia, Sierra Leone, and Botswana are in a similar place – with ethics review operating at different levels but no national ethics guidelines or policies and no legislation in place; in countries like Swaziland, there are guidelines, but these are still at a rudimentary stage.

One of the key findings of the study undertaken here is that governance tools used in African countries are increasingly similar – ethics policies, legislation, ethics review committees, and drug regulatory authorities – with some differences in terms of content and structure. The National Health Research Ethics Committee or Council are policymaking bodies which also have regulatory functions. Thus, South Africa, Nigeria, and Kenya use similar tools, although the arrangements differ in small but significant respects. These mechanisms govern both domestic and internationally sponsored research.

National ethics guidelines are in place in South Africa, Nigeria, and Kenya but not in Egypt. As noted in Chapter 3, national ethics policy may provide a primary reference point for determining the ethical standards to be implemented, where there is disagreement about universal ethical standards. However, analysis of the national ethics codes and the policies in place in the case studies indicates that, while they provide guidance in some areas, in other areas, gaps remain in these pieces of guidance. These gaps include clarity about the place of international guidelines; guidance on access to experimental medicines; issues related to obtaining, storage, and use of biological samples; templates for clinical trials agreements, including with respect to equipment and knowledge transfer, amongst others. Issues such as the sharing of benefit of research, placebo use, and community engagements continue to be thorny issues which ethics review committees struggle with. In some countries, like Nigeria, the focus appears to be on the procedural matters rather than substantive ethical issues, with little attempt made to address the thorny ethical concerns in a domestic context, giving the impression that these issues have been resolved. Social, behavioural, psychological, and qualitative research related to health have also been minimally addressed in ethics guidelines and policy in Africa. The language of most ethics guidelines, the ethical concerns, the levels of risks anticipated, the methods, and the processes lean towards biomedical research, with little specific guidance for researchers and ethics review committees on the ethical concerns, risk management, and protections in social science research related to health. This gap may be related to the focus on the risks of biomedical research, as exposed in research scandals that have taken place on the continent. But this could also be related to the privileging of biomedical research, the funding of biomedical research, and the neglect of qualitative health research and its potential benefits. From a different perspective, it is also not often clear from existing research how ethics review committees apply the existing guidelines and what the challenges of doing so might be in African contexts. The concern that ethics review committees may become too legalistic, leaving no room for full consideration of context, is an ongoing concern. Future research on these issues would be helpful.

Legislation is also another increasingly popular tool. South Africa, Nigeria, and Kenya all currently have legislation that regulates health research involving humans. Egypt only has legislation in relation to drug approvals, but there have been efforts to enact legislation for all health research involving humans. Other African countries, like Zambia (National Health Research Act of Zambia, 2013) and Liberia (National Public Health Institute Act, 2016) are developing similar governance arrangements through the enactment of legislation in recent years. The import of this cannot be underestimated, with its implications for ethics review decisions and the possibility of legal action and sanctions against researchers and even regulatory authorities, as provided by legislation. In terms of sanctions, other methods of enforcement besides legislation remain in practice – withdrawal of funding, refusal of publication of research in top journals, etc.

Ethics review is also a key issue. Since the 2001 WHO study which found that only a quarter of clinical research passed through ethics review, it has become entrenched on the continent. A legal foundation for ethics review is recommended; ethics review is a legal requirement in South Africa and Nigeria. But it is not a legal requirement in other countries (like Egypt). In terms of structure, South Africa, Kenya, and Nigeria have national bodies that act as national ethics review committees which set standards for ethics review and provide general oversight, including through accreditation, standards setting, audit, etc. This is different from the decentralised approach taken in countries like Canada. There are several advantages to this structure – national and others (institutional and regional) (see Chapter 3). However, the literature is also clear on the fact that resources continue to be a challenge for ethics review committees at all levels. This is obvious from the case studies and requires attention. Resources are required for the continued training of members of ethics review committees, office maintenance, honoraria, and so on. At this time, much of the training that does occur is sponsored by donors and as such is short term and irregular, with resultant effects on skill and expertise. In Nigeria, where I am currently a member of the National Health Research Ethics Committee, for example, there is no budget for the national committee or an office. Meetings are not regular and often depend on being able to find a sponsor. This raises the possibility of conflicts of interest. Although fees may be charged for reviews in some countries, this may not provide for all the needs of the ethics review committees, and also raises the spectre of conflict of interest. Not providing some compensation (such as honorariums) for members of ethics review committees, as is currently the case in Nigeria, for example, may also affect their commitment.

The institutional approach to ethics review is now seemingly entrenched with the challenges noted in Chapter 3, including conflicts of interest issues. Ethics shopping remains a possibility in some countries (like Kenya). Although there has been significant improvement, compliance with requirements relating to seeking the approval of ethics review committees is still a challenge in African countries, including those not surveyed here (like Cameroon).[1]

All the countries surveyed have drug regulatory authorities. These are typically established by legislation. They also usually have some working relationship with ethics review committees. In some cases, as in Nigeria, it is not clear from available guidance that the processes of ethics review committees and the guidance are harmonised. What this means for governance is lack of clarity about requirements. Resources for their operations, as with ethics review, can be problematic. While resources are typically provided for through budgetary allocations, drug regulatory authorities often lack sufficient resources for their work, resulting in longer approval times and in some cases a lack of required oversight.[2] Other systemic challenges are noted in Chapter 3.

In addition, professional regulation is a potential tool of governance. However, professional regulatory bodies are not actively part of the regulatory process in many countries, and even where their codes of regulation contain specific requirements on health research, they do not appear to be implemented. The requirements also appear to be a repetition of certain international guidelines,

1 NS Munung et al, "Are Students Kidding with Health Research Ethics? The Case of HIV/AIDS Research in Cameroon" (2012) 13:1 BMC Med Ethics 12. NS Munung et al, "How Often are Ethics Approval and Informed Consent Reported in Publications on Health Research in Cameroon? A five-year review" (2011) 6:3 J Empir Res Hum Res Ethics 93–97. R Fombo, "Review of Research and Research Ethics in Cameroon" (2017) 1:2 Int J Res Cult Soc 19.

2 See, for instance, C Weijer, "Commentary: Ethics in Conduct of Trials in Developing Countries" (2010) 340 BMJ 1373.

without a clear effort to adapt them. This is the case, particularly for Nigeria and Kenya. Egypt has adopted some ethics requirements in its physicians' code, but these are by no means comprehensive. South Africa is an exception, with a careful treatment of health research involving humans in its professional code. It remains to be seen how effective implementation will be.

Clinical trial registries are becoming an important tool of governance, with guidance in some countries requiring them. The importance of this cannot be overemphasised, especially in a context where determining research priorities is crucial. They would, however, be more effective if the research agenda-setting agencies and ethics review committees put them to use, for instance, in terms of determining what has been over-researched and potential research areas where gaps remain. It is interesting also to note that regional clinical trial registry – Pan African Clinical Trials Registry (PACTR) – has significantly fewer African studies registered in it than the NIH-sponsored Clinicaltrials.gov. The reasons for this are open to speculation. For Kenya, for example, there are seven studies in the PACTR and 403 studies in the Clinicaltrials.gov. This may say something about how much ownership African countries still need to take over research. It may relate to issues of perceived researcher prestige or research visibility. More research will help identify why this is so and whether a change is needed.

In general, civil society organisations have had limited participation in health research governance, much less than in other health issues. This suggests that issues relating to health research involving humans are still lower down the scale of priorities. Although donors, including international development agencies, have not been studied extensively in this book, they play a significant role – through funding, influencing of policies, and insistence on some steps being taken. This continues to be the reality of many African countries, nevertheless it is essential for these countries to devote some domestic resources to research governance in their countries. The broader context of research governance appears inescapable – determining who sets the research agenda, inequitable relations between foreign and domestic researchers, the relationships of research institutes funded by foreigners and other domestic entities – are all issues that impact how research governance arrangements are implemented. Civil society organisations' participation in discussions about the context is essential.

How effective are the existing governance frameworks in addressing regulatory challenges? Do the research governance arrangements currently in place meet the three main goals of governance distilled in Chapter 2: namely, ensuring that research is potentially beneficial; minimising risks to protect the safety, dignity, and well-being of research participants; and maintaining trust between the research community and society as a whole? There are certainly efforts to put in place arrangements that seek to address this, using several of the components outlined in Chapter 3. But implementation is a key challenge because of limited resources devoted to the structures in place. For example, there are some provisions mandating registration of clinical trials and health research databases, which, amongst other benefits, would help committees established to develop research priorities, but not all countries have these requirements or monitor implementation. Having made the argument that law should be a part of the arrangement to help meet these goals, in part to mandate ethics review, there are laws which do so directly, as in South Africa, and indirectly, as in Kenya and Nigeria. However, there remain gaps, for example, in mandating that the state budgets monies for the implementation of research governance. From the analyses undertaken here, despite the formal structures now in place for health research governance and regulation, there continue to be allegations of unethical practices and perceptions that governance regimes are still inadequate to protect research participants.[3] The implementation of extant guidelines and law remains patchy and incomplete. While government is a central figure in research governance through the enactment of law and the appointment of key persons (such as in Nigeria, where the Minister appoints the members of the National Health Research Committee and the National Health Research Ethics Committee), there is little effort in terms of bringing resources to the table. Only in Kenya do we currently have a law establishing a fund (the National Research Fund) with a specific per cent of the budget and funding for the key research regulation agency. But ethics review committees in all four countries, typically institutionally based, continue to struggle with limited resources to carry out their work. There are gaps in policy provisions, as I have noted throughout the case studies.

Efficiency, with respect to the manner of protocols submission, communication between ethics review committees and researchers, turnaround times for ethics review, and review times for drug regulatory authorities, is currently poor. Paper-based submissions remain the norm in African countries, providing a level of complexity that is adverse to efficient processes. Archives are also mostly paper-based. Regular meetings are still not the norm, including for national ethics review committees. The result is that turnaround times for ethics review are longer in African countries, by some estimates ranging from 3 to 37 months.[4] Efforts are being made to reduce these timelines, including through web-based platforms,[5] helping reducing workloads and review times. This remains a work in progress.

Thus, despite good intentions and increasing formalisation, several gaps pervade current governance arrangements. From the analysis of the case studies, using the assessment criteria developed in Chapter 2 then, there may be good points for legitimacy and, increasingly, clarity. But adequacy, comprehensiveness, efficiency, adequacy, uniformity, and effectiveness may not get as many points in some countries.

What is clear from the textual approach adopted in this book is that several countries are making requirements clearer and the parameters of engaging in

---

3 See, for example, Embry Howell and Jennifer Obado-Joel, "Human Subjects Protection in the African Context" (2016) 4:1 African Eval J 1.

4 P. Ndebele et al, "Regulatory Challenges Associated with Conducting Multicountry Clinical Trials in Resource-Limited Settings" (2014) 65 J Acquir Immune Defic Syndr 29 at 30.

5 Boitumelo Mokgatla et al, "Enhancing the Efficiency and Quality of African Research Ethics Review Processes – Through an Automated Review Platform" (2017) 8 J AIDS Clin Res 658.

research stricter. It is also apparent that while increasing regulatory requirements may not address all the issues, researchers can be better informed, and citizens can enjoy better protections while participating in relevant health research.

Some recommendations

On the whole, the move towards the formalisation of health research governance is seemingly inexorable. The full complement of research governance instruments, via ethical, legal, and institutional frameworks, are on display. As health research governance arrangements solidify in African countries, there is need for in-country evaluation of these arrangements to help address gaps and ongoing challenges. The criteria for a systems evaluation identified in Chapter 2 would be necessary for this assessment – legitimacy, adequacy, uniformity, comprehensiveness, clarity, simplicity, efficiency, and effectiveness.

Such systems analysis will help identify areas requiring improvement, in particular improving synergies between the various components of the research governance system. For instance, evaluating the structure of ethics review – whether to adopt a regional system where provinces and states host ethics review committees rather than institutions, and whether this might help provide the resources required for the effective implementation of their functions, taking into account the sociopolitical context of the country. There is need for research within country settings to study the work of ethics review committees: for example, their difficulties in providing ongoing monitoring for approved research, interpreting the guidelines, or providing decisions in a more efficient manner.

Such evaluation could also help determine what capacity gaps currently exist in the work that drug regulatory authorities do in regulating clinical trials, not only of drugs but also devices. Moreover, some of the gaps in ethics guidance, in the legal framework or implementation, will become clearer with such periodic evaluation. Such gaps as have been mentioned within the approaches taken, (for instance, the need to develop a more synergistic relationship between drug regulatory authorities and ethics review committees or in promoting and regulating qualitative, social sciences research), will also become apparent and provoke discussion and possibly change. Research such as that on the impact of mental health on work, the intersections of domestic violence and the mental health of women, the migration and health of trafficked persons, the health impact of state-perpetrated human rights violations on marginalised groups, and the psychosocial aspects of patient safety, just to name a few examples, and other similar projects are necessary and relevant. Ethics guidance both for researchers and ethics review committees need to be reconsidered. Evaluations of the research governance sometimes take place at the behest of a donor, or for academic research, but this needs to become part of the fabric of research governance, sponsored by national authorities and undertaken for the purpose of improving the system.

Another key issue that arises from a new and hybrid governance perspective is the need for greater legitimacy. Thus there is a need to engage the public more in matters relating to research ethics and research regulation. Transparency can be engendered by mandating that national ethics committees make publications about key issues available on their websites, as is currently being done to some degree. But this can be extended. At the present time, research governance issues typically make their way into the news through the publication of allegations of unethical conduct. More public education about the benefits of health research and research ethics, aside from such allegations, is needed. This will encourage greater transparency and accountability, and may also be beneficial to the willingness of communities to participate in research. Another way of engaging the community is by engaging community members on ethics review committees. While several of the guidelines reviewed in this book have provisions for lay membership or community membership, in some cases this is ill-defined and in other cases it is simply not implemented. Active steps by national ethics review committees to make this a part of their accreditation requirements would be helpful. Stakeholder engagement and public consultations should also be a part of the process of reviewing the guidelines. Civil society organisations should be welcomed into these processes to enlarge the engagement space. The media should also be actively engaged in these process of awareness creation, not only by providing details of the allegations of unethical practices but also by having the knowledge to ask the right questions. Reports of magical cures for HIV and other diseases remain, and questions on the processes of reaching such conclusions are typically not asked by reporters. This can be remedied by a deliberate effort to educate health journalists and other on research governance. In short, health research governance should increasingly become a societal endeavour rather than the exclusive preserve of public health officials, biomedical scientists, researchers, research sponsors, and civil servants.

Likewise, health professionals, through their regulatory bodies, should become an active part of the governance process. The aim should, of course, not be to bring in the professional rivalry that is frequently rampant in medical practice but for each regulatory body to increase the capacity of its members to conduct themselves in accordance with ethics requirements. Capacity building on the governance arrangements, including the law and ethics of research as it applies within African countries and internationally, should be a requirement in the continuing professional development framework of each professional regulatory body. More should be made of incorporating the national and international code into codes of conduct and ethics. Beyond this, professional regulatory bodies should be willing to discipline erring members for flouting research ethics principles or other research governance requirements.

There are other areas that require attention. Clinical trials registries have the potential to provide the database for monitoring but also for determining the kinds of clinical trials that have been, or are being, undertaken. The slight research undertaken here suggests that local/domestic registries are not being fully utilised by researchers. Future research would be necessary to clarify this. What gaps are being experienced in this area, and what can be done to address them? I have recommended a legal mandate here (as in South Africa), but there may be other avenues of support. It is also crucial to create databases for other kinds of health research. It is a notorious fact that in many African countries, health research is not adequately employed to inform and influence policy. One way to change this would be to have a database of health research. The Kenya approach of requiring institutions to establish such database may be one way to go. National Health Research Committees who work on research prioritisation would certainly find such a resource useful. Another issue is expertise in ethics. Health ethics or bioethics scholarship is relatively new in African countries. This is an area that requires attention. It is one way to address some of the concerns that have been raised elsewhere about the focus on the bricks and mortar of health research governance – guidelines, laws, committees, etc., with the resulting effect that researchers and ethics review committees are engaged in mere rule-following and checking off SOPs checklists, and not in true reflection on the ethics of the research. Ethics scholarship would help provide a base to build the capacity of ethics review committees and researchers engaged in health research to reflect on what they are doing, why they are doing it, the communities they are working in, the benefits and disadvantages to those communities, and the ethical issues at stake.

Finally, resources are required to sustain the emergent domestic governance regimes. While there may be design problems and policy gaps as identified in this book, many of the challenges of health research governance in African countries are increasingly implementation problems. Devoting resources to research governance should therefore be a priority, alongside making efforts to increase domestically funded research. In other words, establishing domestic research governance mechanisms in Africa is important, but implementation or effectiveness, requires resources. These resources cannot only come from foreign countries or external sources. As I argued in Chapter 2, the state is important, including through its enactment and wielding of the blunt instrument of legislation, but it must bring more than that to the table of health research governance. It must bring resources. This allows it to take ownership of the protection of research participants and build its research governance infrastructure. Economic constraints may limit what resources are made available to research. However, complete or predominant reliance on donor support, as is the case for many African countries, speaks to the value placed on research and research governance, and is not a long-term or sustainable strategy. While not eschewing external support, domestic resources are crucial to demonstrating ownership of the promotion of research and protection of citizens as well as to promoting sustainability. To ensure that resources are made available, legal mandates and continued political engagement are necessary. Resources are required to identify and implement health research priorities, to actualise health research governance procedures and arrangements with the aim of benefiting the people, potential research participants, in a way that protects them from harm and promotes their well-being.

Index

Printed in the United States
by Baker & Taylor Publisher Services